IDOL dreams

& ART BY

ARINA TANEMURA

4

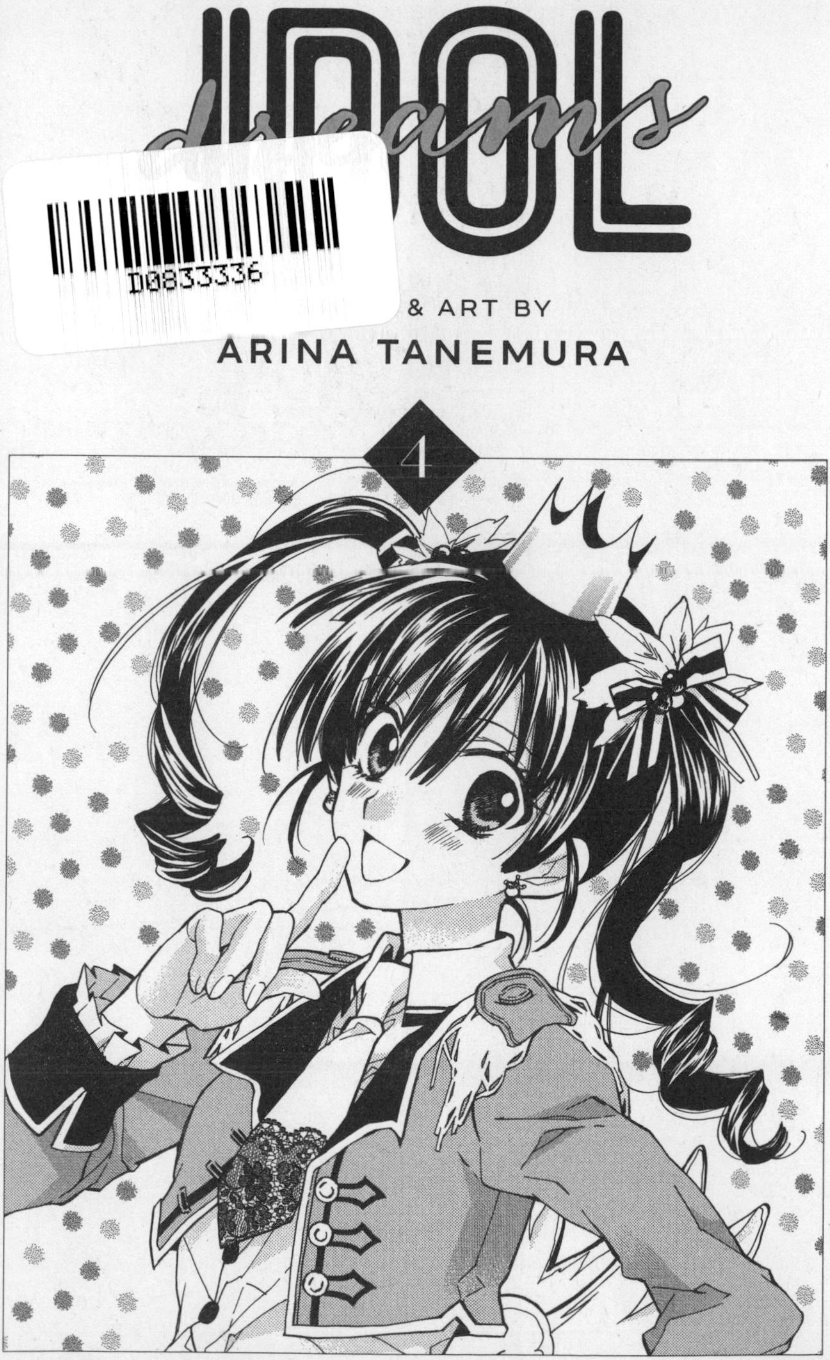

CONTENTS

Chapter 16......3

Chapter 17......35

Chapter 18......67

Chapter 19......99

Chapter 20......131

The Mysterious
Pipikopiko!......163

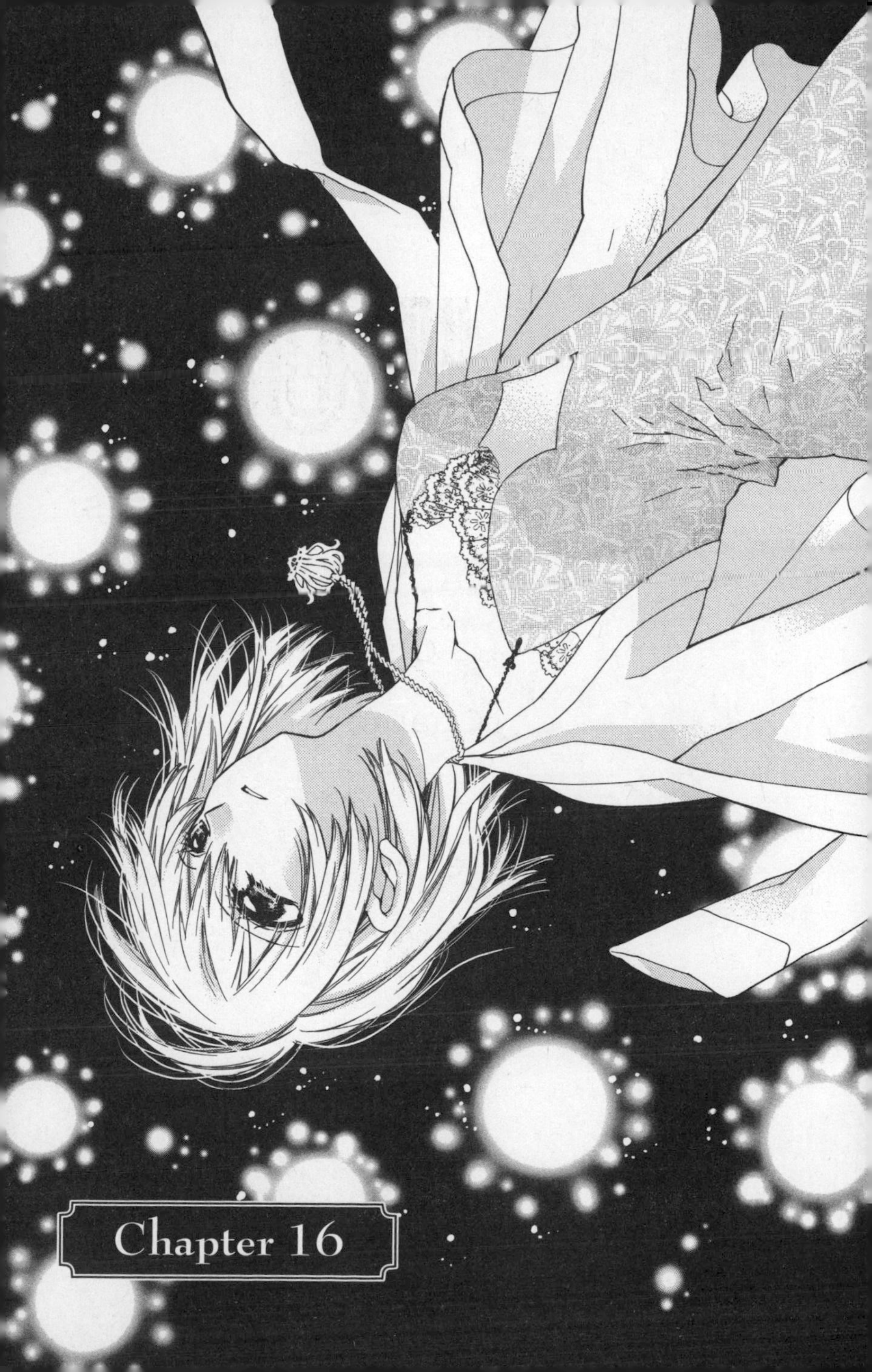
Chapter 16

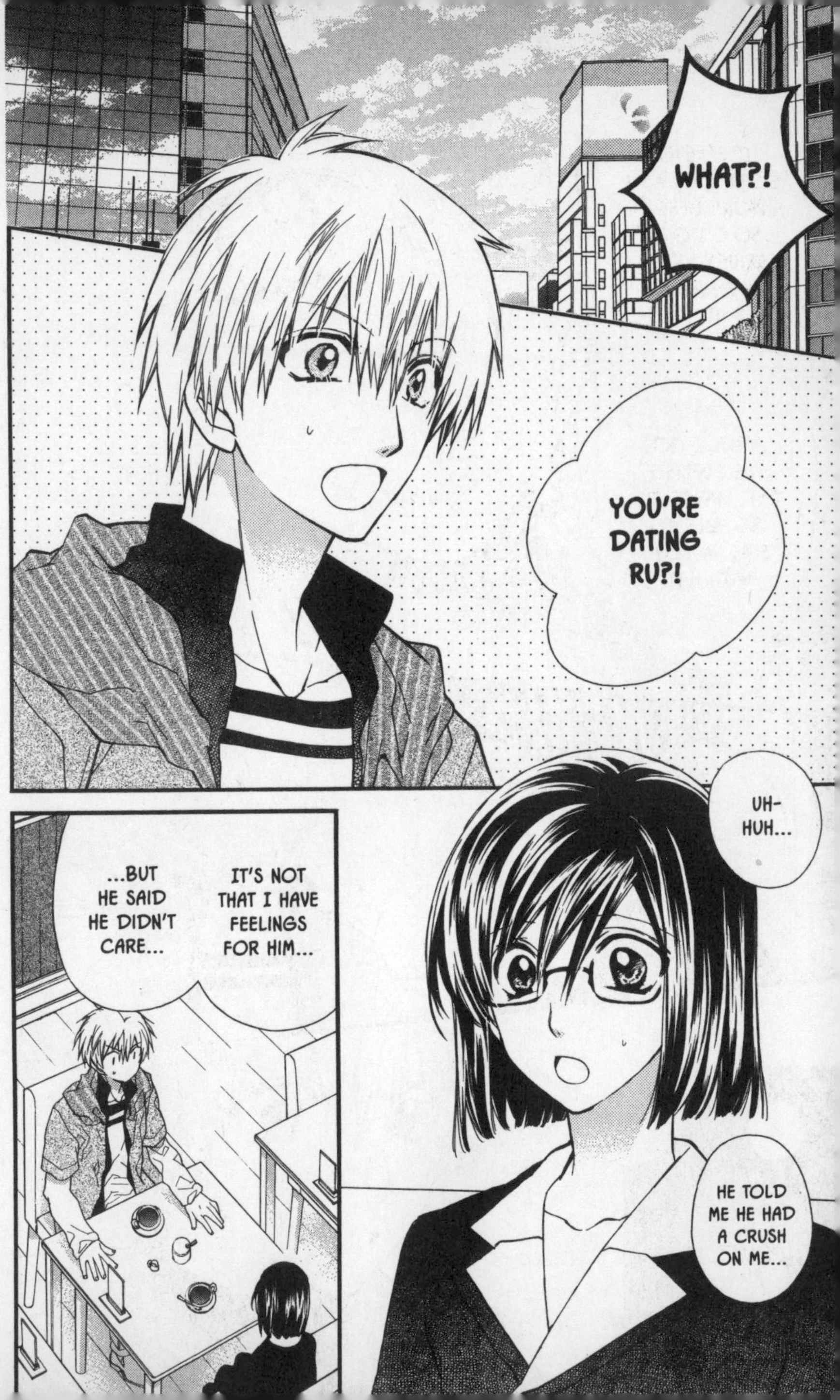
WHAT?!
YOU'RE DATING RU?!
UH-HUH...
HE TOLD ME HE HAD A CRUSH ON ME...
IT'S NOT THAT I HAVE FEELINGS FOR HIM...
...BUT HE SAID HE DIDN'T CARE...

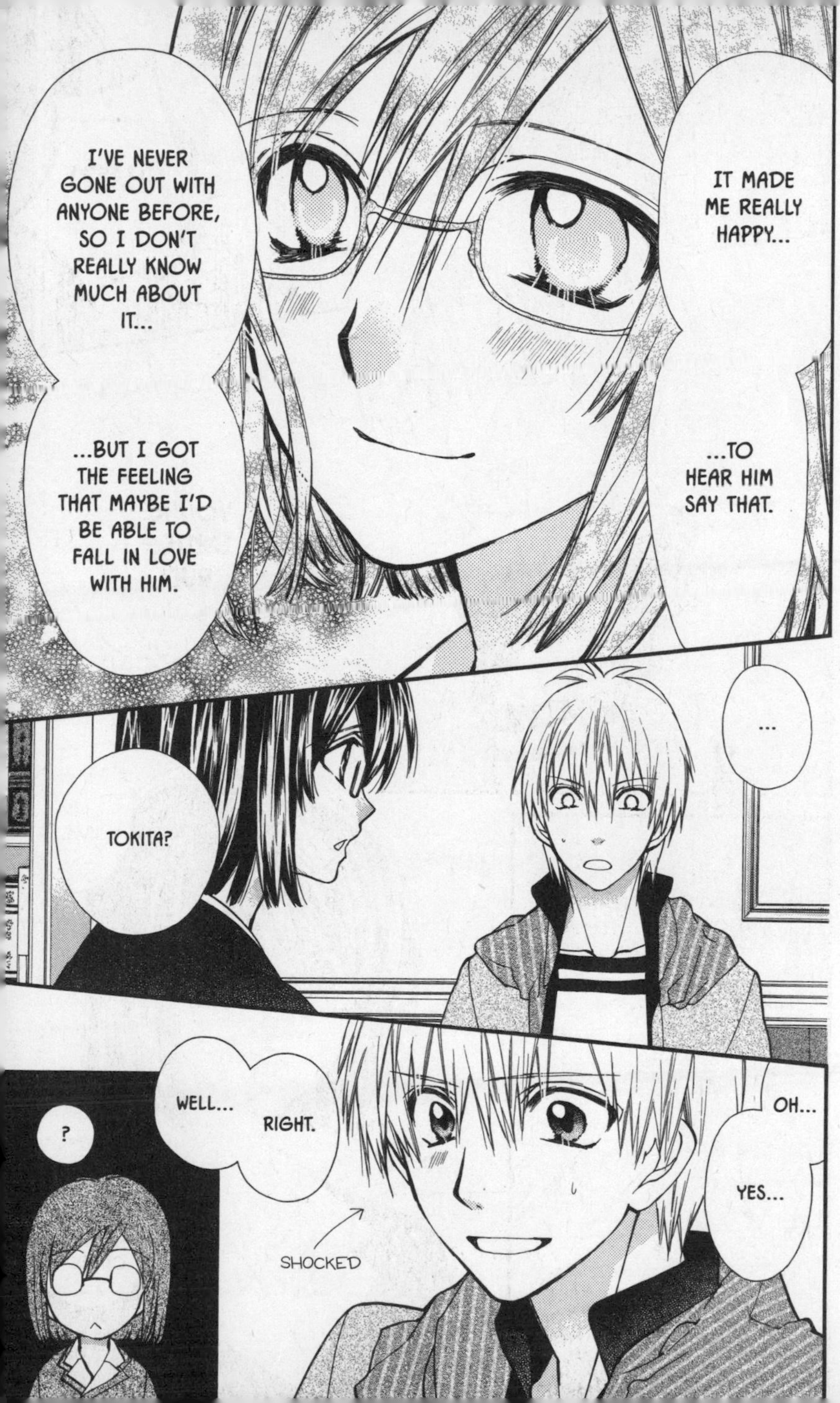
IT MADE ME REALLY HAPPY...
...TO HEAR HIM SAY THAT.
I'VE NEVER GONE OUT WITH ANYONE BEFORE, SO I DON'T REALLY KNOW MUCH ABOUT IT...
...BUT I GOT THE FEELING THAT MAYBE I'D BE ABLE TO FALL IN LOVE WITH HIM.
...
TOKITA?
OH...
YES...
WELL...
RIGHT.
SHOCKED
?

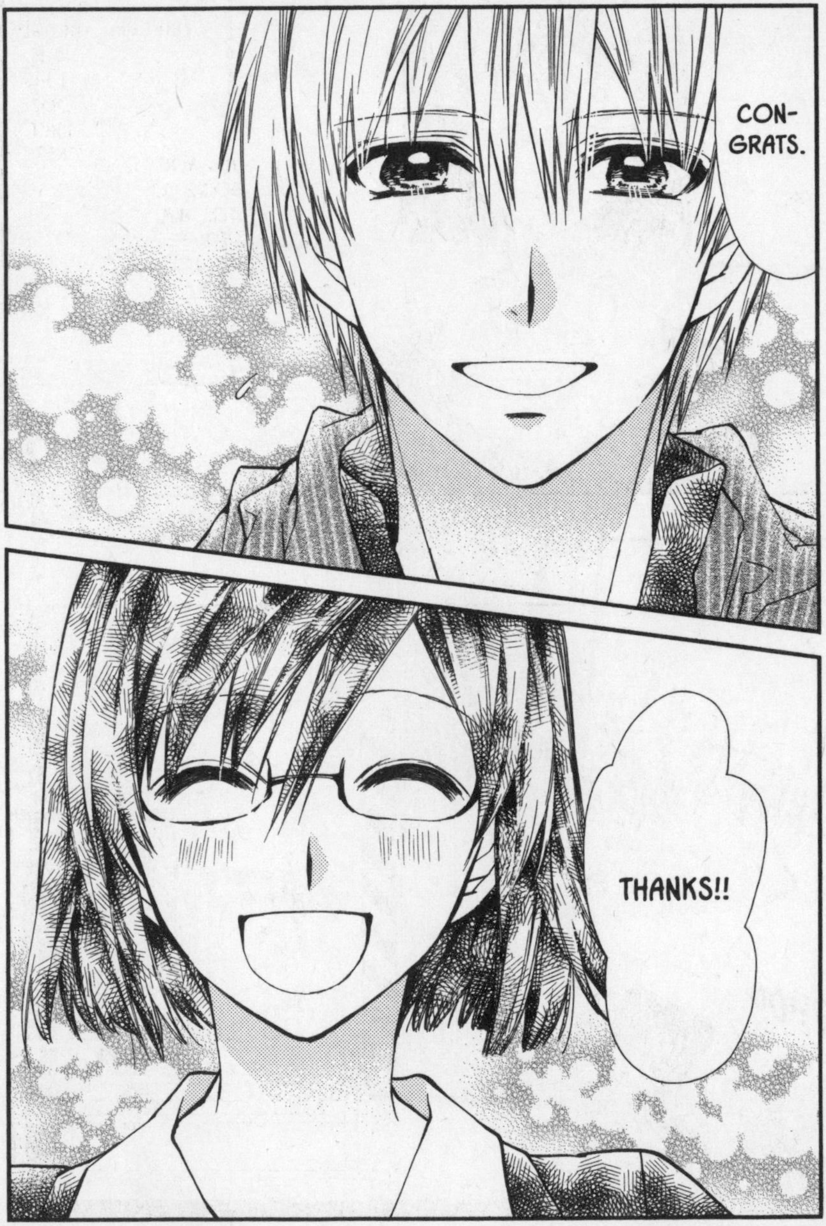
CON-
GRATS.
THANKS!!

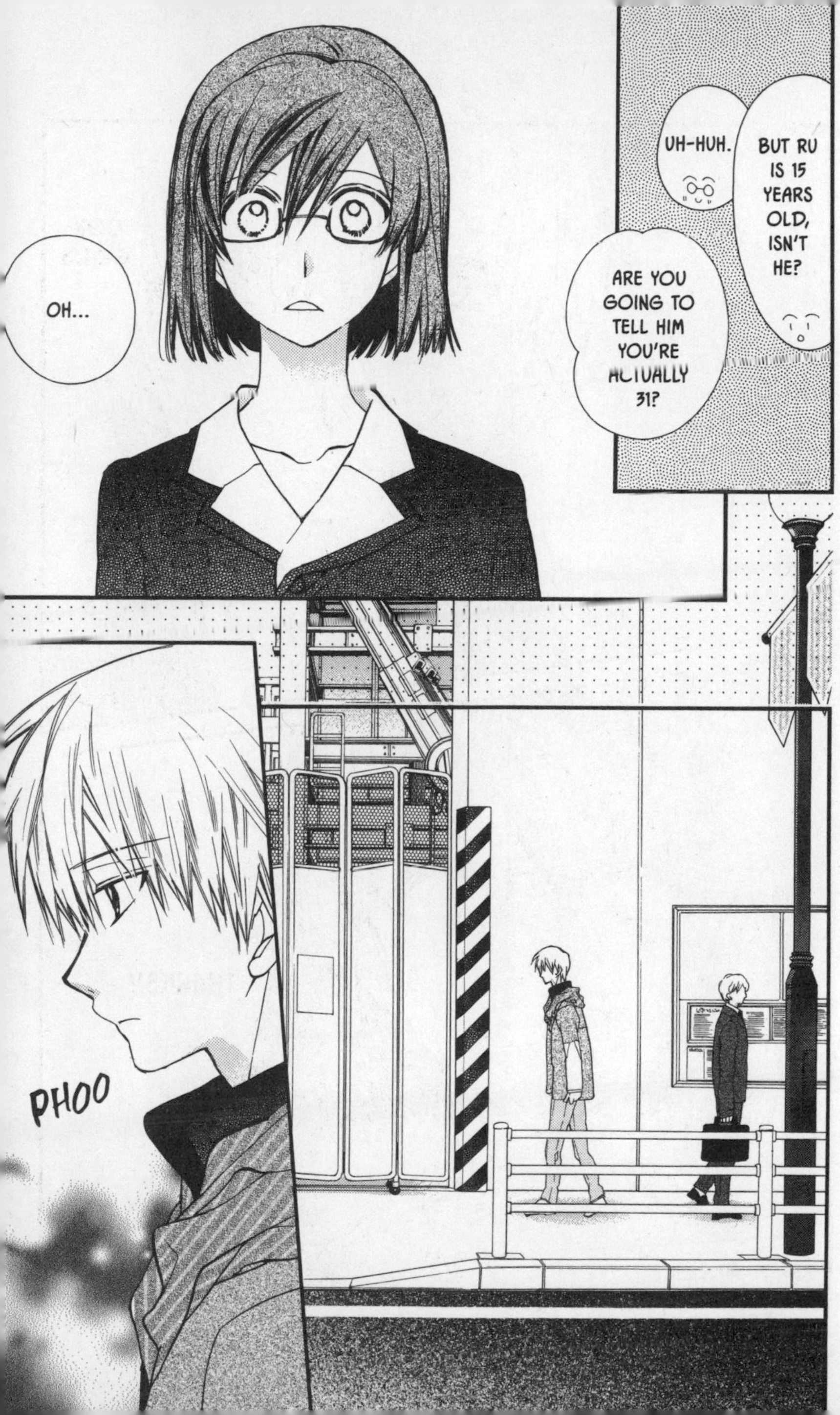
BUT RU IS 15 YEARS OLD, ISN'T HE?
UH-HUH.
ARE YOU GOING TO TELL HIM YOU'RE ACTUALLY 31?
OH...
PHOO

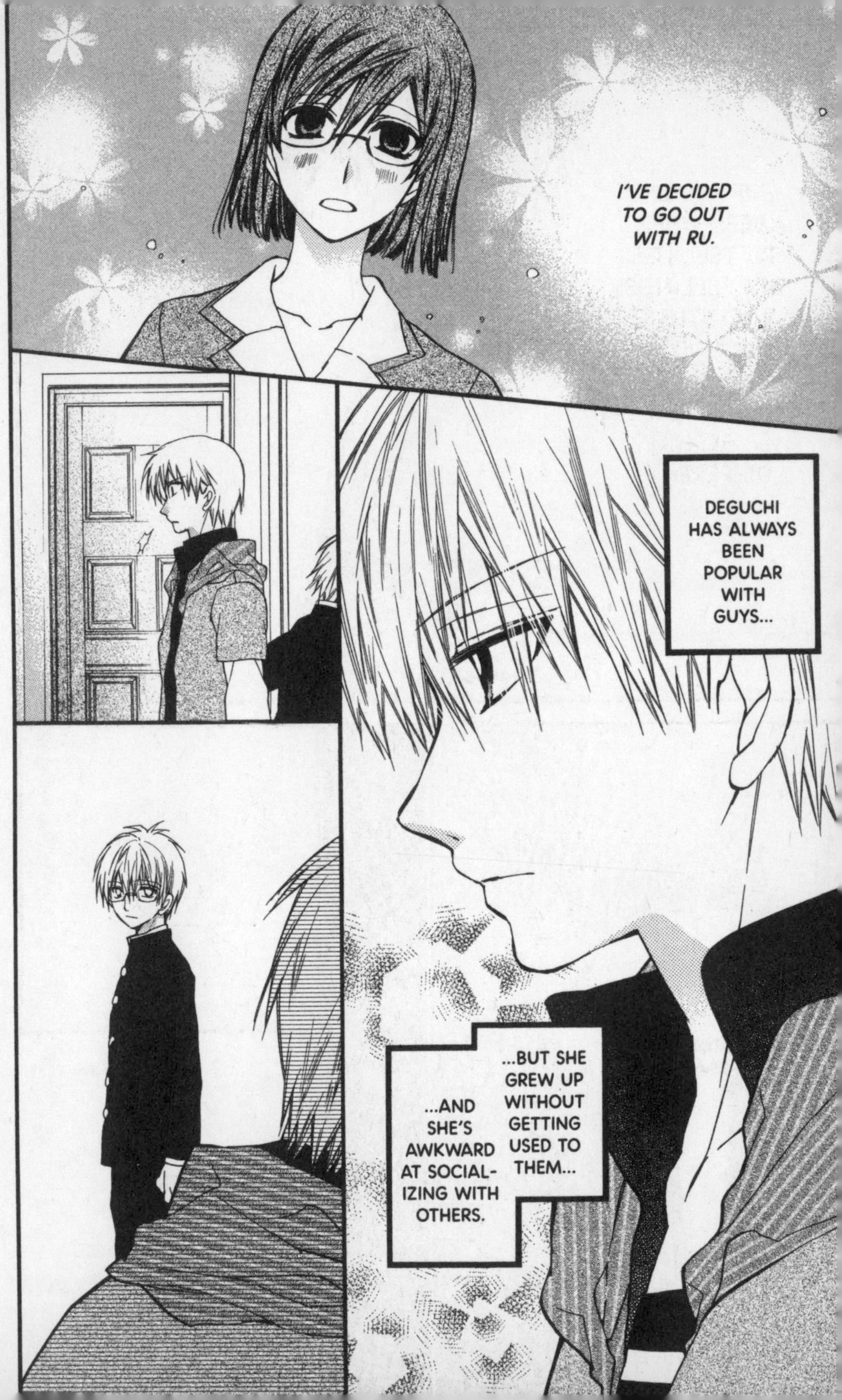
I'VE DECIDED TO GO OUT WITH RU.
DEGUCHI HAS ALWAYS BEEN POPULAR WITH GUYS...
...BUT SHE GREW UP WITHOUT GETTING USED TO THEM...
...AND SHE'S AWKWARD AT SOCIAL-IZING WITH OTHERS.

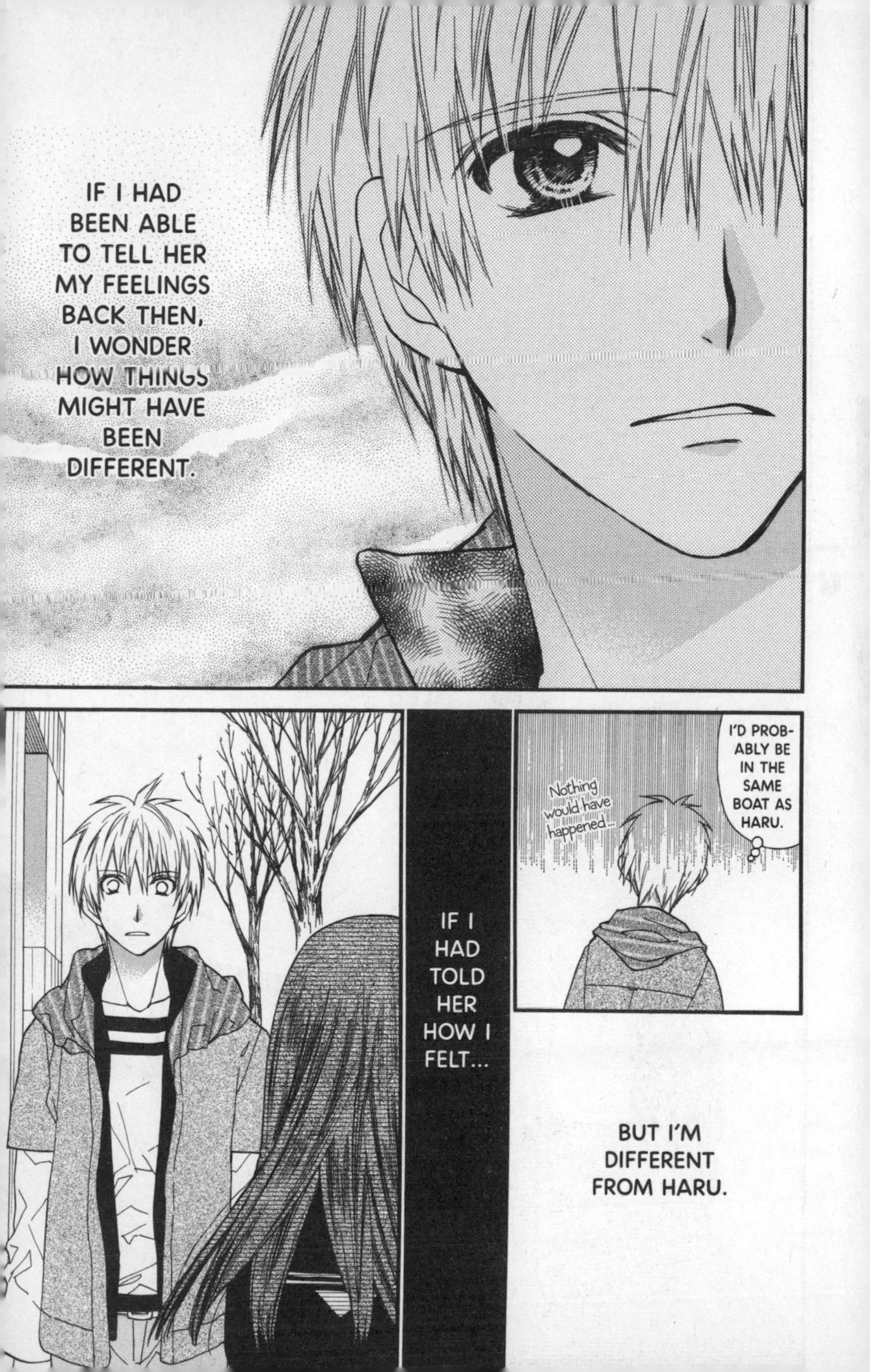
IF I HAD BEEN ABLE TO TELL HER MY FEELINGS BACK THEN, I WONDER HOW THINGS MIGHT HAVE BEEN DIFFERENT.
I'D PROB-ABLY BE IN THE SAME BOAT AS HARU.
Nothing would have happened...
BUT I'M DIFFERENT FROM HARU.
IF I HAD TOLD HER HOW I FELT...

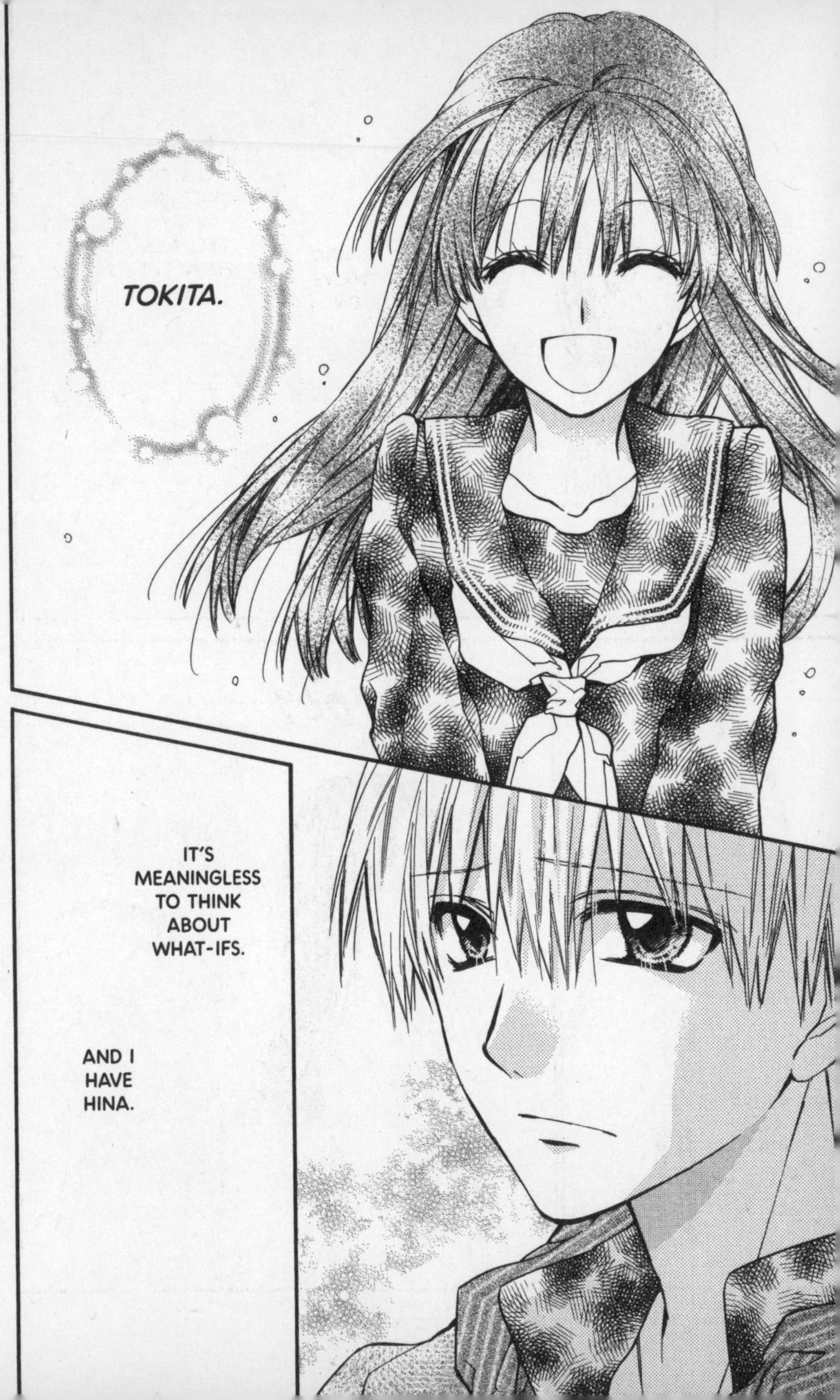
TOKITA.
IT'S MEANINGLESS TO THINK ABOUT WHAT-IFS.
AND I HAVE HINA.

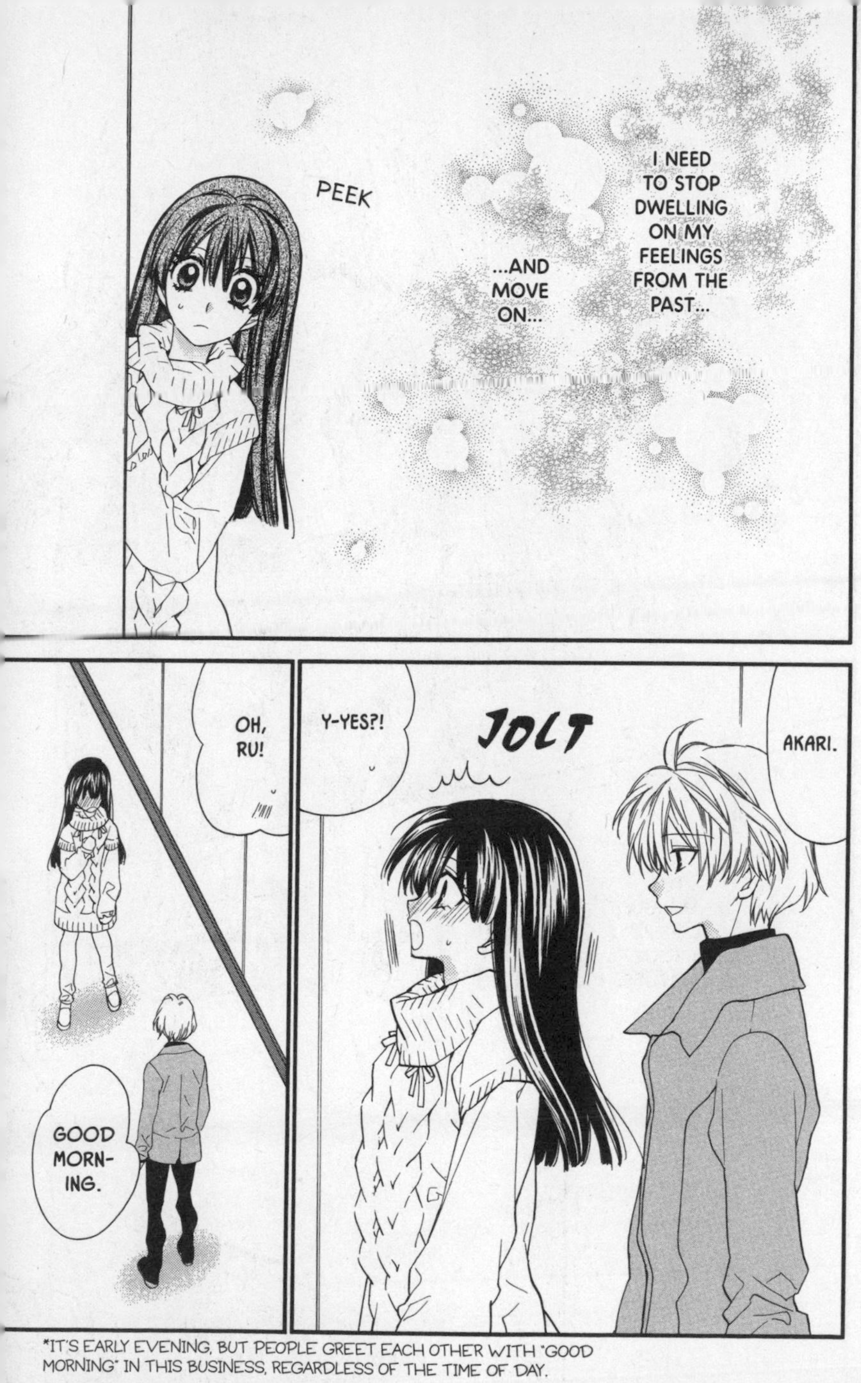
I NEED TO STOP DWELLING ON MY FEELINGS FROM THE PAST...
...AND MOVE ON...
PEEK
AKARI.
JOLT
Y-YES?!
OH, RU!
GOOD MORN-ING.

*IT'S EARLY EVENING, BUT PEOPLE GREET EACH OTHER WITH "GOOD MORNING" IN THIS BUSINESS, REGARDLESS OF THE TIME OF DAY.

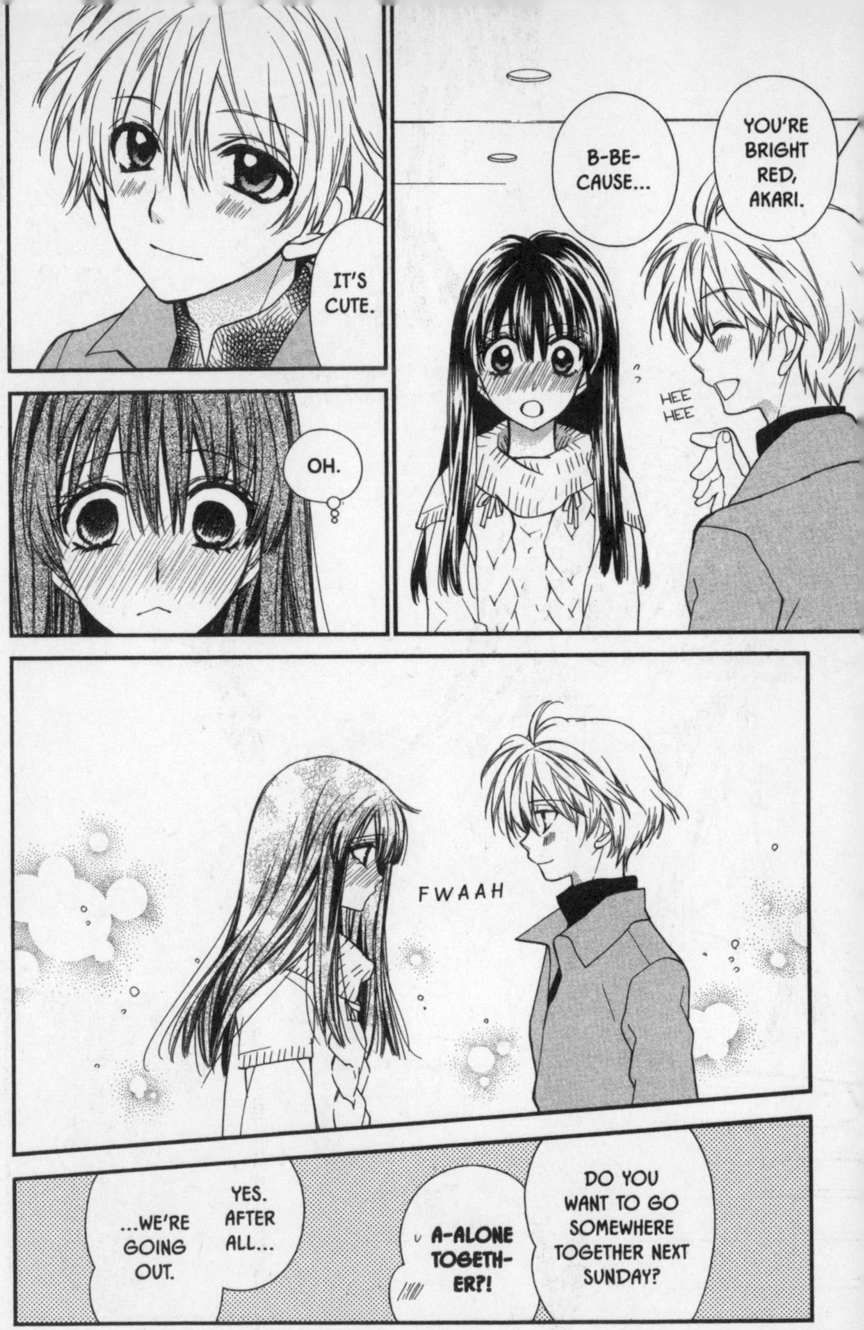
YOU'RE BRIGHT RED, AKARI.
B-BE-CAUSE...
HEE HEE
IT'S CUTE.
OH.
FWAAH
DO YOU WANT TO GO SOMEWHERE TOGETHER NEXT SUNDAY?
A-ALONE TOGETH-ER?!
YES. AFTER ALL...
...WE'RE GOING OUT.

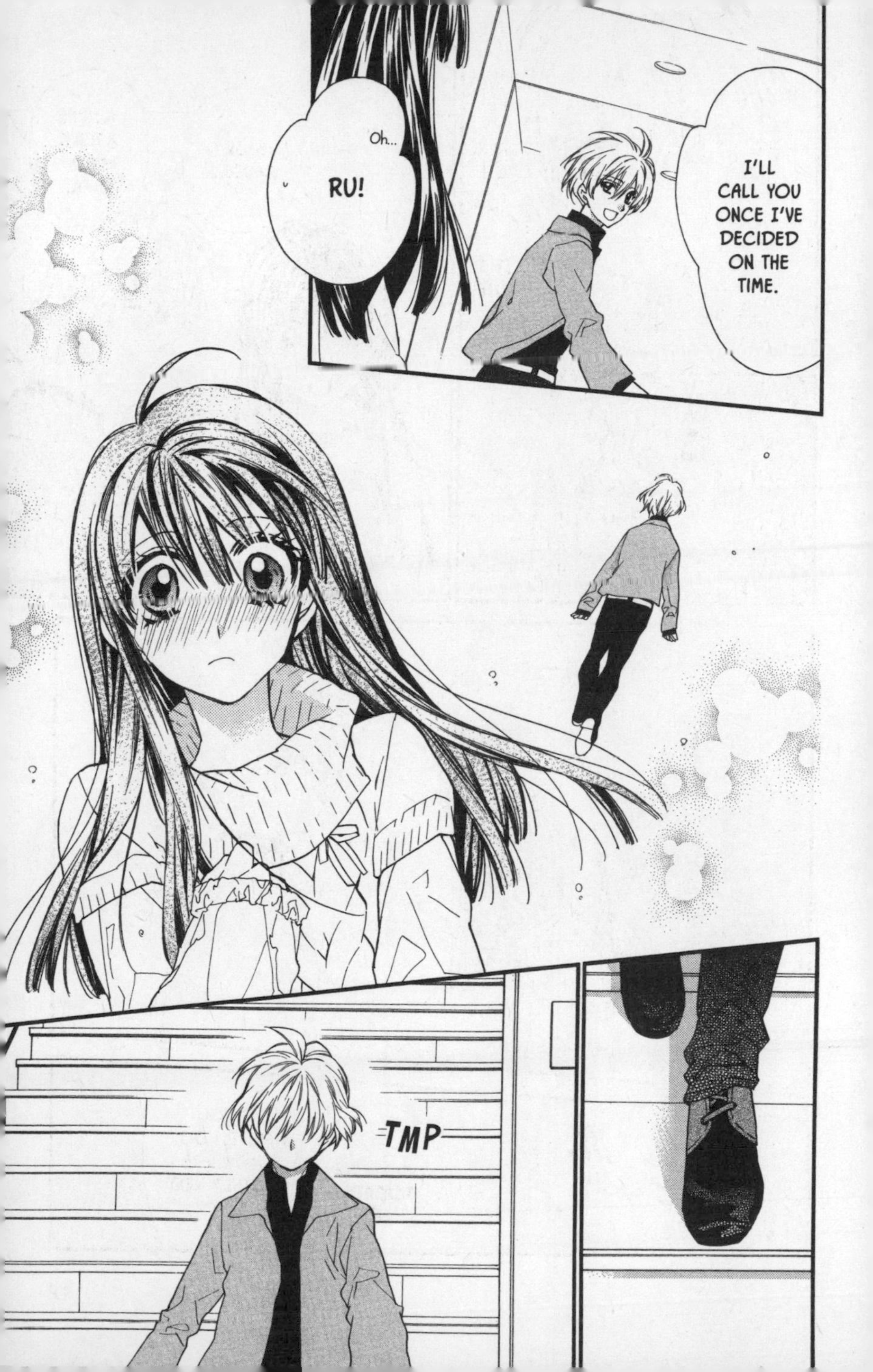
I'LL CALL YOU ONCE I'VE DECIDED ON THE TIME.
Oh... RU!
TMP

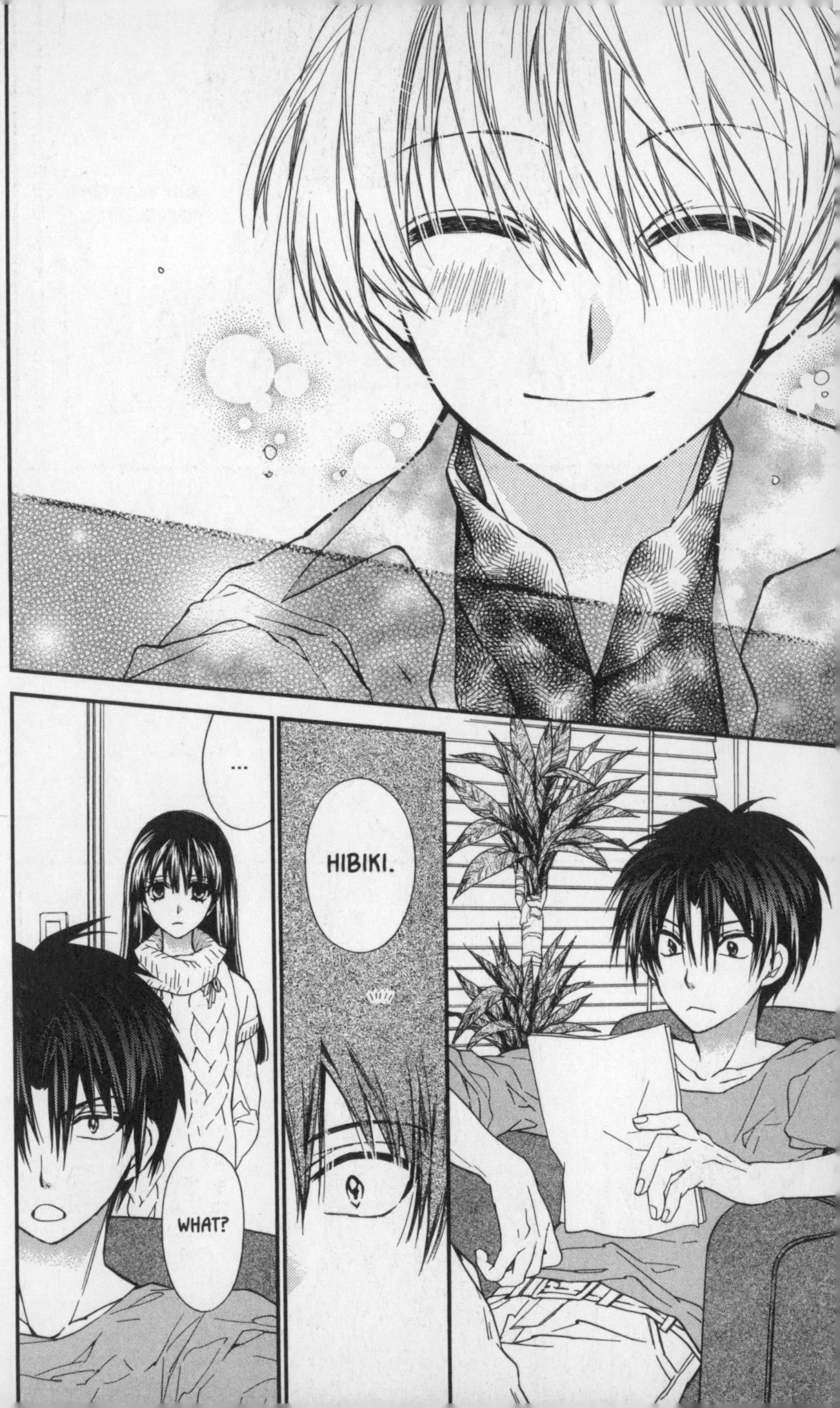
HIBIKI.
...
WHAT?

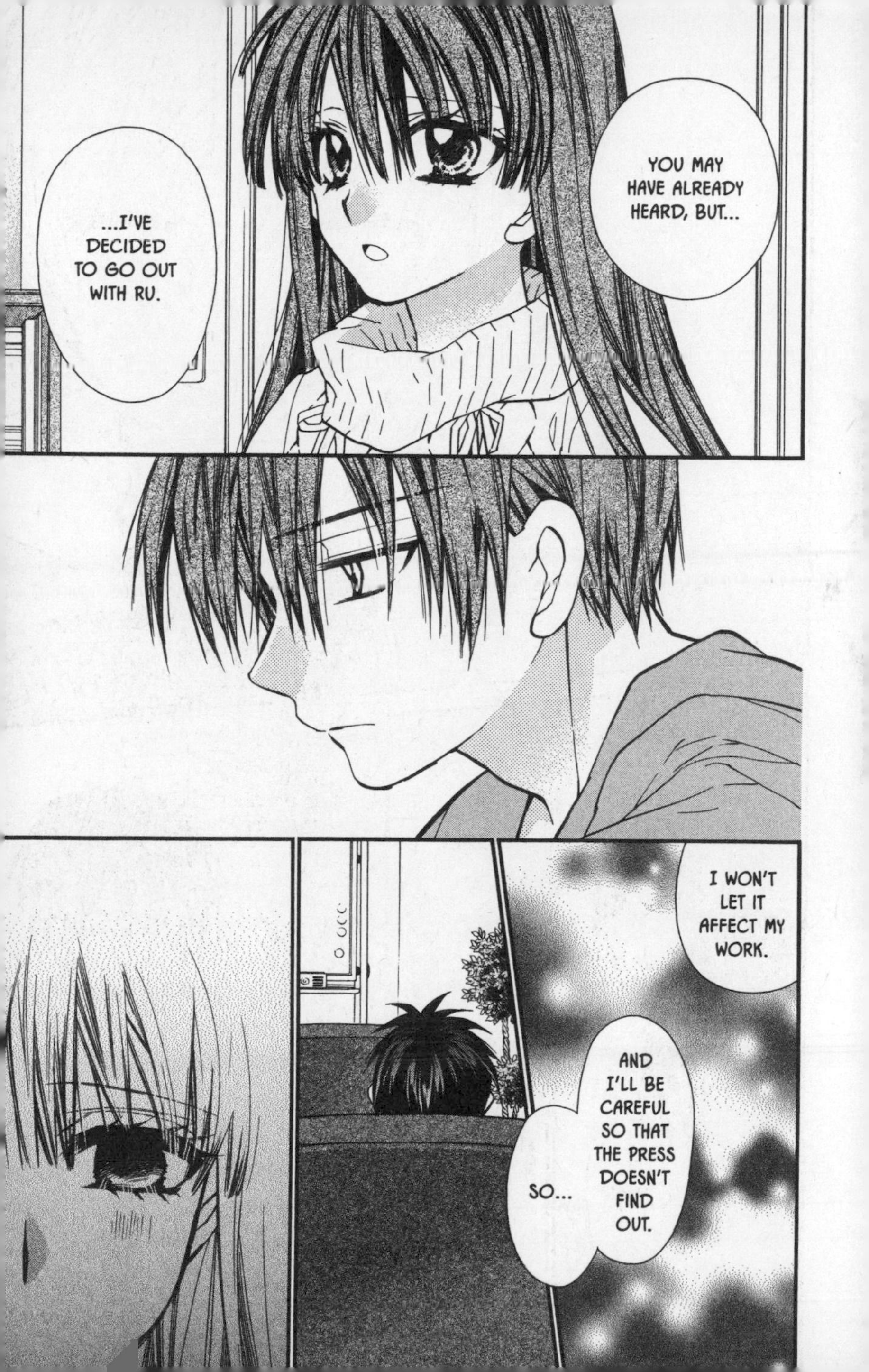
YOU MAY HAVE ALREADY HEARD, BUT...
...I'VE DECIDED TO GO OUT WITH RU.
I WON'T LET IT AFFECT MY WORK.
AND I'LL BE CAREFUL SO THAT THE PRESS DOESN'T FIND OUT.
SO...

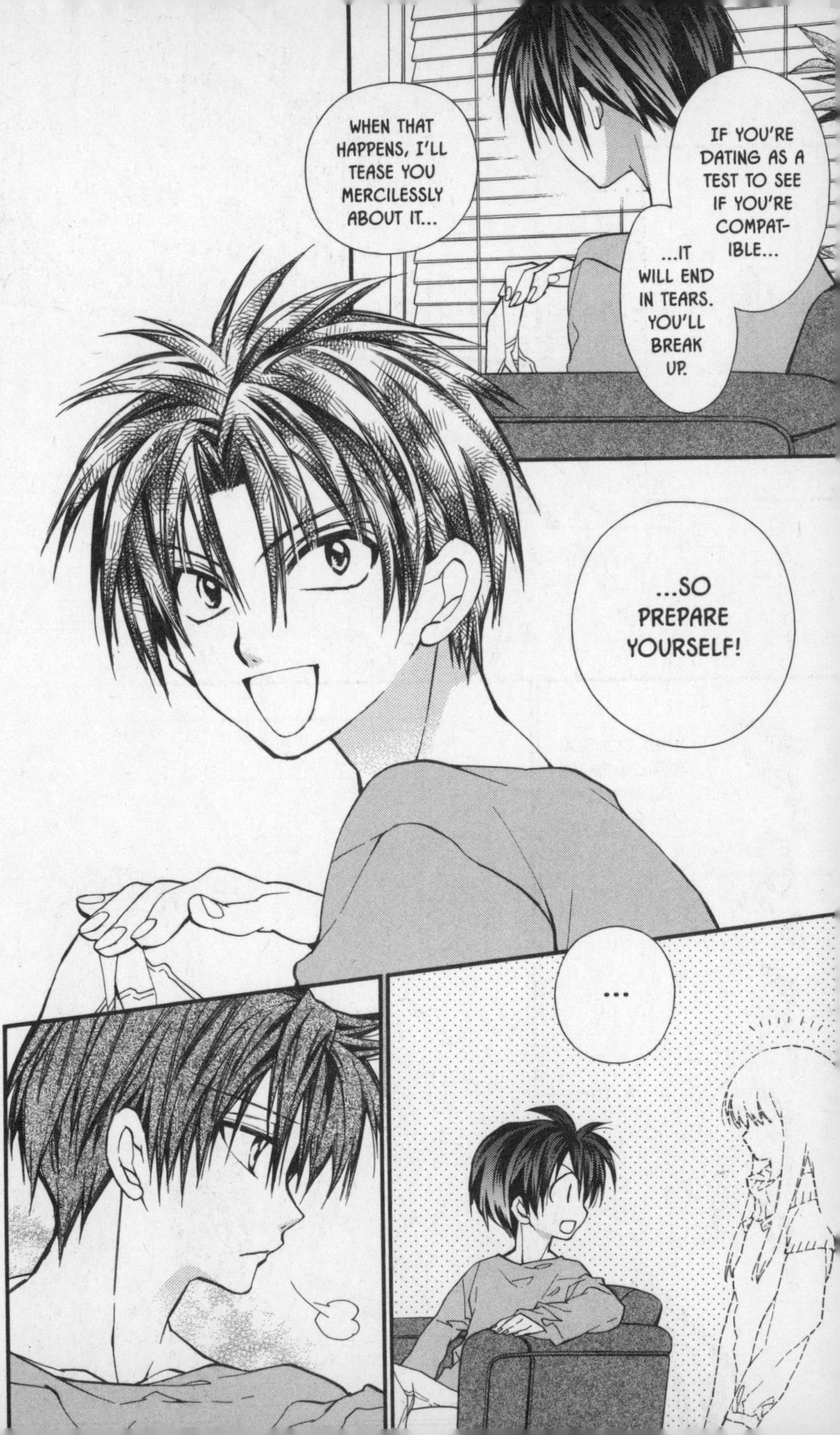
IF YOU'RE DATING AS A TEST TO SEE IF YOU'RE COMPAT-IBLE...
...IT WILL END IN TEARS. YOU'LL BREAK UP.
WHEN THAT HAPPENS, I'LL TEASE YOU MERCILESSLY ABOUT IT...
...SO PREPARE YOURSELF!
...

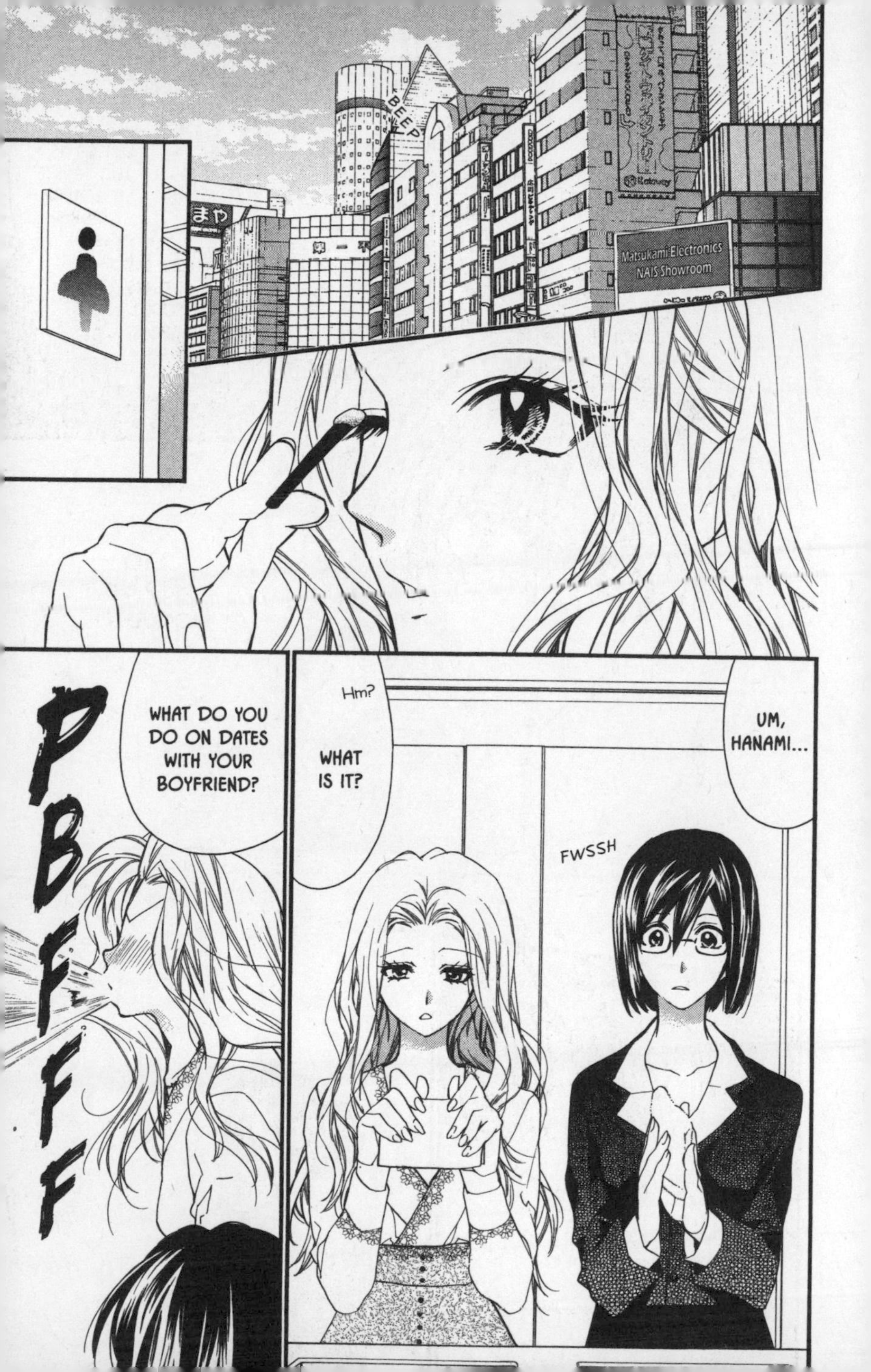
BEEP
Matsukami Electronics
NAIS Showroom
UM, HANAMI...
Hm?
WHAT IS IT?
FWSSH
WHAT DO YOU DO ON DATES WITH YOUR BOYFRIEND?
PBFFFF

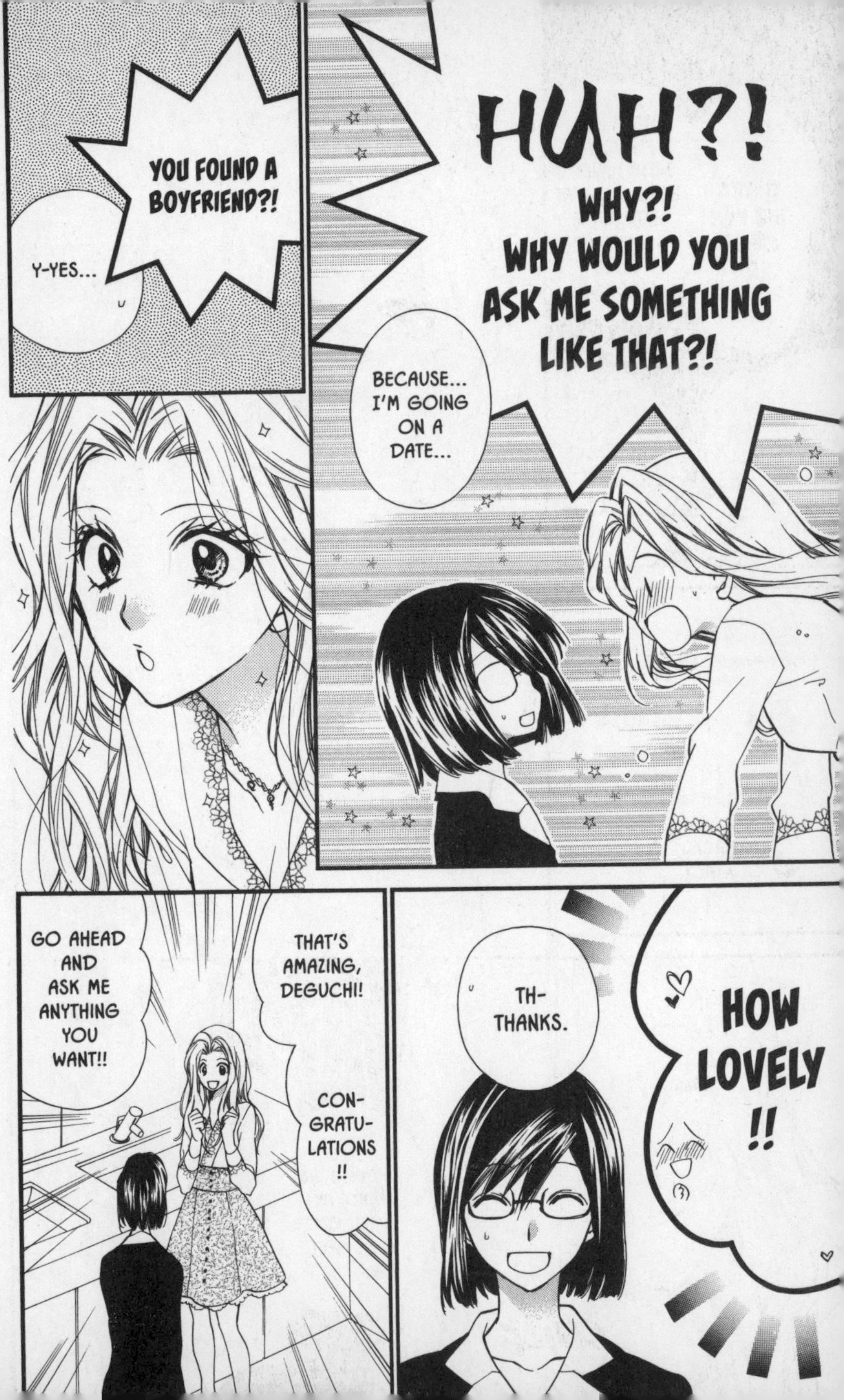
HUH?!
WHY?! WHY WOULD YOU ASK ME SOMETHING LIKE THAT?!
BECAUSE... I'M GOING ON A DATE...
YOU FOUND A BOYFRIEND?!
Y-YES...
HOW LOVELY!!
TH-THANKS.
THAT'S AMAZING, DEGUCHI!
CON-GRATU-LATIONS!!
GO AHEAD AND ASK ME ANYTHING YOU WANT!!

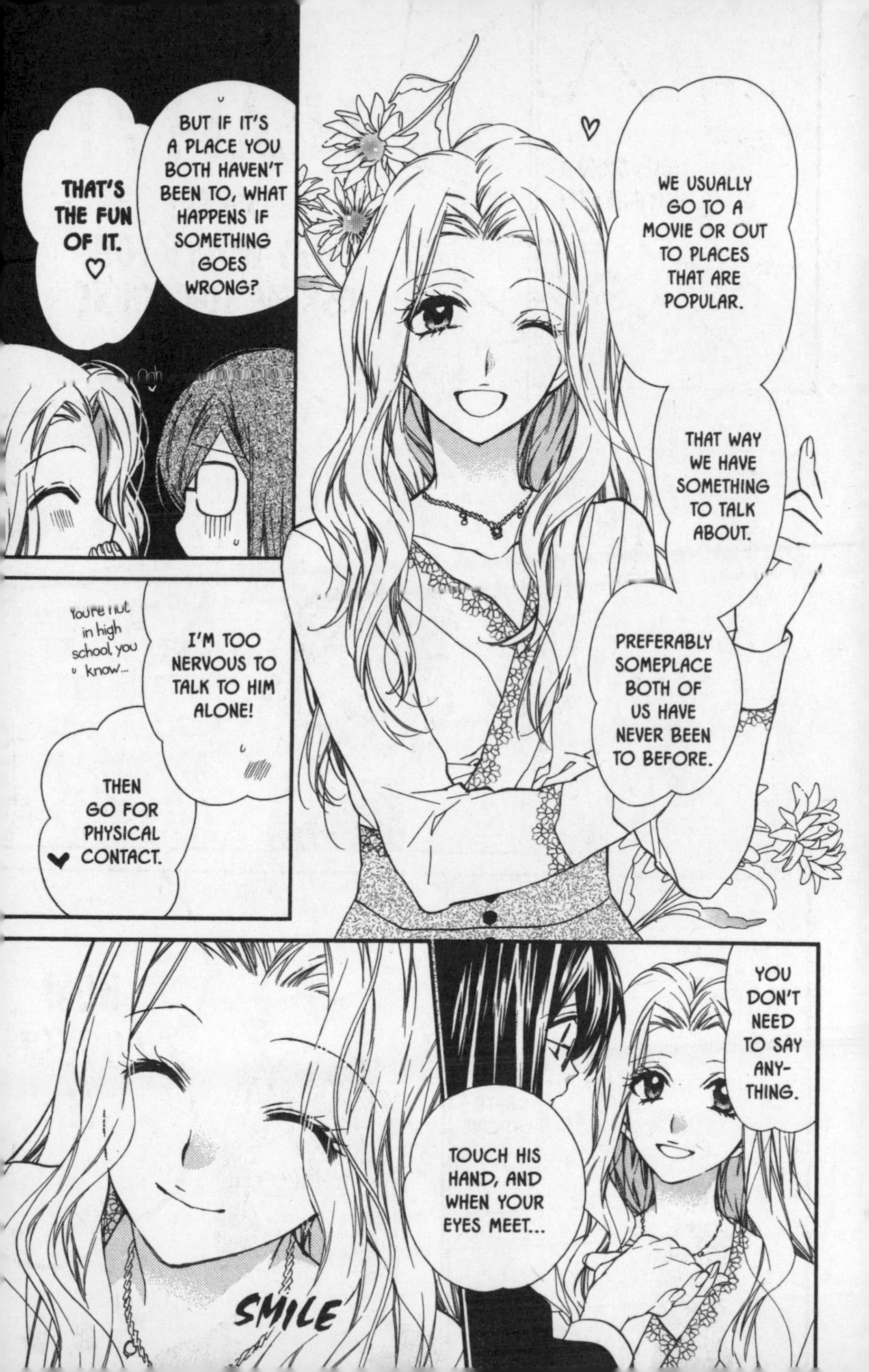
WE USUALLY GO TO A MOVIE OR OUT TO PLACES THAT ARE POPULAR.
THAT WAY WE HAVE SOMETHING TO TALK ABOUT.
PREFERABLY SOMEPLACE BOTH OF US HAVE NEVER BEEN TO BEFORE.
BUT IF IT'S A PLACE YOU BOTH HAVEN'T BEEN TO, WHAT HAPPENS IF SOMETHING GOES WRONG?
THAT'S THE FUN OF IT. ♡
I'M TOO NERVOUS TO TALK TO HIM ALONE!
You're not in high school, you know...
THEN GO FOR PHYSICAL CONTACT. ❤
YOU DON'T NEED TO SAY ANY-THING.
TOUCH HIS HAND, AND WHEN YOUR EYES MEET...
SMILE

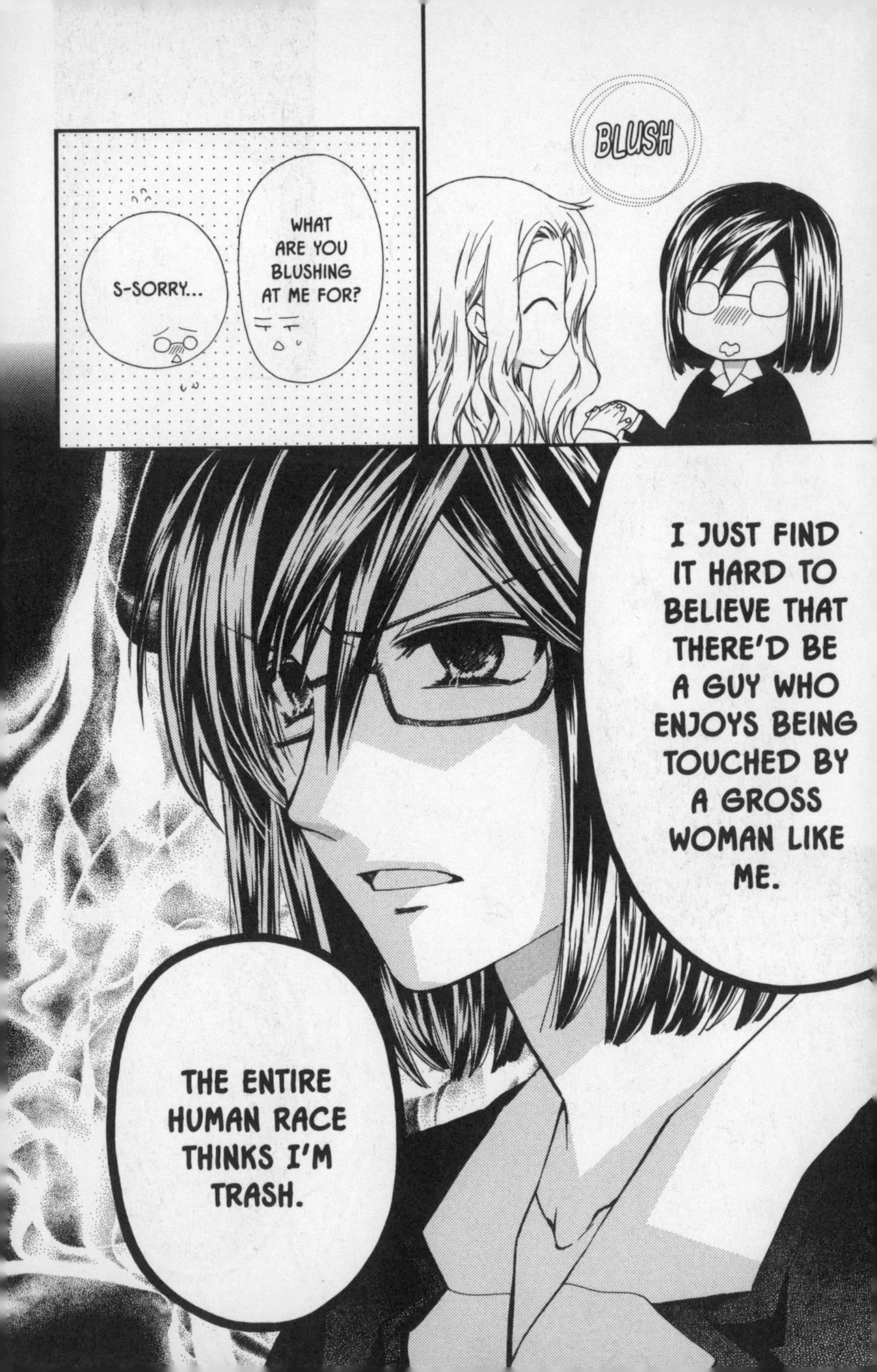
BLUSH
WHAT ARE YOU BLUSHING AT ME FOR?
S-SORRY...
I JUST FIND IT HARD TO BELIEVE THAT THERE'D BE A GUY WHO ENJOYS BEING TOUCHED BY A GROSS WOMAN LIKE ME.
THE ENTIRE HUMAN RACE THINKS I'M TRASH.

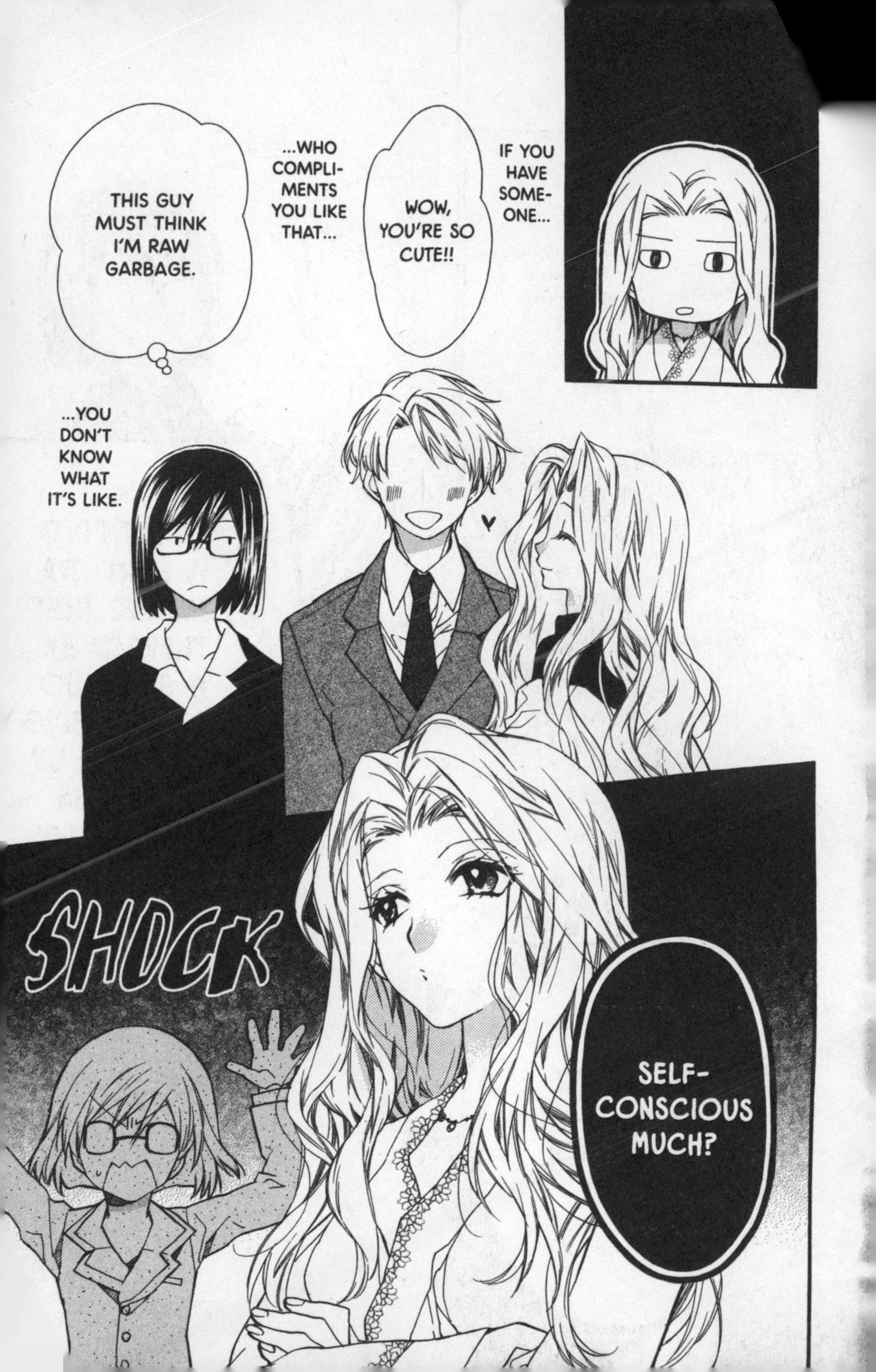
IF YOU HAVE SOME-ONE...
WOW, YOU'RE SO CUTE!!
...WHO COMPLI-MENTS YOU LIKE THAT...
THIS GUY MUST THINK I'M RAW GARBAGE.
...YOU DON'T KNOW WHAT IT'S LIKE.
SELF-CONSCIOUS MUCH?
SHOCK

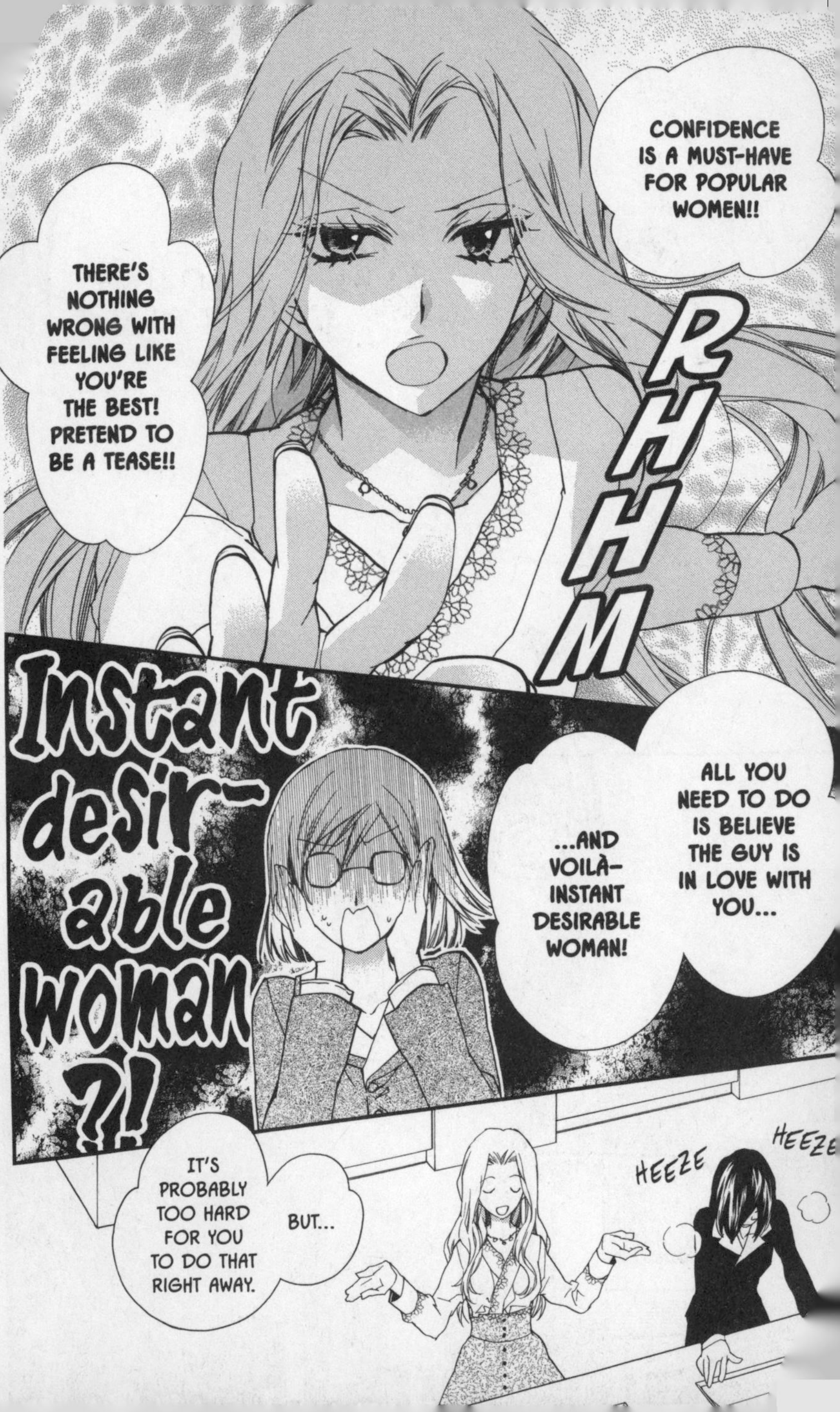
CONFIDENCE IS A MUST-HAVE FOR POPULAR WOMEN!!
THERE'S NOTHING WRONG WITH FEELING LIKE YOU'RE THE BEST! PRETEND TO BE A TEASE!!
RHHHM
ALL YOU NEED TO DO IS BELIEVE THE GUY IS IN LOVE WITH YOU...
...AND VOILÀ—INSTANT DESIRABLE WOMAN!
Instant desir-able woman?!
HEEZE
HEEZE
IT'S PROBABLY TOO HARD FOR YOU TO DO THAT RIGHT AWAY.
BUT...

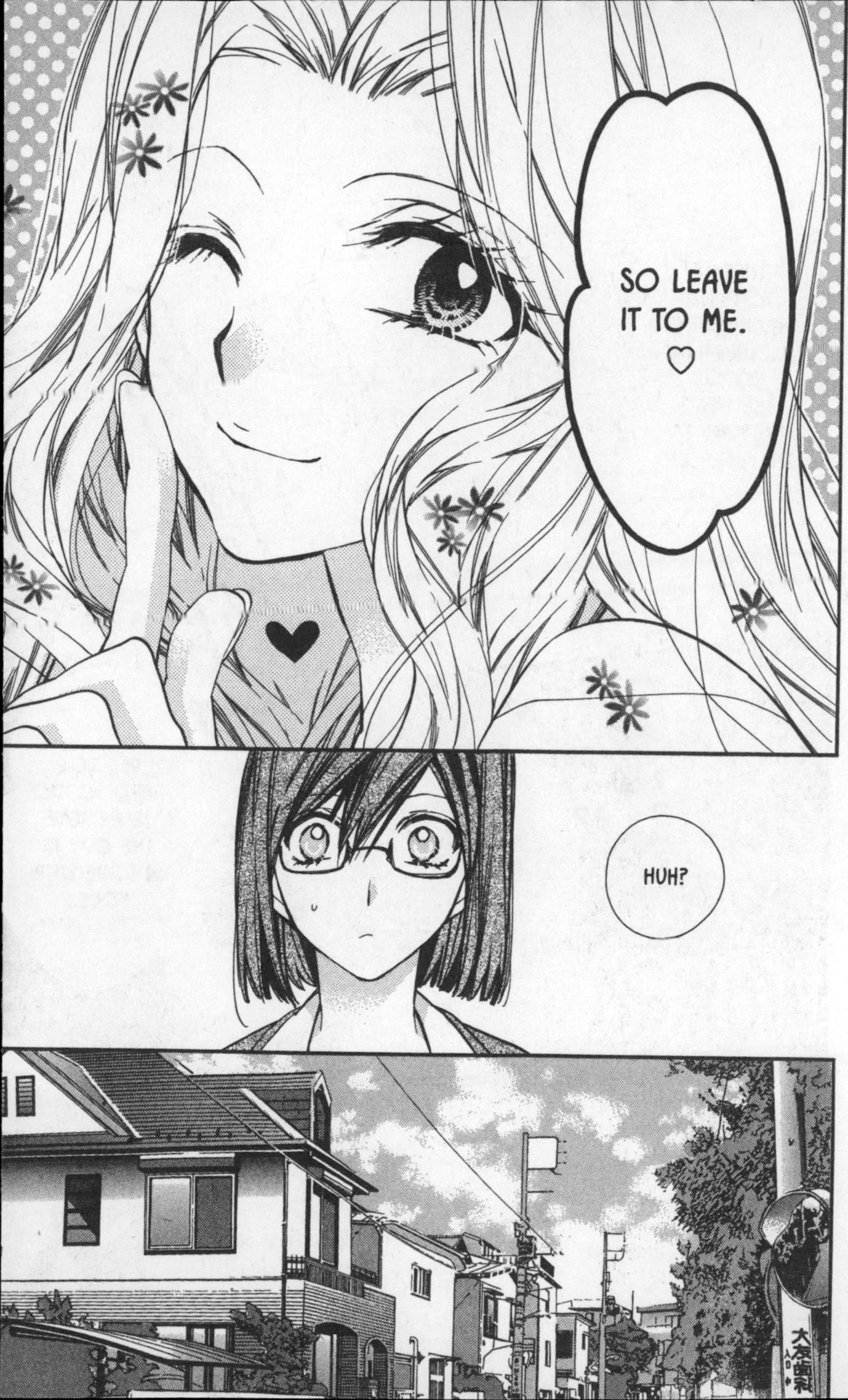
SO LEAVE IT TO ME. ♡
HUH?

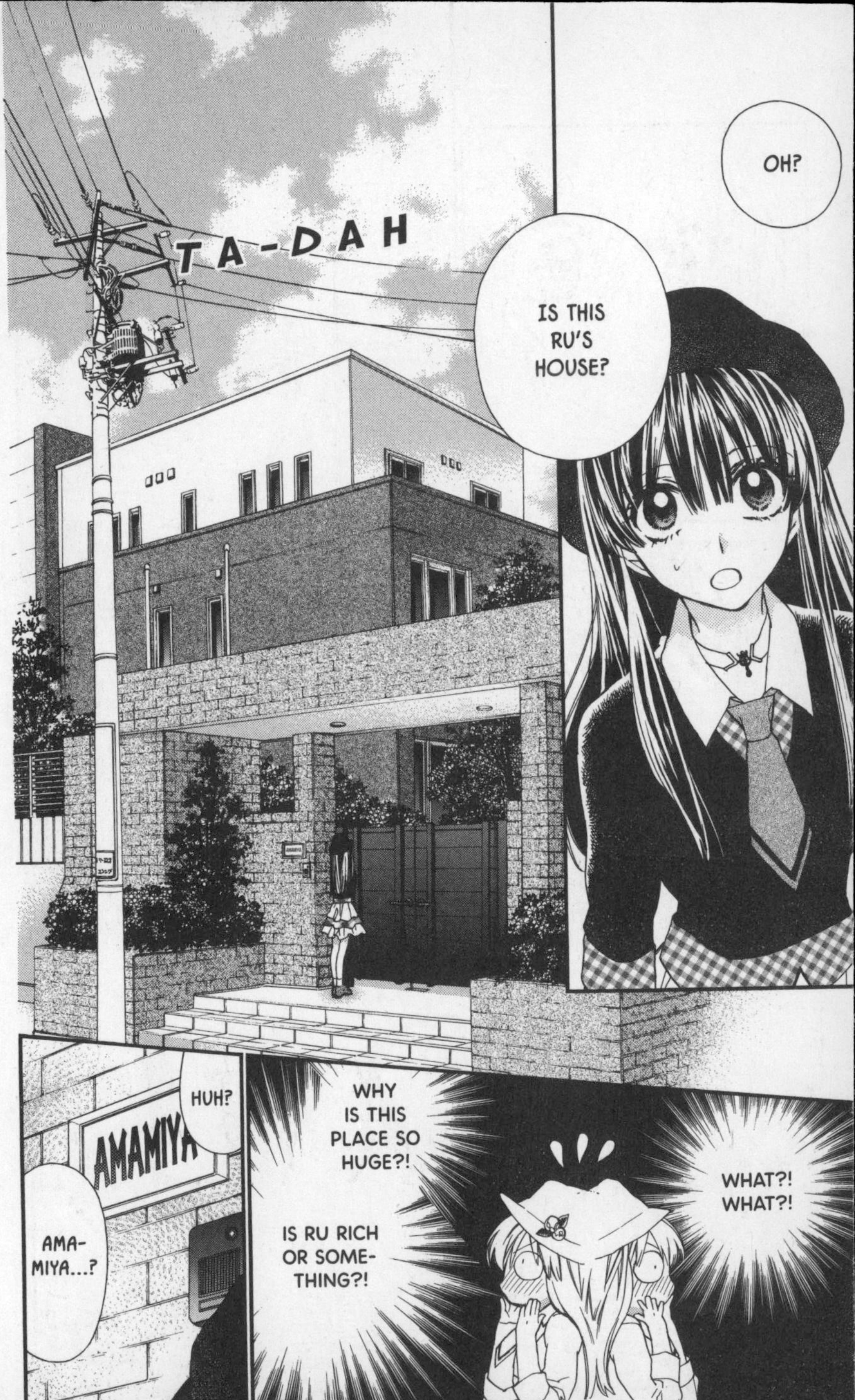
OH?
IS THIS RU'S HOUSE?
TA-DAH
WHAT?! WHAT?!
WHY IS THIS PLACE SO HUGE?!
IS RU RICH OR SOMETHING?!
HUH?
AMAMIYA
AMA-MIYA...?

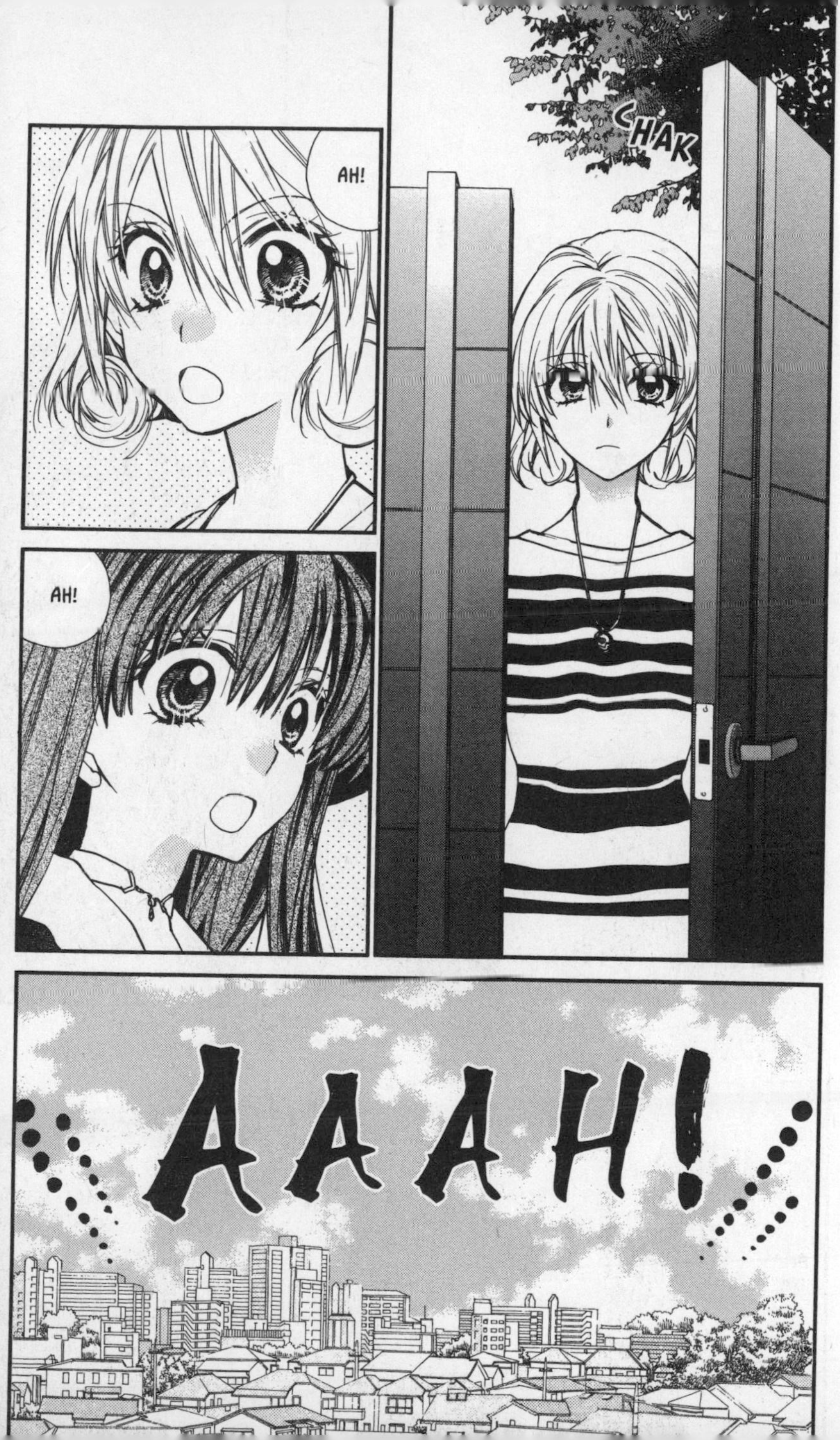
CHAK
AH!
AH!
AAAH!

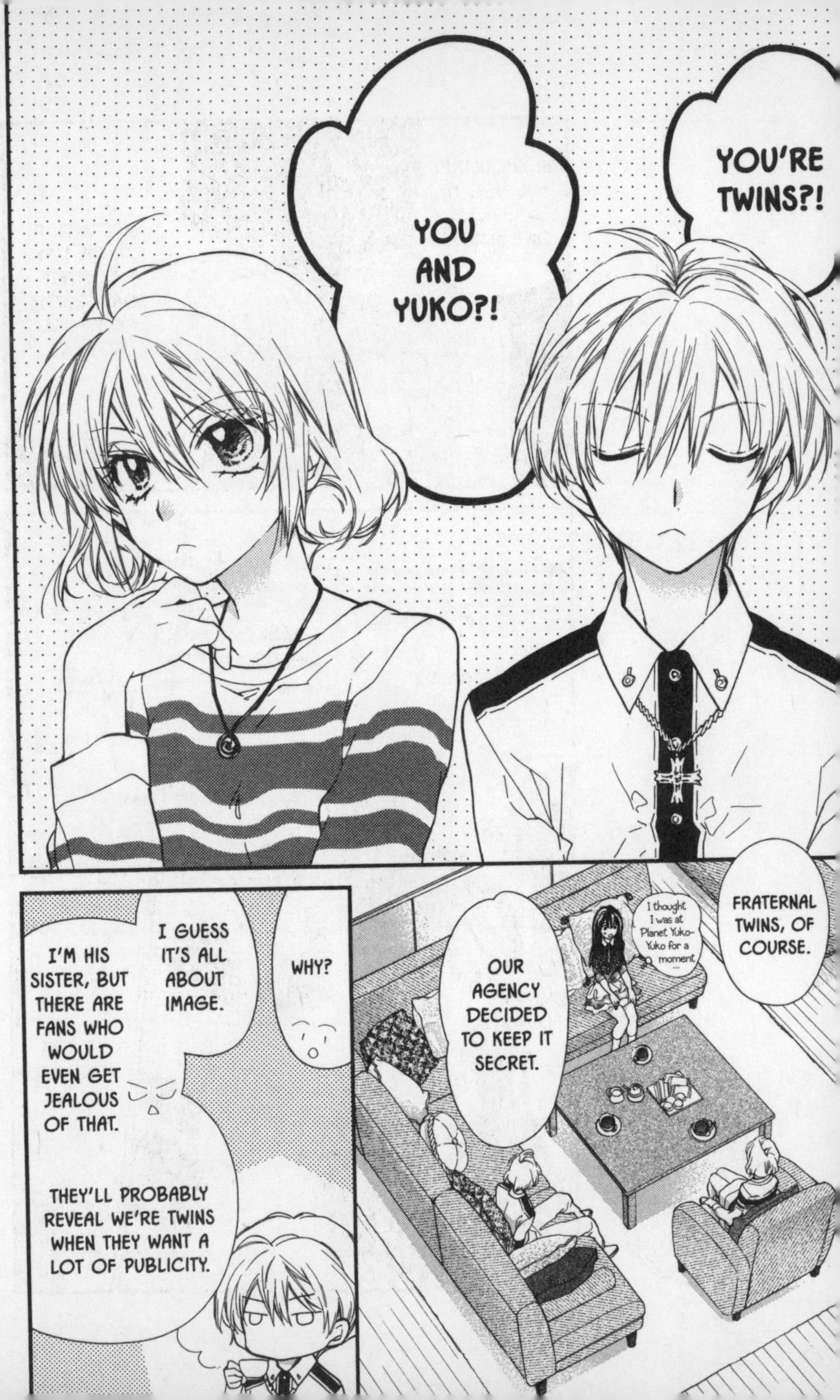
YOU'RE TWINS?!
YOU AND YUKO?!
FRATERNAL TWINS, OF COURSE.
I thought I was at Planet Yuko-Yuko for a moment...
OUR AGENCY DECIDED TO KEEP IT SECRET.
WHY?
I GUESS IT'S ALL ABOUT IMAGE.
I'M HIS SISTER, BUT THERE ARE FANS WHO WOULD EVEN GET JEALOUS OF THAT.
THEY'LL PROBABLY REVEAL WE'RE TWINS WHEN THEY WANT A LOT OF PUBLICITY.

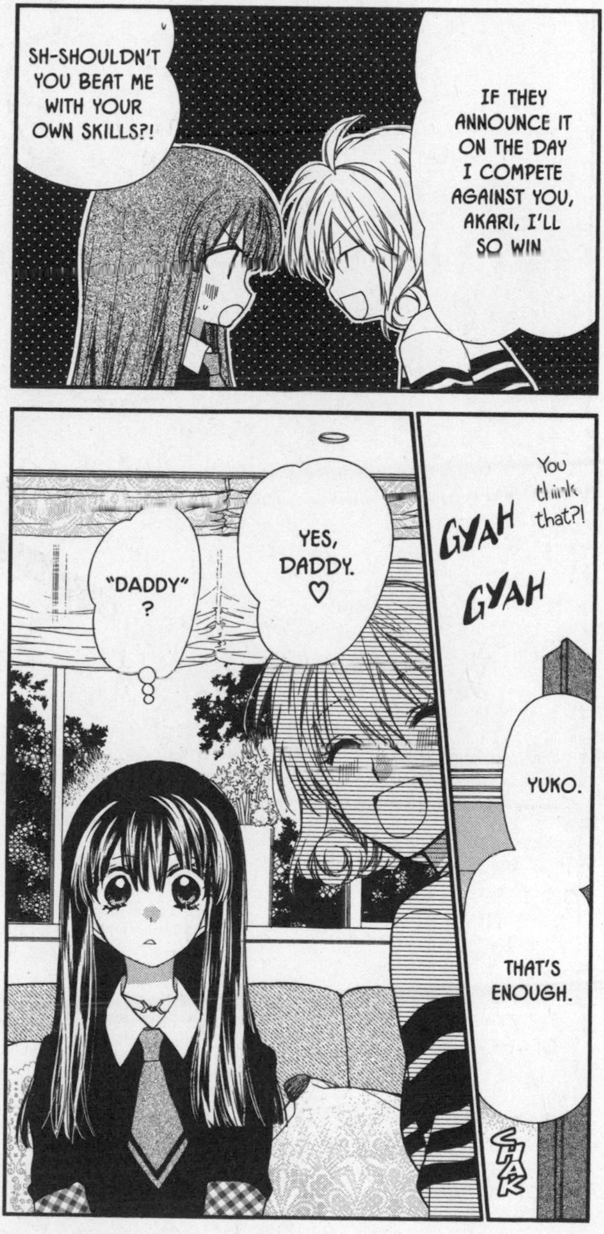
IF THEY ANNOUNCE IT ON THE DAY I COMPETE AGAINST YOU, AKARI, I'LL SO WIN
SH-SHOULDN'T YOU BEAT ME WITH YOUR OWN SKILLS?!
You think that?!
GYAH
GYAH
YUKO.
THAT'S ENOUGH.
CHAK
YES, DADDY. ♡
"DADDY"?

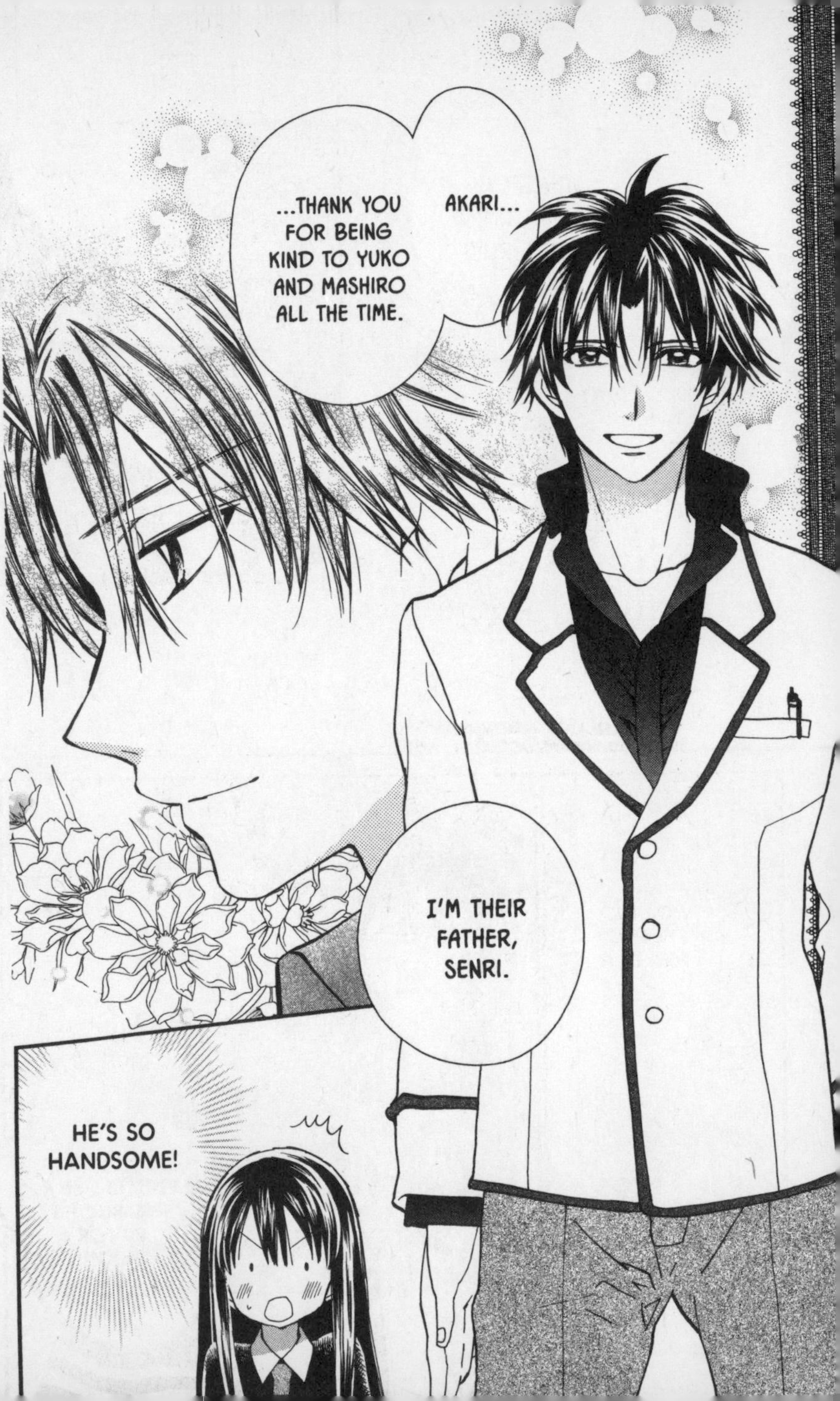
AKARI...
...THANK YOU FOR BEING KIND TO YUKO AND MASHIRO ALL THE TIME.
I'M THEIR FATHER, SENRI.
HE'S SO HANDSOME!

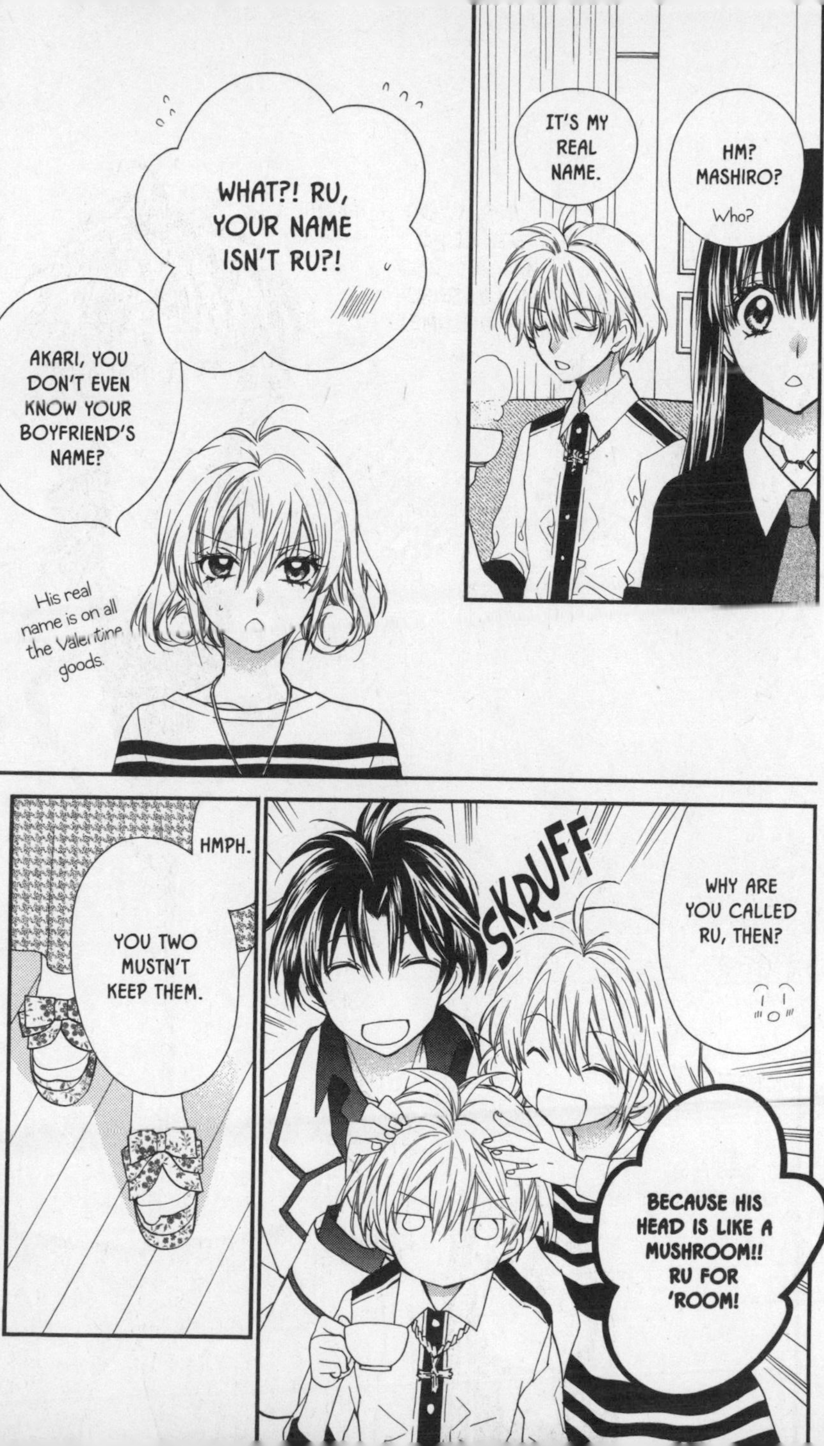
HM? MASHIRO?
Who?
IT'S MY REAL NAME.
WHAT?! RU, YOUR NAME ISN'T RU?!
AKARI, YOU DON'T EVEN KNOW YOUR BOYFRIEND'S NAME?
His real name is on all the Valentine goods.
WHY ARE YOU CALLED RU, THEN?
SKRUFF
BECAUSE HIS HEAD IS LIKE A MUSHROOM!! RU FOR 'ROOM!
HMPH.
YOU TWO MUSTN'T KEEP THEM.

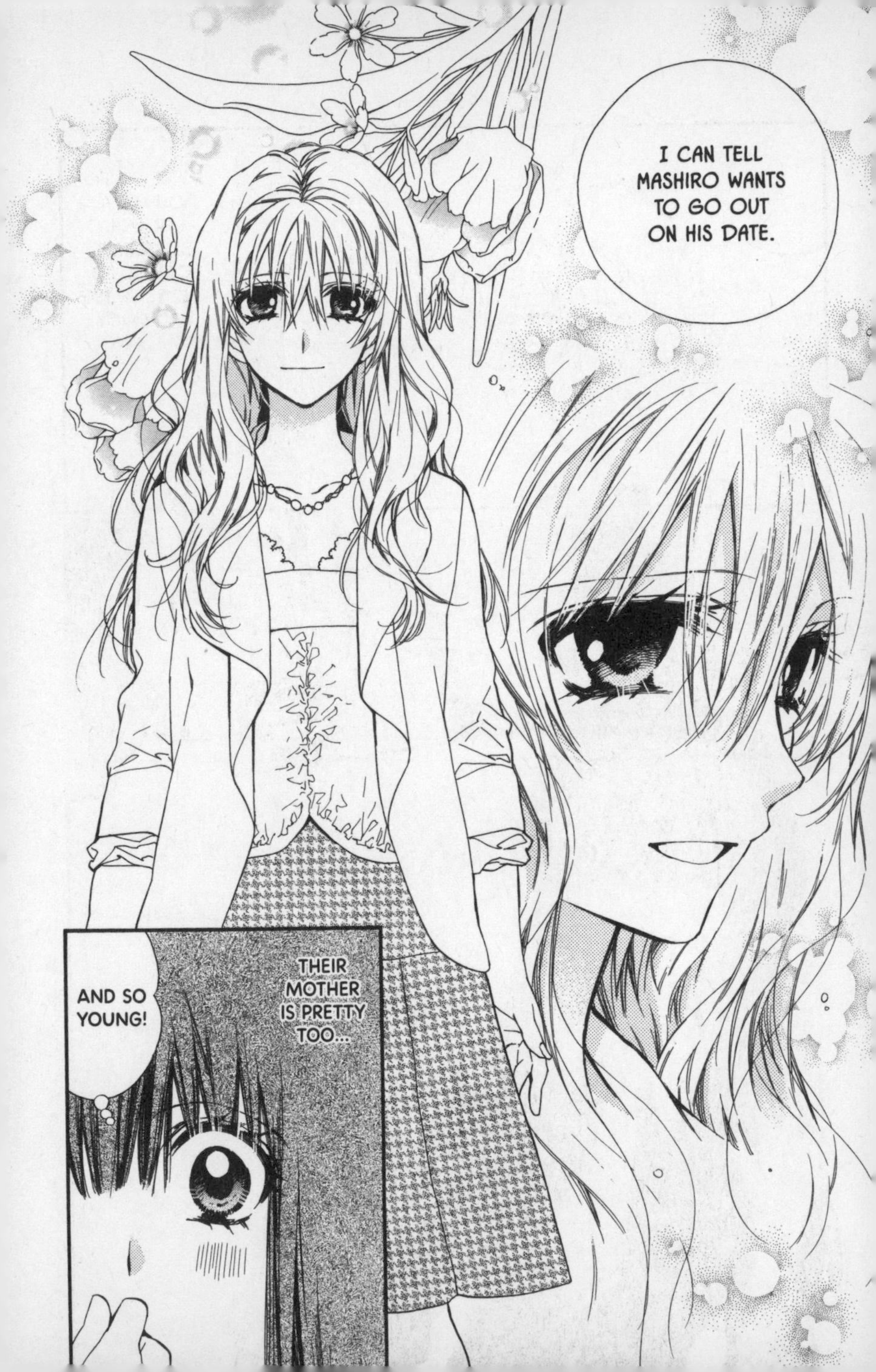
I CAN TELL MASHIRO WANTS TO GO OUT ON HIS DATE.
THEIR MOTHER IS PRETTY TOO...
AND SO YOUNG!

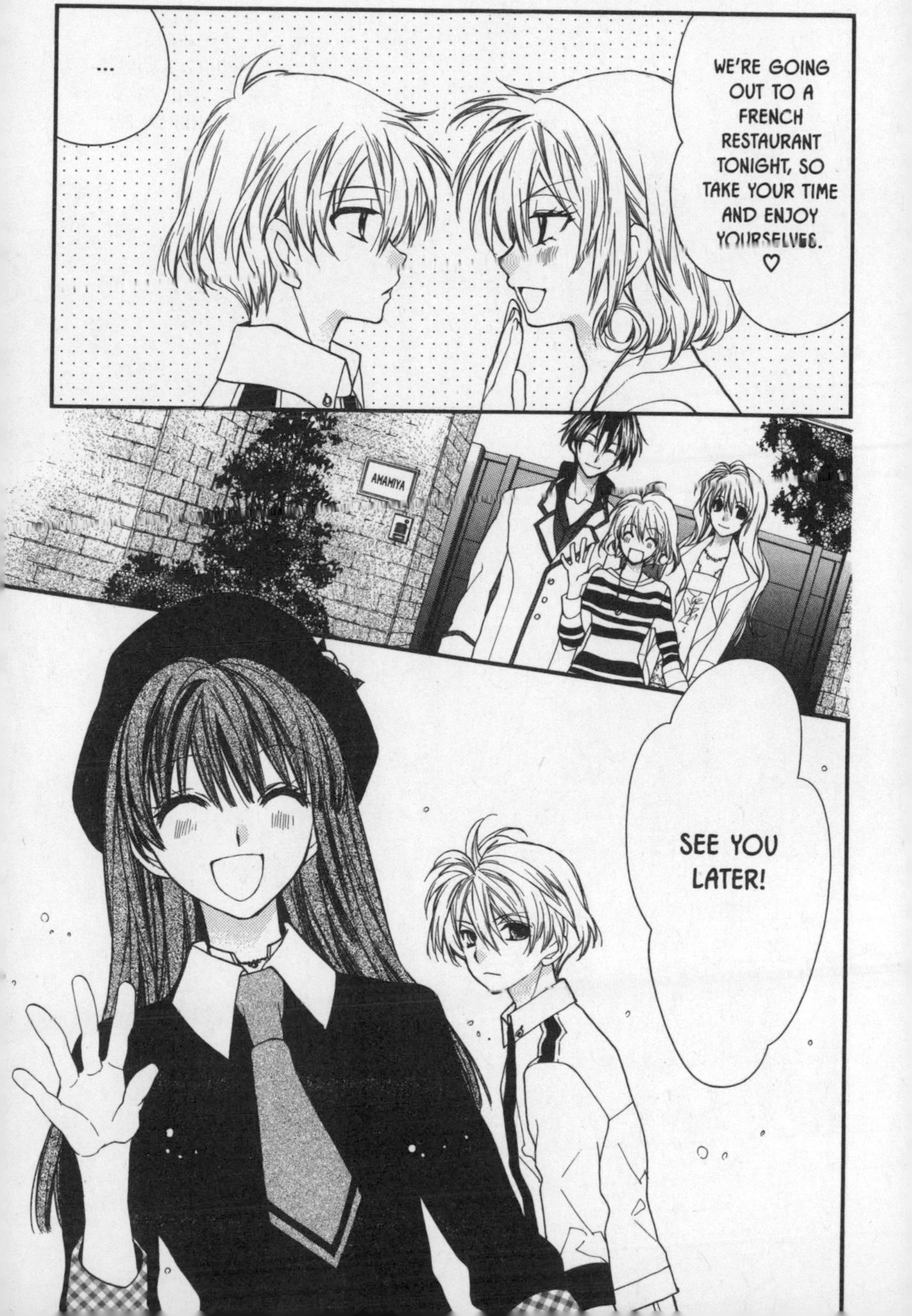
WE'RE GOING OUT TO A FRENCH RESTAURANT TONIGHT, SO TAKE YOUR TIME AND ENJOY YOURSELVES. ♡
...
AMAMIYA
SEE YOU LATER!

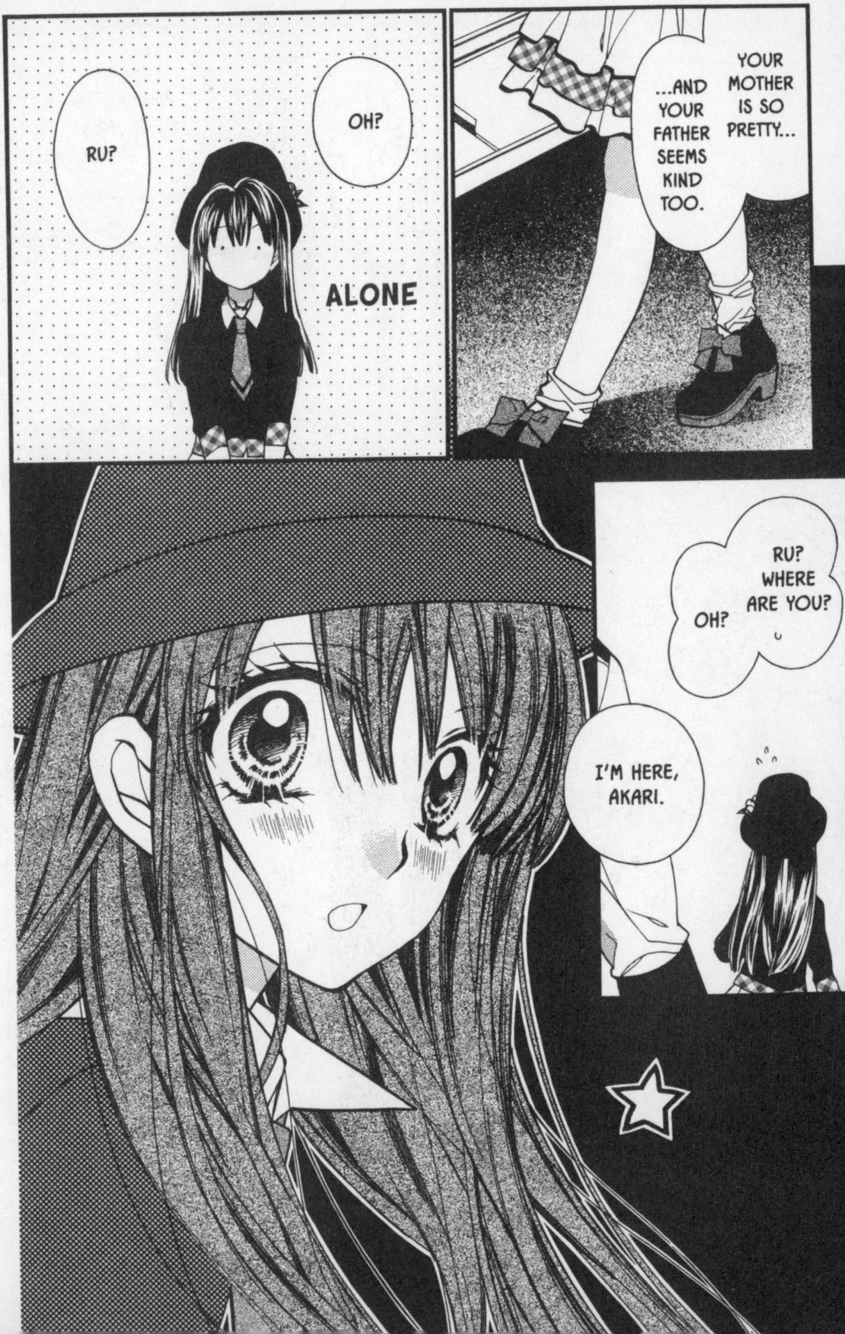
YOUR MOTHER IS SO PRETTY...
...AND YOUR FATHER SEEMS KIND TOO.
OH?
RU?
ALONE
OH?
RU? WHERE ARE YOU?
I'M HERE, AKARI.

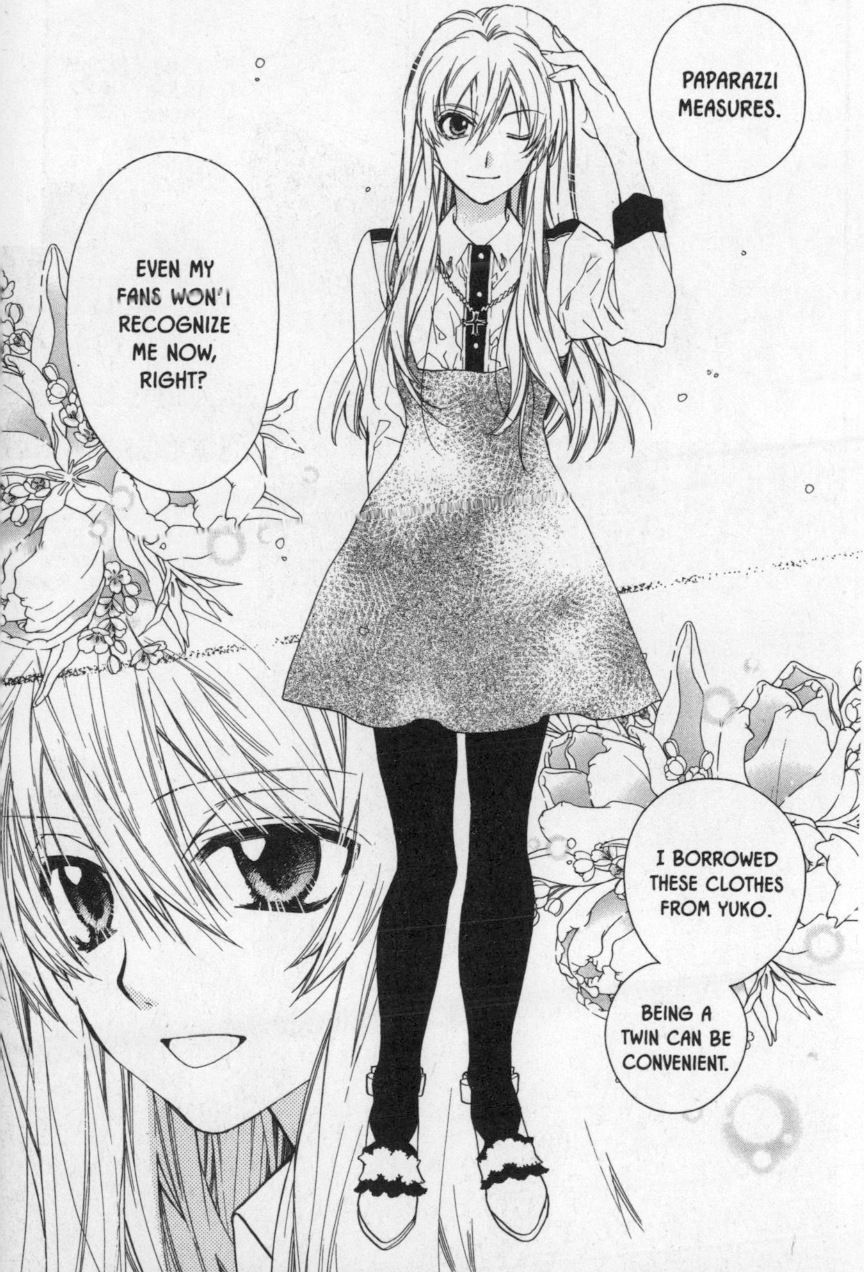
PAPARAZZI MEASURES.
EVEN MY FANS WON'T RECOGNIZE ME NOW, RIGHT?
I BORROWED THESE CLOTHES FROM YUKO.
BEING A TWIN CAN BE CONVENIENT.

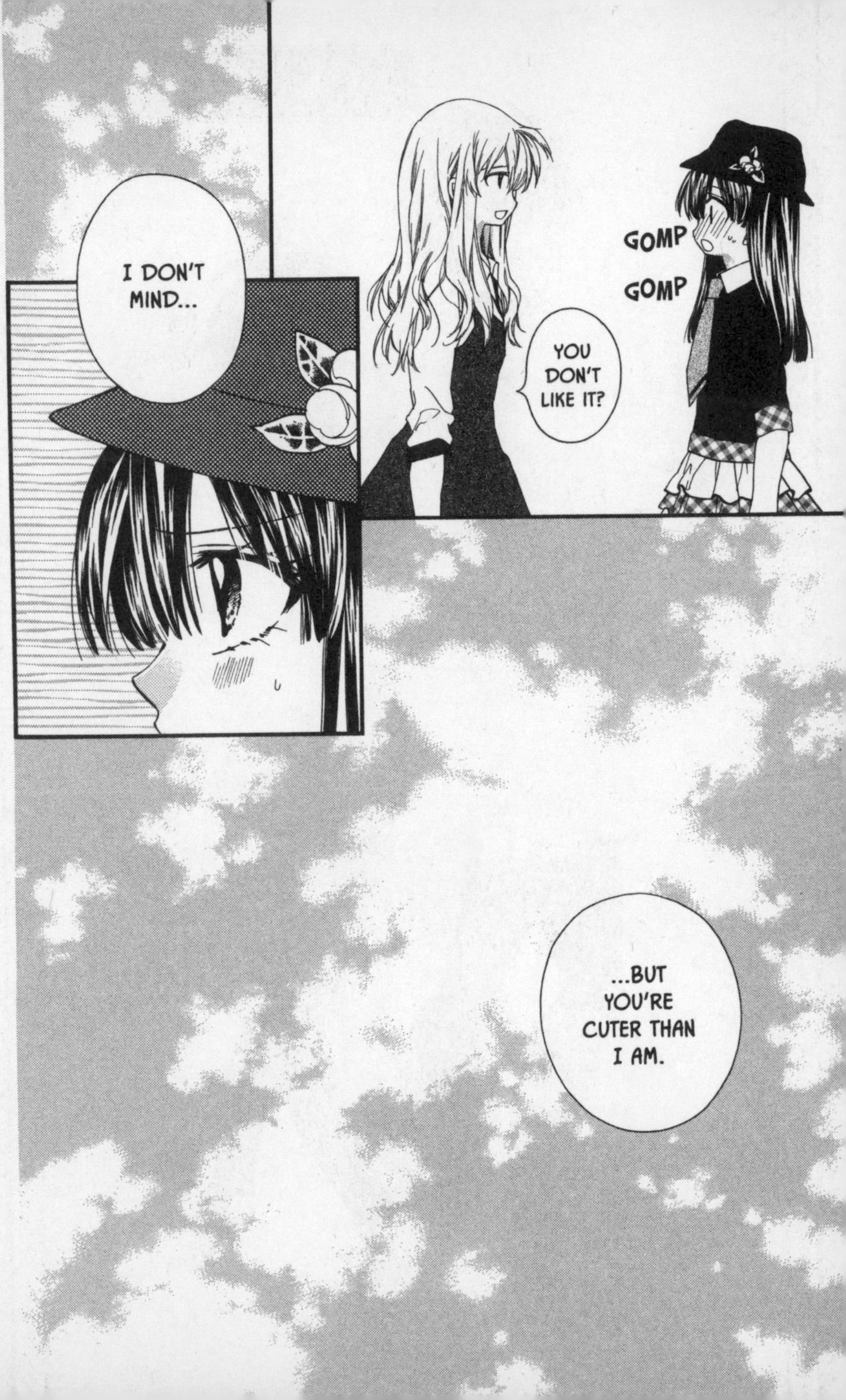
GOMP
GOMP
YOU DON'T LIKE IT?
I DON'T MIND...
...BUT YOU'RE CUTER THAN I AM.

Chapter 17

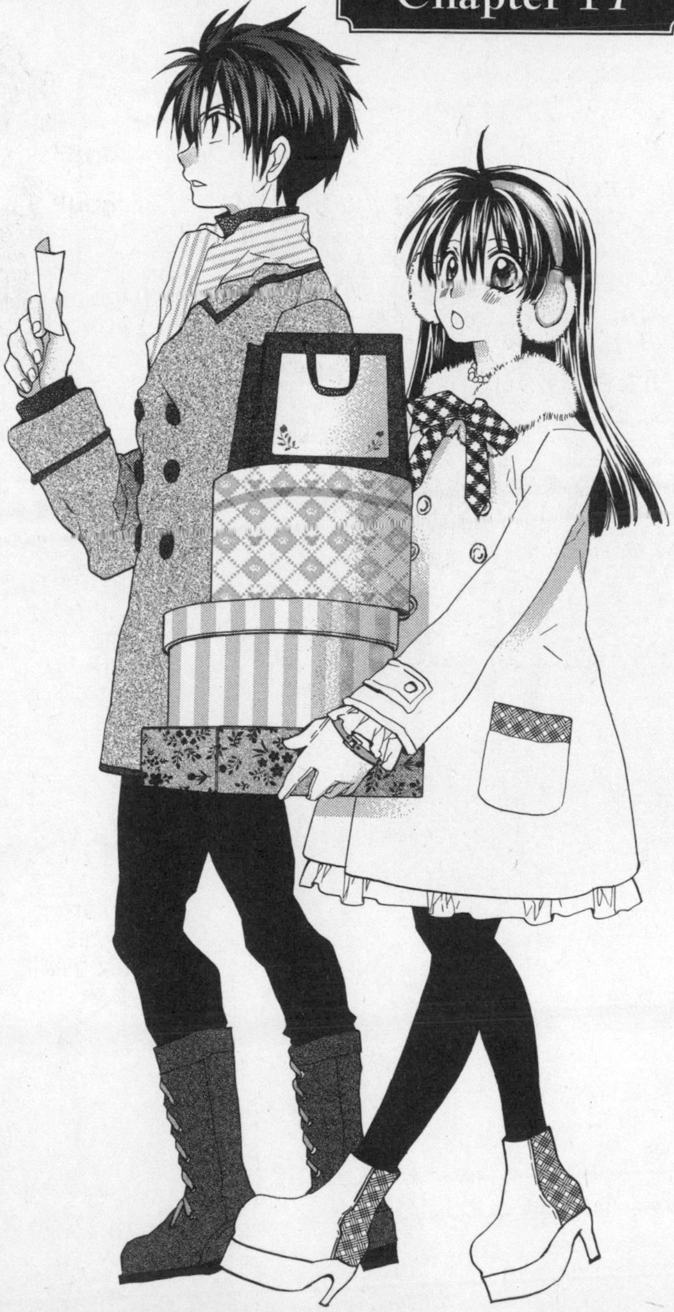

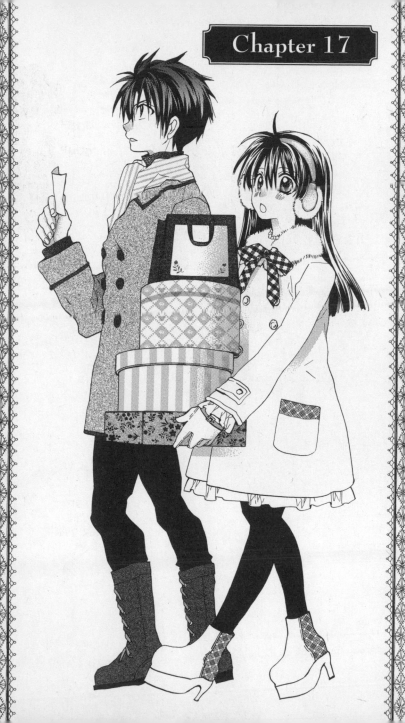

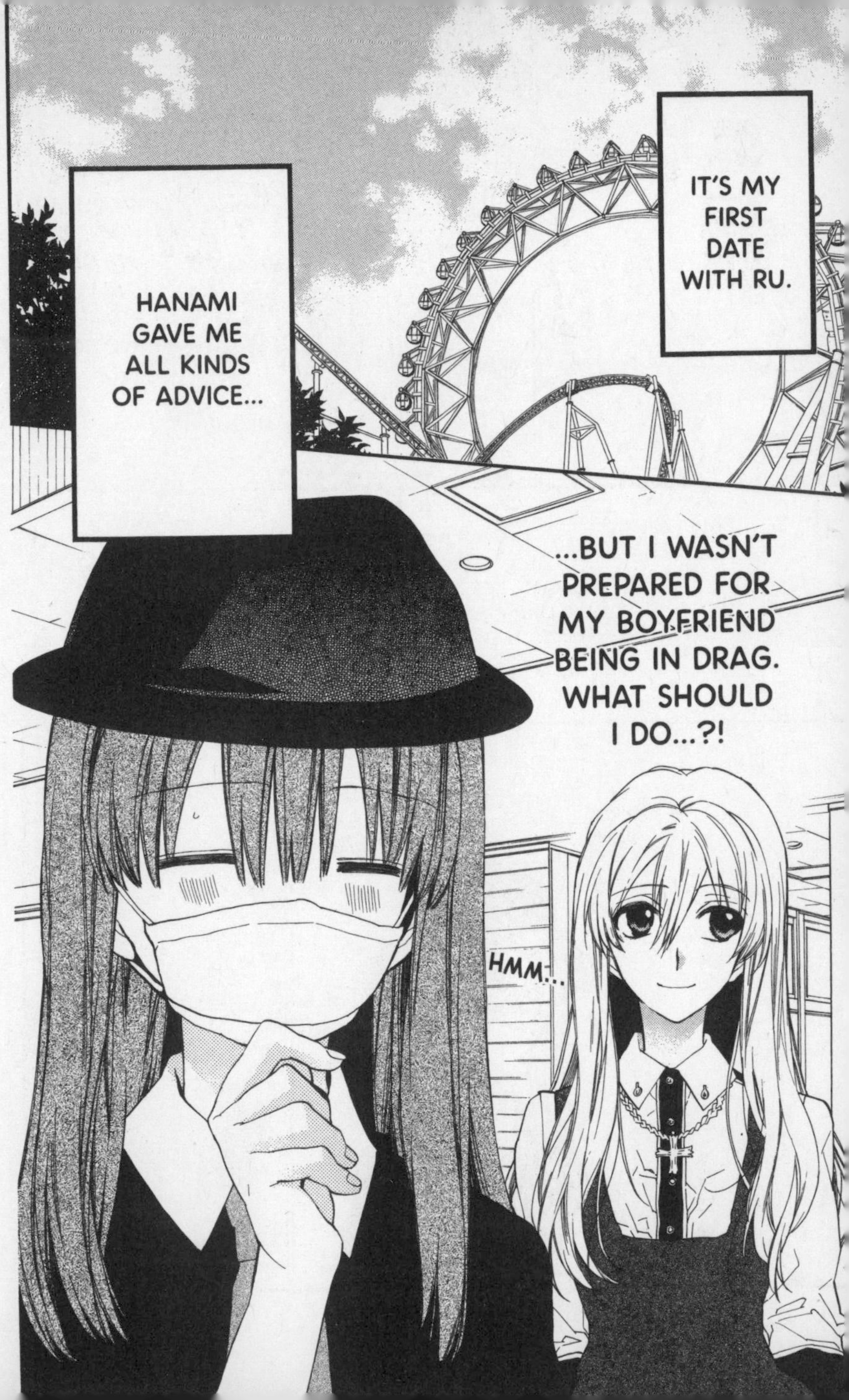
IT'S MY FIRST DATE WITH RU.
HANAMI GAVE ME ALL KINDS OF ADVICE...
...BUT I WASN'T PREPARED FOR MY BOYFRIEND BEING IN DRAG. WHAT SHOULD I DO...?!
HMM...

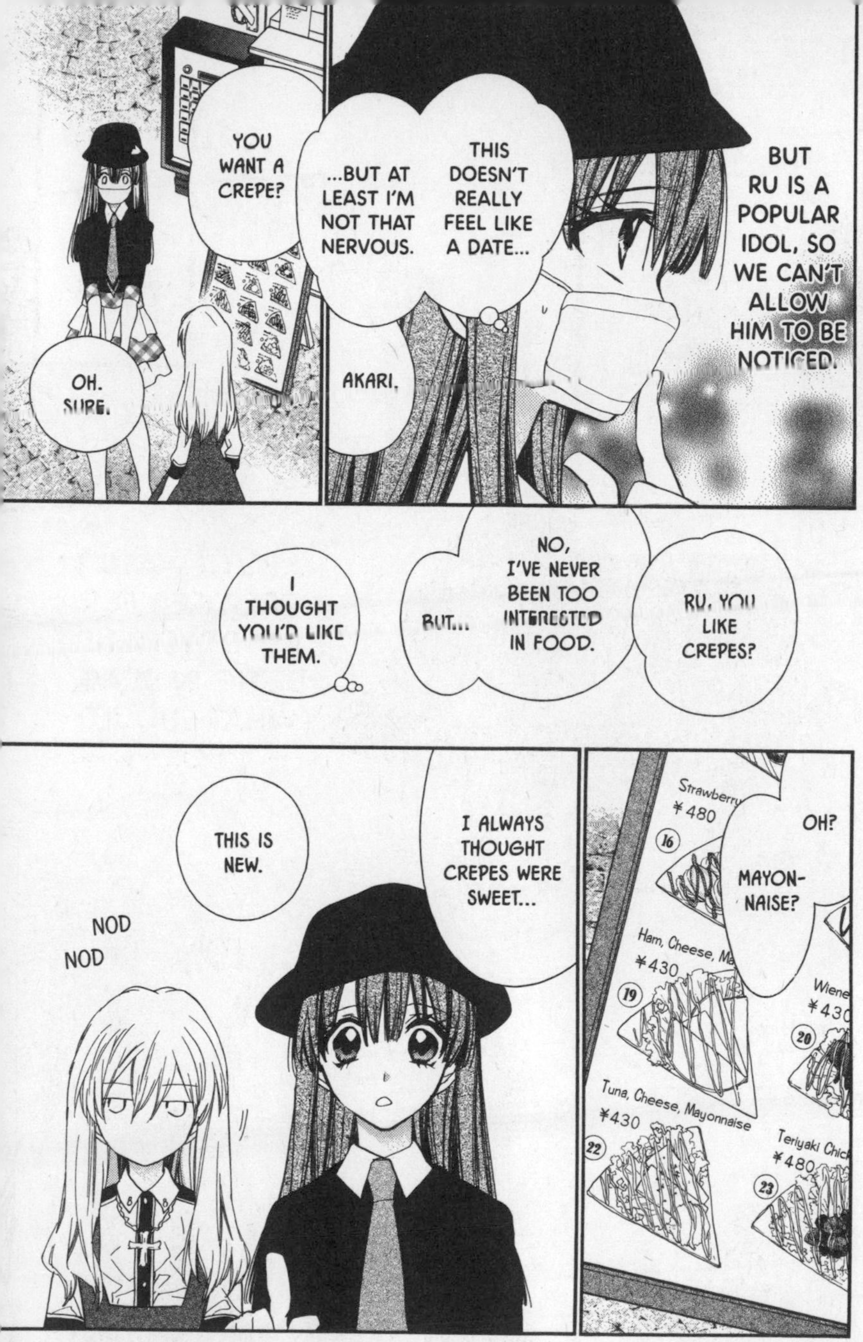
BUT RU IS A POPULAR IDOL, SO WE CAN'T ALLOW HIM TO BE NOTICED.
THIS DOESN'T REALLY FEEL LIKE A DATE...
...BUT AT LEAST I'M NOT THAT NERVOUS.
AKARI.
YOU WANT A CREPE?
OH. SURE.
RU, YOU LIKE CREPES?
NO, I'VE NEVER BEEN TOO INTERESTED IN FOOD.
BUT...
I THOUGHT YOU'D LIKE THEM.
OH?
MAYONNAISE?
Strawberry
¥480
Tuna, Cheese, Mayonnaise
¥430
I ALWAYS THOUGHT CREPES WERE SWEET...
THIS IS NEW.
NOD
NOD

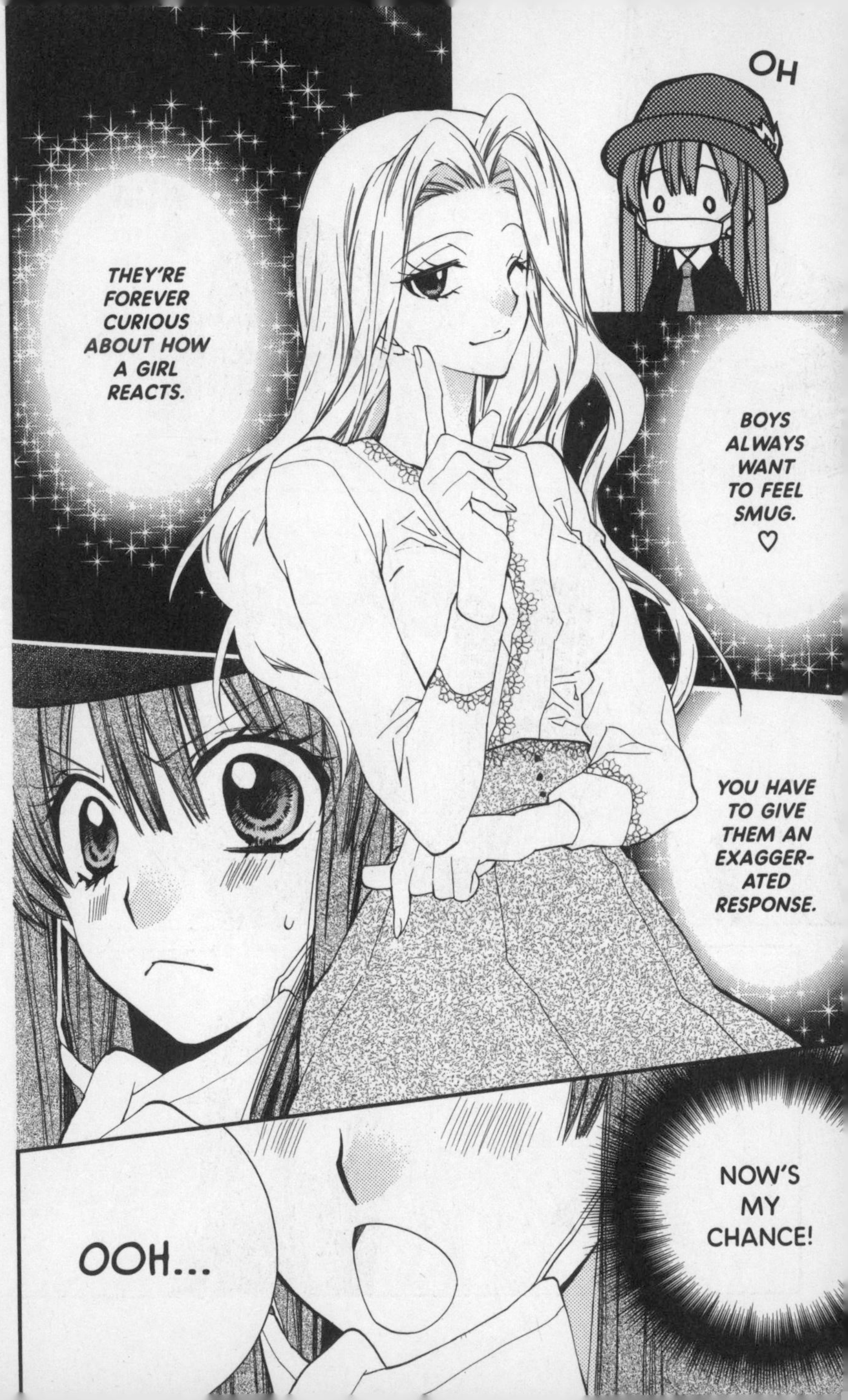
OH
BOYS ALWAYS WANT TO FEEL SMUG. ♡
THEY'RE FOREVER CURIOUS ABOUT HOW A GIRL REACTS.
YOU HAVE TO GIVE THEM AN EXAGGER-ATED RESPONSE.
NOW'S MY CHANCE!
OOH...

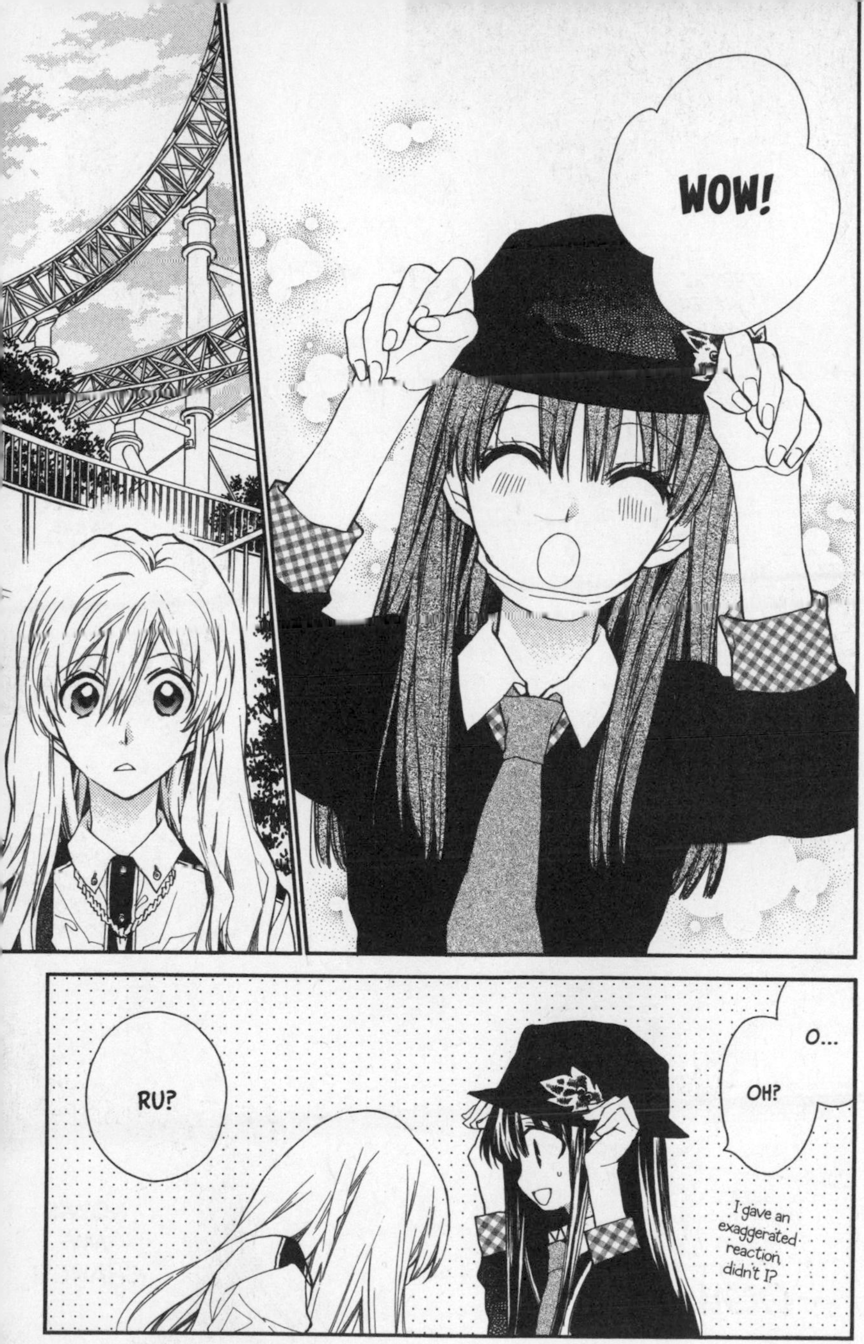
WOW!
O...
OH?
RU?
I gave an exaggerated reaction, didn't I?

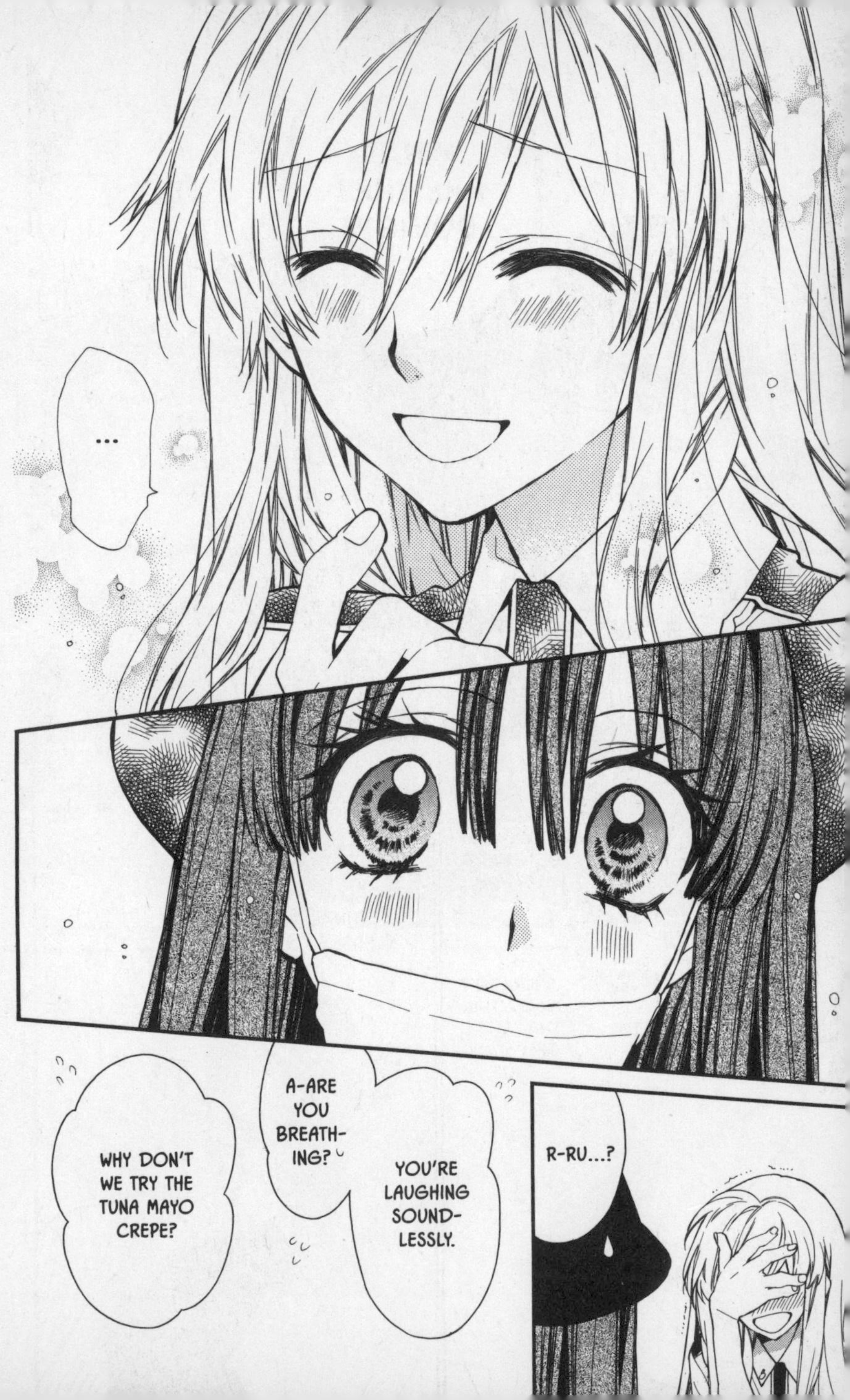
...
R-RU...?
YOU'RE LAUGHING SOUND-LESSLY.
A-ARE YOU BREATH-ING?
WHY DON'T WE TRY THE TUNA MAYO CREPE?

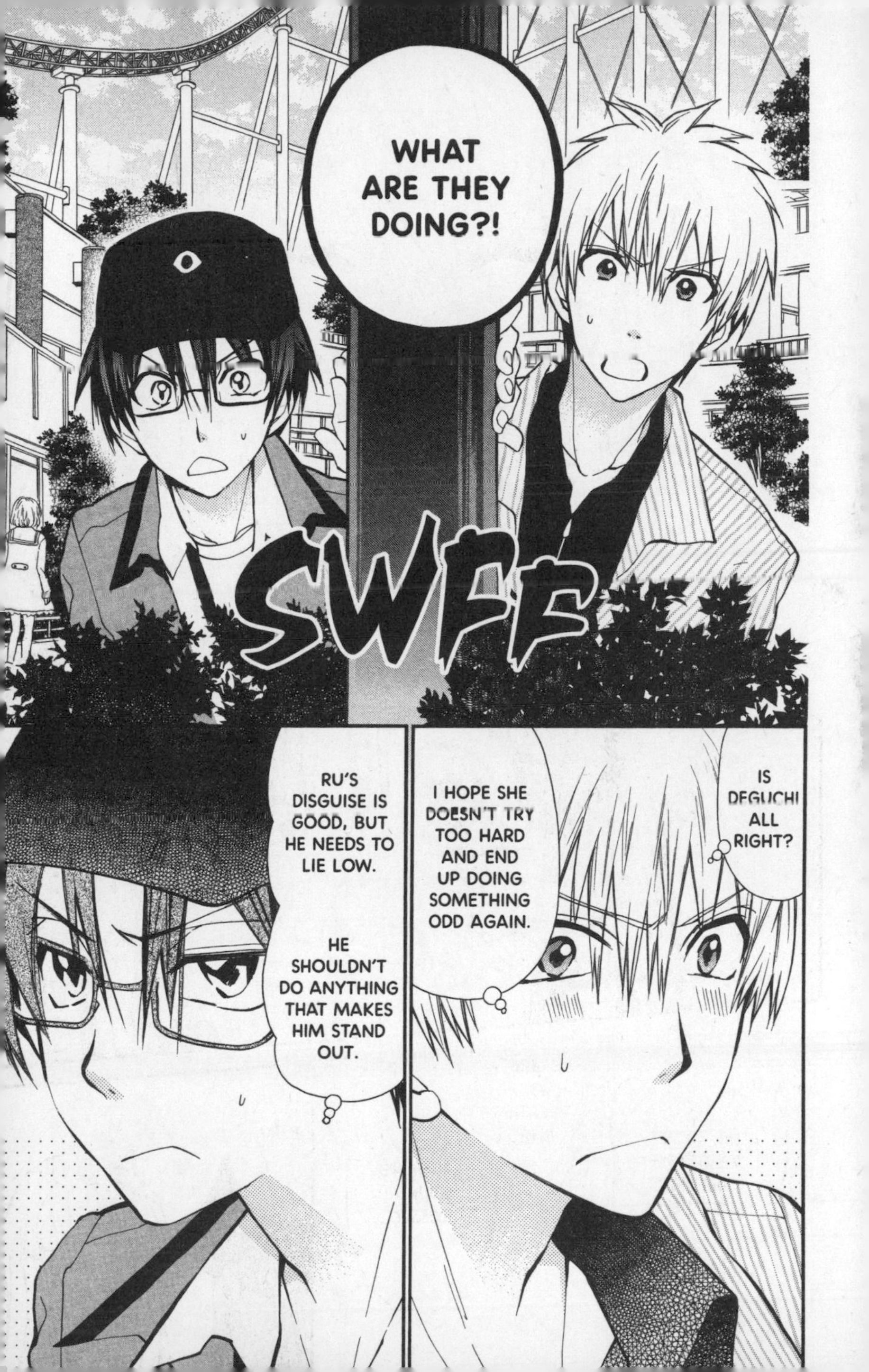
WHAT ARE THEY DOING?!
SWFF
IS DEGUCHI ALL RIGHT?
I HOPE SHE DOESN'T TRY TOO HARD AND END UP DOING SOMETHING ODD AGAIN.
RU'S DISGUISE IS GOOD, BUT HE NEEDS TO LIE LOW.
HE SHOULDN'T DO ANYTHING THAT MAKES HIM STAND OUT.

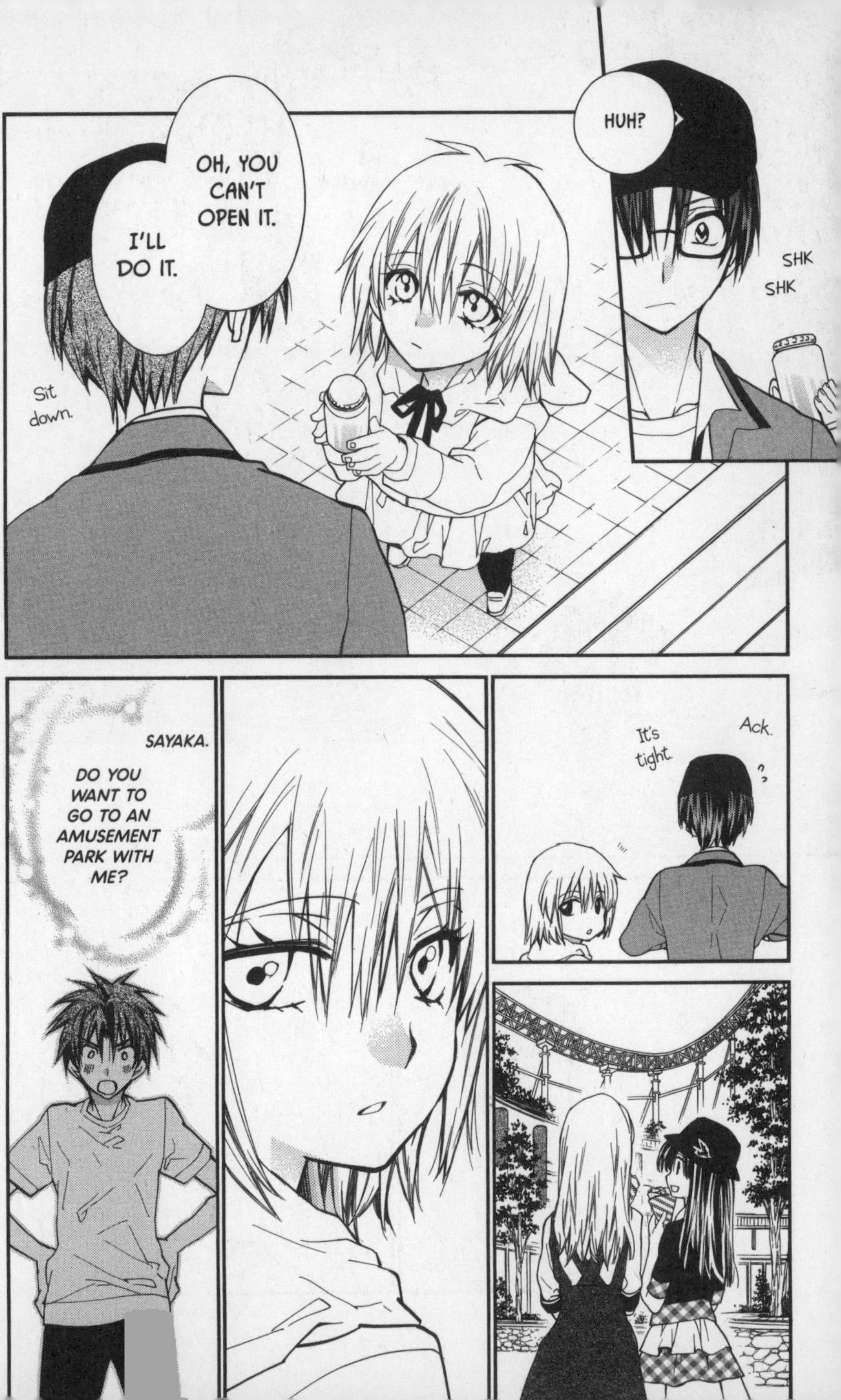
HUH?
SHK
SHK
OH, YOU CAN'T OPEN IT.
I'LL DO IT.
Sit down.
Ack.
It's tight.
SAYAKA.
DO YOU WANT TO GO TO AN AMUSEMENT PARK WITH ME?

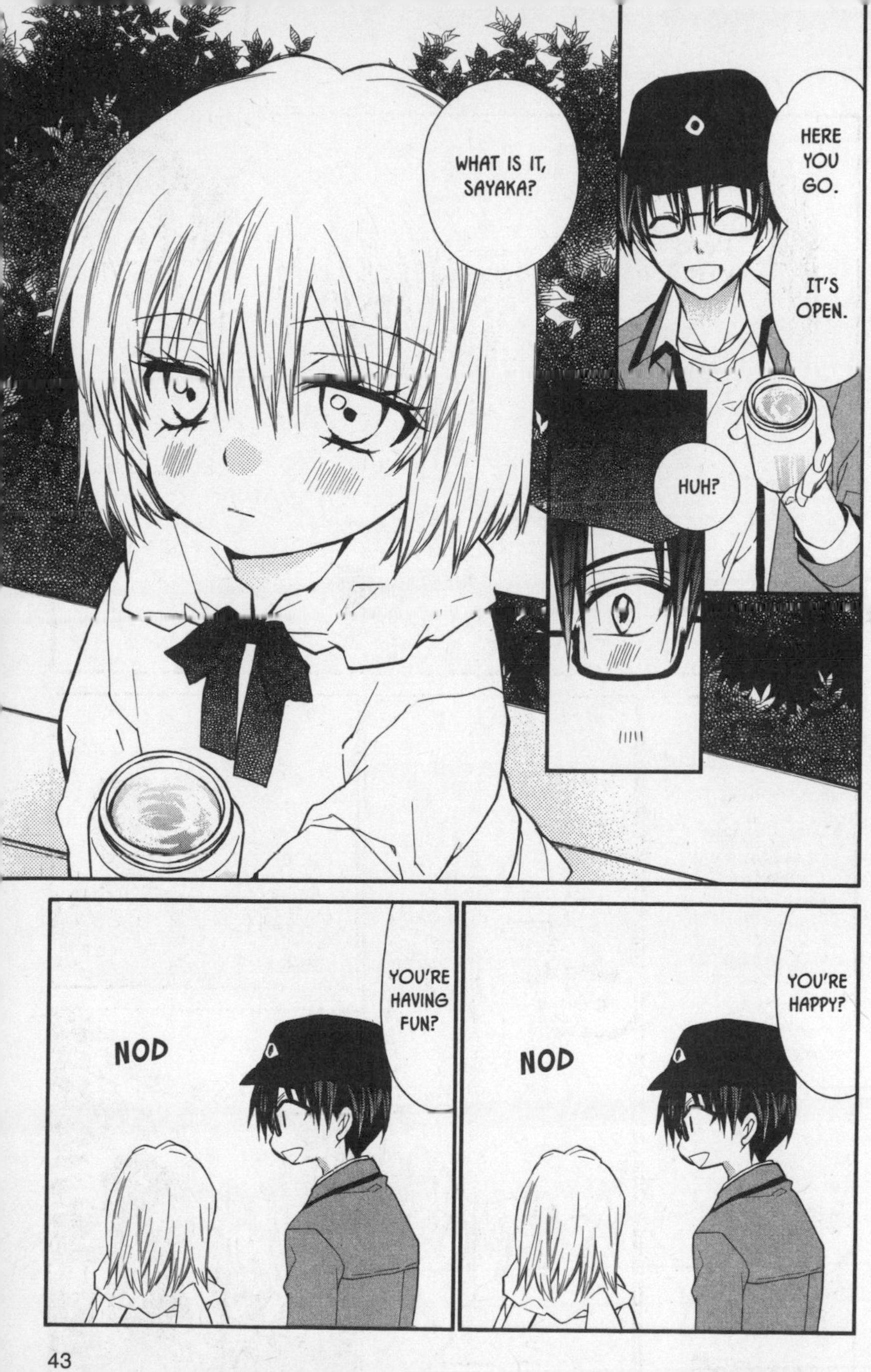
HERE YOU GO.
IT'S OPEN.
HUH?
WHAT IS IT, SAYAKA?
YOU'RE HAPPY?
NOD
YOU'RE HAVING FUN?
NOD

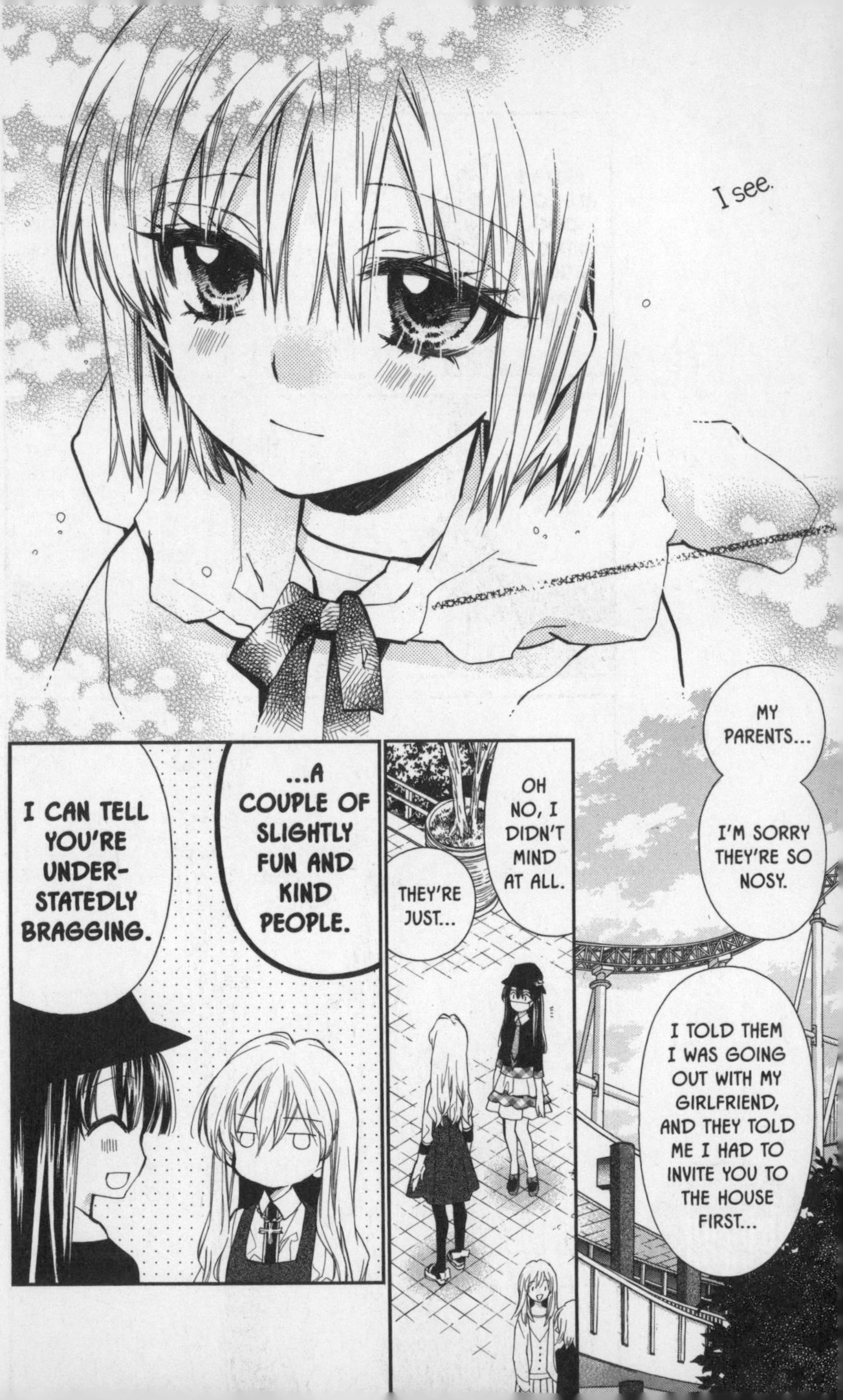
I see.
MY PARENTS...
I'M SORRY THEY'RE SO NOSY.
I TOLD THEM I WAS GOING OUT WITH MY GIRLFRIEND, AND THEY TOLD ME I HAD TO INVITE YOU TO THE HOUSE FIRST...
OH NO, I DIDN'T MIND AT ALL.
THEY'RE JUST...
...A COUPLE OF SLIGHTLY FUN AND KIND PEOPLE.
I CAN TELL YOU'RE UNDER-STATEDLY BRAGGING.

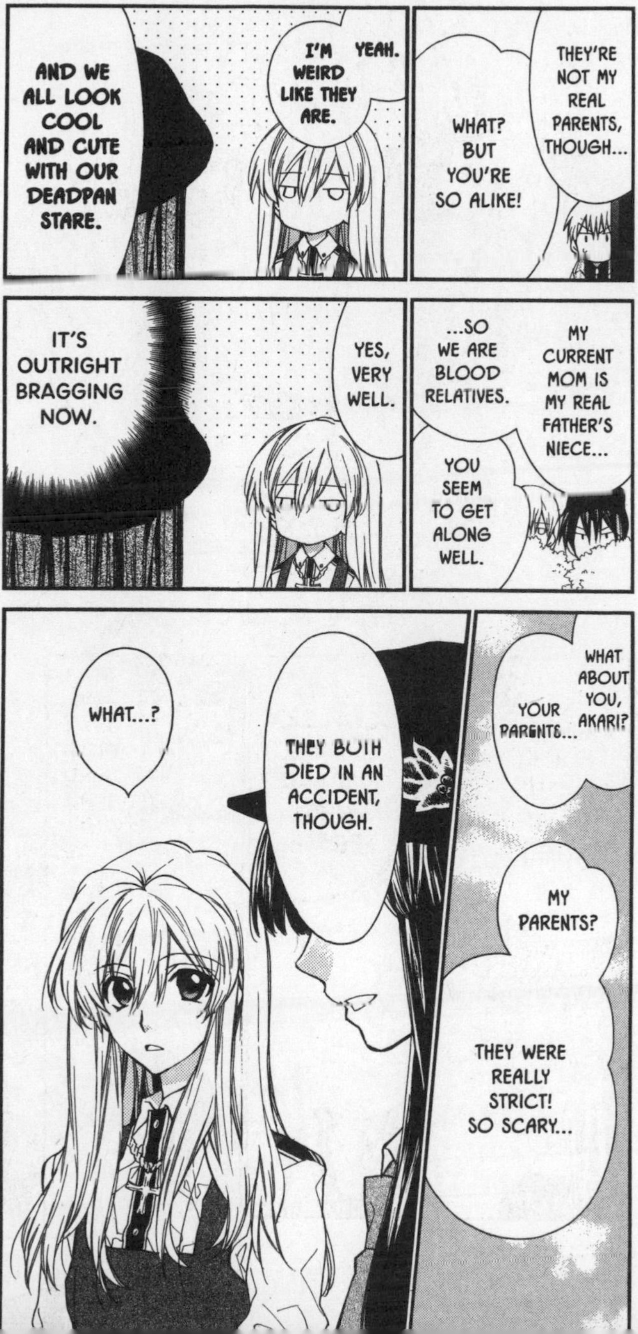
THEY'RE NOT MY REAL PARENTS, THOUGH...
WHAT? BUT YOU'RE SO ALIKE!
YEAH.
I'M WEIRD LIKE THEY ARE.
AND WE ALL LOOK COOL AND CUTE WITH OUR DEADPAN STARE.
MY CURRENT MOM IS MY REAL FATHER'S NIECE...
...SO WE ARE BLOOD RELATIVES.
YOU SEEM TO GET ALONG WELL.
YES, VERY WELL.
IT'S OUTRIGHT BRAGGING NOW.
WHAT ABOUT YOU, AKARI?
YOUR PARENTS...
MY PARENTS?
THEY WERE REALLY STRICT! SO SCARY...
THEY BOTH DIED IN AN ACCIDENT, THOUGH.
WHAT...?

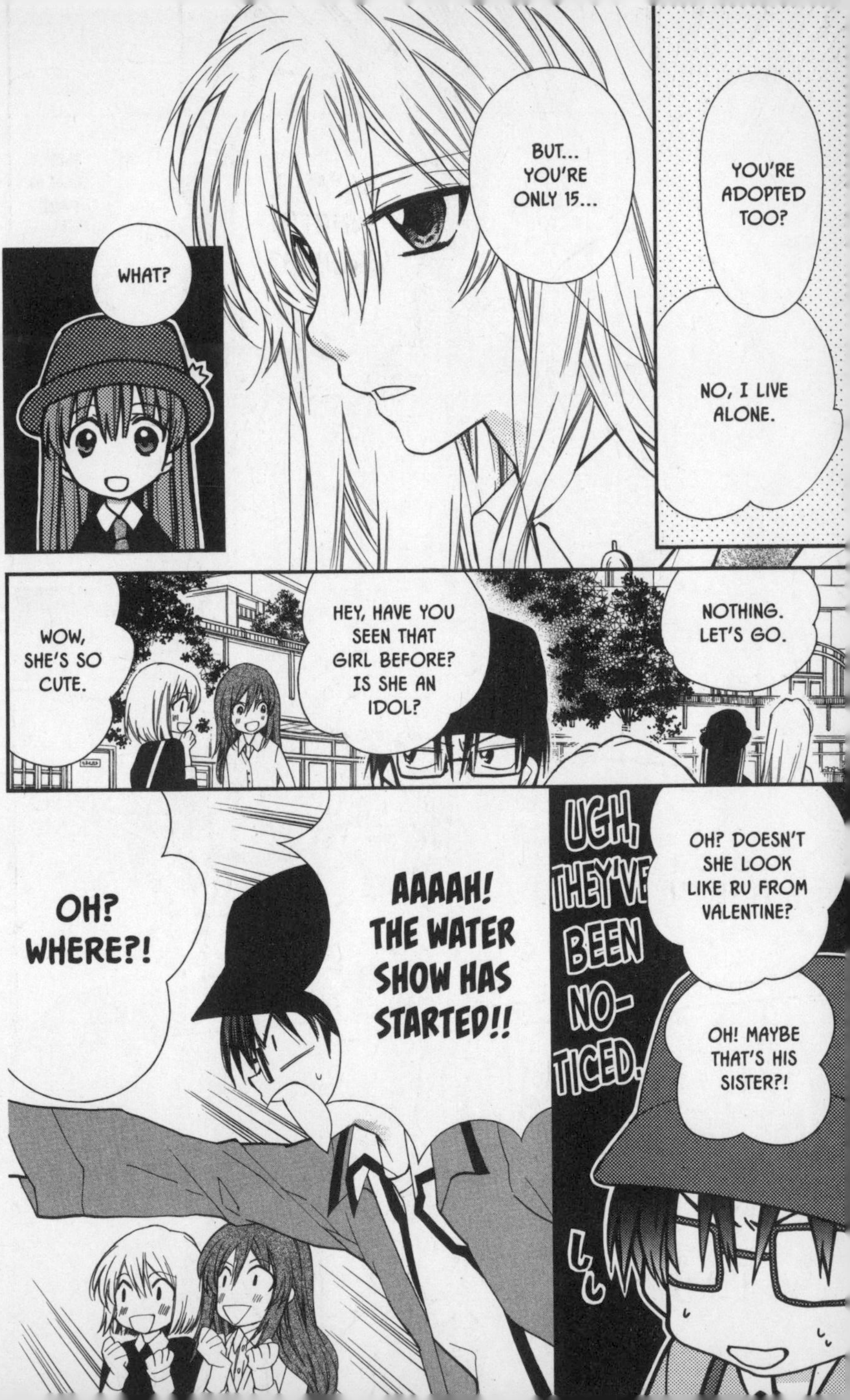
YOU'RE ADOPTED TOO?
NO, I LIVE ALONE.
BUT... YOU'RE ONLY 15...
WHAT?
NOTHING. LET'S GO.
HEY, HAVE YOU SEEN THAT GIRL BEFORE? IS SHE AN IDOL?
WOW, SHE'S SO CUTE.
OH? DOESN'T SHE LOOK LIKE RU FROM VALENTINE?
OH! MAYBE THAT'S HIS SISTER?!
UGH, THEY'VE BEEN NO-TICED.
AAAAH! THE WATER SHOW HAS STARTED!!
OH? WHERE?!

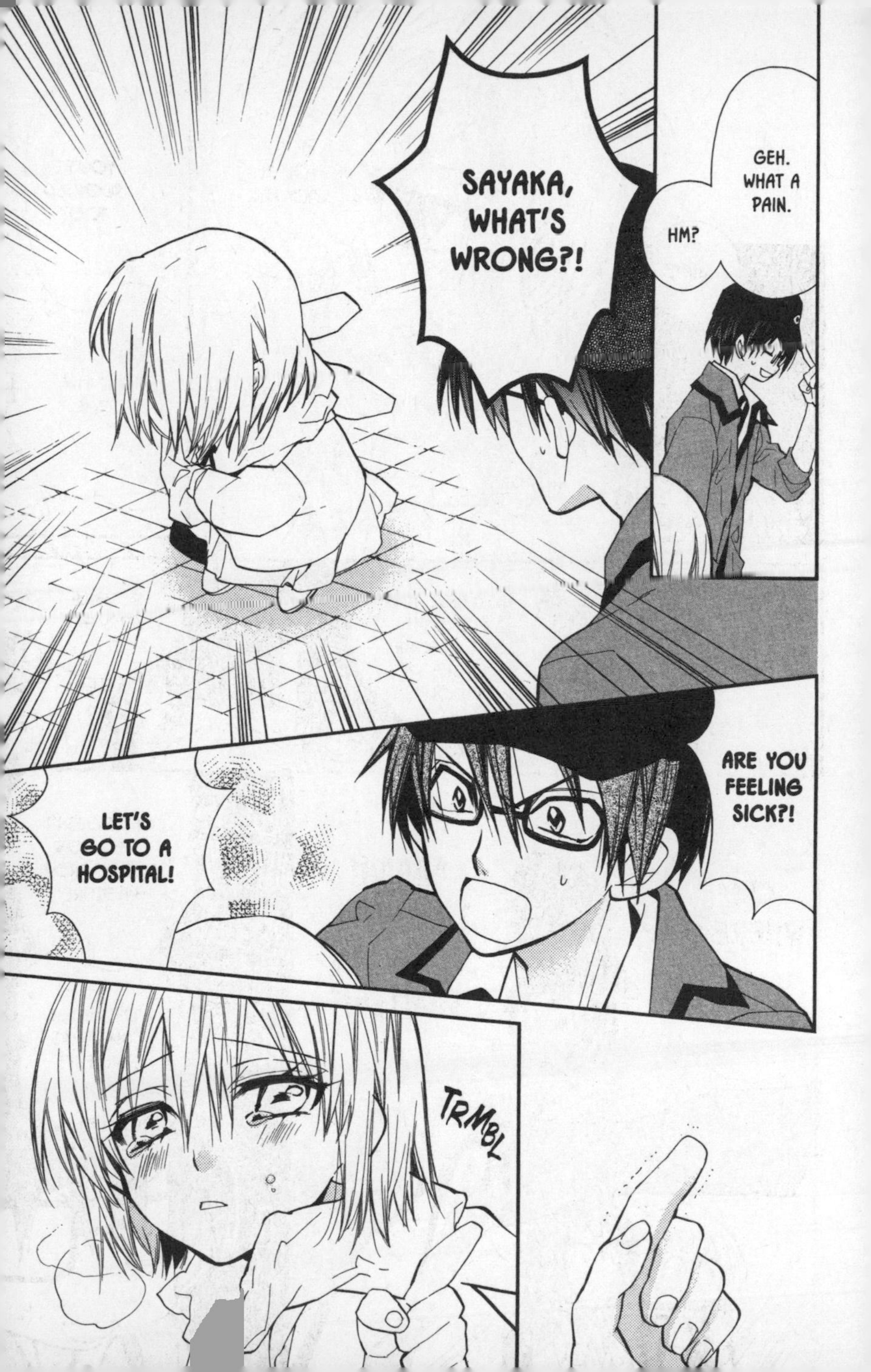
GEH. WHAT A PAIN.
HM?
SAYAKA, WHAT'S WRONG?!
ARE YOU FEELING SICK?!
LET'S GO TO A HOSPITAL!
TRMBL

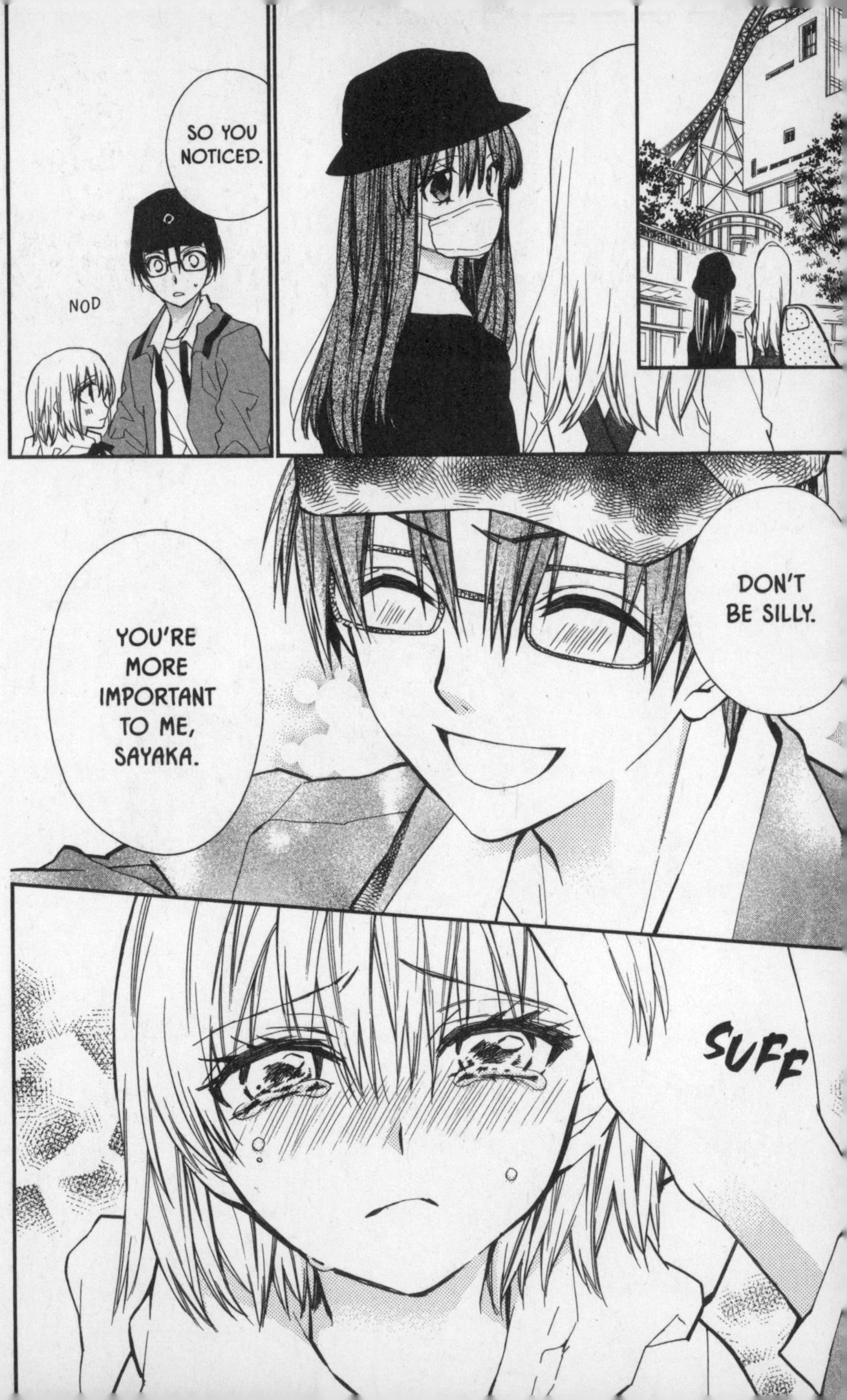
SO YOU NOTICED.
NOD
DON'T BE SILLY.
YOU'RE MORE IMPORTANT TO ME, SAYAKA.
SUFF

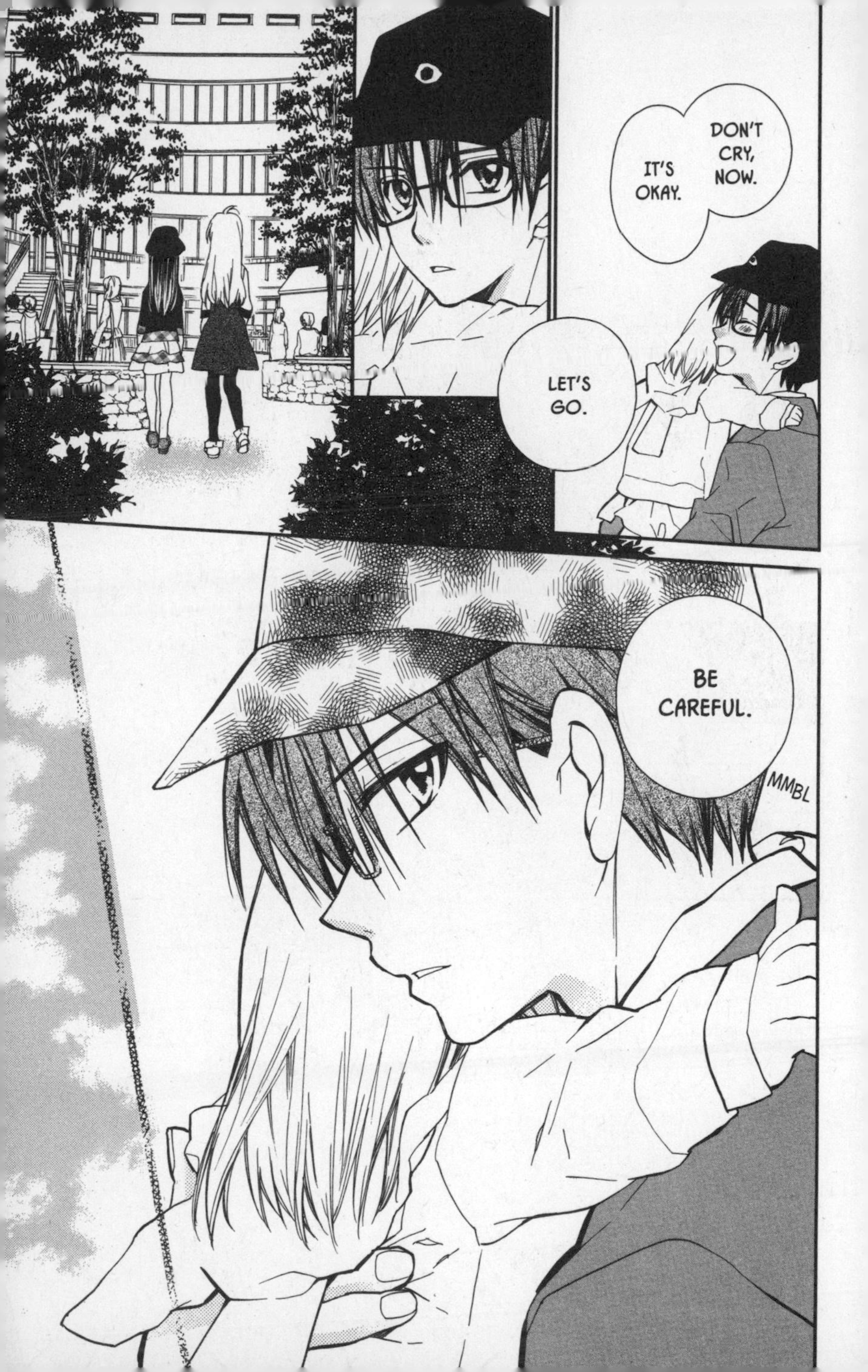
DON'T CRY, NOW.
IT'S OKAY.
LET'S GO.
BE CAREFUL.
MMBL

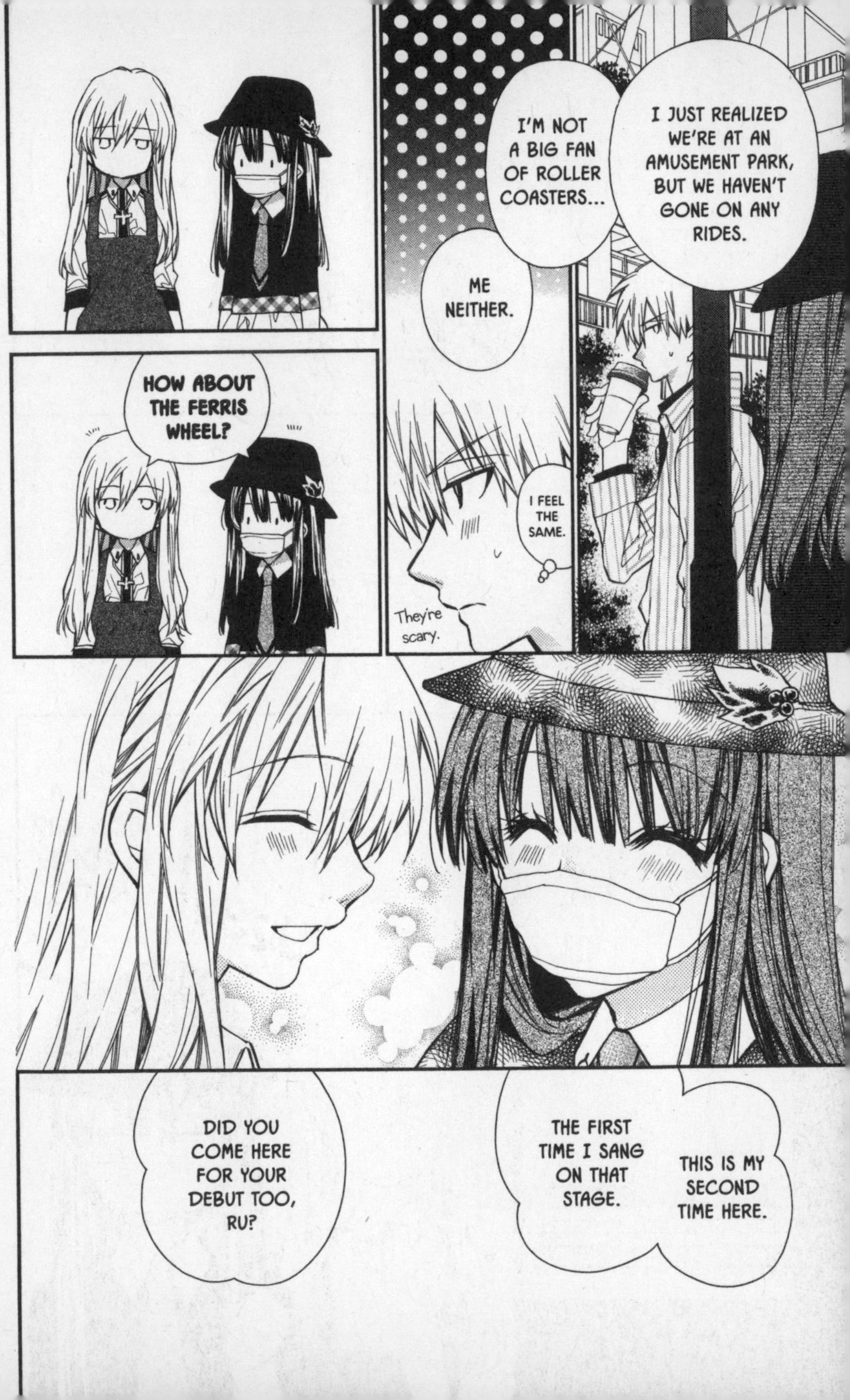
I JUST REALIZED WE'RE AT AN AMUSEMENT PARK, BUT WE HAVEN'T GONE ON ANY RIDES.
I'M NOT A BIG FAN OF ROLLER COASTERS...
ME NEITHER.
I FEEL THE SAME.
They're scary.
HOW ABOUT THE FERRIS WHEEL?
THIS IS MY SECOND TIME HERE.
THE FIRST TIME I SANG ON THAT STAGE.
DID YOU COME HERE FOR YOUR DEBUT TOO, RU?

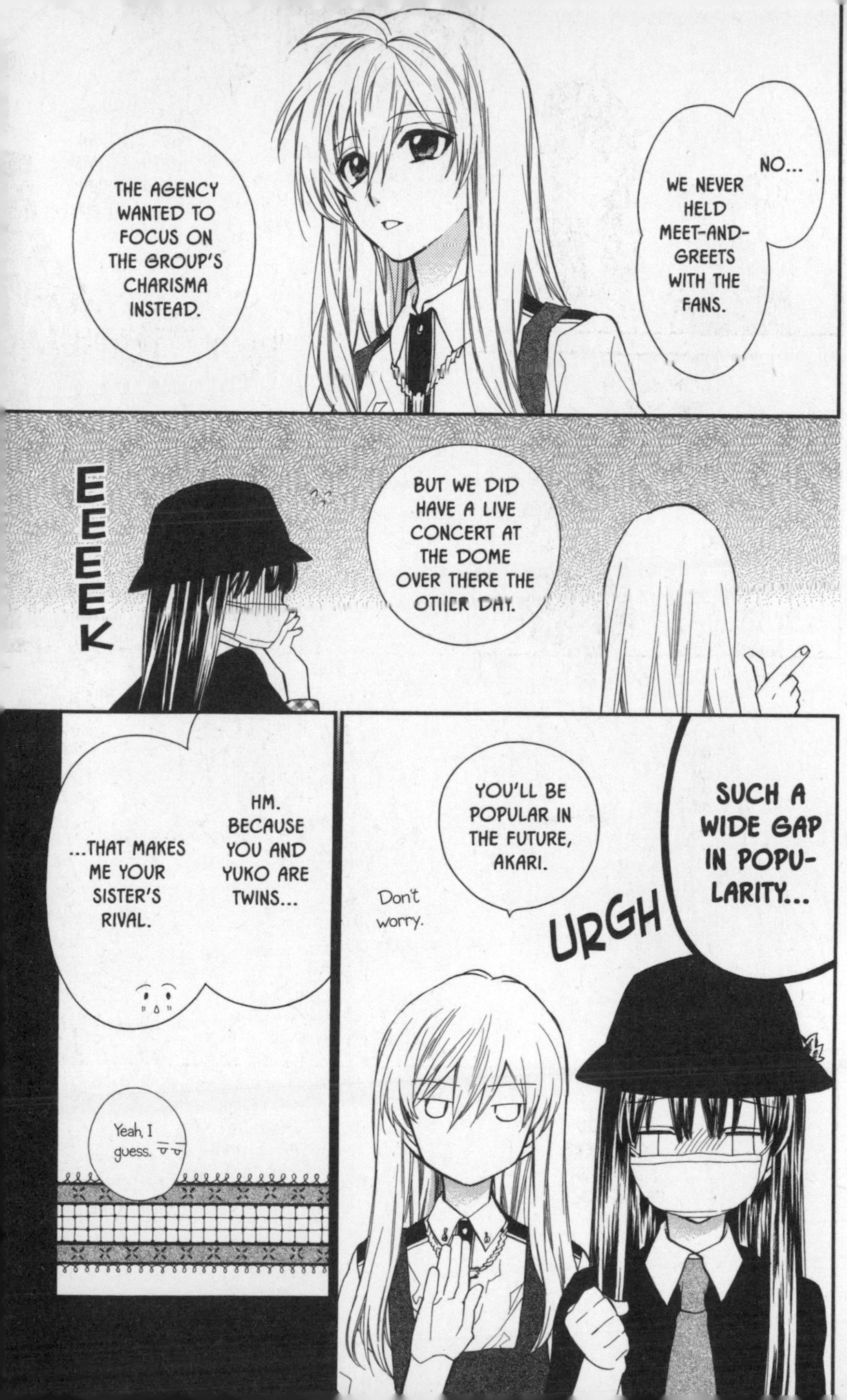
NO... WE NEVER HELD MEET-AND-GREETS WITH THE FANS.
THE AGENCY WANTED TO FOCUS ON THE GROUP'S CHARISMA INSTEAD.
BUT WE DID HAVE A LIVE CONCERT AT THE DOME OVER THERE THE OTHER DAY.
EEEEK
SUCH A WIDE GAP IN POPU-LARITY...
URGH
YOU'LL BE POPULAR IN THE FUTURE, AKARI.
Don't worry.
HM. BECAUSE YOU AND YUKO ARE TWINS...
...THAT MAKES ME YOUR SISTER'S RIVAL.
Yeah, I guess.

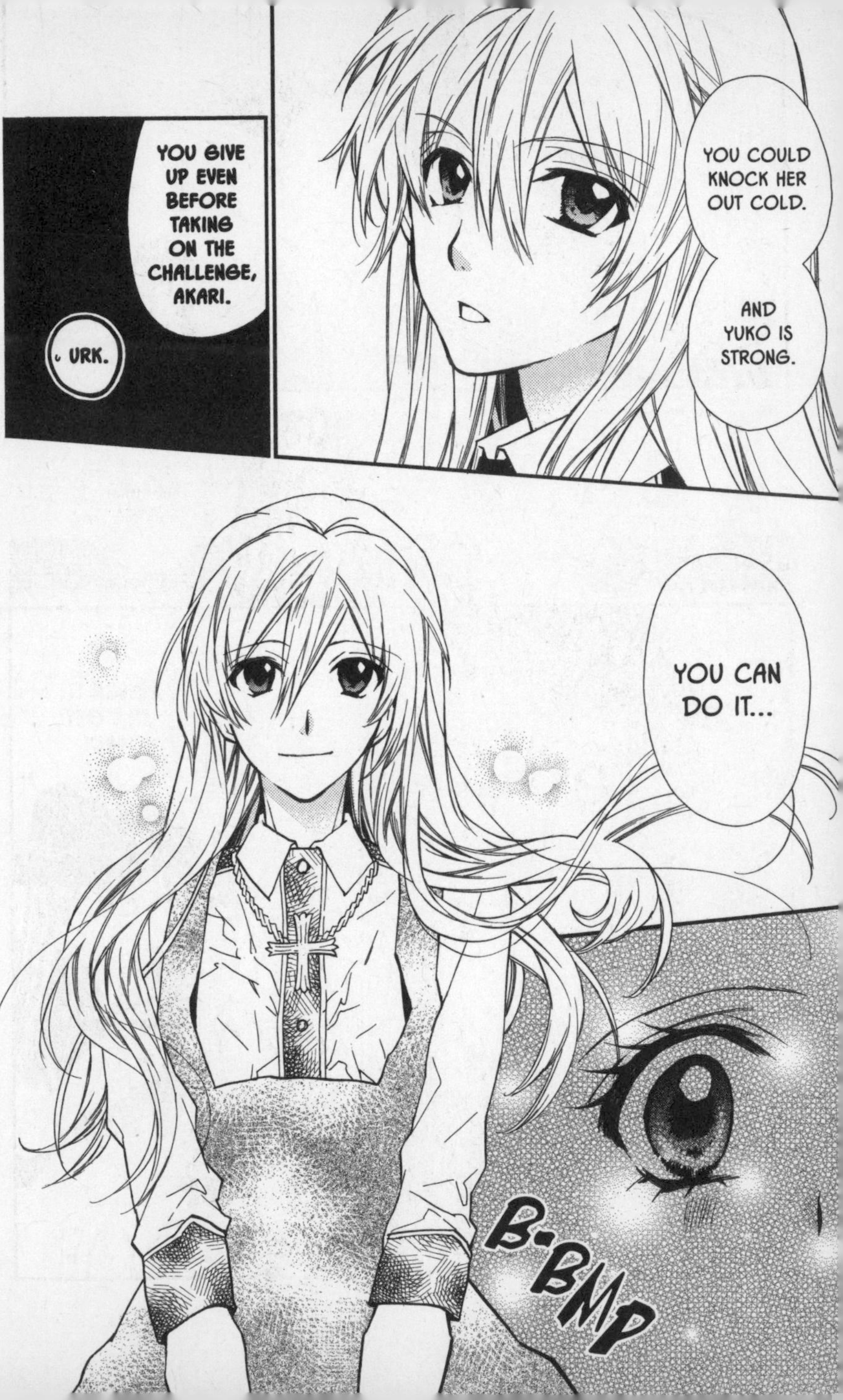
YOU COULD KNOCK HER OUT COLD.
AND YUKO IS STRONG.
YOU GIVE UP EVEN BEFORE TAKING ON THE CHALLENGE, AKARI.
URK.
YOU CAN DO IT...
B-BMP

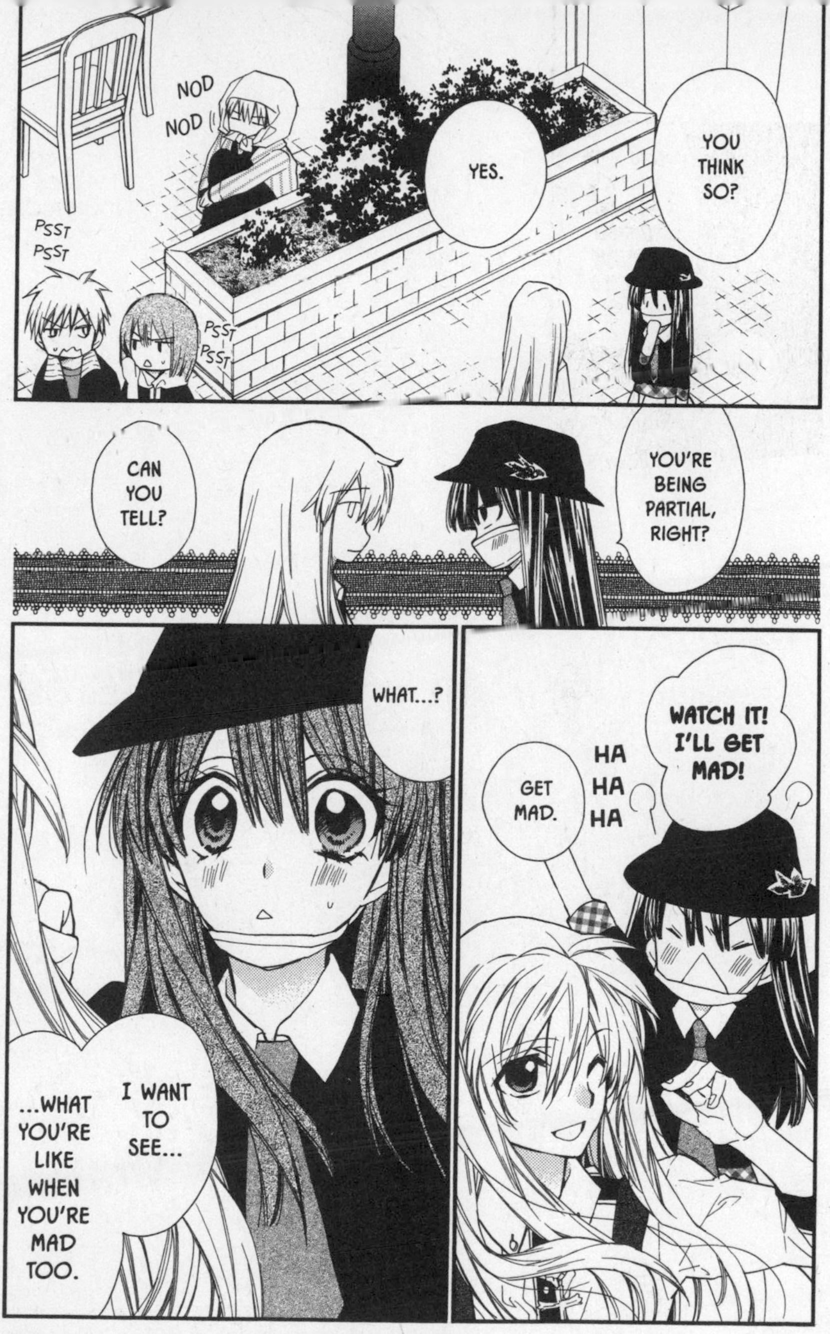
YOU THINK SO?
YES.
NOD NOD
PSST PSST
PSST PSST
YOU'RE BEING PARTIAL, RIGHT?
CAN YOU TELL?
WATCH IT! I'LL GET MAD!
HA HA HA
GET MAD.
WHAT...?
I WANT TO SEE...
...WHAT YOU'RE LIKE WHEN YOU'RE MAD TOO.

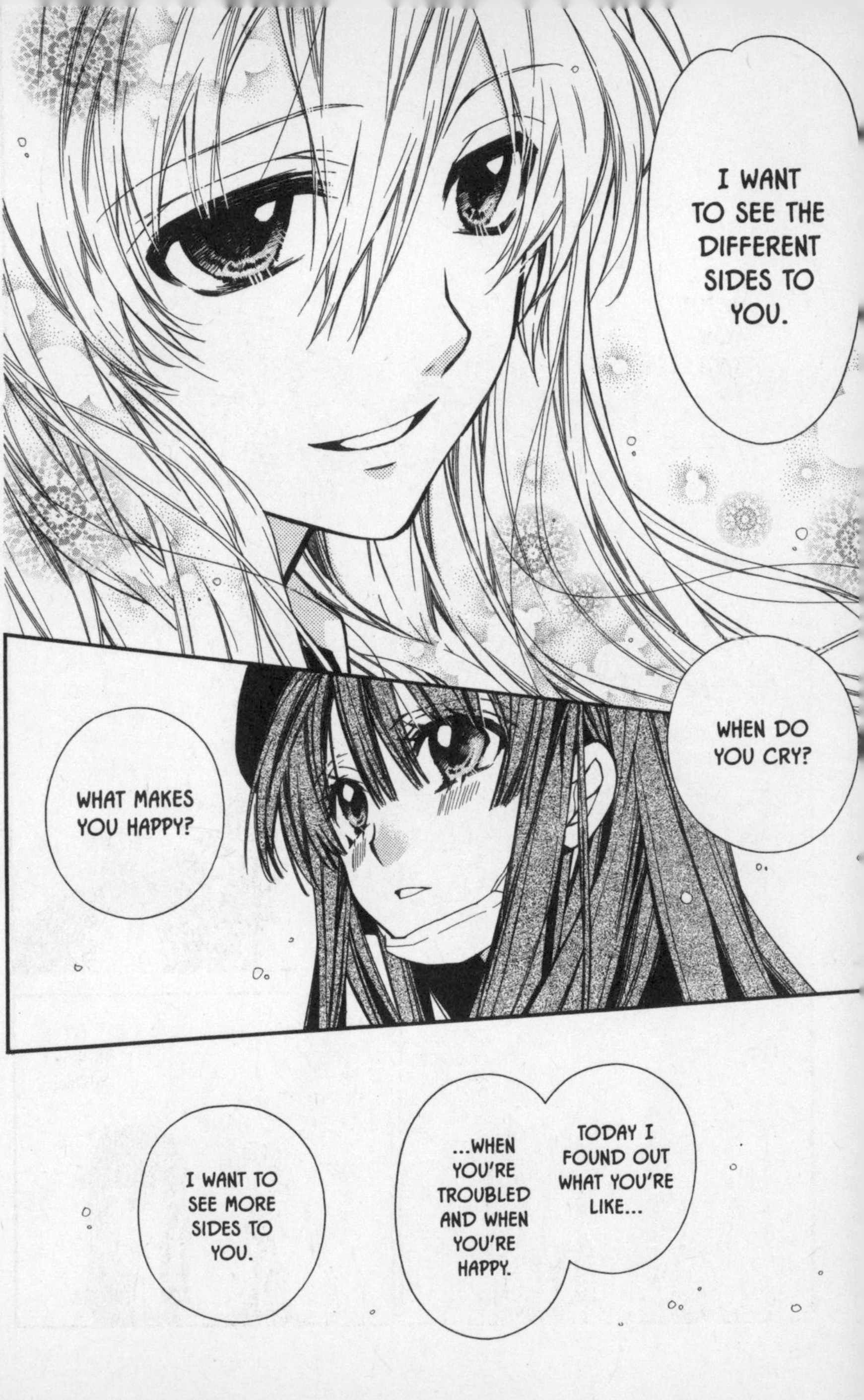
I WANT TO SEE THE DIFFERENT SIDES TO YOU.
WHEN DO YOU CRY?
WHAT MAKES YOU HAPPY?
TODAY I FOUND OUT WHAT YOU'RE LIKE...
...WHEN YOU'RE TROUBLED AND WHEN YOU'RE HAPPY.
I WANT TO SEE MORE SIDES TO YOU.

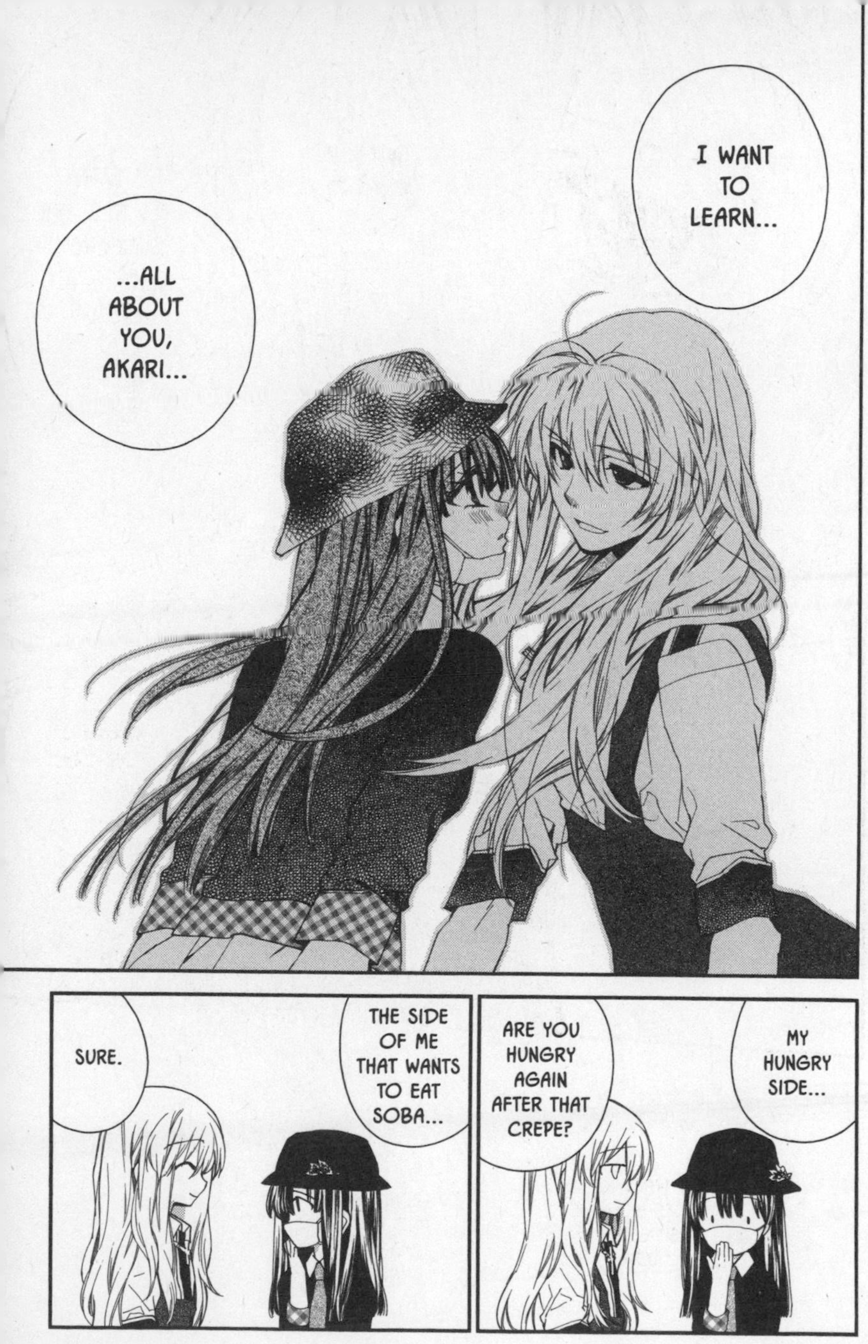
I WANT TO LEARN...
...ALL ABOUT YOU, AKARI...
MY HUNGRY SIDE...
ARE YOU HUNGRY AGAIN AFTER THAT CREPE?
THE SIDE OF ME THAT WANTS TO EAT SOBA...
SURE.

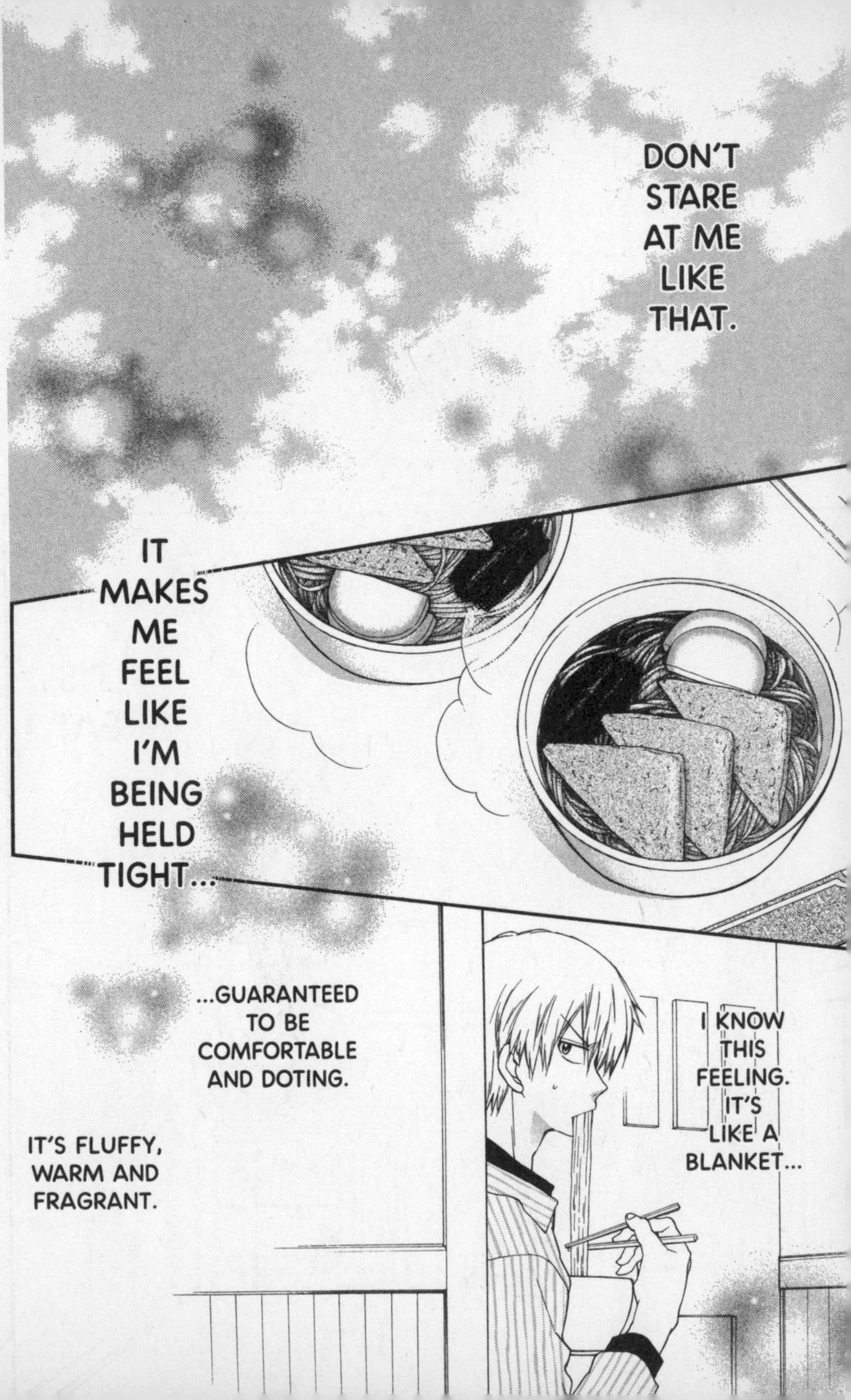
DON'T STARE AT ME LIKE THAT.
IT MAKES ME FEEL LIKE I'M BEING HELD TIGHT...
I KNOW THIS FEELING. IT'S LIKE A BLANKET...
...GUARANTEED TO BE COMFORTABLE AND DOTING.
IT'S FLUFFY, WARM AND FRAGRANT.

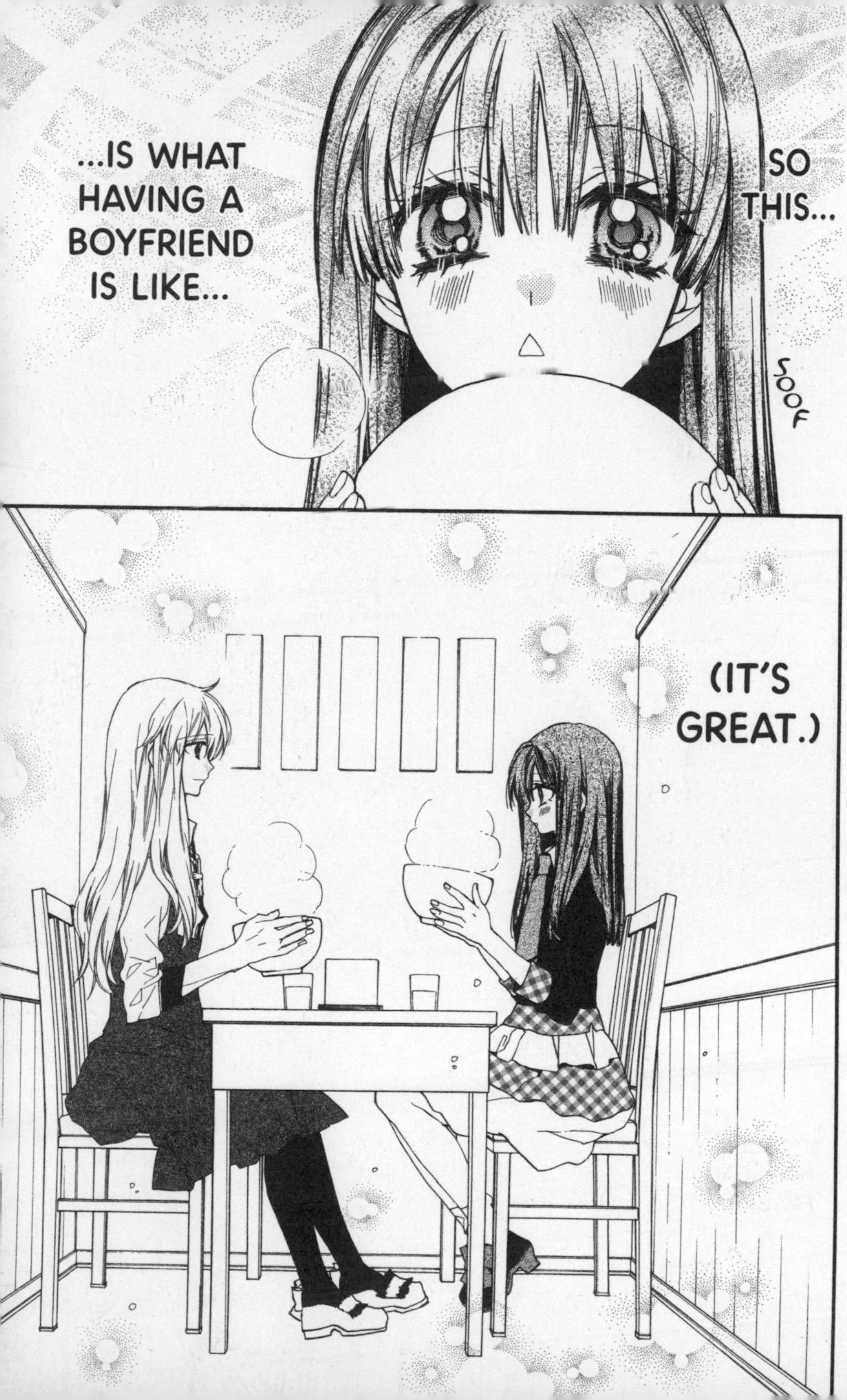
SO THIS...
...IS WHAT HAVING A BOYFRIEND IS LIKE...
SOOF
(IT'S GREAT.)

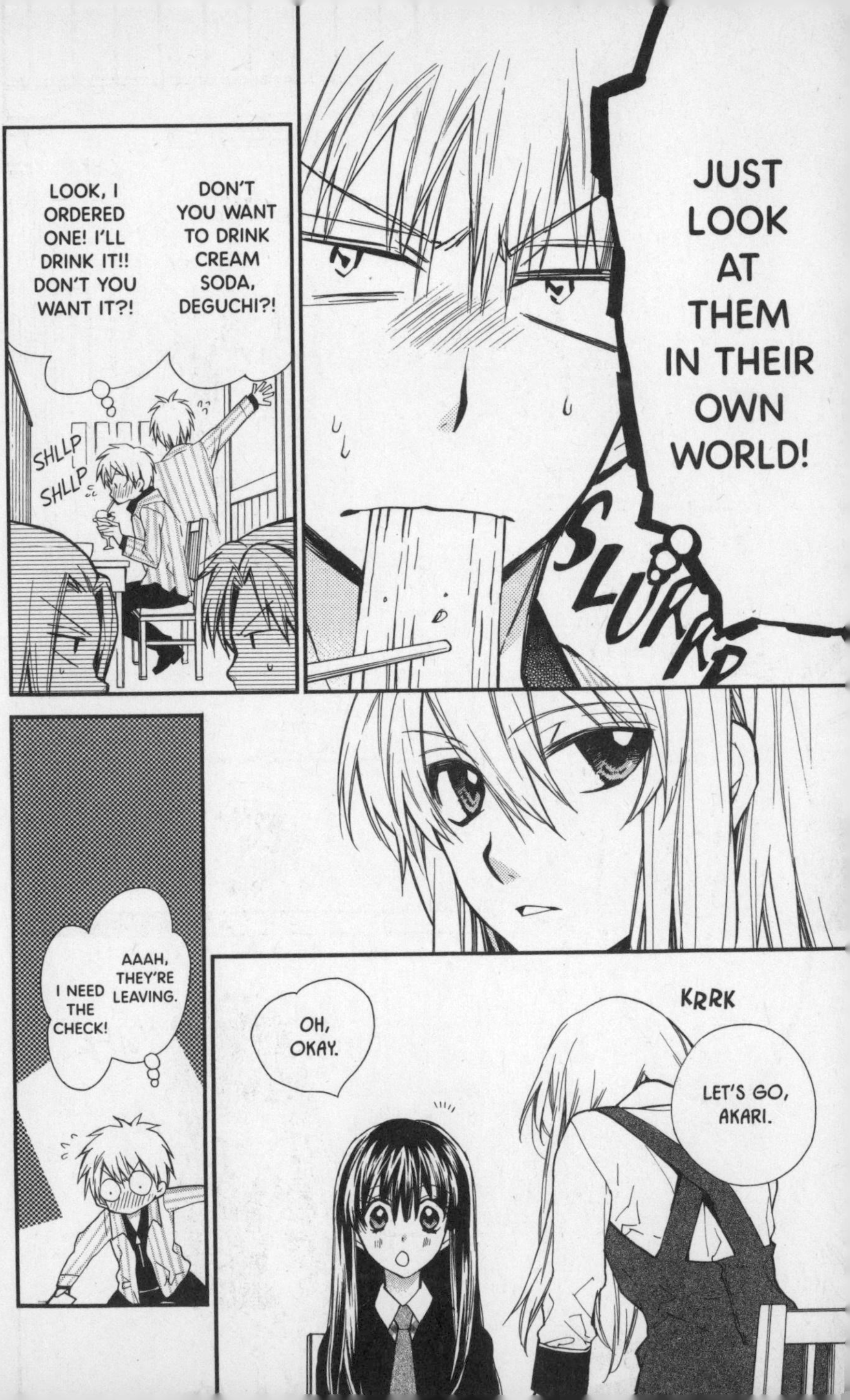
JUST LOOK AT THEM IN THEIR OWN WORLD!
SLURRP
DON'T YOU WANT TO DRINK CREAM SODA, DEGUCHI?!
LOOK, I ORDERED ONE! I'LL DRINK IT!! DON'T YOU WANT IT?!
SHLLP SHLLP
KRRK
LET'S GO, AKARI.
OH, OKAY.
AAAH, THEY'RE LEAVING.
I NEED THE CHECK!

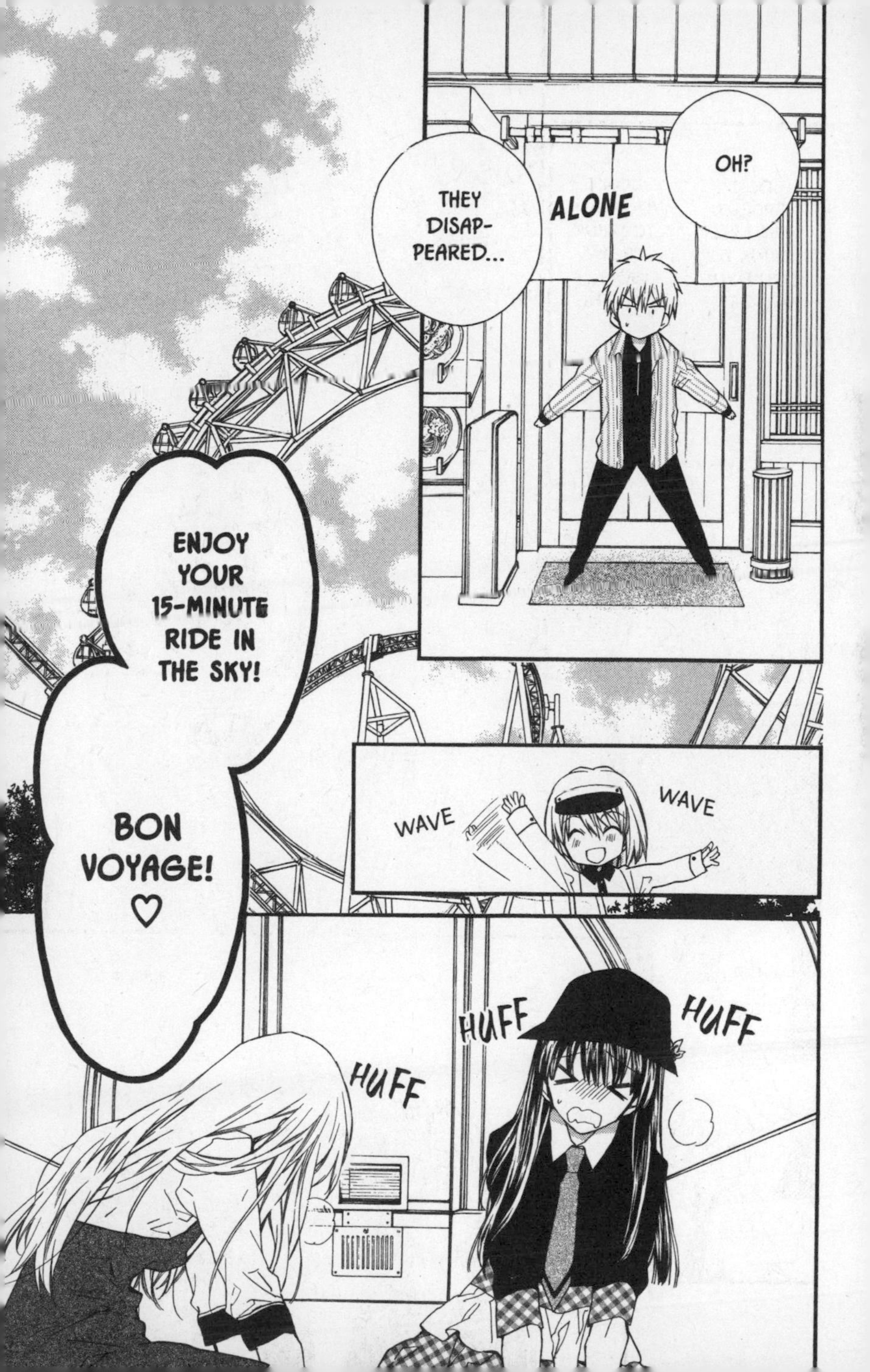
OH?
ALONE
THEY DISAP-PEARED...
WAVE
WAVE
ENJOY YOUR 15-MINUTE RIDE IN THE SKY!
BON VOYAGE! ♡
HUFF
HUFF
HUFF

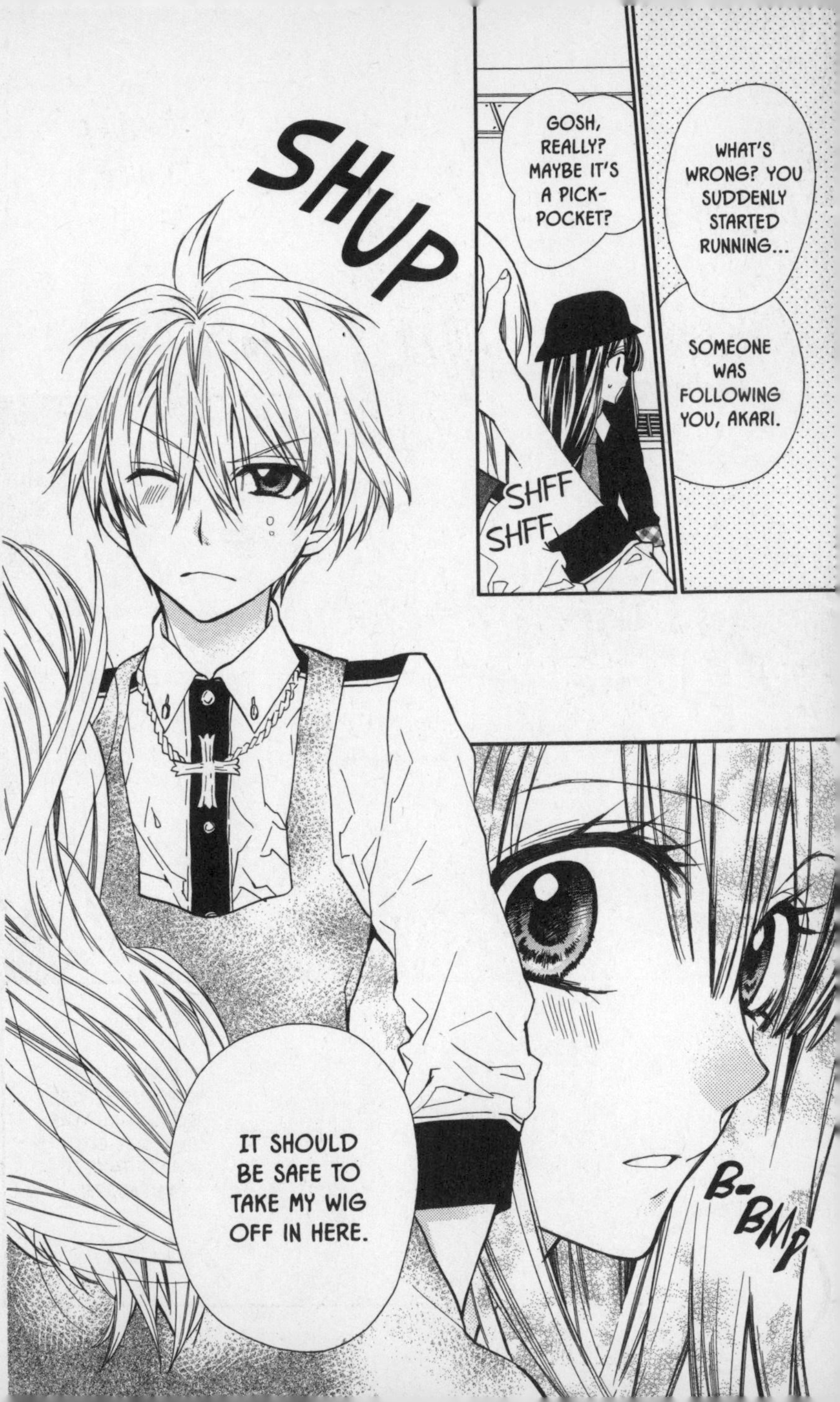
WHAT'S WRONG? YOU SUDDENLY STARTED RUNNING...
SOMEONE WAS FOLLOWING YOU, AKARI.
GOSH, REALLY? MAYBE IT'S A PICK-POCKET?
SHFF SHFF
B-BMP
SHUP
IT SHOULD BE SAFE TO TAKE MY WIG OFF IN HERE.

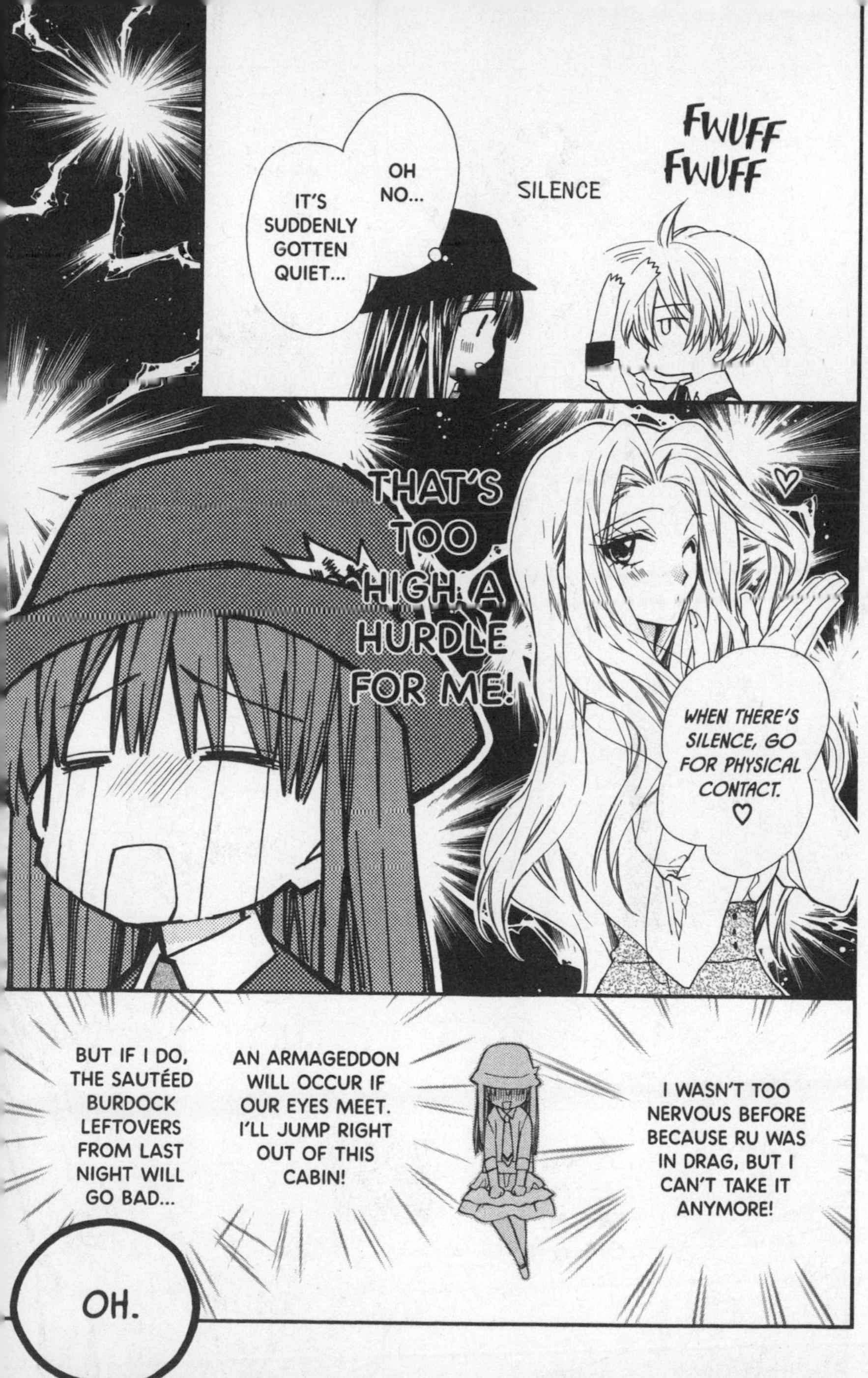
FWUFF FWUFF
SILENCE
OH NO... IT'S SUDDENLY GOTTEN QUIET...
WHEN THERE'S SILENCE, GO FOR PHYSICAL CONTACT. ♡
THAT'S TOO HIGH A HURDLE FOR ME!
I WASN'T TOO NERVOUS BEFORE BECAUSE RU WAS IN DRAG, BUT I CAN'T TAKE IT ANYMORE!
AN ARMAGEDDON WILL OCCUR IF OUR EYES MEET. I'LL JUMP RIGHT OUT OF THIS CABIN!
BUT IF I DO, THE SAUTÉED BURDOCK LEFTOVERS FROM LAST NIGHT WILL GO BAD...
OH.

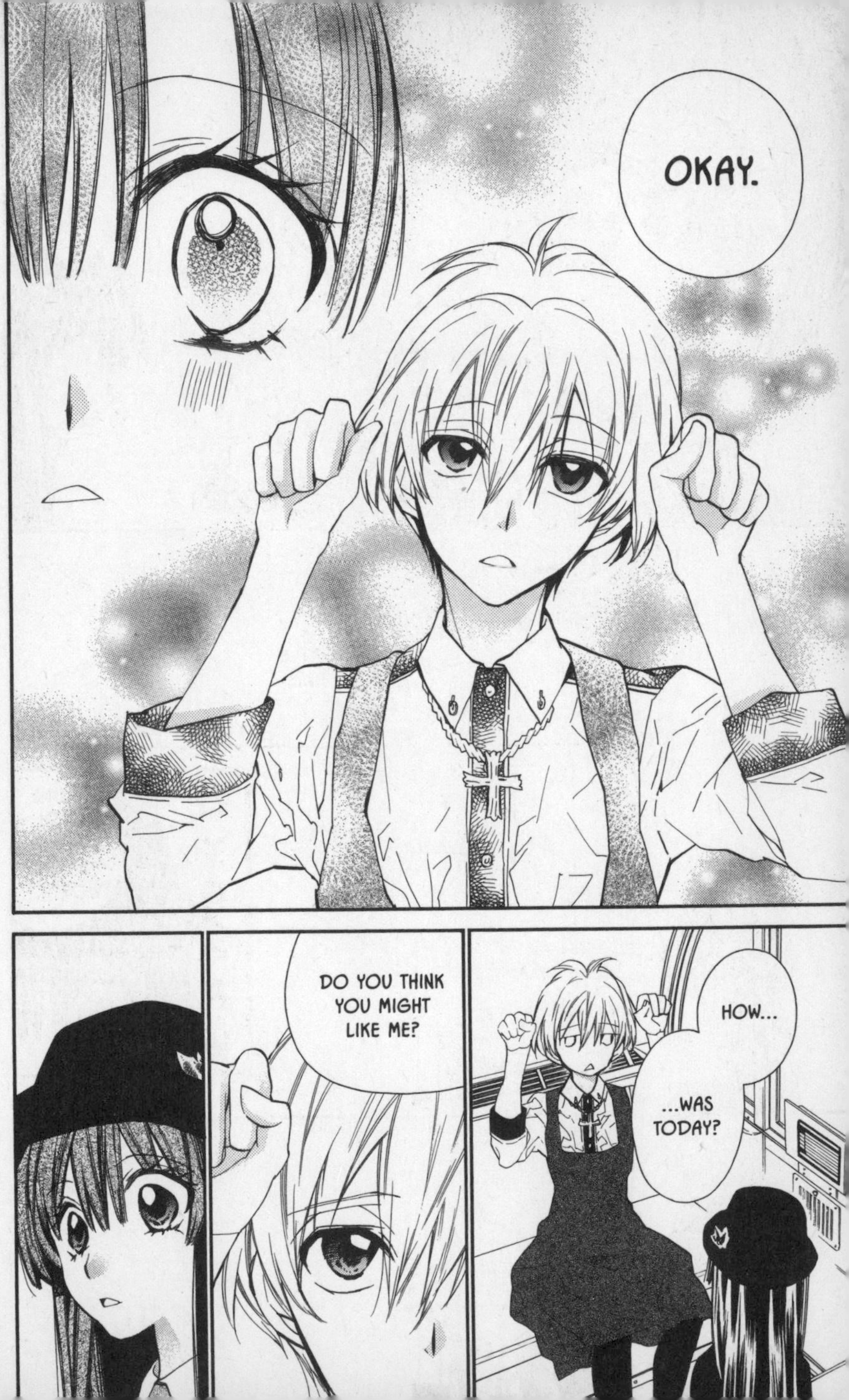
OKAY.
HOW...
...WAS TODAY?
DO YOU THINK YOU MIGHT LIKE ME?

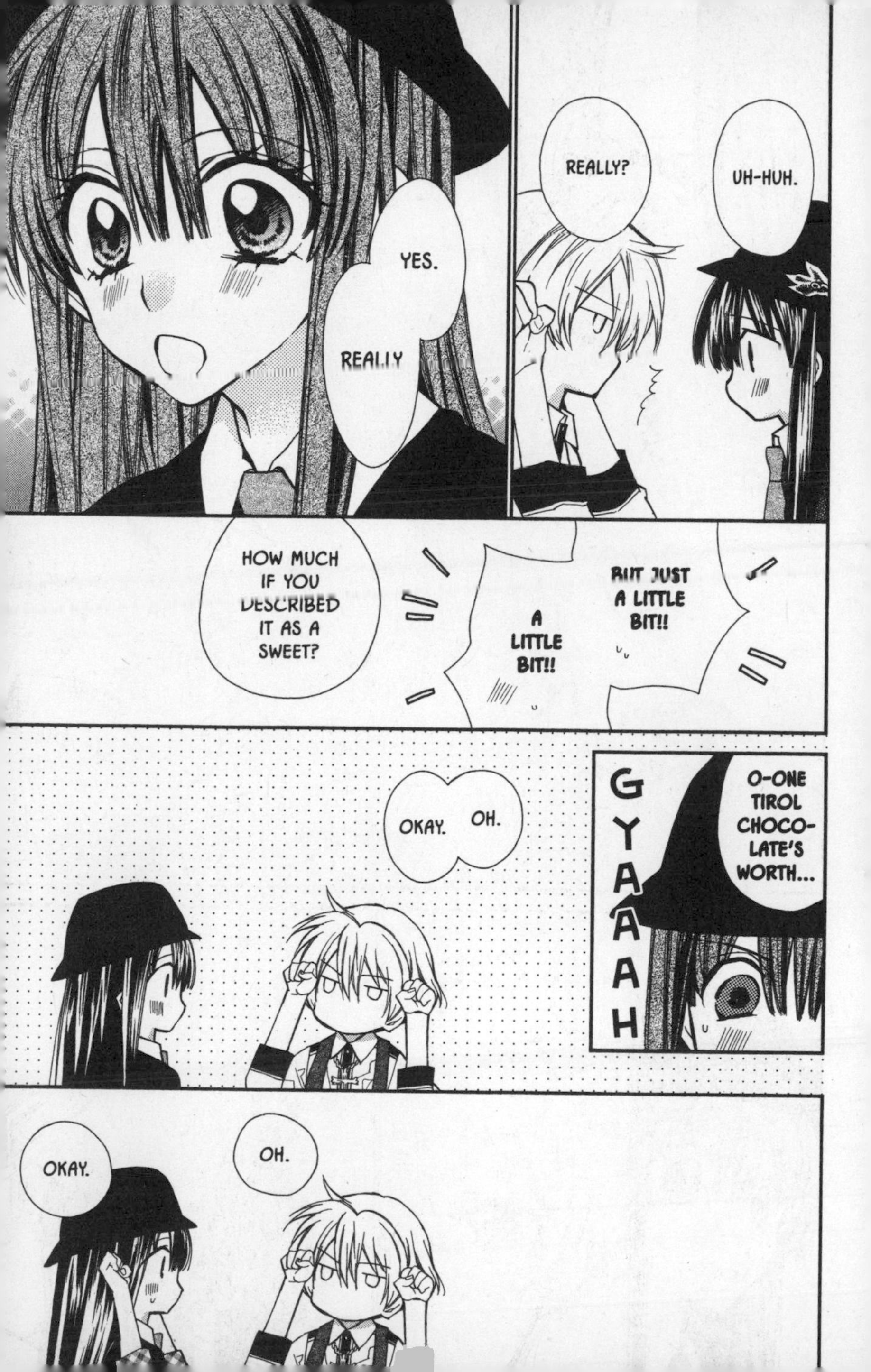
UH-HUH.
REALLY?
YES.
REALLY
BUT JUST A LITTLE BIT!!
A LITTLE BIT!!
HOW MUCH IF YOU DESCRIBED IT AS A SWEET?
O-ONE TIROL CHOCO-LATE'S WORTH...
GYAAAH
OH.
OKAY.
OH.
OKAY.

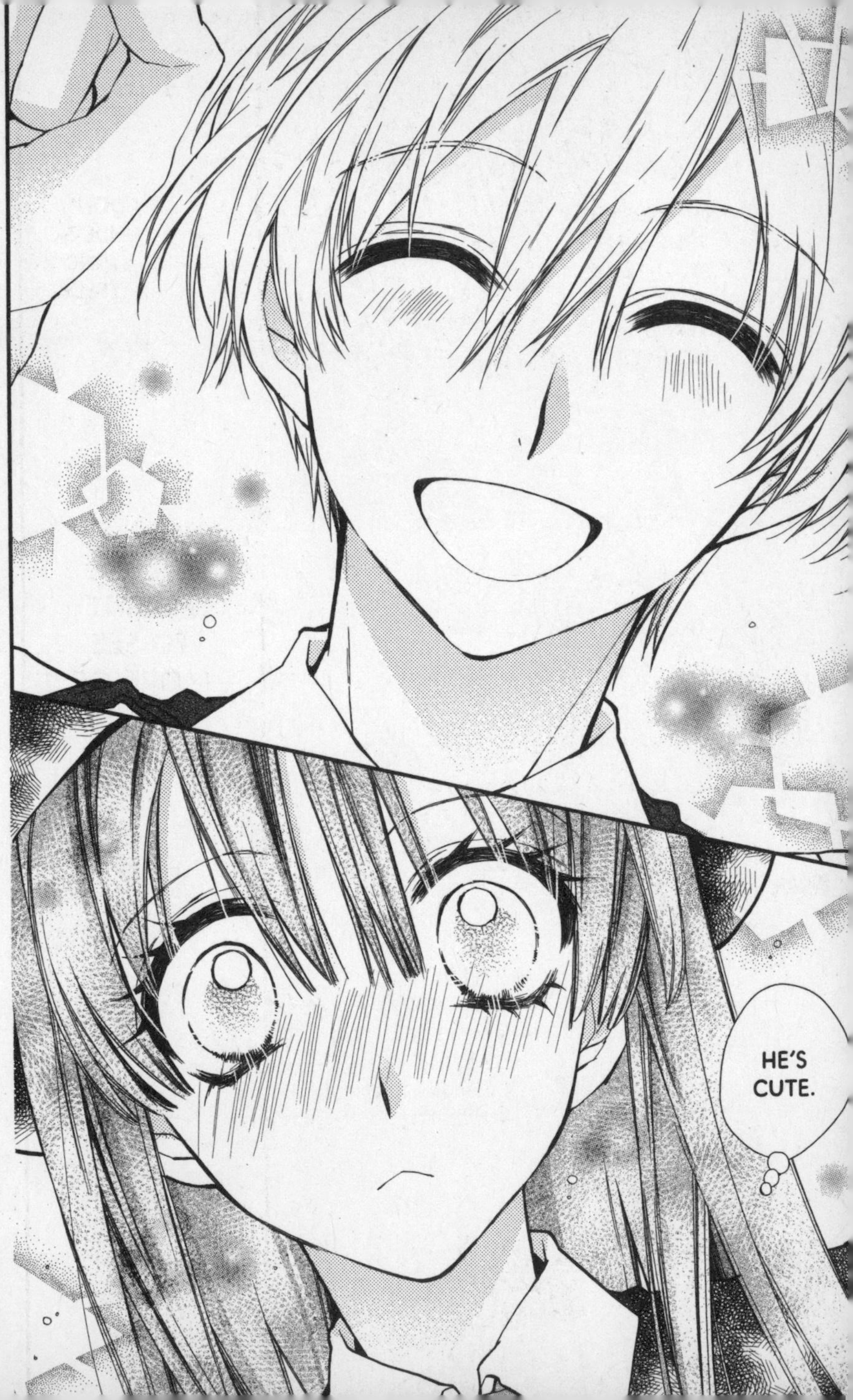
HE'S CUTE.

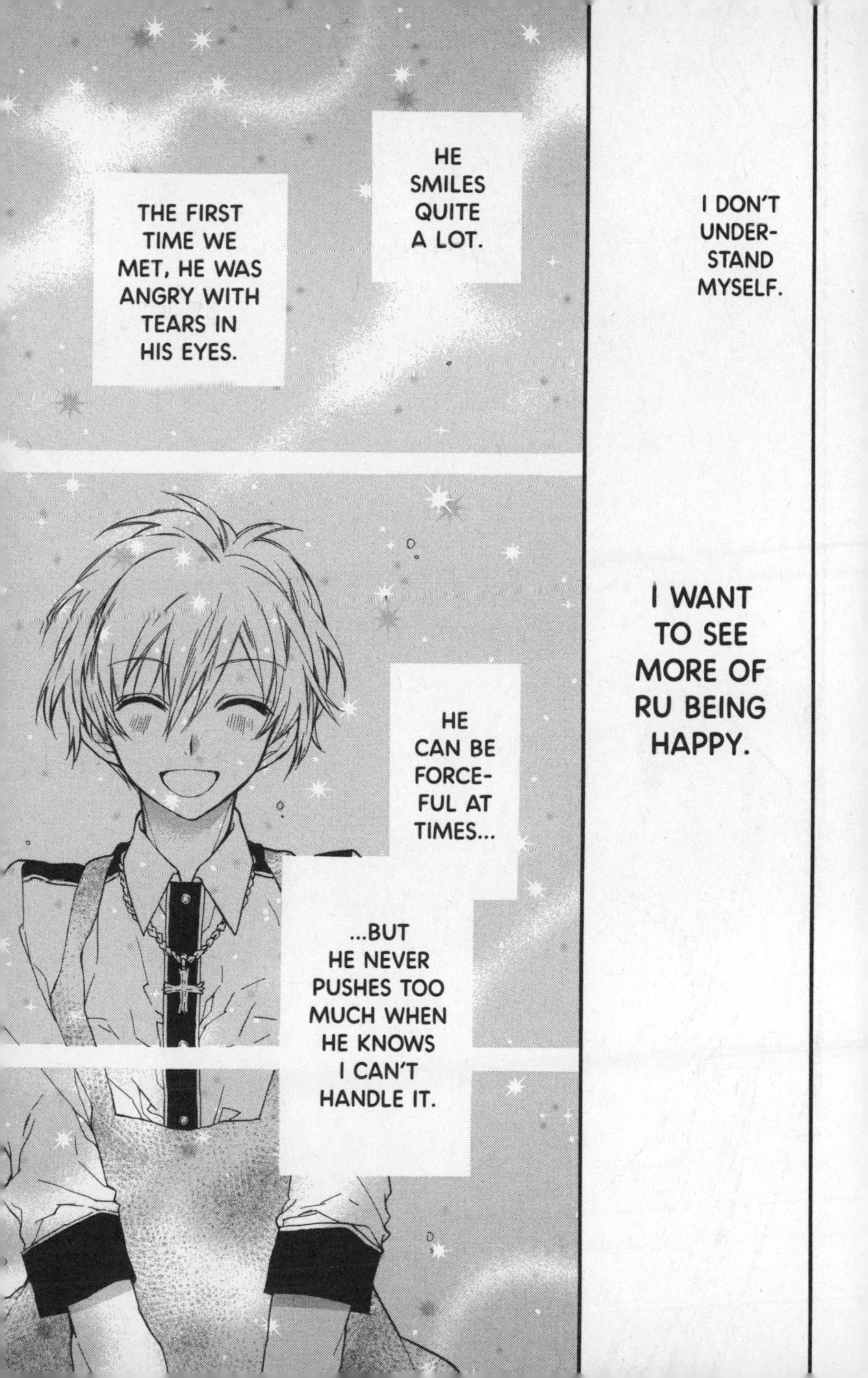
I DON'T UNDER-STAND MYSELF.
I WANT TO SEE MORE OF RU BEING HAPPY.
HE SMILES QUITE A LOT.
THE FIRST TIME WE MET, HE WAS ANGRY WITH TEARS IN HIS EYES.
HE CAN BE FORCE-FUL AT TIMES...
...BUT HE NEVER PUSHES TOO MUCH WHEN HE KNOWS I CAN'T HANDLE IT.

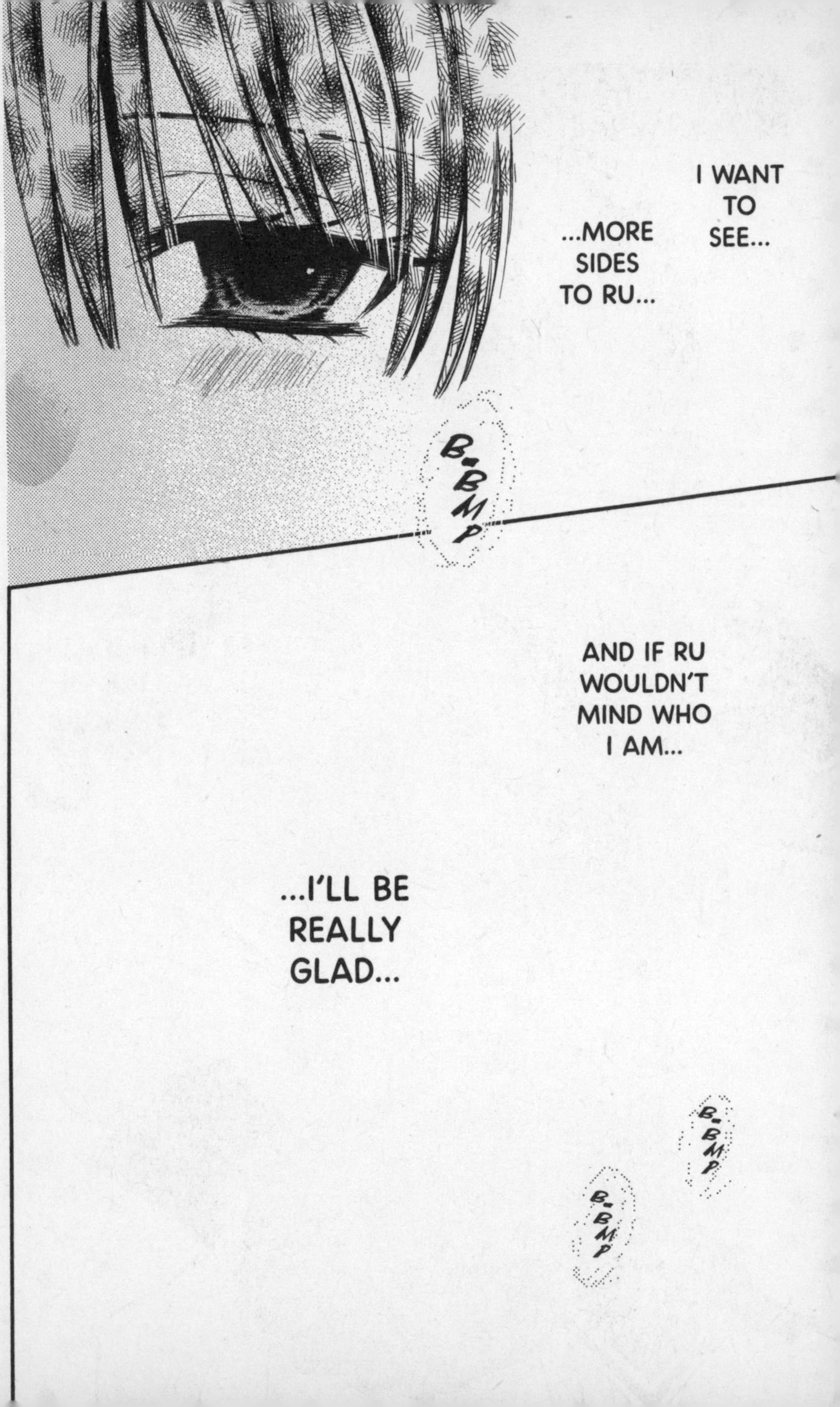
I WANT TO SEE...
...MORE SIDES TO RU...
B-BMP
AND IF RU WOULDN'T MIND WHO I AM...
...I'LL BE REALLY GLAD...
B-BMP
B-BMP

Chapter 18

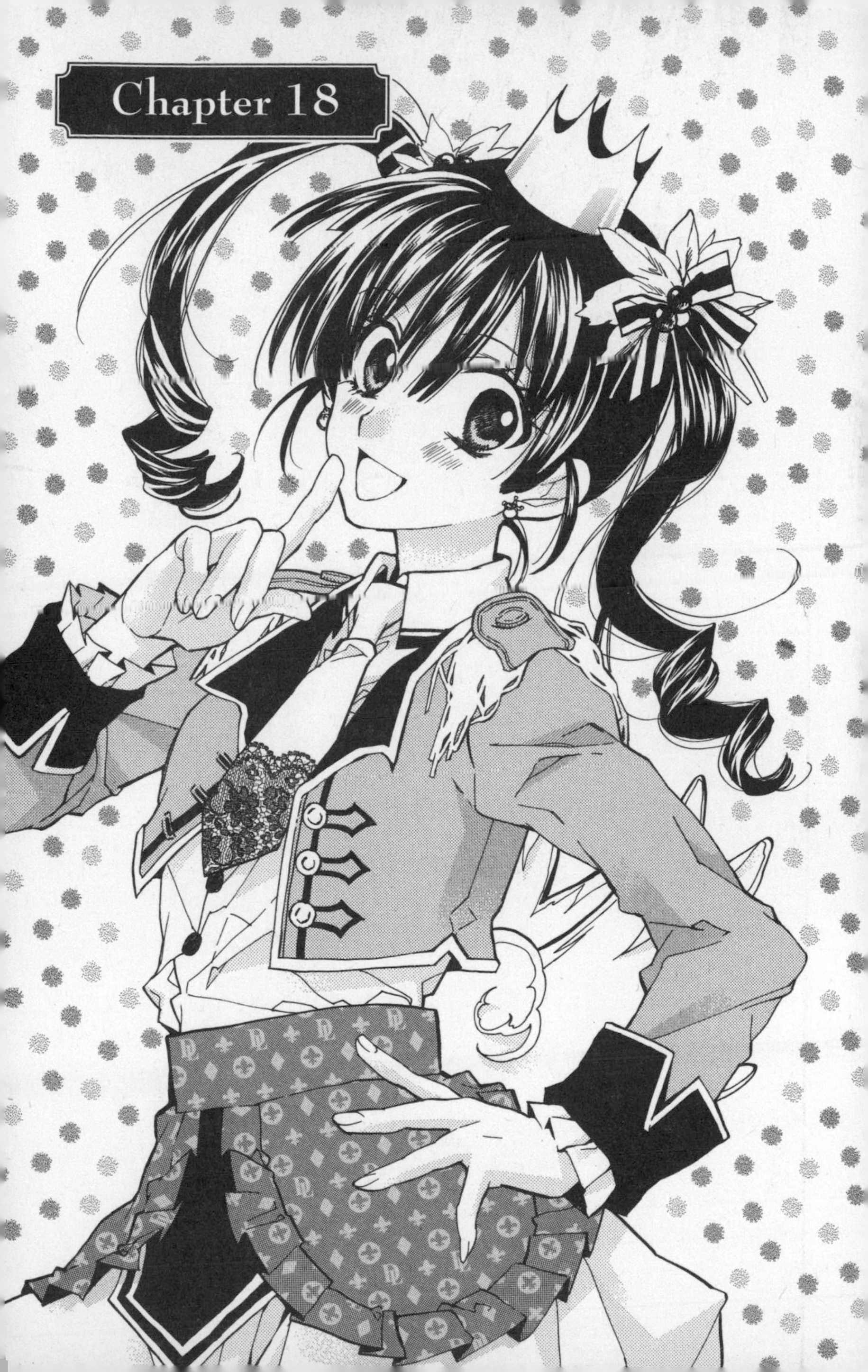

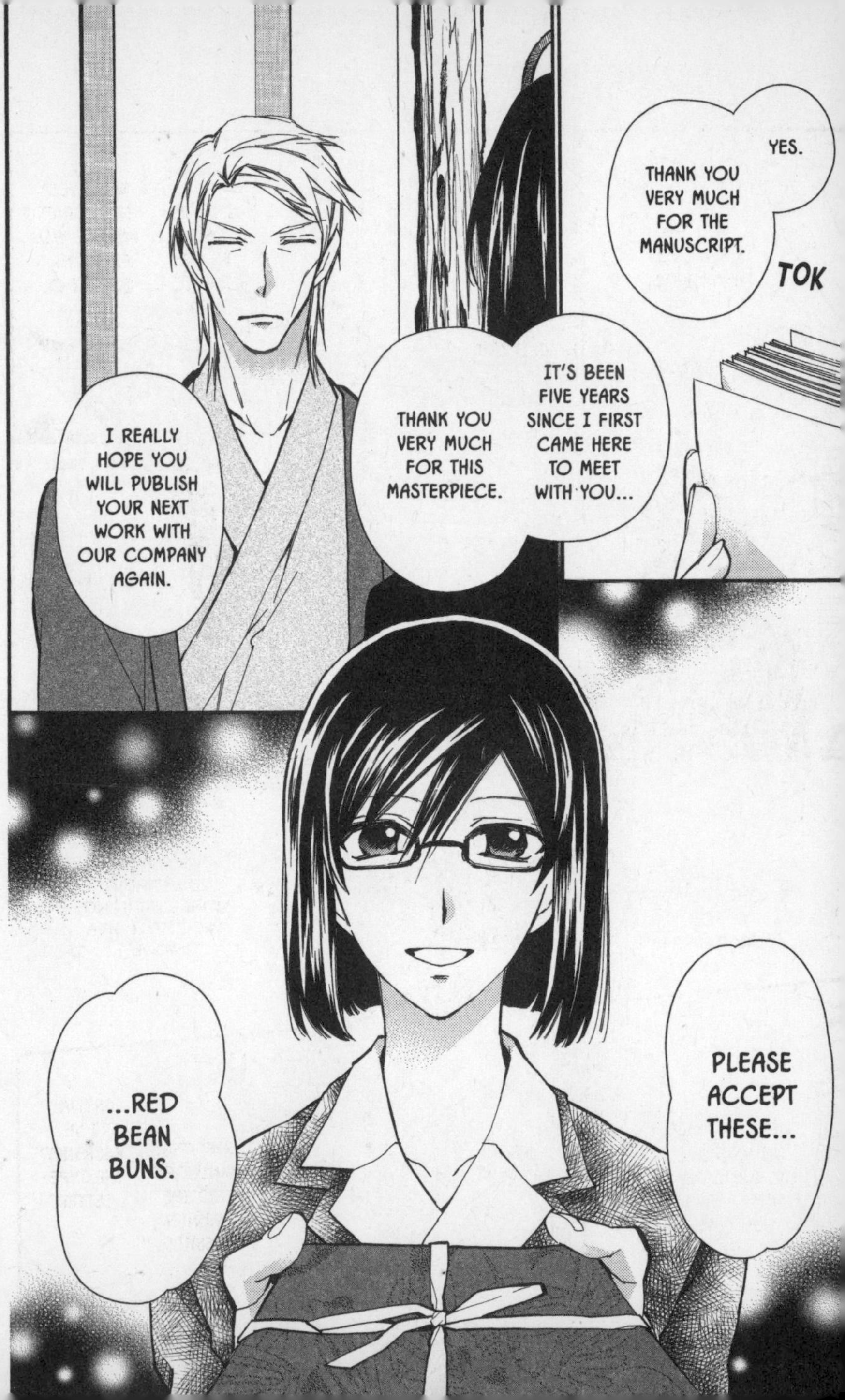
YES.
THANK YOU VERY MUCH FOR THE MANUSCRIPT.
TOK
IT'S BEEN FIVE YEARS SINCE I FIRST CAME HERE TO MEET WITH YOU...
THANK YOU VERY MUCH FOR THIS MASTERPIECE.
I REALLY HOPE YOU WILL PUBLISH YOUR NEXT WORK WITH OUR COMPANY AGAIN.
PLEASE ACCEPT THESE...
...RED BEAN BUNS.

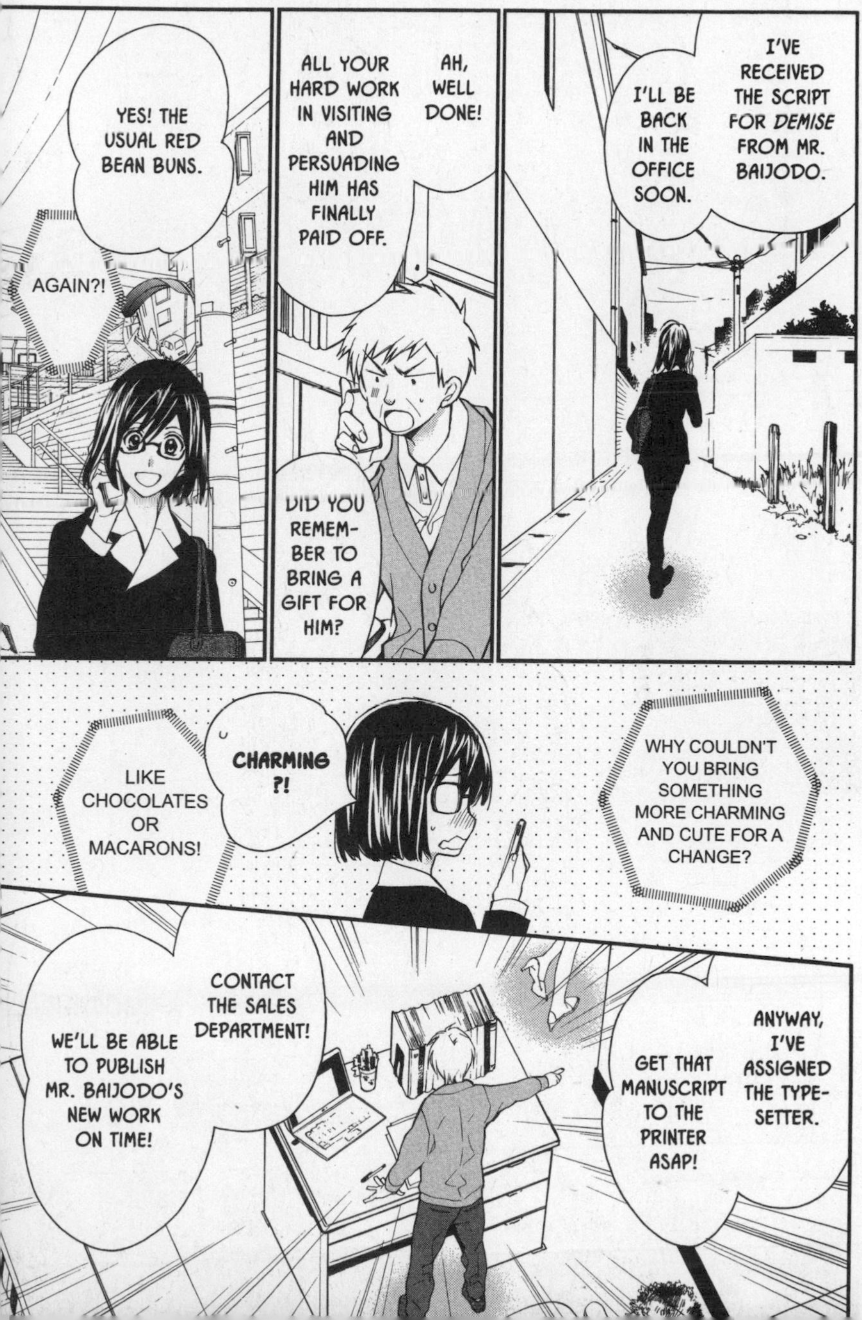
I'VE RECEIVED THE SCRIPT FOR *DEMISE* FROM MR. BAIJODO.
I'LL BE BACK IN THE OFFICE SOON.
AH, WELL DONE!
ALL YOUR HARD WORK IN VISITING AND PERSUADING HIM HAS FINALLY PAID OFF.
DID YOU REMEMBER TO BRING A GIFT FOR HIM?
YES! THE USUAL RED BEAN BUNS.
AGAIN?!
WHY COULDN'T YOU BRING SOMETHING MORE CHARMING AND CUTE FOR A CHANGE?
CHARMING?!
LIKE CHOCOLATES OR MACARONS!
ANYWAY, I'VE ASSIGNED THE TYPE-SETTER.
GET THAT MANUSCRIPT TO THE PRINTER ASAP!
CONTACT THE SALES DEPARTMENT!
WE'LL BE ABLE TO PUBLISH MR. BAIJODO'S NEW WORK ON TIME!

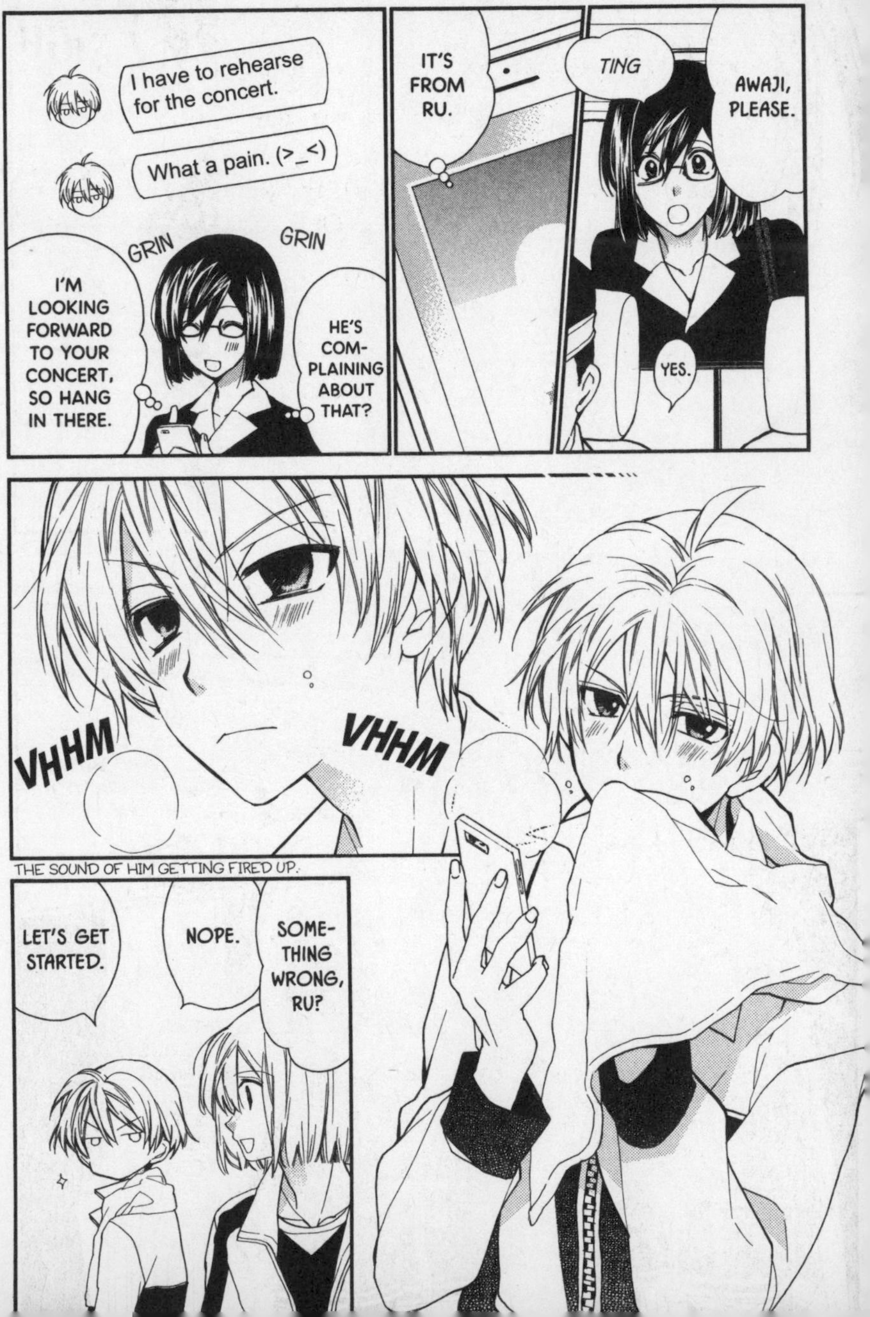
TING
AWAJI, PLEASE.
YES.
IT'S FROM RU.
I have to rehearse for the concert.
What a pain. (>_<)
GRIN
GRIN
HE'S COM-PLAINING ABOUT THAT?
I'M LOOKING FORWARD TO YOUR CONCERT, SO HANG IN THERE.
VHHM
VHHM
THE SOUND OF HIM GETTING FIRED UP.
SOME-THING WRONG, RU?
NOPE.
LET'S GET STARTED.

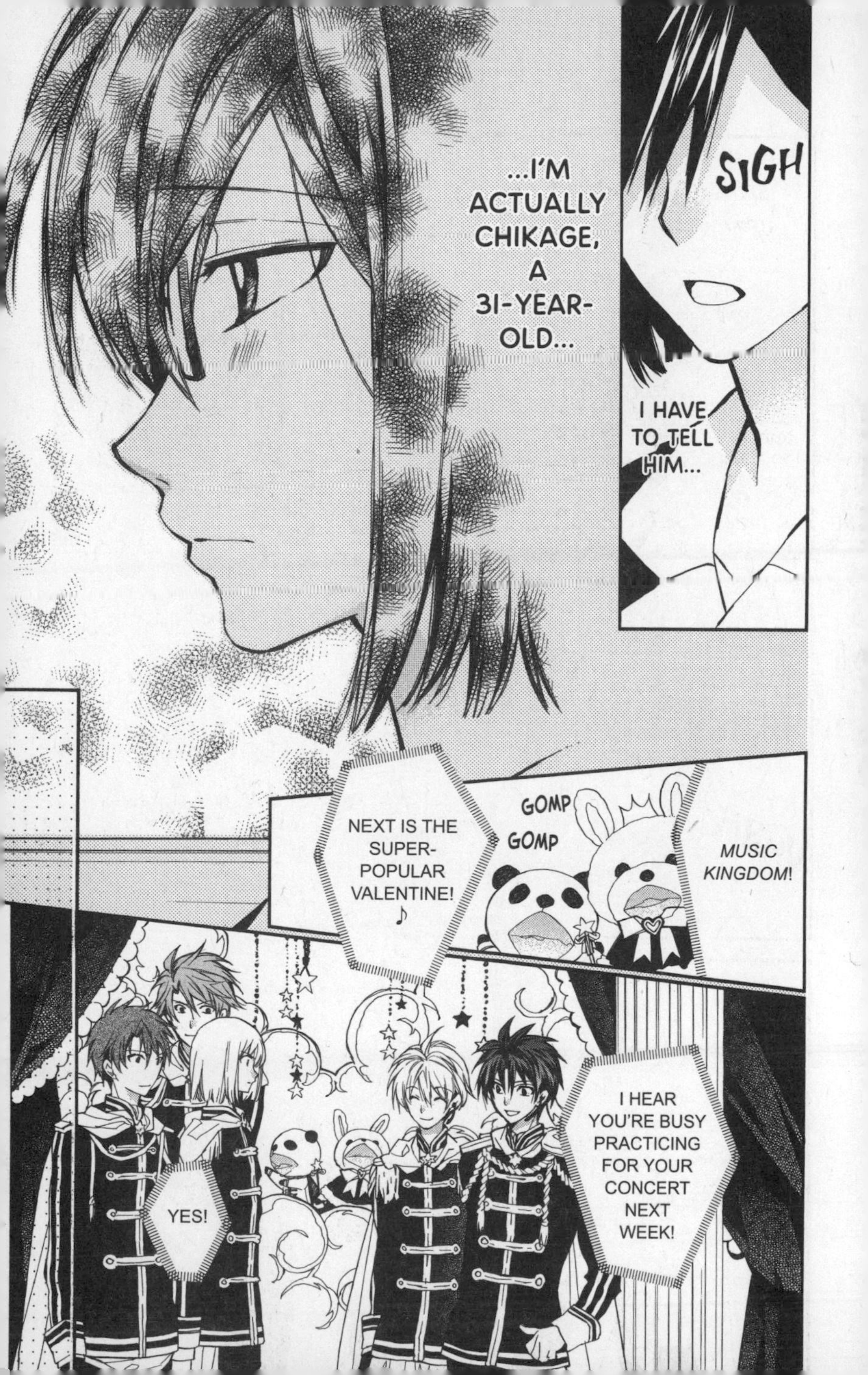
SIGH
I HAVE TO TELL HIM...
...I'M ACTUALLY CHIKAGE, A 31-YEAR-OLD...
MUSIC KINGDOM!
GOMP GOMP
NEXT IS THE SUPER-POPULAR VALENTINE! ♪
I HEAR YOU'RE BUSY PRACTICING FOR YOUR CONCERT NEXT WEEK!
YES!

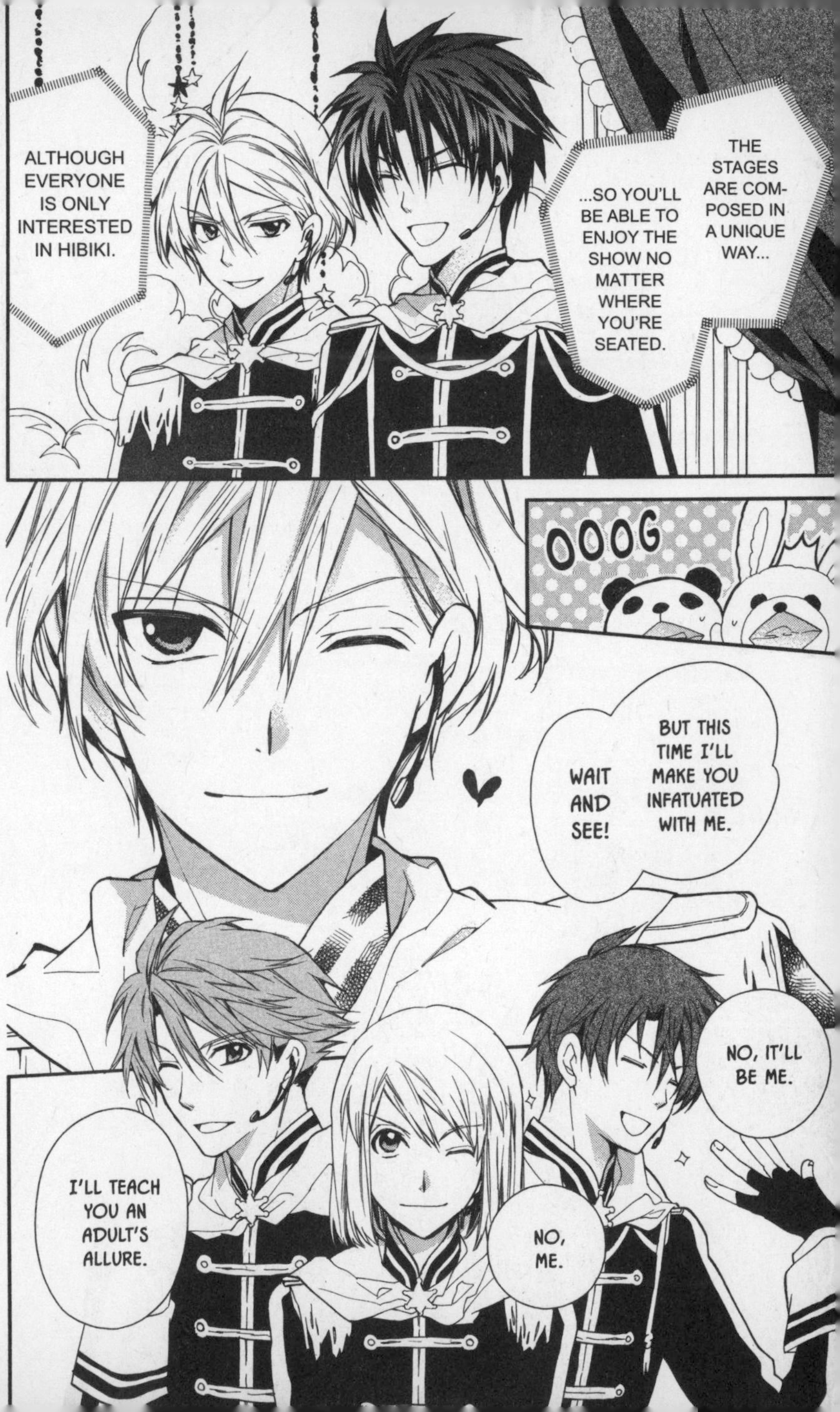
THE STAGES ARE COMPOSED IN A UNIQUE WAY...
...SO YOU'LL BE ABLE TO ENJOY THE SHOW NO MATTER WHERE YOU'RE SEATED.
ALTHOUGH EVERYONE IS ONLY INTERESTED IN HIBIKI.
OOOG
BUT THIS TIME I'LL MAKE YOU INFATUATED WITH ME.
WAIT AND SEE!
NO, IT'LL BE ME.
NO, ME.
I'LL TEACH YOU AN ADULT'S ALLURE.

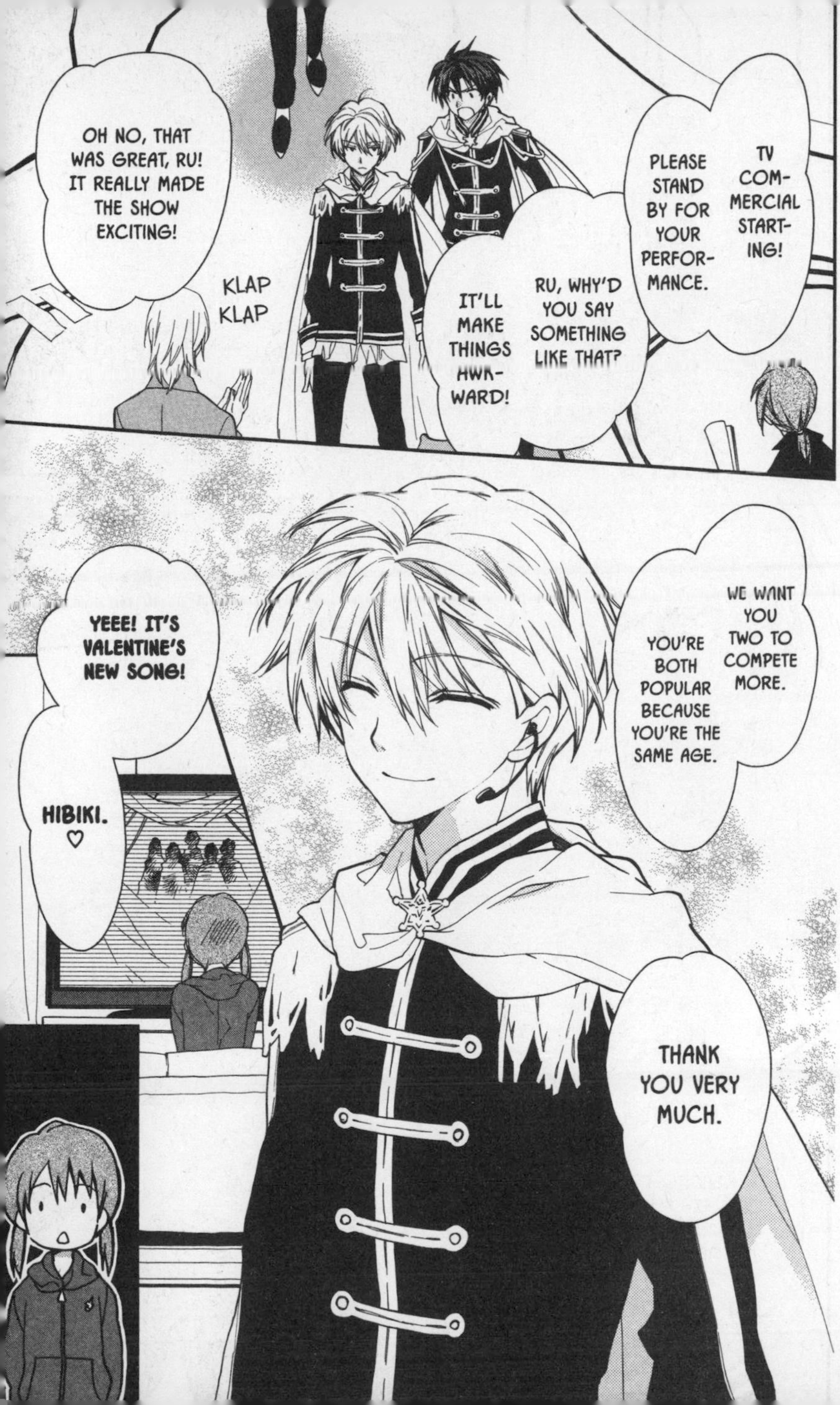
TV COMMERCIAL STARTING!
PLEASE STAND BY FOR YOUR PERFORMANCE.
RU, WHY'D YOU SAY SOMETHING LIKE THAT?
IT'LL MAKE THINGS AWKWARD!
KLAP KLAP
OH NO, THAT WAS GREAT, RU! IT REALLY MADE THE SHOW EXCITING!
WE WANT YOU TWO TO COMPETE MORE.
YOU'RE BOTH POPULAR BECAUSE YOU'RE THE SAME AGE.
THANK YOU VERY MUCH.
YEEE! IT'S VALENTINE'S NEW SONG!
HIBIKI. ♡

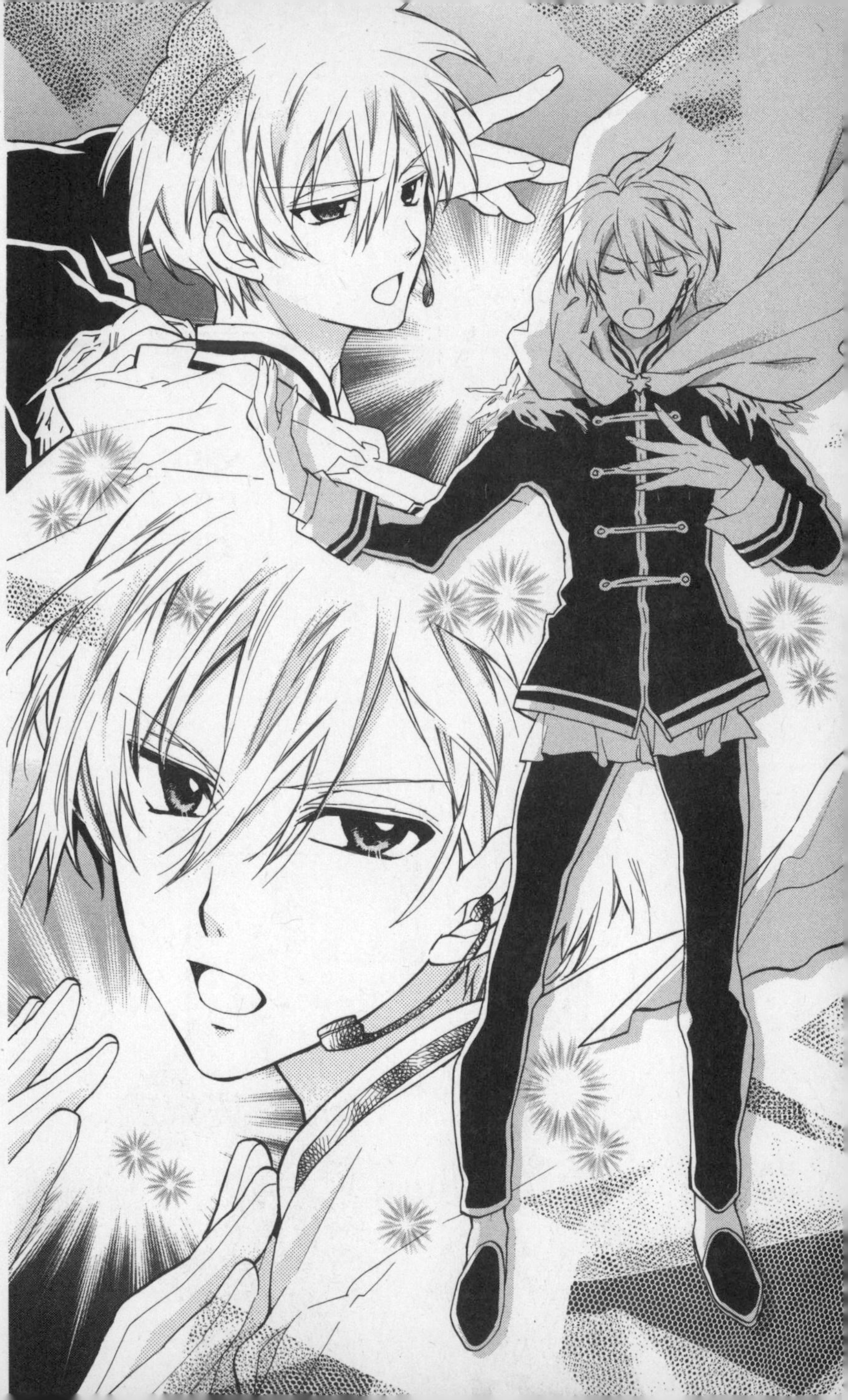

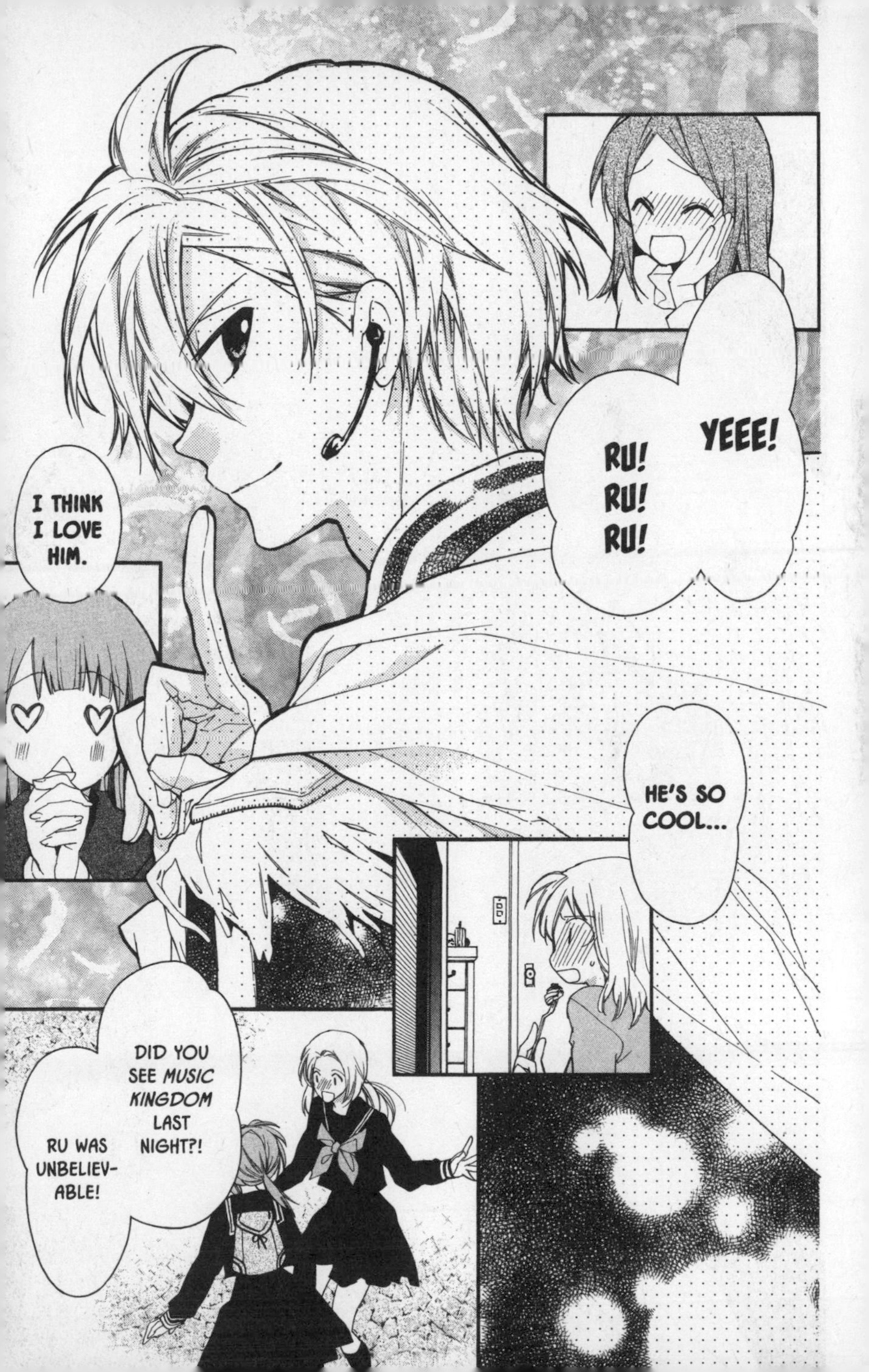
RU! RU! RU! YEEE!
I THINK I LOVE HIM.
HE'S SO COOL...
DID YOU SEE *MUSIC KINGDOM* LAST NIGHT?!
RU WAS UNBELIEV-ABLE!

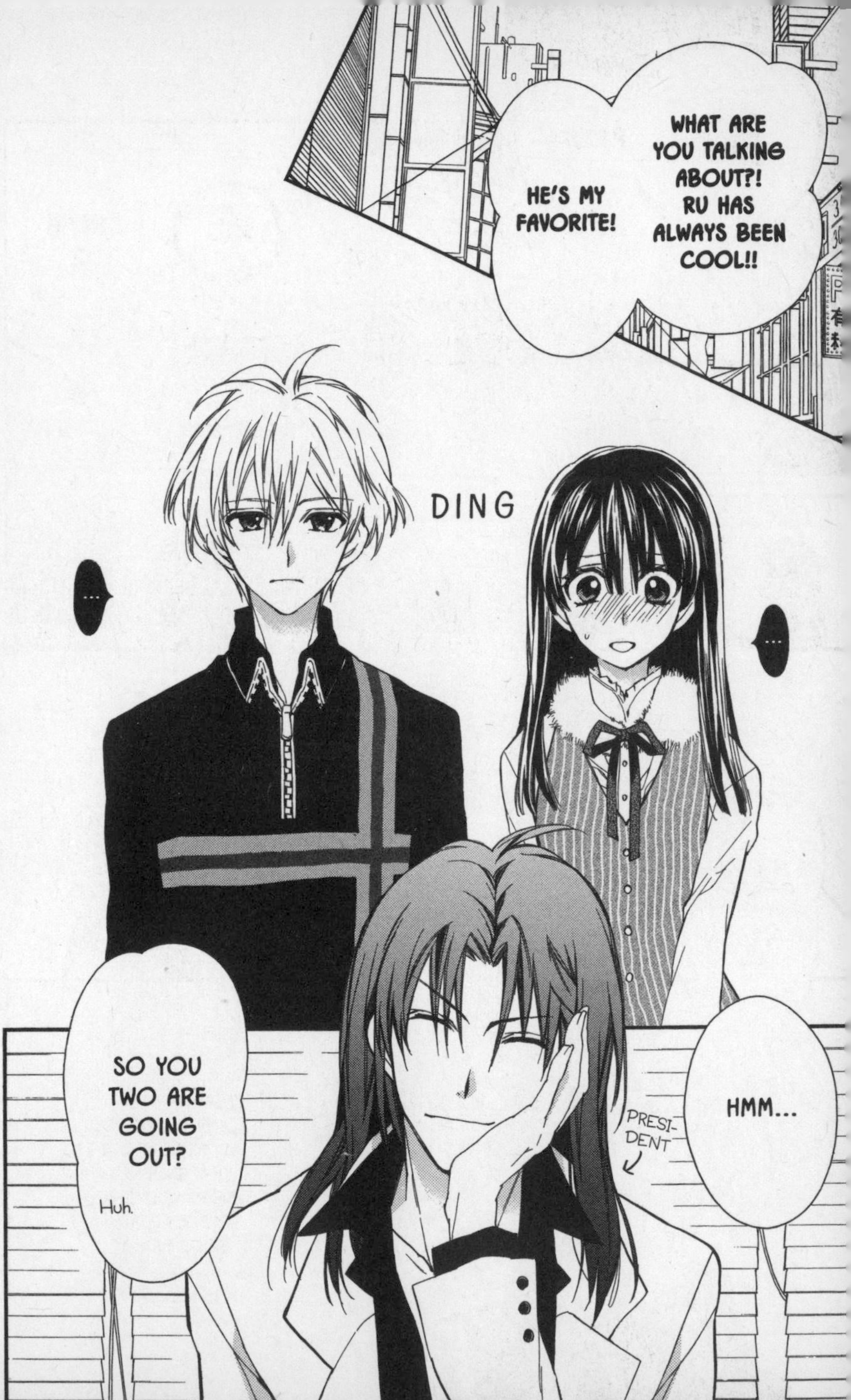
WHAT ARE YOU TALKING ABOUT?! RU HAS ALWAYS BEEN COOL!!
HE'S MY FAVORITE!
DING
...
...
HMM...
PRESI-DENT
SO YOU TWO ARE GOING OUT?
Huh.

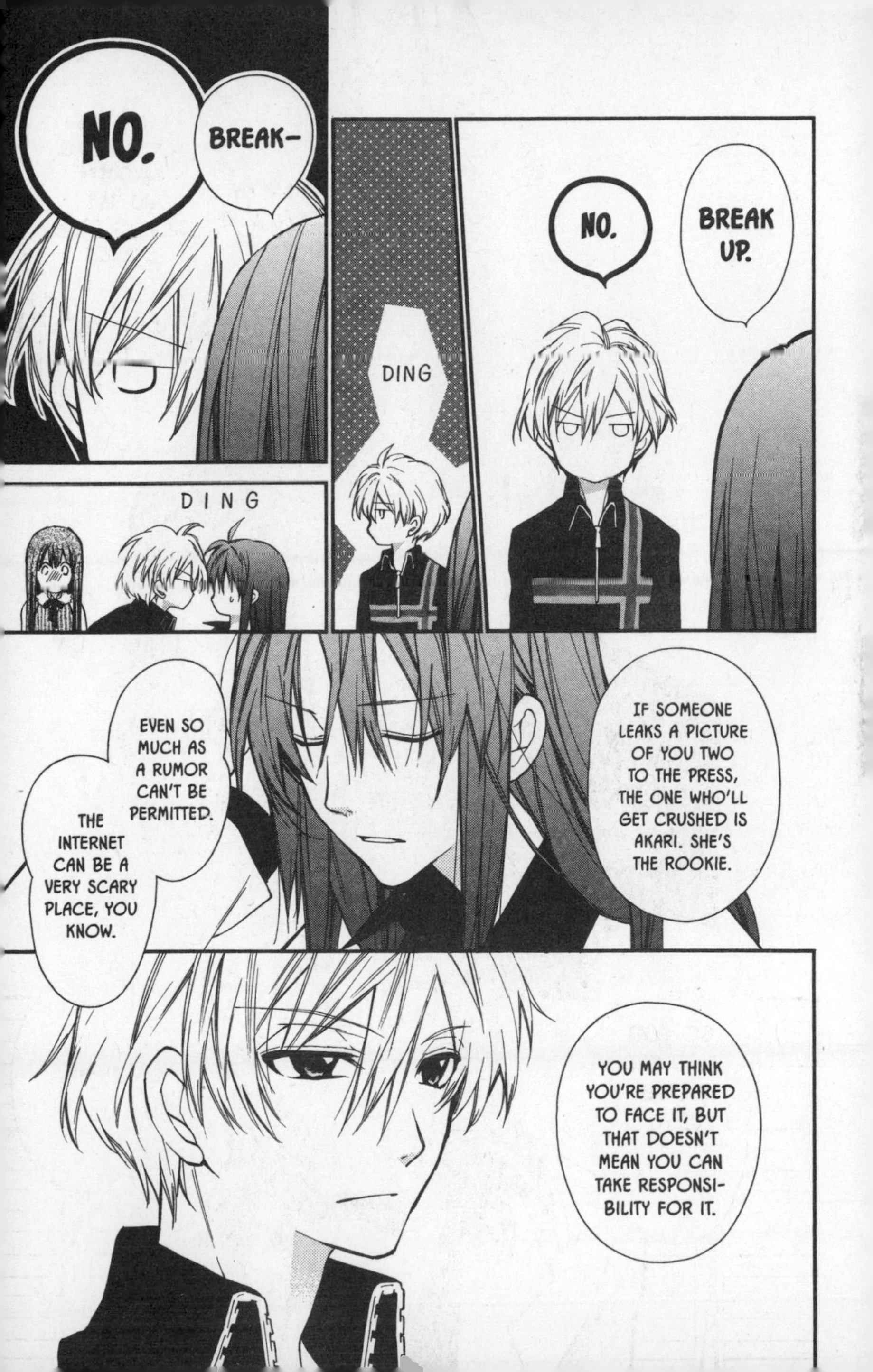
BREAK UP.
NO.
DING
BREAK-
NO.
DING
IF SOMEONE LEAKS A PICTURE OF YOU TWO TO THE PRESS, THE ONE WHO'LL GET CRUSHED IS AKARI. SHE'S THE ROOKIE.
EVEN SO MUCH AS A RUMOR CAN'T BE PERMITTED.
THE INTERNET CAN BE A VERY SCARY PLACE, YOU KNOW.
YOU MAY THINK YOU'RE PREPARED TO FACE IT, BUT THAT DOESN'T MEAN YOU CAN TAKE RESPONSI-BILITY FOR IT.

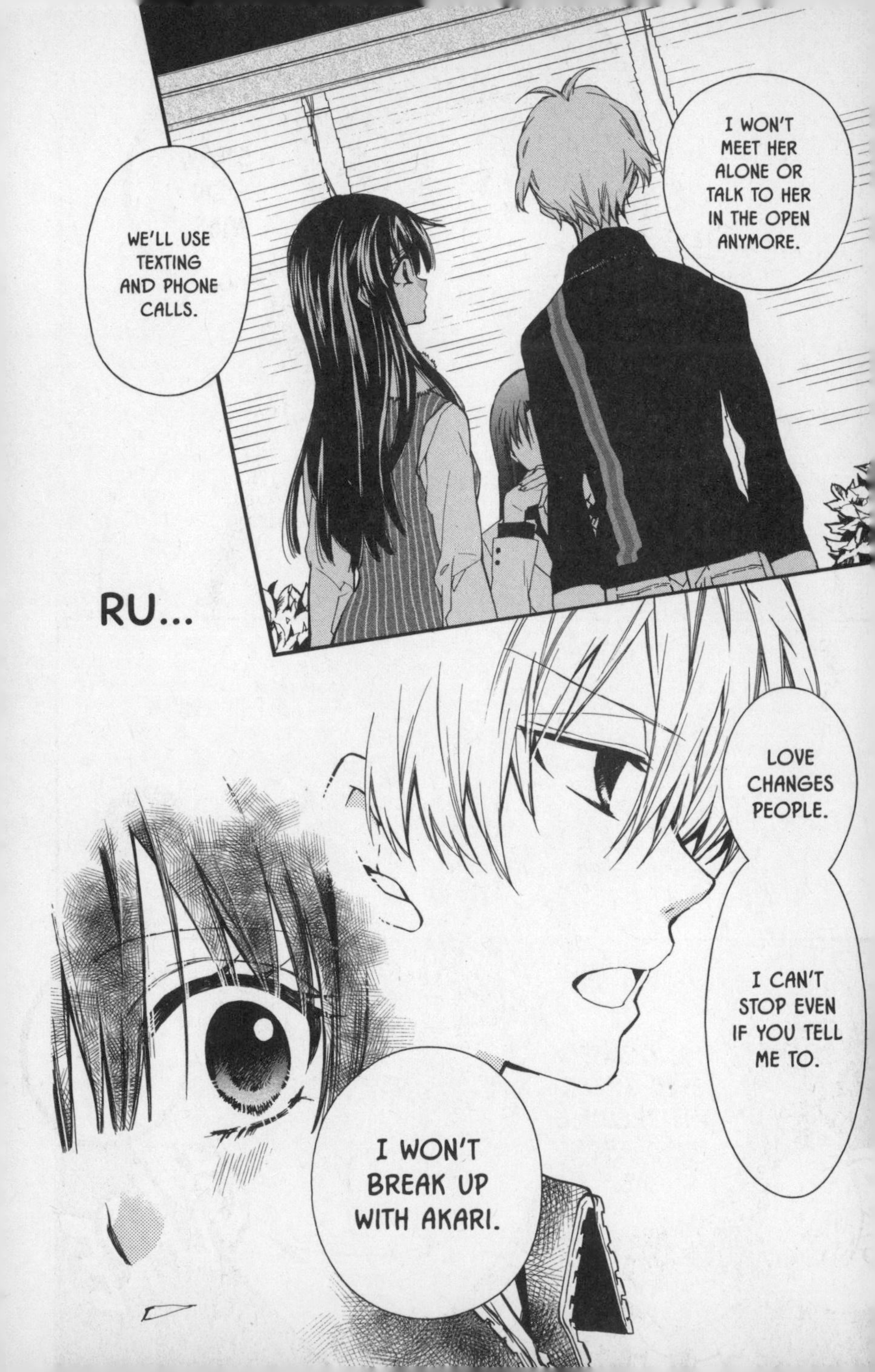
I WON'T MEET HER ALONE OR TALK TO HER IN THE OPEN ANYMORE.
WE'LL USE TEXTING AND PHONE CALLS.
RU...
LOVE CHANGES PEOPLE.
I CAN'T STOP EVEN IF YOU TELL ME TO.
I WON'T BREAK UP WITH AKARI.

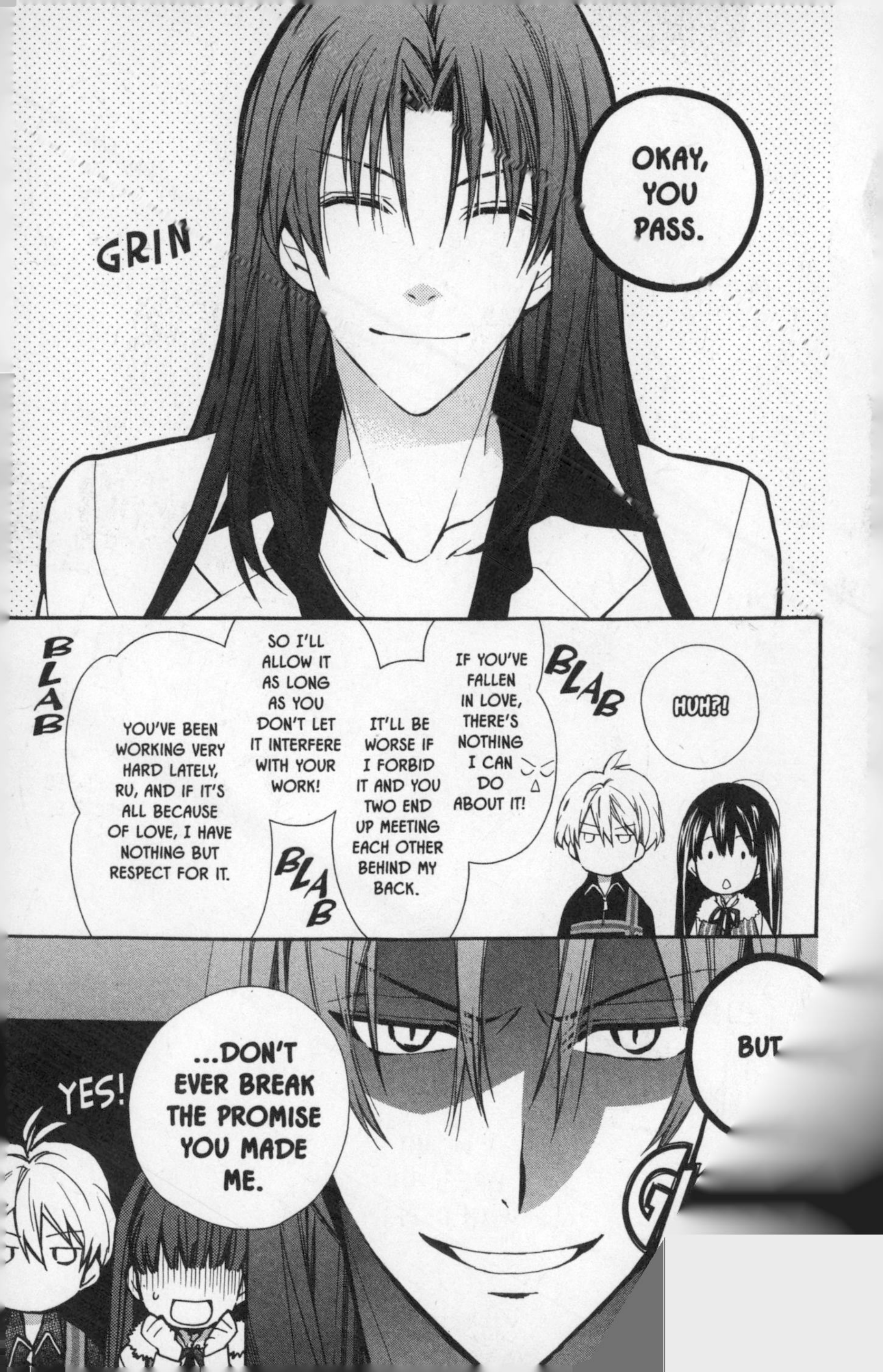
OKAY, YOU PASS.
GRIN
HUH?!
BLAB
IF YOU'VE FALLEN IN LOVE, THERE'S NOTHING I CAN DO ABOUT IT!
IT'LL BE WORSE IF I FORBID IT AND YOU TWO END UP MEETING EACH OTHER BEHIND MY BACK.
BLAB
SO I'LL ALLOW IT AS LONG AS YOU DON'T LET IT INTERFERE WITH YOUR WORK!
YOU'VE BEEN WORKING VERY HARD LATELY, RU, AND IF IT'S ALL BECAUSE OF LOVE, I HAVE NOTHING BUT RESPECT FOR IT.
BLAB
BUT
...DON'T EVER BREAK THE PROMISE YOU MADE ME.
YES!

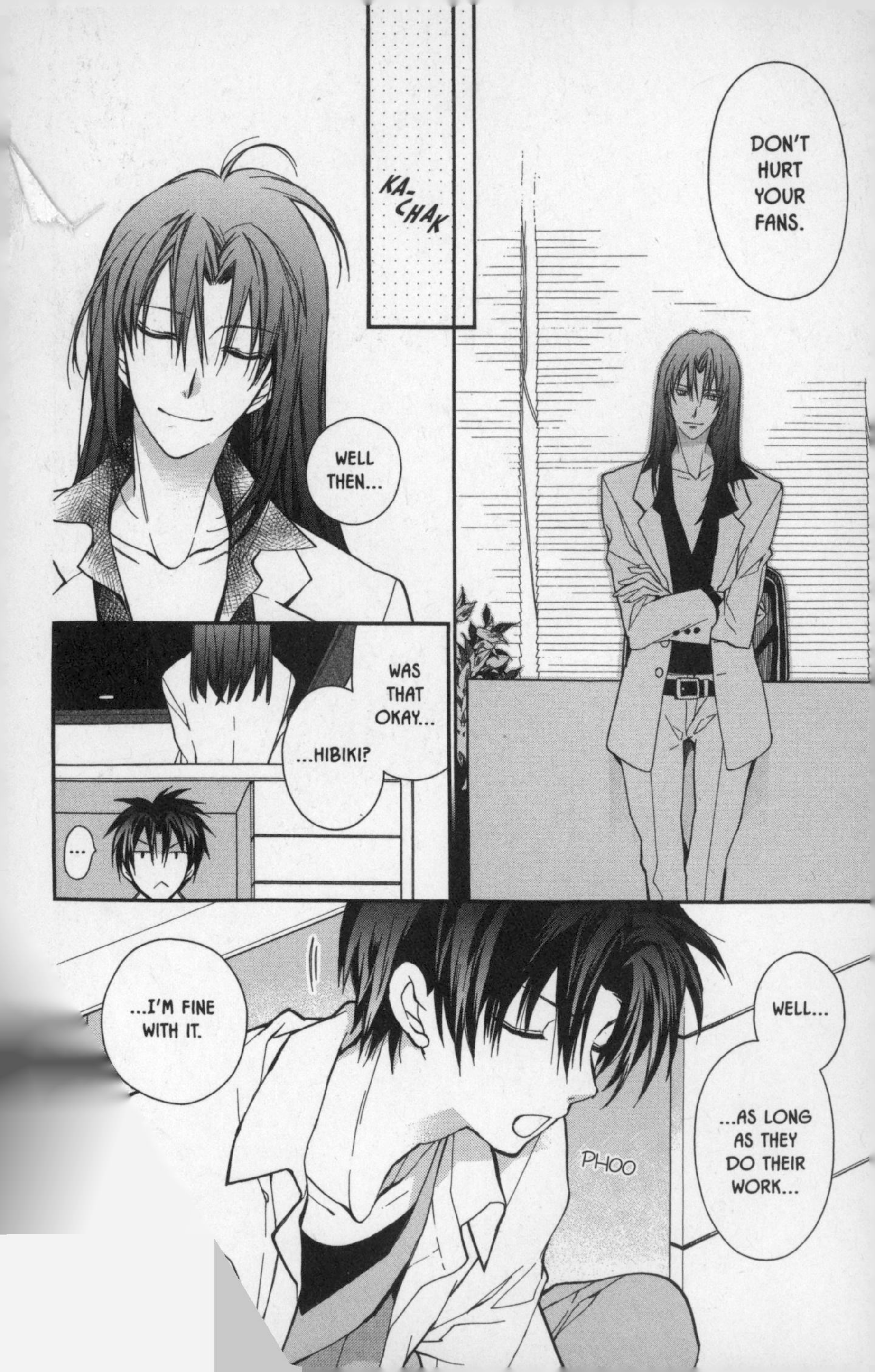
DON'T HURT YOUR FANS.
KA-CHAK
WELL THEN...
WAS THAT OKAY...
...HIBIKI?
...
WELL...
...AS LONG AS THEY DO THEIR WORK...
PHOO
...I'M FINE WITH IT.

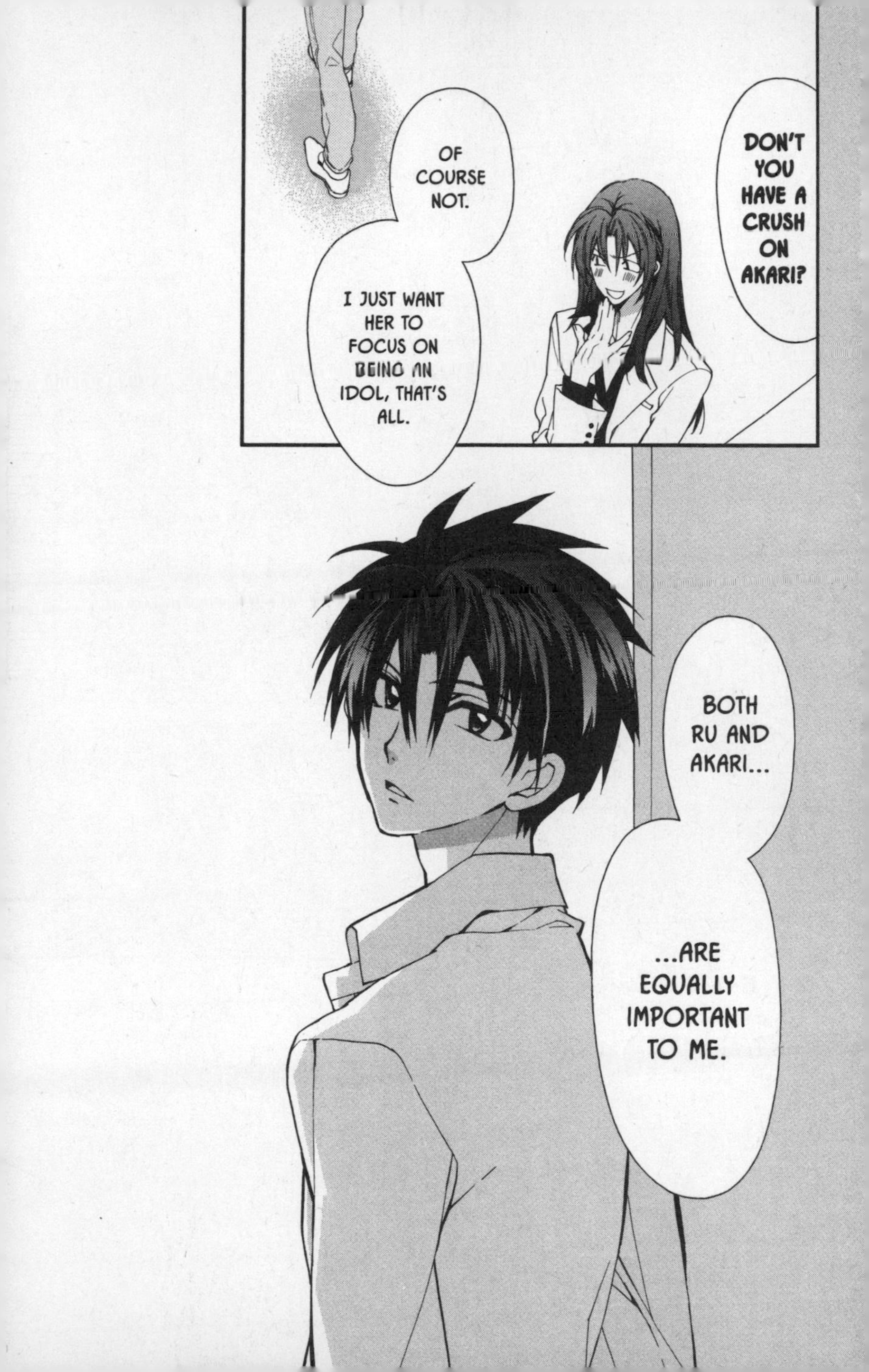
DON'T YOU HAVE A CRUSH ON AKARI?
OF COURSE NOT.
I JUST WANT HER TO FOCUS ON BEING AN IDOL, THAT'S ALL.
BOTH RU AND AKARI...
...ARE EQUALLY IMPORTANT TO ME.

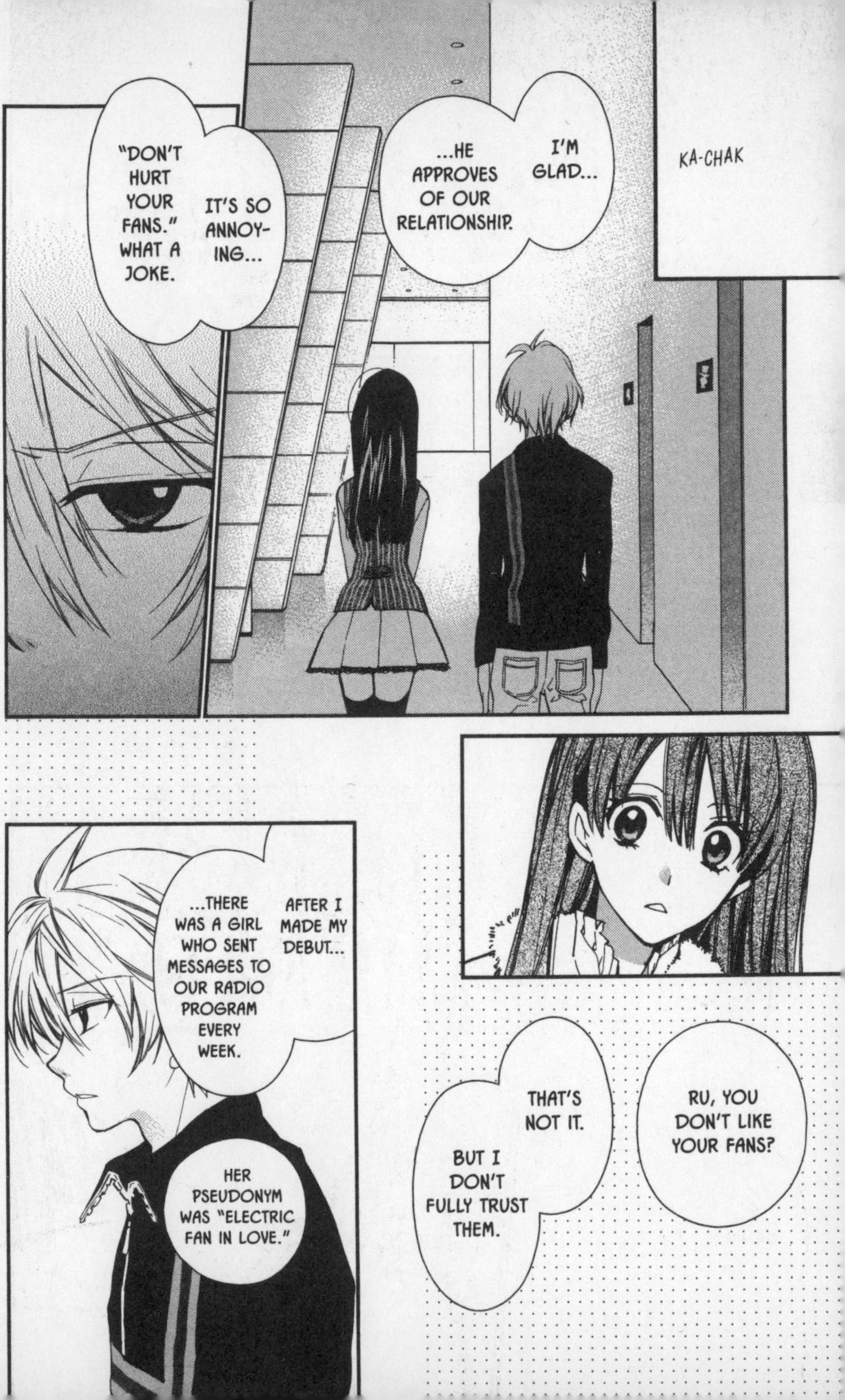
KA-CHAK
I'M GLAD...
...HE APPROVES OF OUR RELATIONSHIP.
IT'S SO ANNOY-ING...
"DON'T HURT YOUR FANS." WHAT A JOKE.
RU, YOU DON'T LIKE YOUR FANS?
THAT'S NOT IT.
BUT I DON'T FULLY TRUST THEM.
AFTER I MADE MY DEBUT...
...THERE WAS A GIRL WHO SENT MESSAGES TO OUR RADIO PROGRAM EVERY WEEK.
HER PSEUDONYM WAS "ELECTRIC FAN IN LOVE."

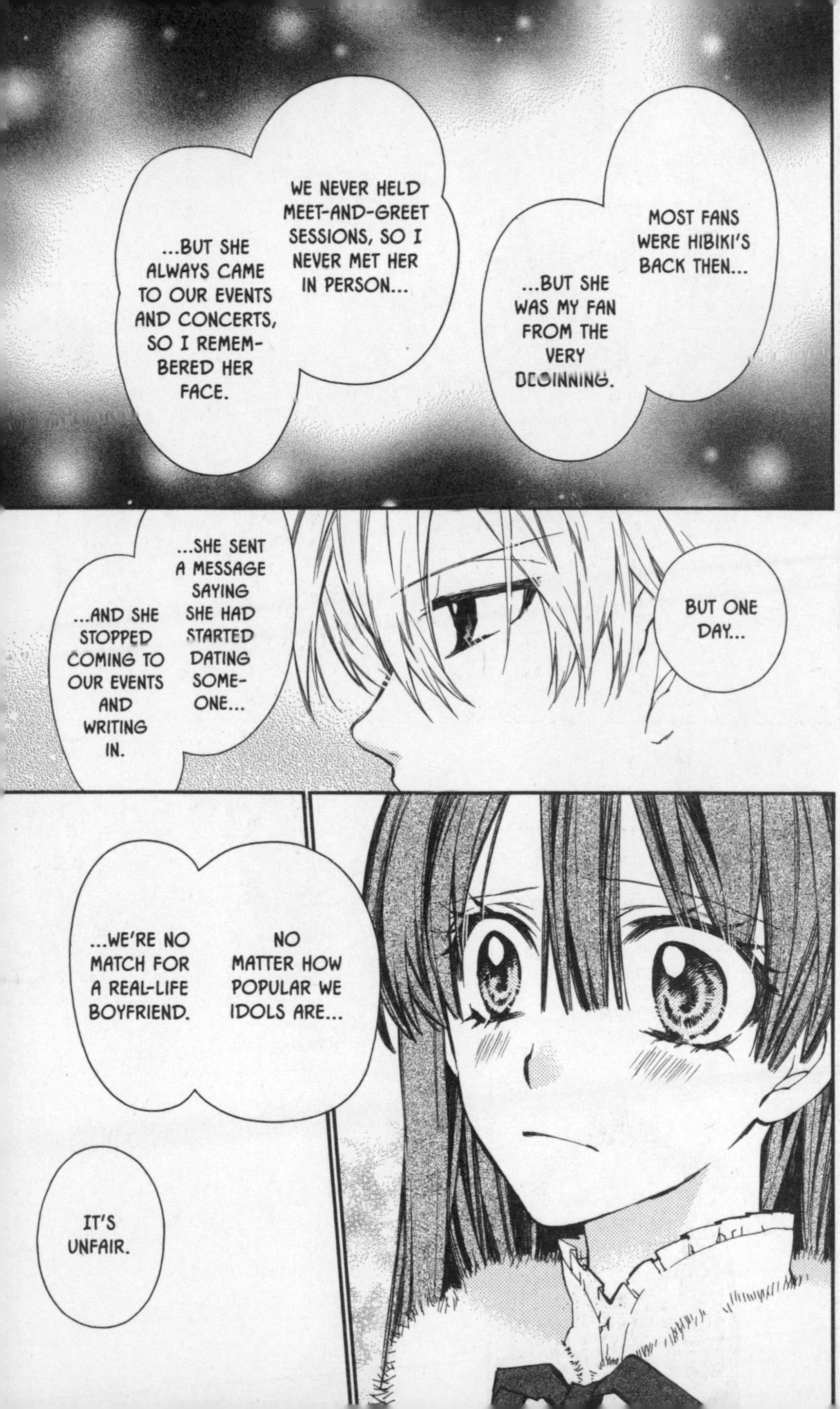
MOST FANS WERE HIBIKI'S BACK THEN...
...BUT SHE WAS MY FAN FROM THE VERY BEGINNING.
WE NEVER HELD MEET-AND-GREET SESSIONS, SO I NEVER MET HER IN PERSON...
...BUT SHE ALWAYS CAME TO OUR EVENTS AND CONCERTS, SO I REMEMBERED HER FACE.
BUT ONE DAY...
...SHE SENT A MESSAGE SAYING SHE HAD STARTED DATING SOMEONE...
...AND SHE STOPPED COMING TO OUR EVENTS AND WRITING IN.
NO MATTER HOW POPULAR WE IDOLS ARE...
...WE'RE NO MATCH FOR A REAL-LIFE BOYFRIEND.
IT'S UNFAIR.

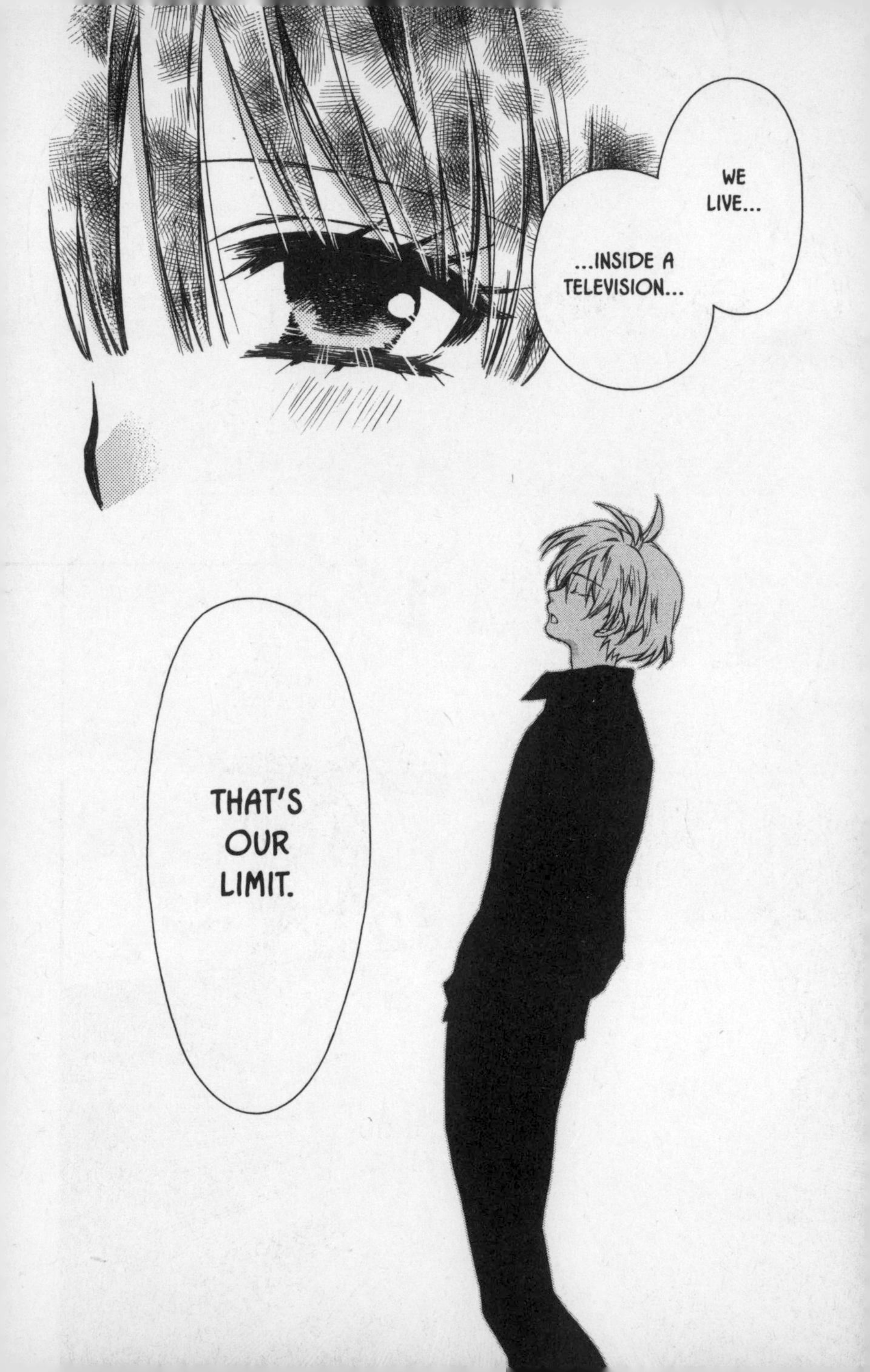
WE LIVE...
...INSIDE A TELEVISION...
THAT'S OUR LIMIT.

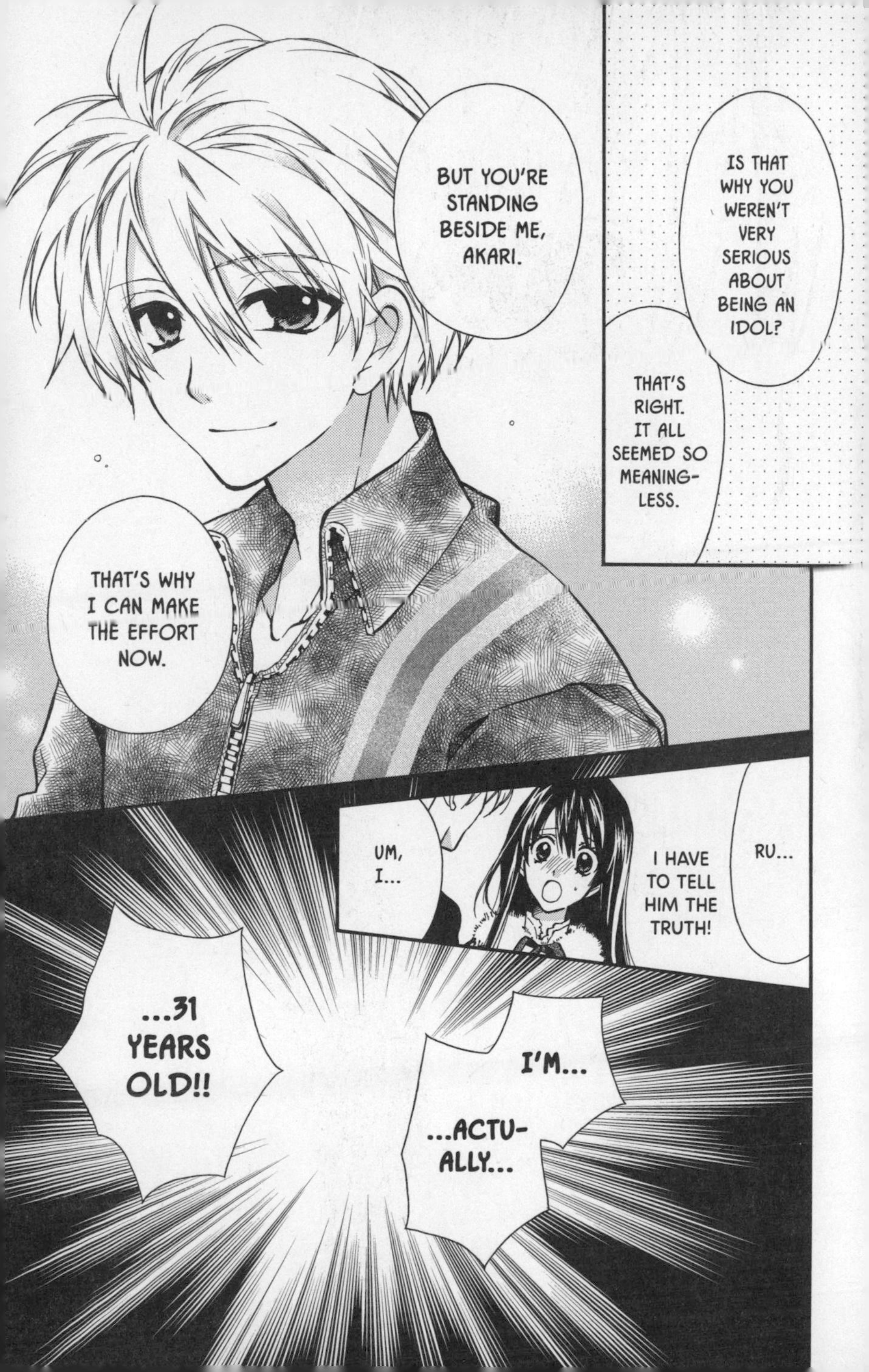
IS THAT WHY YOU WEREN'T VERY SERIOUS ABOUT BEING AN IDOL?
THAT'S RIGHT. IT ALL SEEMED SO MEANING-LESS.
BUT YOU'RE STANDING BESIDE ME, AKARI.
THAT'S WHY I CAN MAKE THE EFFORT NOW.
RU...
I HAVE TO TELL HIM THE TRUTH!
UM, I...
I'M...
...ACTU-ALLY...
...31 YEARS OLD!!

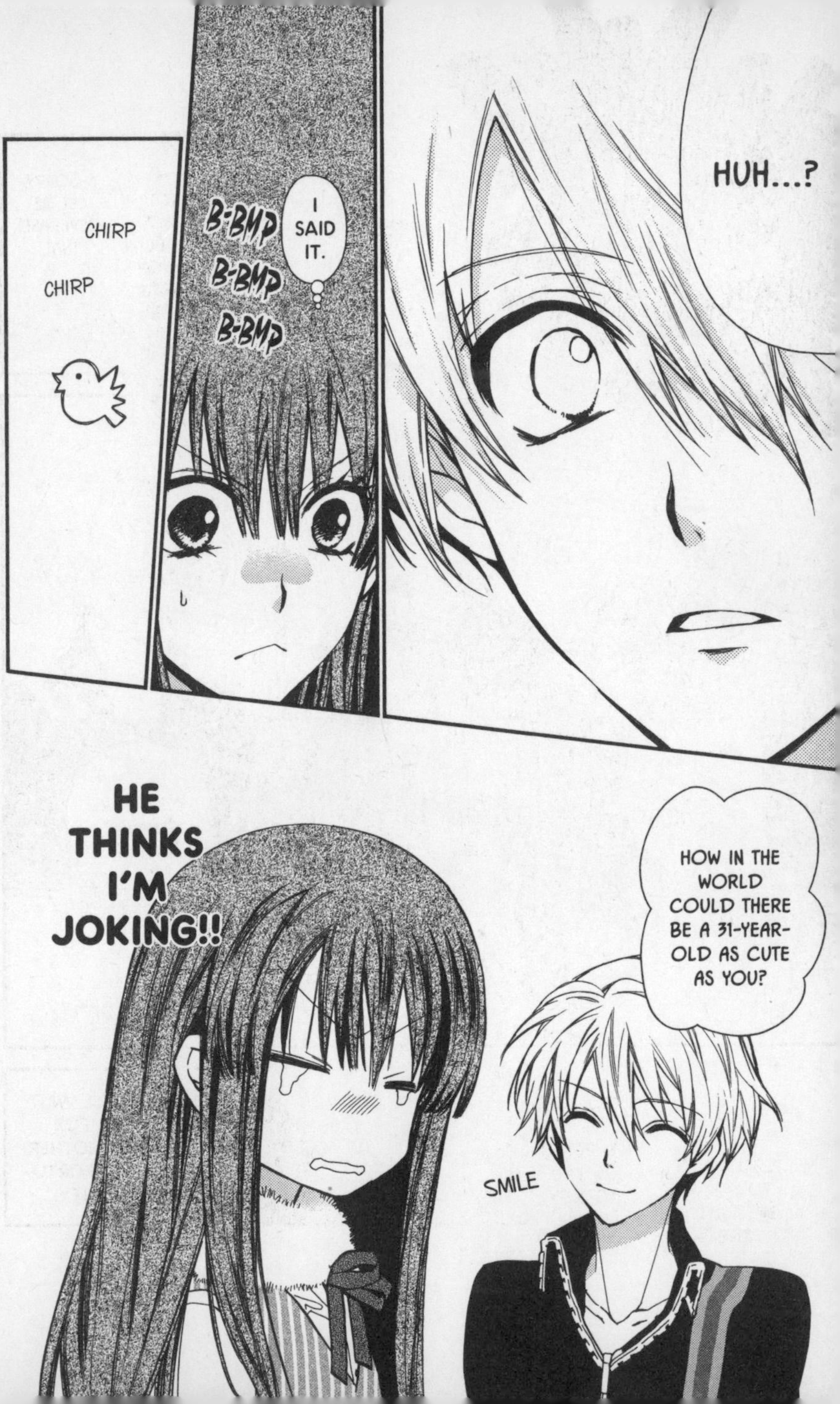
HUH...?
I SAID IT.
B-BMP B-BMP B-BMP
CHIRP
CHIRP
HOW IN THE WORLD COULD THERE BE A 31-YEAR-OLD AS CUTE AS YOU?
SMILE
HE THINKS I'M JOKING!!

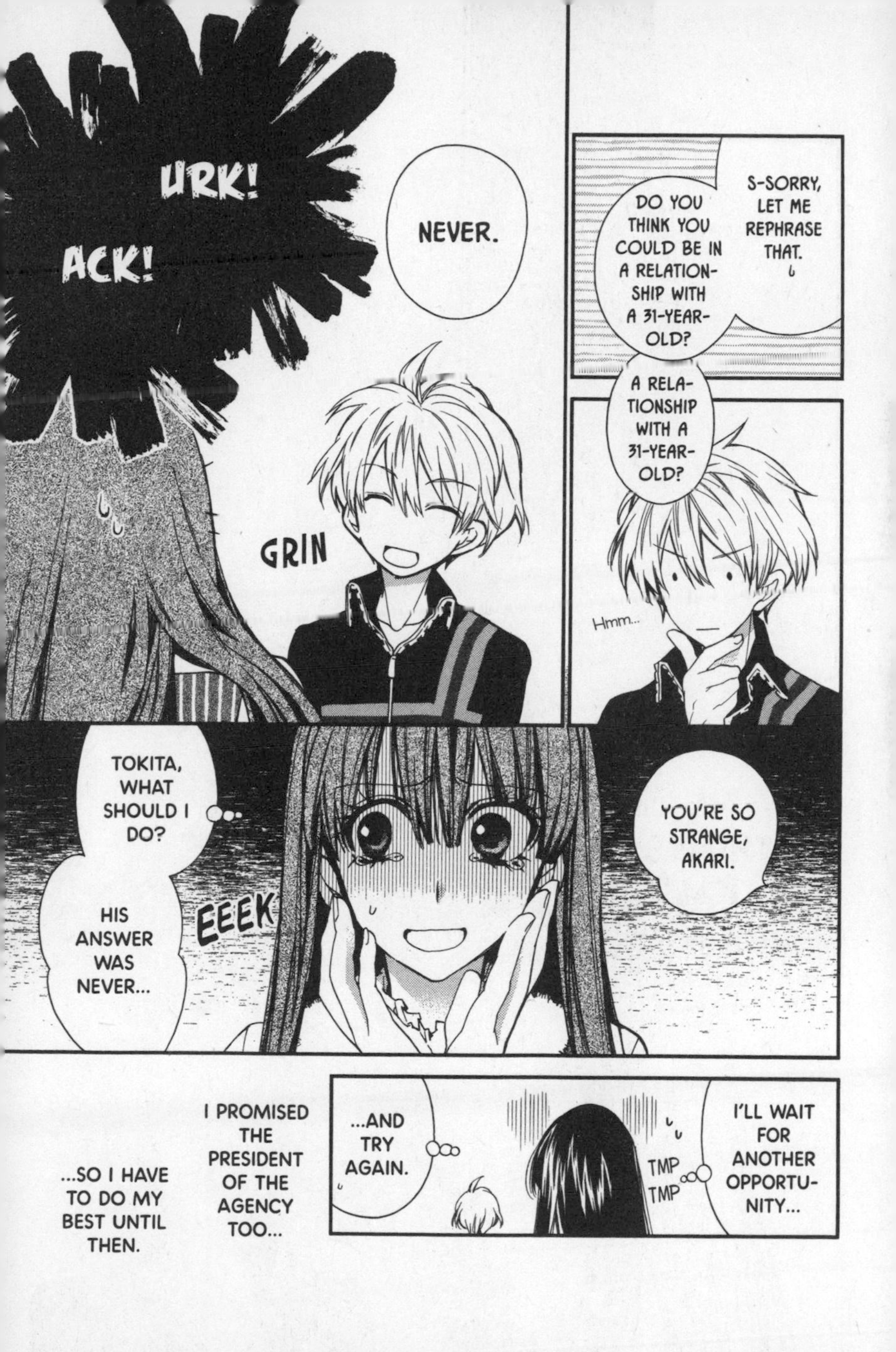
S-SORRY, LET ME REPHRASE THAT.
DO YOU THINK YOU COULD BE IN A RELATIONSHIP WITH A 31-YEAR-OLD?
A RELATIONSHIP WITH A 31-YEAR-OLD?
Hmm...
NEVER.
GRIN
URK!
ACK!
YOU'RE SO STRANGE, AKARI.
TOKITA, WHAT SHOULD I DO?
HIS ANSWER WAS NEVER...
EEEK
I'LL WAIT FOR ANOTHER OPPORTUNITY...
TMP TMP
...AND TRY AGAIN.
I PROMISED THE PRESIDENT OF THE AGENCY TOO...
...SO I HAVE TO DO MY BEST UNTIL THEN.

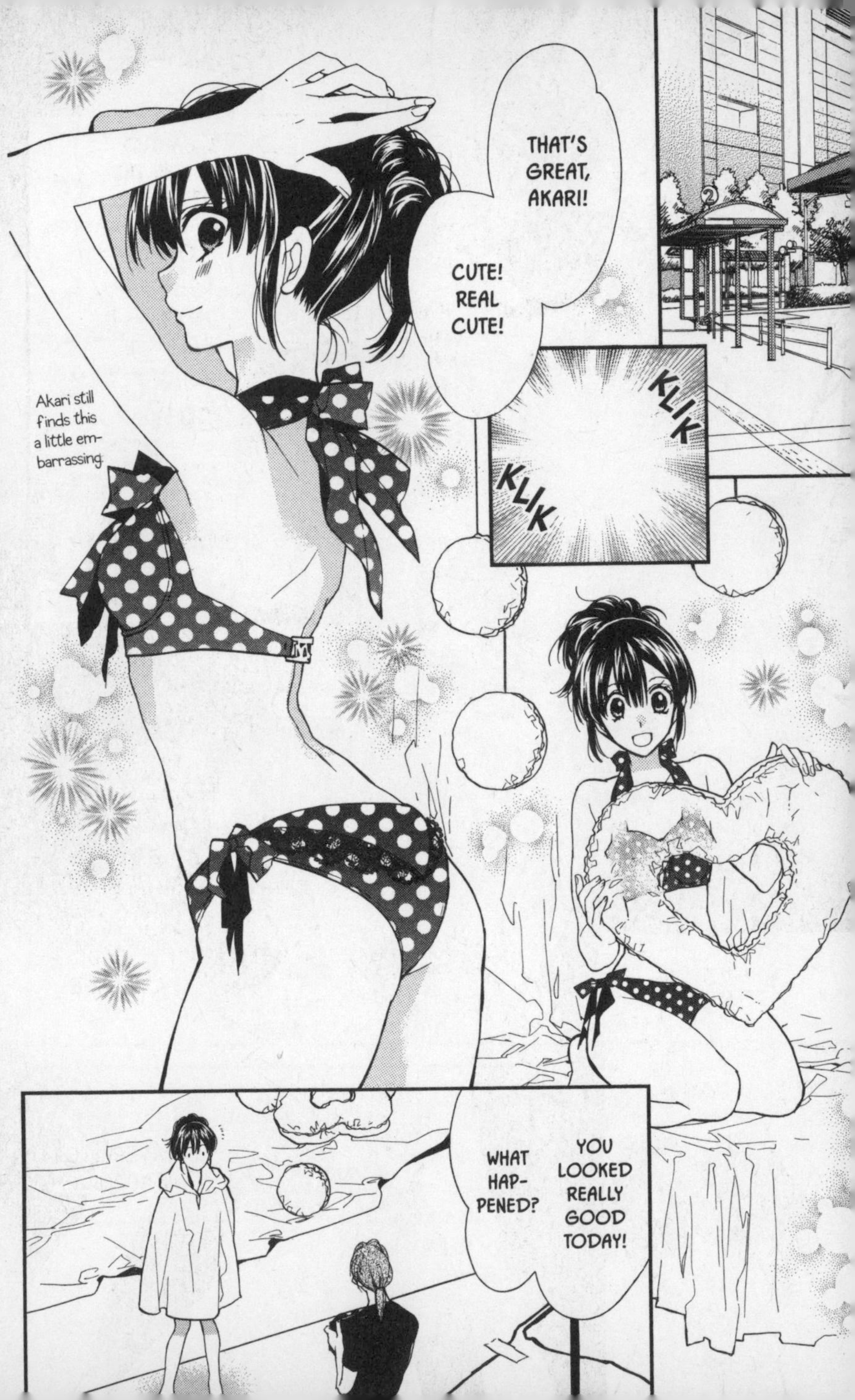
THAT'S GREAT, AKARI!
CUTE! REAL CUTE!
KLIK KLIK
Akari still finds this a little embarrassing.
YOU LOOKED REALLY GOOD TODAY!
WHAT HAPPENED?

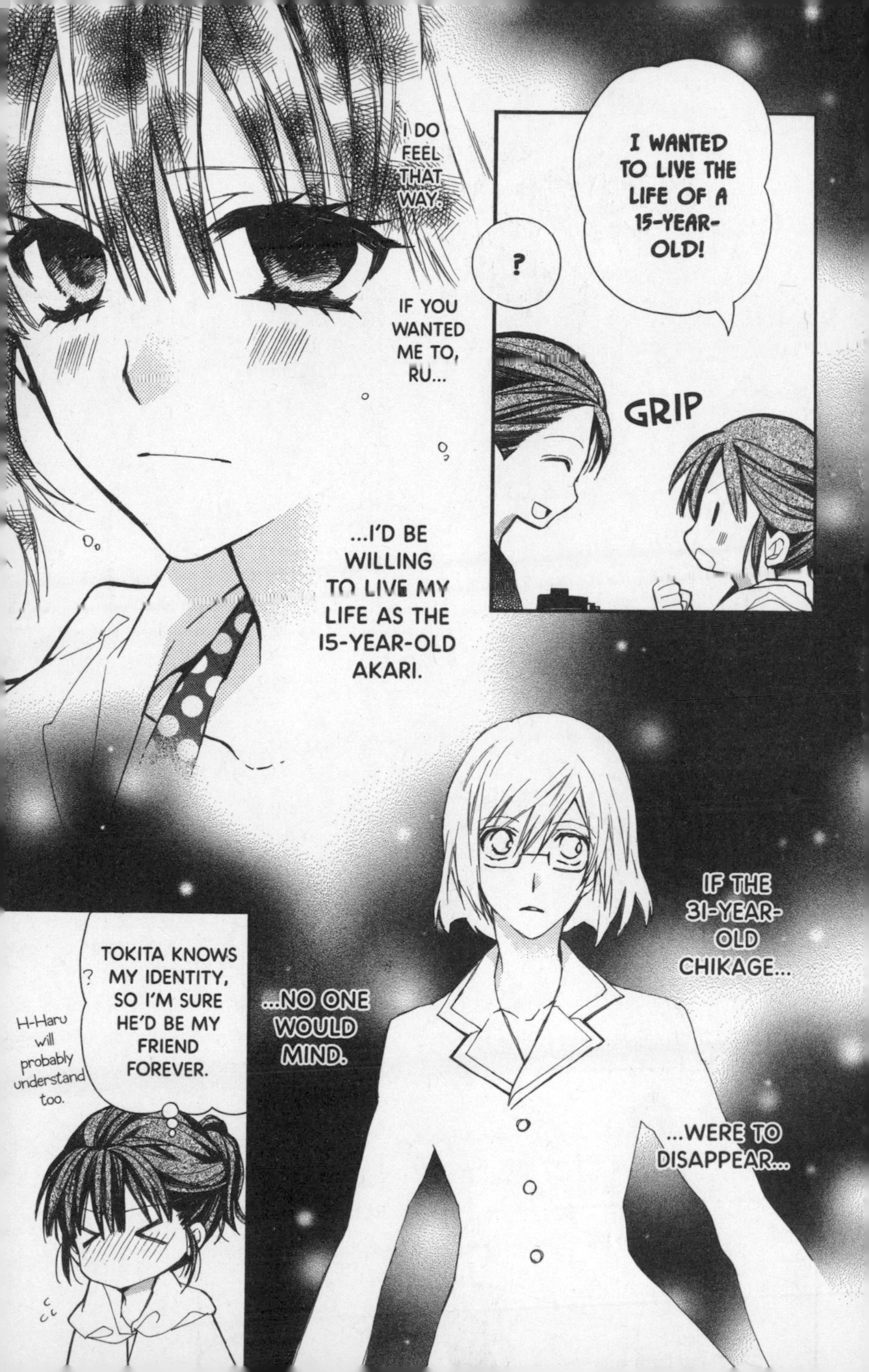
I WANTED TO LIVE THE LIFE OF A 15-YEAR-OLD!
?
GRIP
I DO FEEL THAT WAY.
IF YOU WANTED ME TO, RU...
...I'D BE WILLING TO LIVE MY LIFE AS THE 15-YEAR-OLD AKARI.
IF THE 31-YEAR-OLD CHIKAGE...
...WERE TO DISAPPEAR...
...NO ONE WOULD MIND.
TOKITA KNOWS MY IDENTITY, SO I'M SURE HE'D BE MY FRIEND FOREVER.
?
H-Haru will probably understand too.

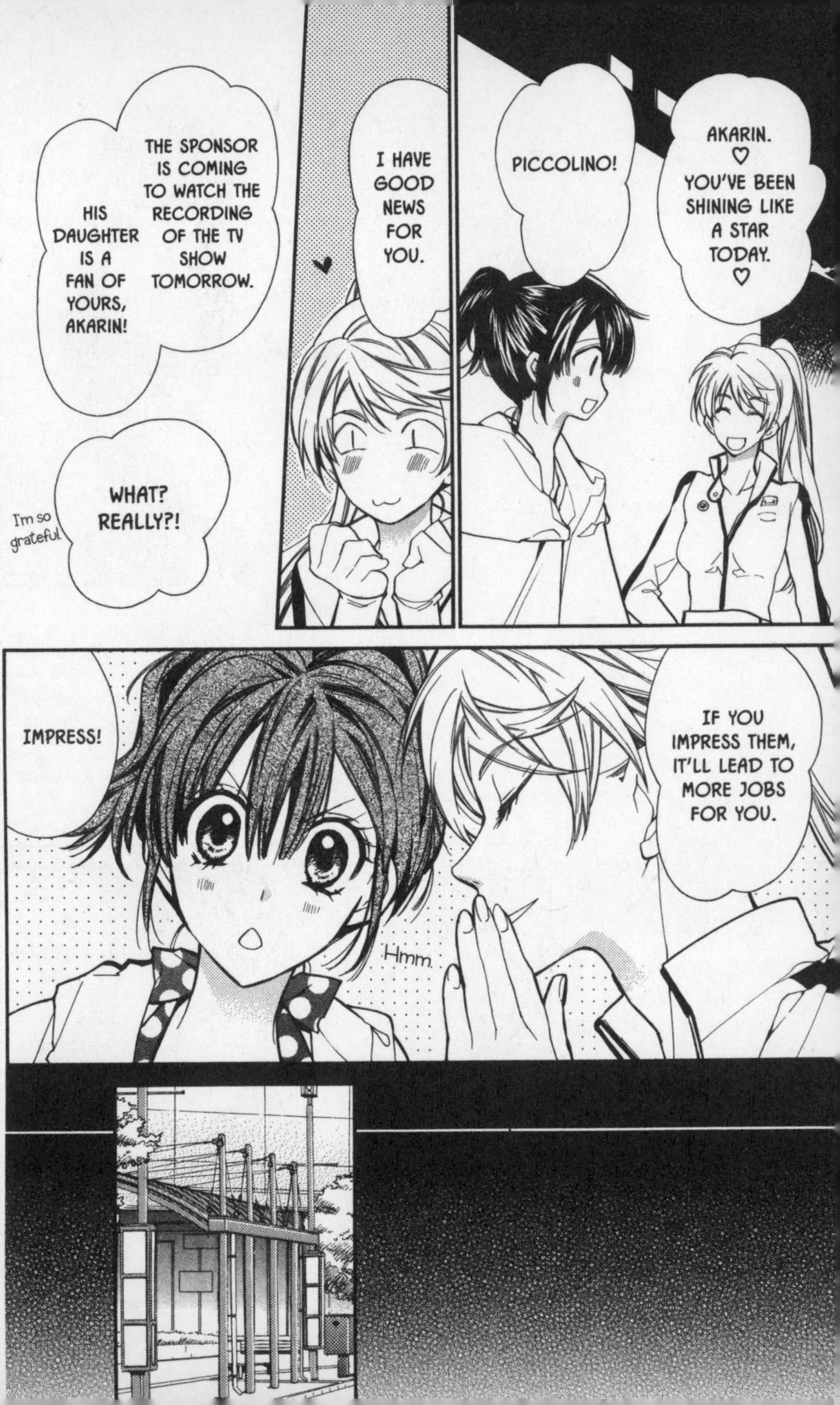
AKARIN. ♡ YOU'VE BEEN SHINING LIKE A STAR TODAY. ♡
PICCOLINO!
I HAVE GOOD NEWS FOR YOU.
THE SPONSOR IS COMING TO WATCH THE RECORDING OF THE TV SHOW TOMORROW.
HIS DAUGHTER IS A FAN OF YOURS, AKARIN!
WHAT? REALLY?!
I'm so grateful.
IF YOU IMPRESS THEM, IT'LL LEAD TO MORE JOBS FOR YOU.
Hmm.
IMPRESS!

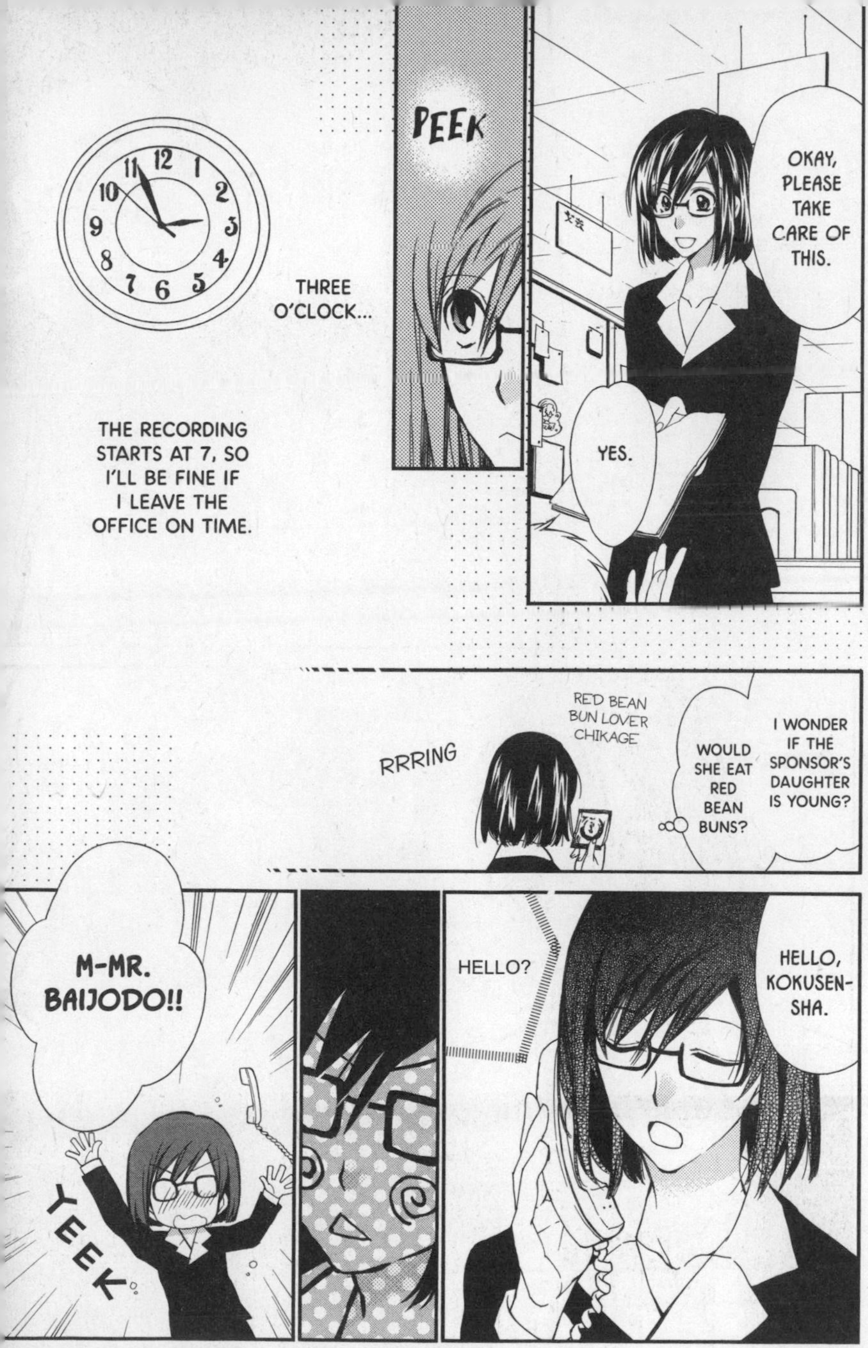
OKAY, PLEASE TAKE CARE OF THIS.
YES.
PEEK
THREE O'CLOCK...
THE RECORDING STARTS AT 7, SO I'LL BE FINE IF I LEAVE THE OFFICE ON TIME.
I WONDER IF THE SPONSOR'S DAUGHTER IS YOUNG?
WOULD SHE EAT RED BEAN BUNS?
RED BEAN BUN LOVER CHIKAGE
RRRING
HELLO, KOKUSEN-SHA.
HELLO?
M-MR. BAIJODO!!
YEEK

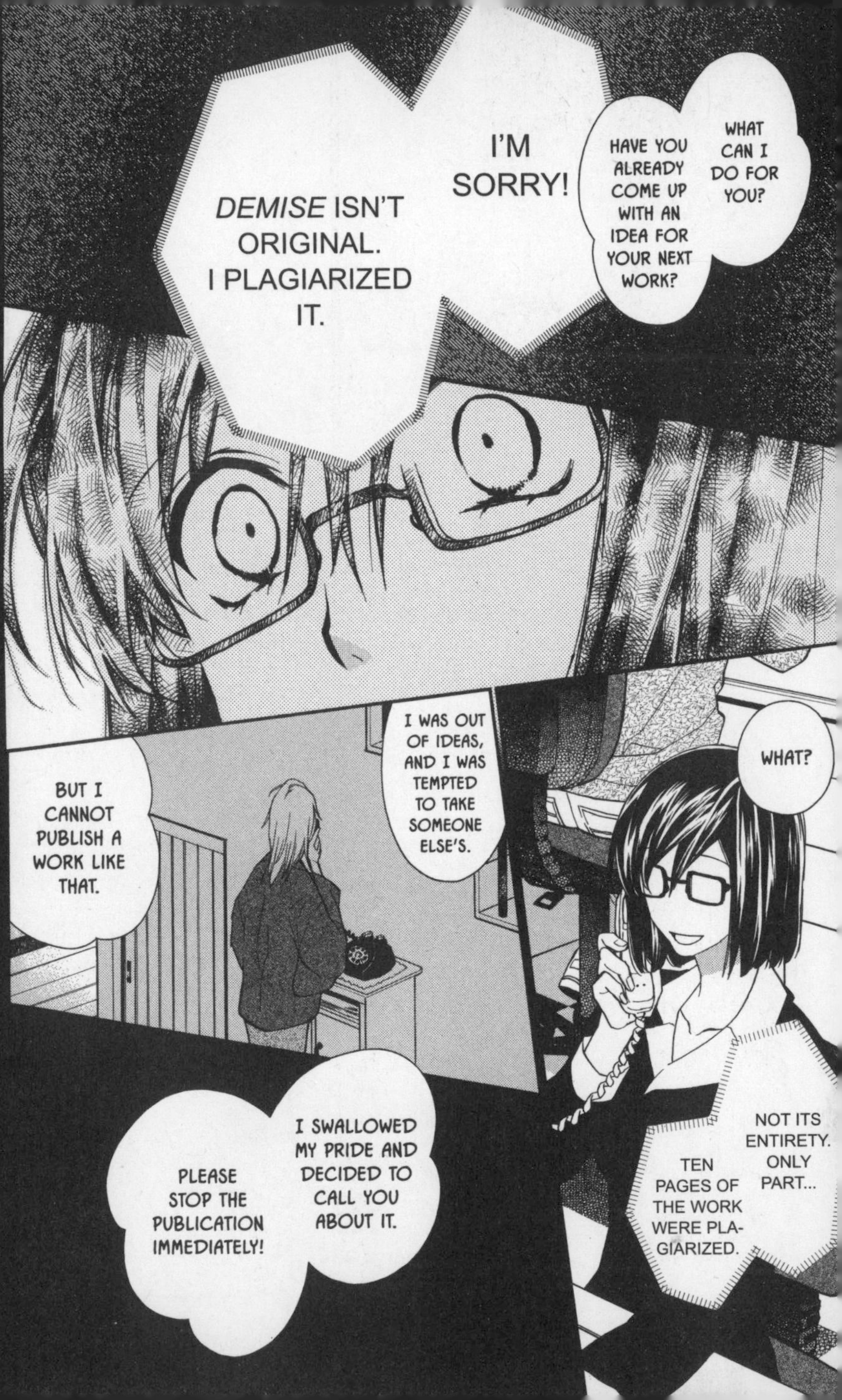
WHAT CAN I DO FOR YOU?
HAVE YOU ALREADY COME UP WITH AN IDEA FOR YOUR NEXT WORK?
I'M SORRY!
DEMISE ISN'T ORIGINAL. I PLAGIARIZED IT.
WHAT?
I WAS OUT OF IDEAS, AND I WAS TEMPTED TO TAKE SOMEONE ELSE'S.
BUT I CANNOT PUBLISH A WORK LIKE THAT.
NOT ITS ENTIRETY. ONLY PART...
TEN PAGES OF THE WORK WERE PLA-GIARIZED.
I SWALLOWED MY PRIDE AND DECIDED TO CALL YOU ABOUT IT.
PLEASE STOP THE PUBLICATION IMMEDIATELY!

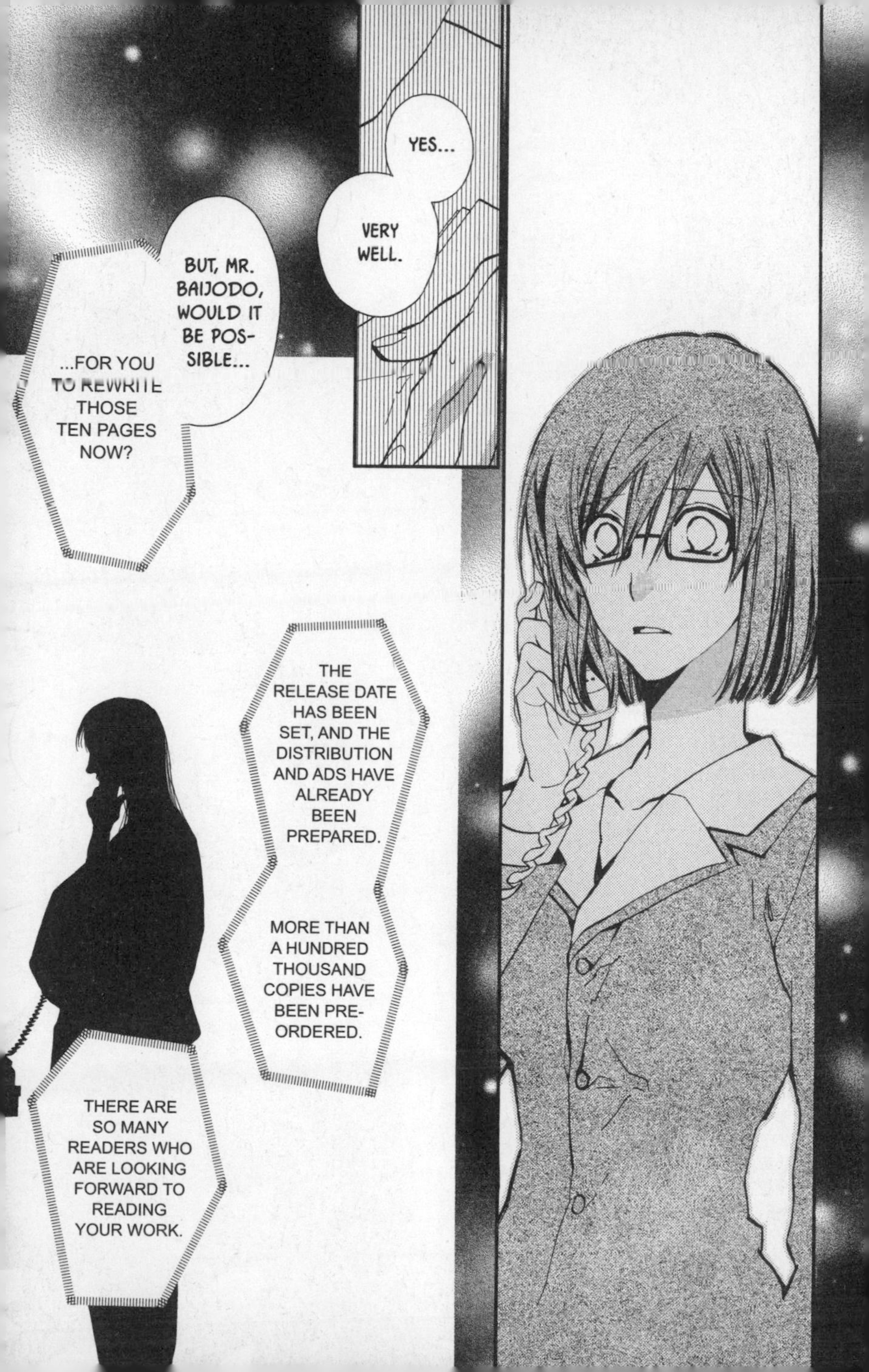
YES...
VERY WELL.
BUT, MR. BAIJODO, WOULD IT BE POS- SIBLE...
...FOR YOU TO REWRITE THOSE TEN PAGES NOW?
THE RELEASE DATE HAS BEEN SET, AND THE DISTRIBUTION AND ADS HAVE ALREADY BEEN PREPARED.
MORE THAN A HUNDRED THOUSAND COPIES HAVE BEEN PRE- ORDERED.
THERE ARE SO MANY READERS WHO ARE LOOKING FORWARD TO READING YOUR WORK.

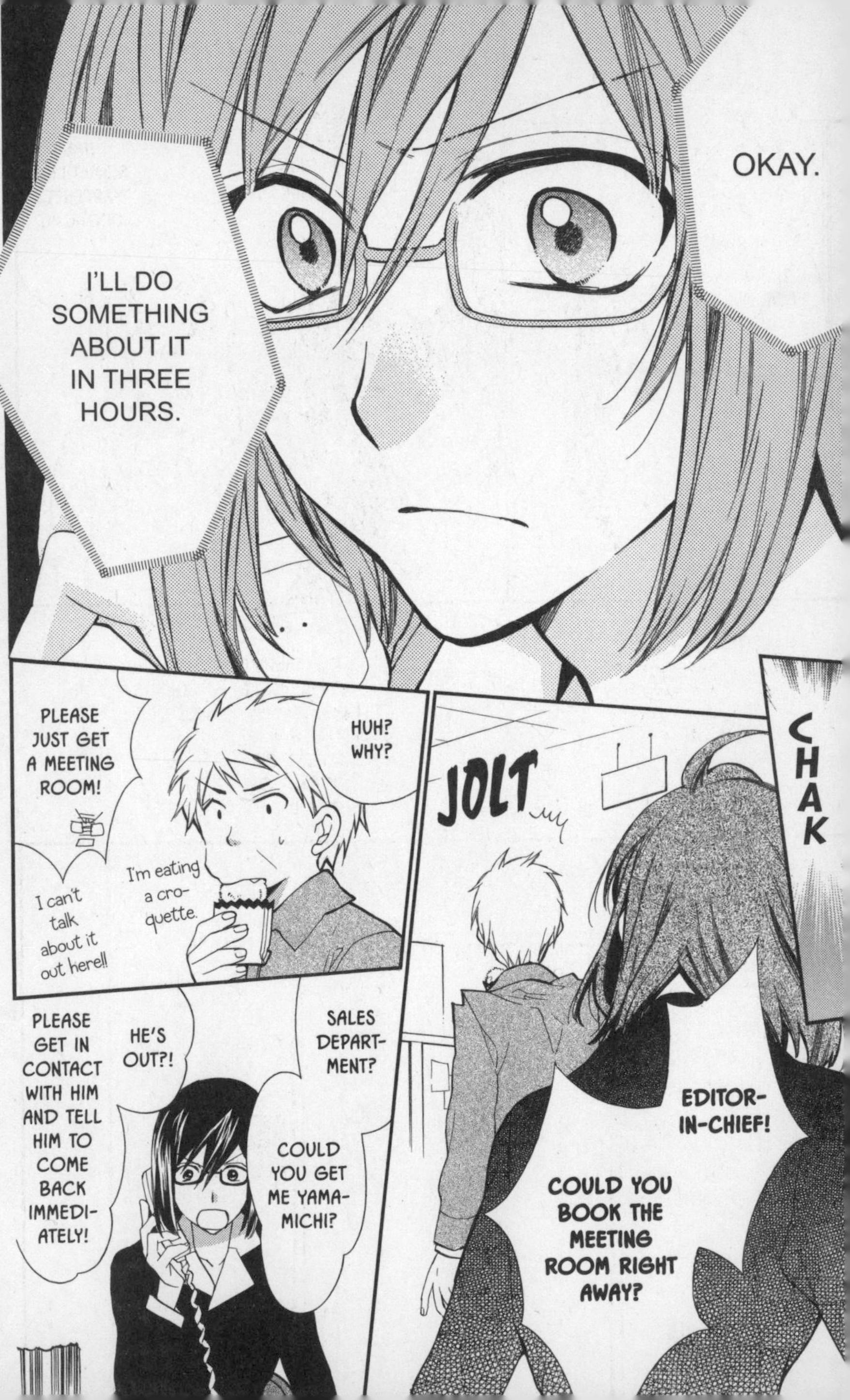
OKAY.
I'LL DO SOMETHING ABOUT IT IN THREE HOURS.
CHAK
JOLT
EDITOR-IN-CHIEF!
COULD YOU BOOK THE MEETING ROOM RIGHT AWAY?
HUH? WHY?
PLEASE JUST GET A MEETING ROOM!
I'm eating a croquette.
I can't talk about it out here!!
SALES DEPARTMENT?
COULD YOU GET ME YAMAMICHI?
HE'S OUT?!
PLEASE GET IN CONTACT WITH HIM AND TELL HIM TO COME BACK IMMEDIATELY!

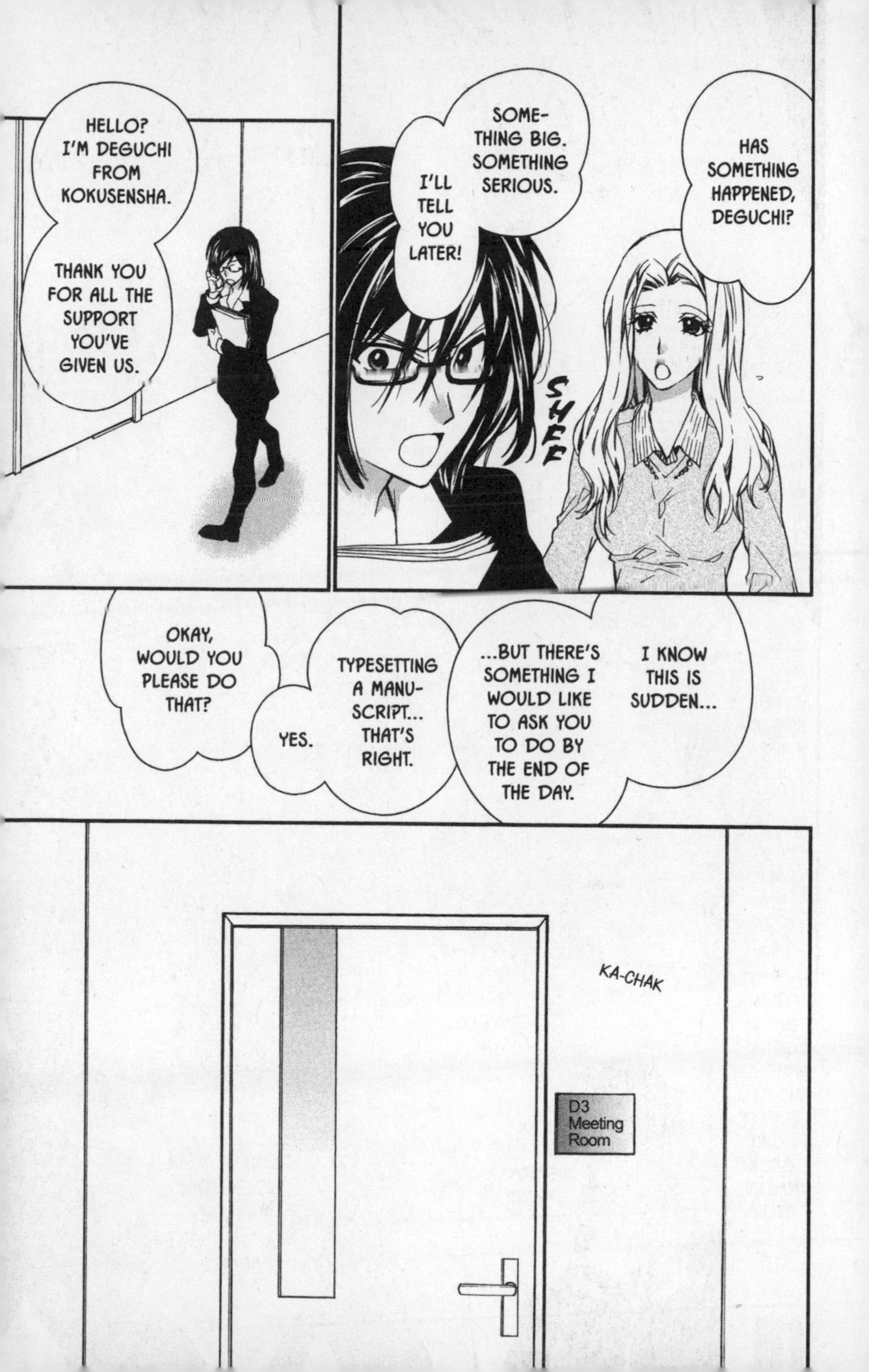
HAS SOMETHING HAPPENED, DEGUCHI?
SOME-THING BIG. SOMETHING SERIOUS.
I'LL TELL YOU LATER!
SHFF
HELLO? I'M DEGUCHI FROM KOKUSENSHA.
THANK YOU FOR ALL THE SUPPORT YOU'VE GIVEN US.
I KNOW THIS IS SUDDEN...
...BUT THERE'S SOMETHING I WOULD LIKE TO ASK YOU TO DO BY THE END OF THE DAY.
TYPESETTING A MANU-SCRIPT... THAT'S RIGHT.
YES.
OKAY, WOULD YOU PLEASE DO THAT?
KA-CHAK
D3 Meeting Room

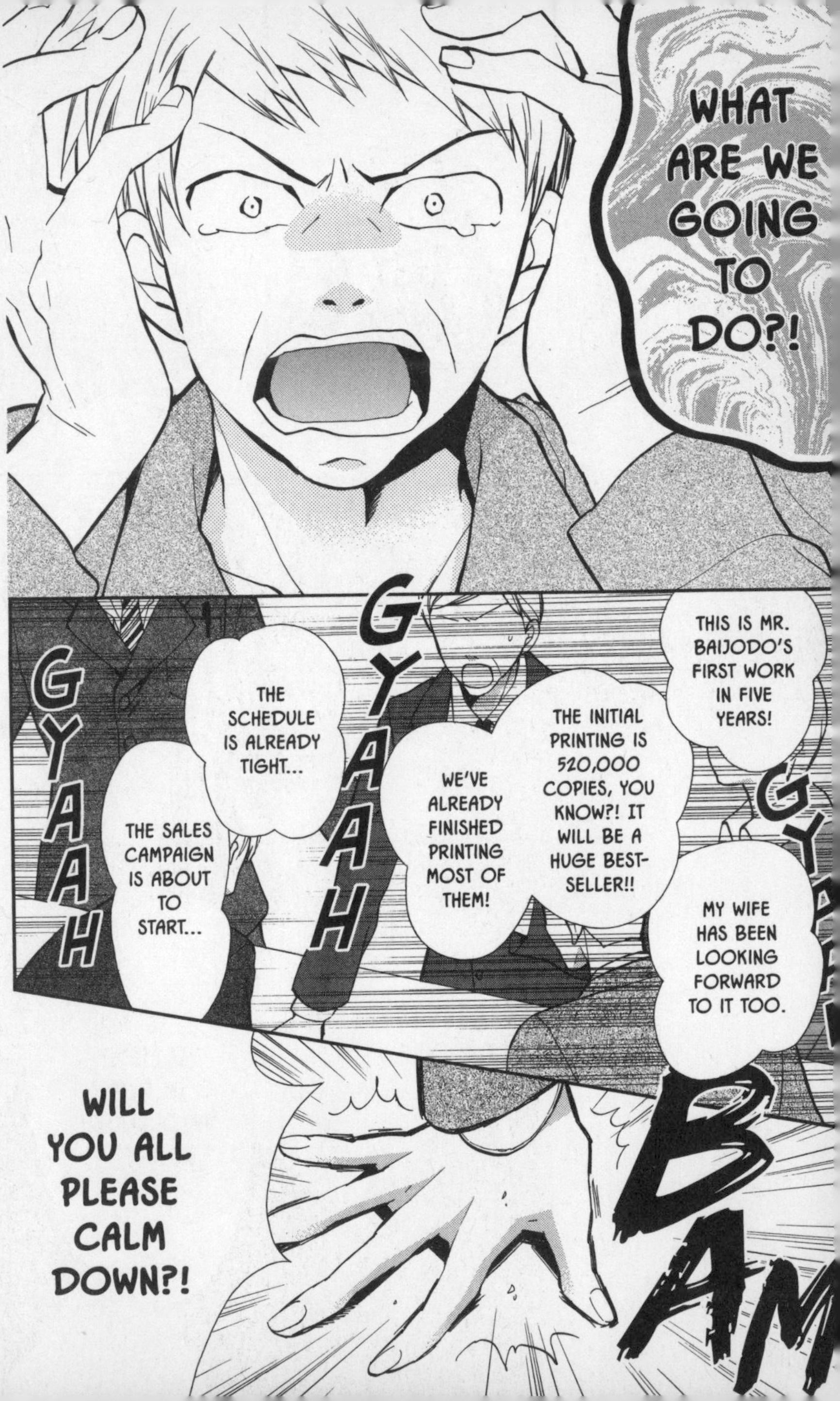
WHAT ARE WE GOING TO DO?!
THIS IS MR. BAIJODO'S FIRST WORK IN FIVE YEARS!
GYA
MY WIFE HAS BEEN LOOKING FORWARD TO IT TOO.
THE INITIAL PRINTING IS 520,000 COPIES, YOU KNOW?! IT WILL BE A HUGE BEST-SELLER!!
WE'VE ALREADY FINISHED PRINTING MOST OF THEM!
GYAAH
THE SCHEDULE IS ALREADY TIGHT...
THE SALES CAMPAIGN IS ABOUT TO START...
GYAAH
BAM
WILL YOU ALL PLEASE CALM DOWN?!

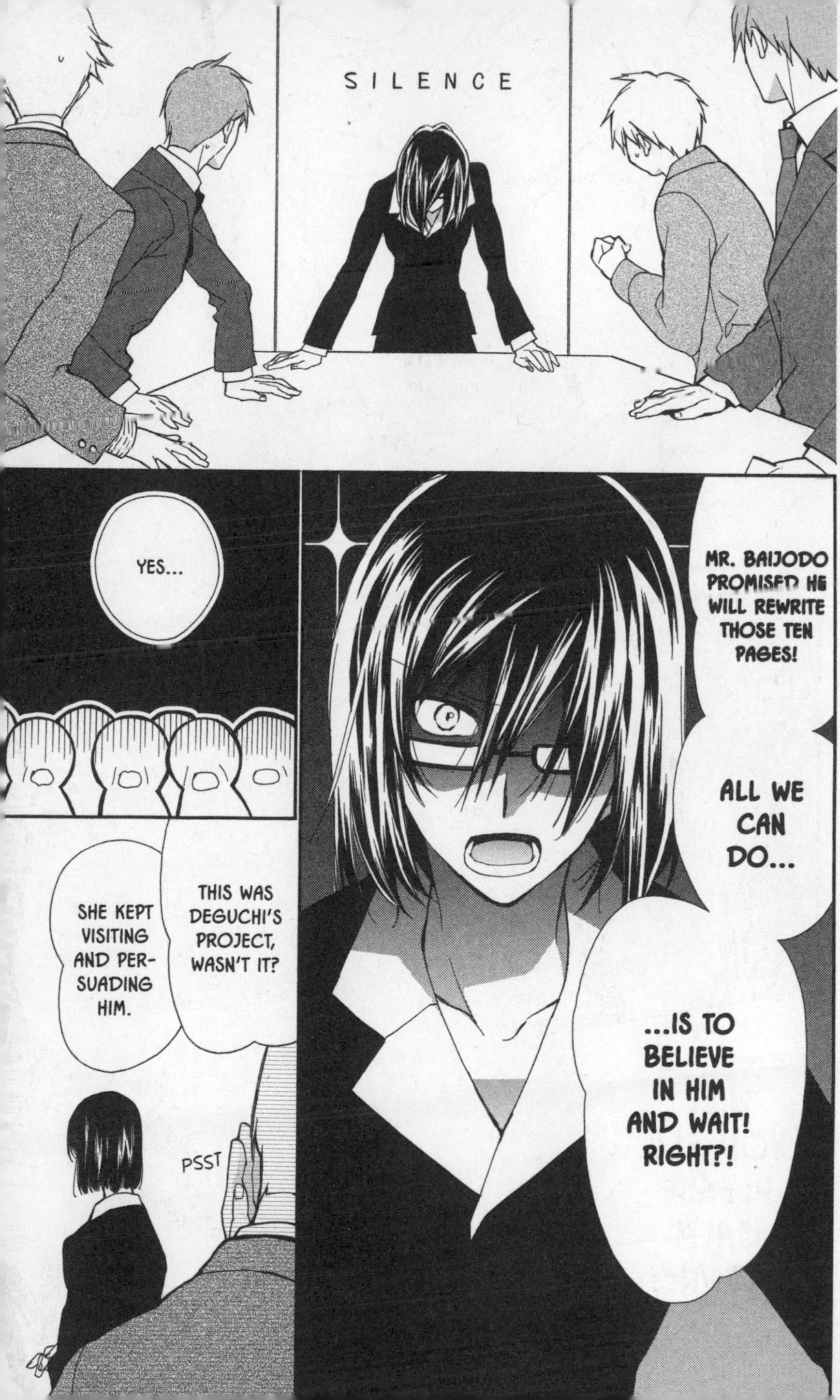
SILENCE
MR. BAIJODO PROMISED HE WILL REWRITE THOSE TEN PAGES!
ALL WE CAN DO...
...IS TO BELIEVE IN HIM AND WAIT! RIGHT?!
YES...
THIS WAS DEGUCHI'S PROJECT, WASN'T IT?
SHE KEPT VISITING AND PERSUADING HIM.
PSST

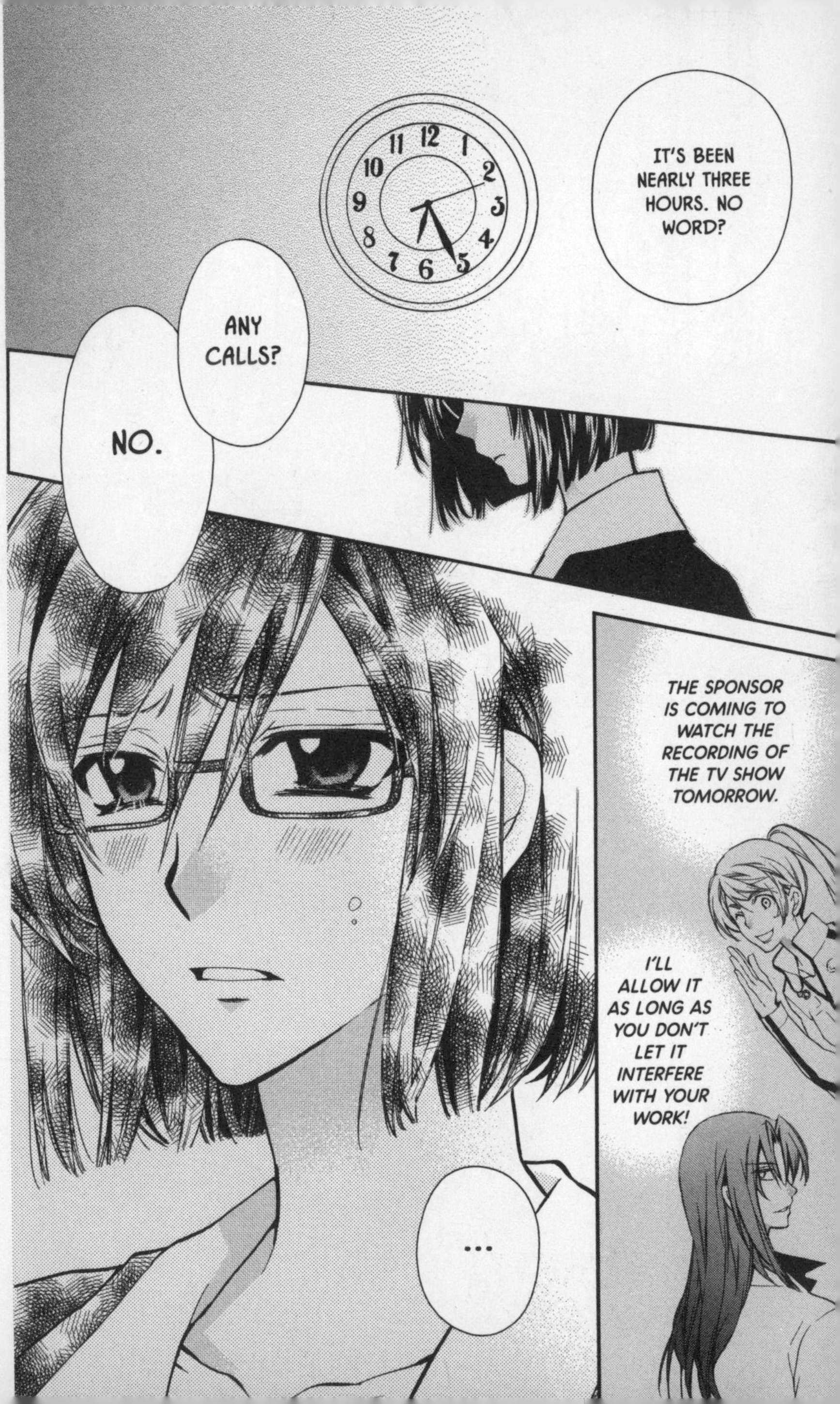
IT'S BEEN NEARLY THREE HOURS. NO WORD?
ANY CALLS?
NO.
THE SPONSOR IS COMING TO WATCH THE RECORDING OF THE TV SHOW TOMORROW.
I'LL ALLOW IT AS LONG AS YOU DON'T LET IT INTERFERE WITH YOUR WORK!
...

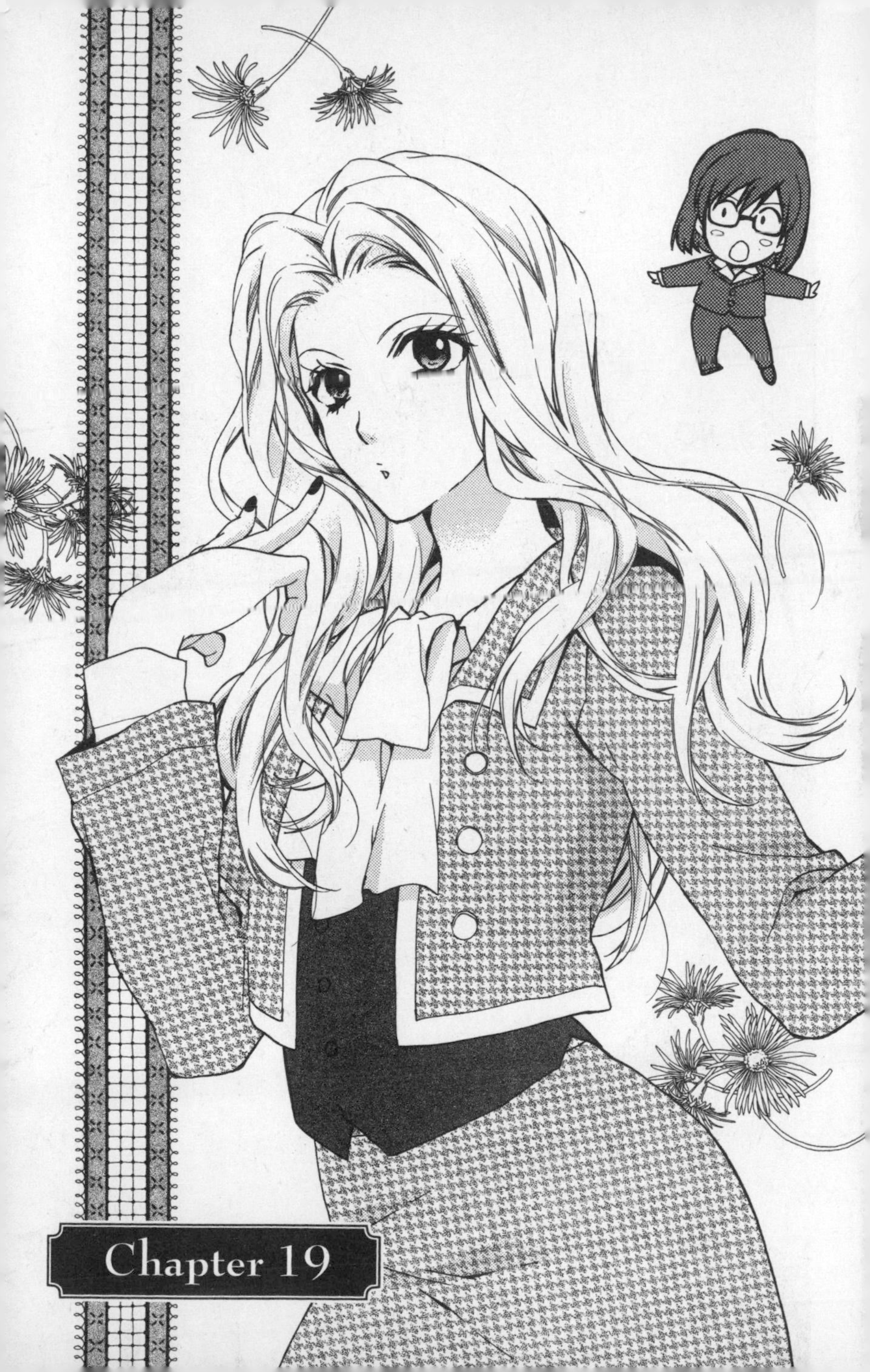
Chapter 19

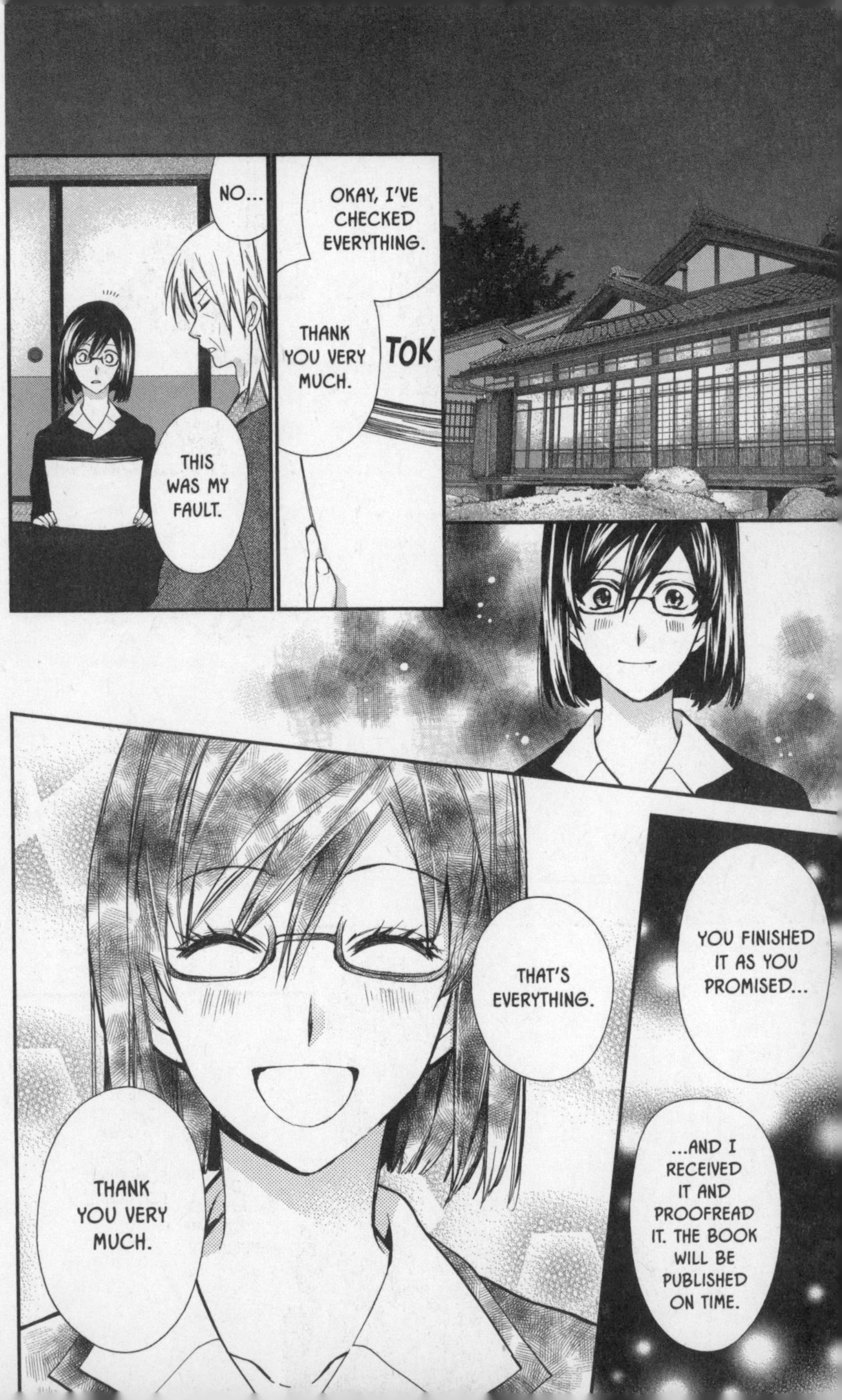
OKAY, I'VE CHECKED EVERYTHING.
THANK YOU VERY MUCH.
TOK
NO...
THIS WAS MY FAULT.
YOU FINISHED IT AS YOU PROMISED...
...AND I RECEIVED IT AND PROOFREAD IT. THE BOOK WILL BE PUBLISHED ON TIME.
THAT'S EVERYTHING.
THANK YOU VERY MUCH.

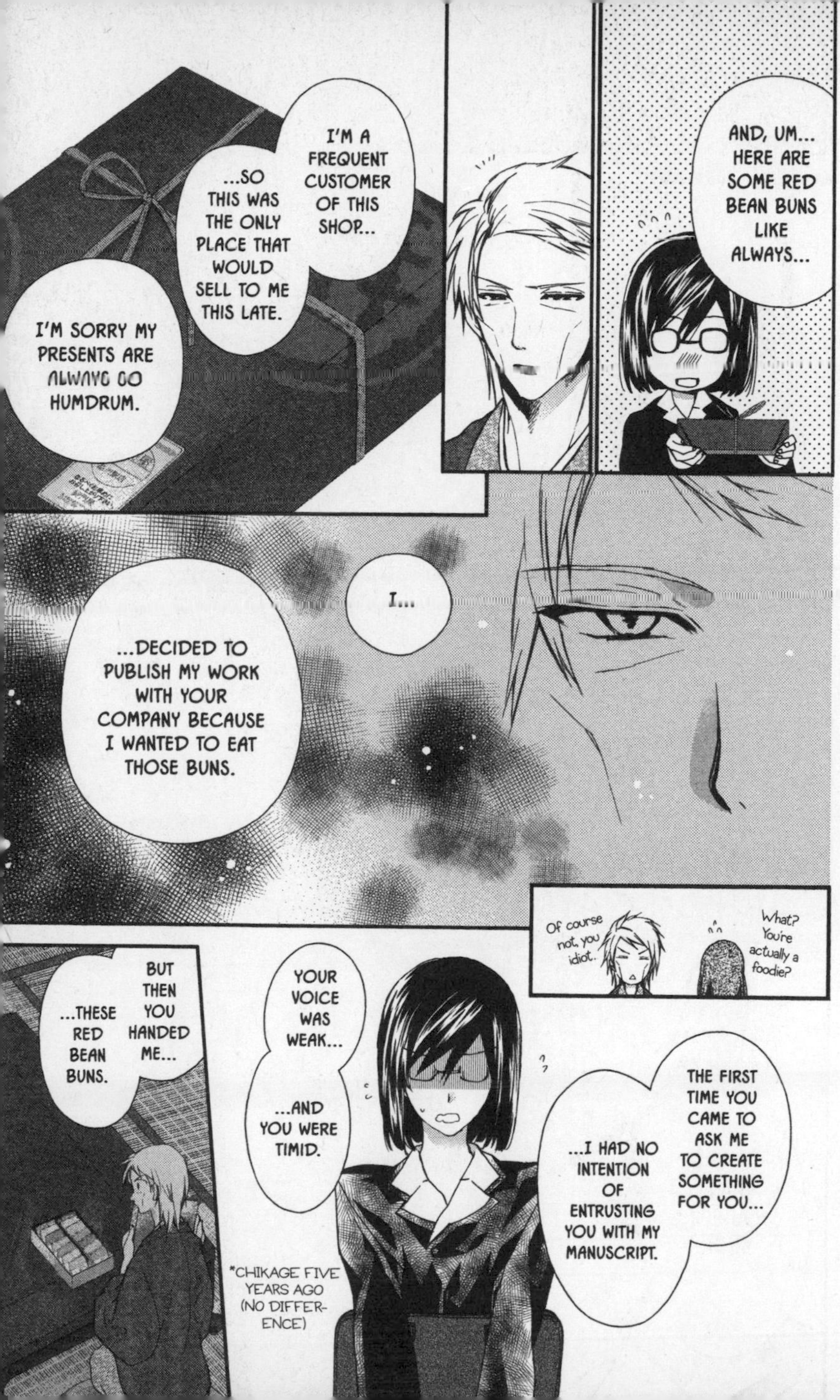
AND, UM... HERE ARE SOME RED BEAN BUNS LIKE ALWAYS...
I'M A FREQUENT CUSTOMER OF THIS SHOP...
...SO THIS WAS THE ONLY PLACE THAT WOULD SELL TO ME THIS LATE.
I'M SORRY MY PRESENTS ARE ALWAYS SO HUMDRUM.
I...
...DECIDED TO PUBLISH MY WORK WITH YOUR COMPANY BECAUSE I WANTED TO EAT THOSE BUNS.
What? You're actually a foodie?
Of course not, you idiot.
THE FIRST TIME YOU CAME TO ASK ME TO CREATE SOMETHING FOR YOU...
...I HAD NO INTENTION OF ENTRUSTING YOU WITH MY MANUSCRIPT.
YOUR VOICE WAS WEAK...
...AND YOU WERE TIMID.
*CHIKAGE FIVE YEARS AGO (NO DIFFERENCE)
BUT THEN YOU HANDED ME...
...THESE RED BEAN BUNS.

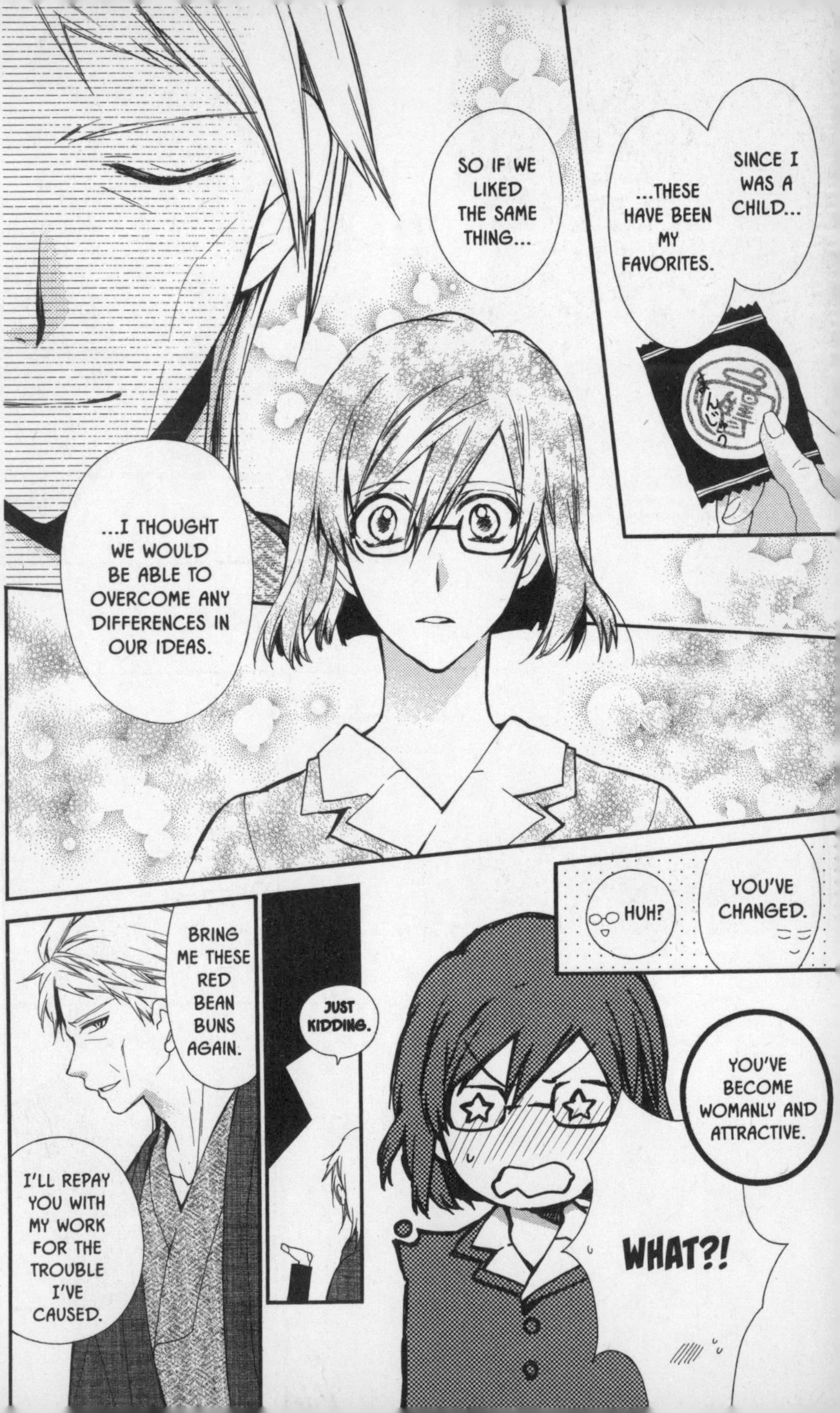
SINCE I WAS A CHILD...
...THESE HAVE BEEN MY FAVORITES.
SO IF WE LIKED THE SAME THING...
...I THOUGHT WE WOULD BE ABLE TO OVERCOME ANY DIFFERENCES IN OUR IDEAS.
YOU'VE CHANGED.
HUH?
YOU'VE BECOME WOMANLY AND ATTRACTIVE.
WHAT?!
JUST KIDDING.
BRING ME THESE RED BEAN BUNS AGAIN.
I'LL REPAY YOU WITH MY WORK FOR THE TROUBLE I'VE CAUSED.

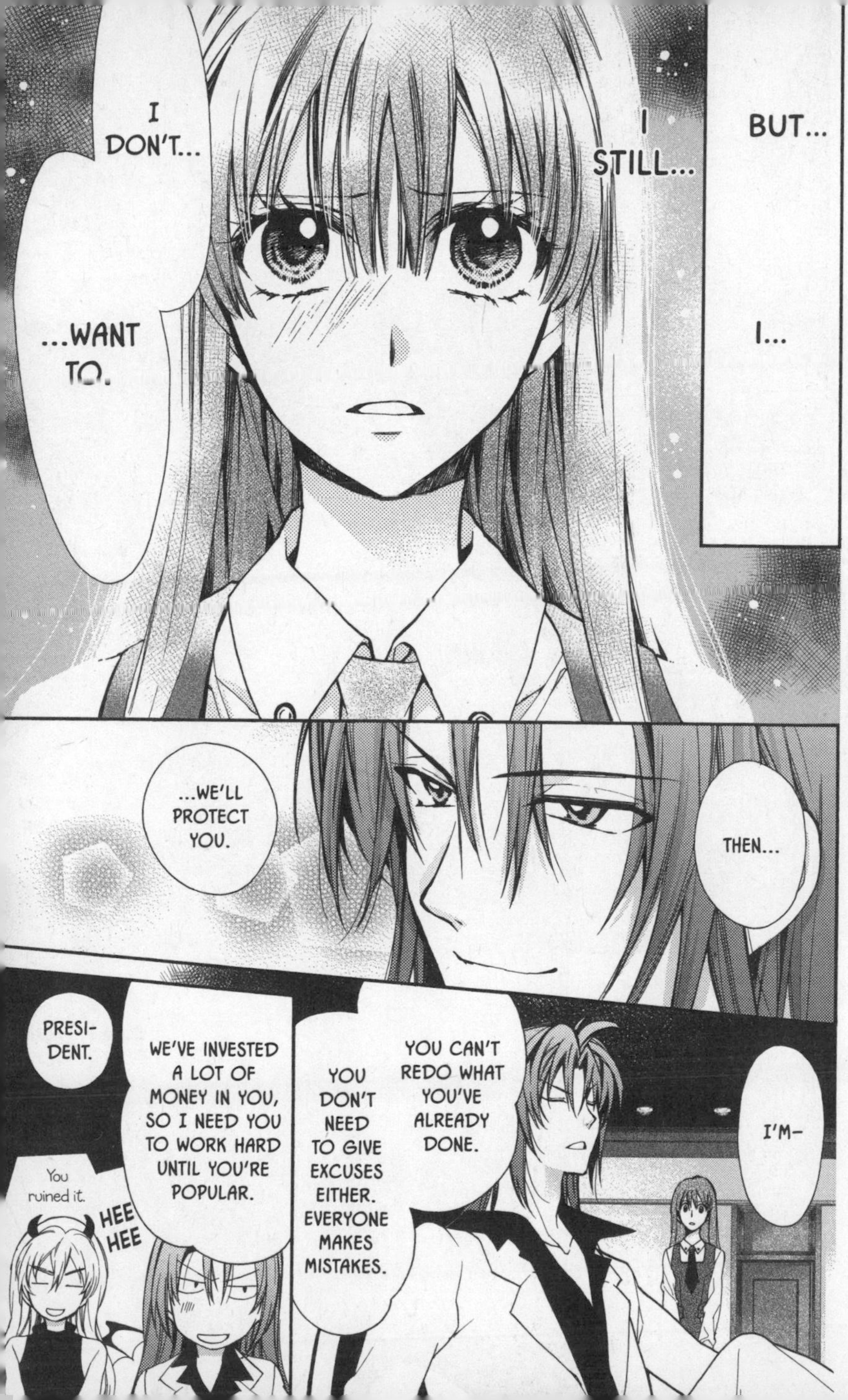
BUT... I...
I STILL...
I DON'T... ...WANT TO.
THEN...
...WE'LL PROTECT YOU.
I'M–
YOU CAN'T REDO WHAT YOU'VE ALREADY DONE.
YOU DON'T NEED TO GIVE EXCUSES EITHER. EVERYONE MAKES MISTAKES.
WE'VE INVESTED A LOT OF MONEY IN YOU, SO I NEED YOU TO WORK HARD UNTIL YOU'RE POPULAR.
PRESI-DENT.
HEE HEE
You ruined it.

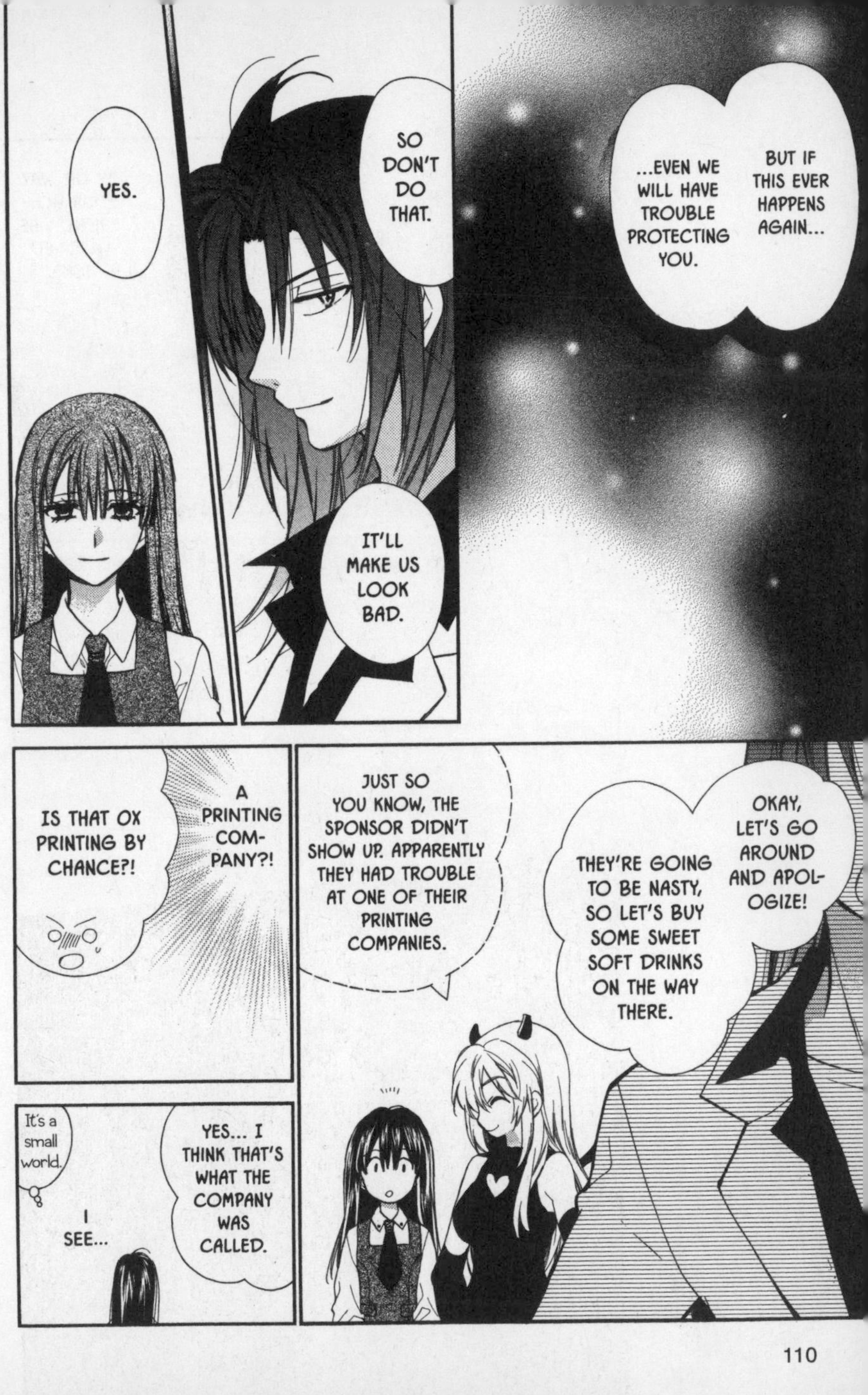
BUT IF THIS EVER HAPPENS AGAIN...
...EVEN WE WILL HAVE TROUBLE PROTECTING YOU.
SO DON'T DO THAT.
IT'LL MAKE US LOOK BAD.
YES.
OKAY, LET'S GO AROUND AND APOLOGIZE!
THEY'RE GOING TO BE NASTY, SO LET'S BUY SOME SWEET SOFT DRINKS ON THE WAY THERE.
JUST SO YOU KNOW, THE SPONSOR DIDN'T SHOW UP. APPARENTLY THEY HAD TROUBLE AT ONE OF THEIR PRINTING COMPANIES.
A PRINTING COMPANY?!
IS THAT OX PRINTING BY CHANCE?!
YES... I THINK THAT'S WHAT THE COMPANY WAS CALLED.
I SEE...
It's a small world.

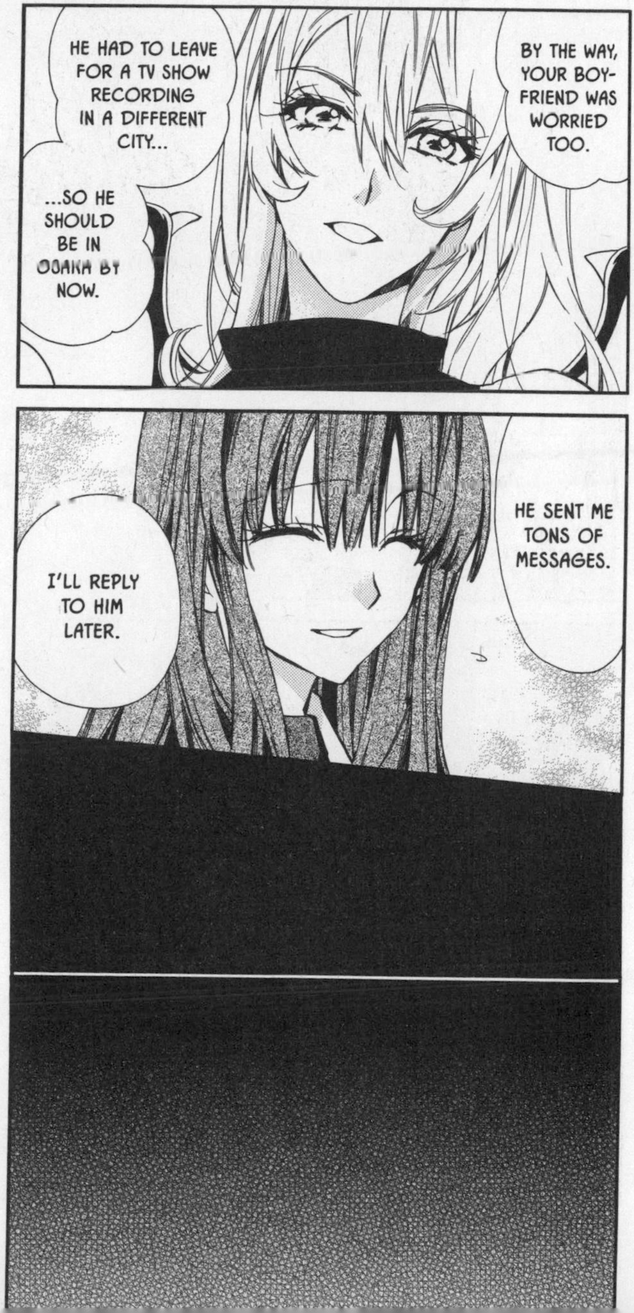
BY THE WAY, YOUR BOY-FRIEND WAS WORRIED TOO.
HE HAD TO LEAVE FOR A TV SHOW RECORDING IN A DIFFERENT CITY...
...SO HE SHOULD BE IN OSAKA BY NOW.
HE SENT ME TONS OF MESSAGES.
I'LL REPLY TO HIM LATER.

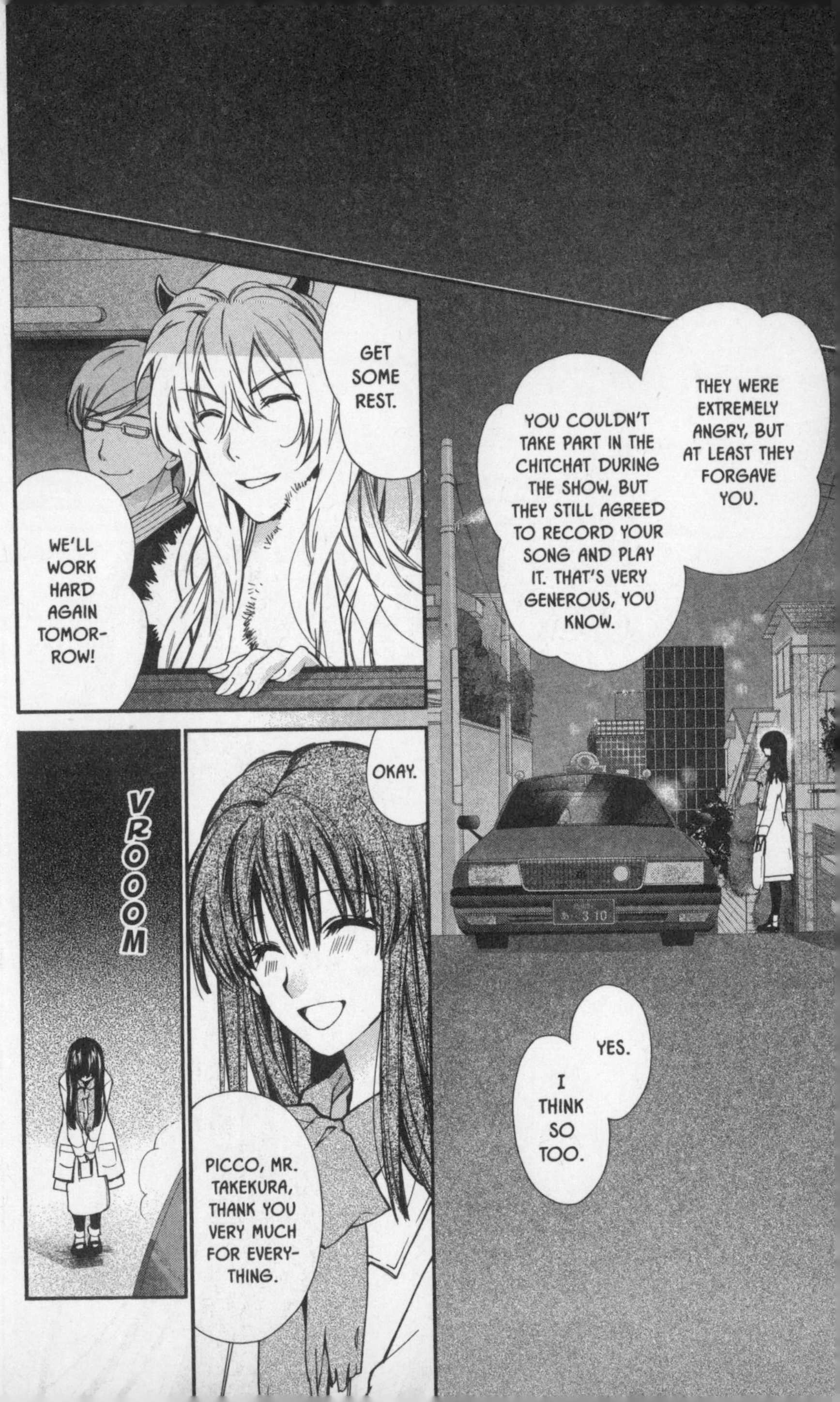
THEY WERE EXTREMELY ANGRY, BUT AT LEAST THEY FORGAVE YOU.
YOU COULDN'T TAKE PART IN THE CHITCHAT DURING THE SHOW, BUT THEY STILL AGREED TO RECORD YOUR SONG AND PLAY IT. THAT'S VERY GENEROUS, YOU KNOW.
YES.
I THINK SO TOO.
GET SOME REST.
WE'LL WORK HARD AGAIN TOMORROW!
OKAY.
PICCO, MR. TAKEKURA, THANK YOU VERY MUCH FOR EVERYTHING.
VROOOOM

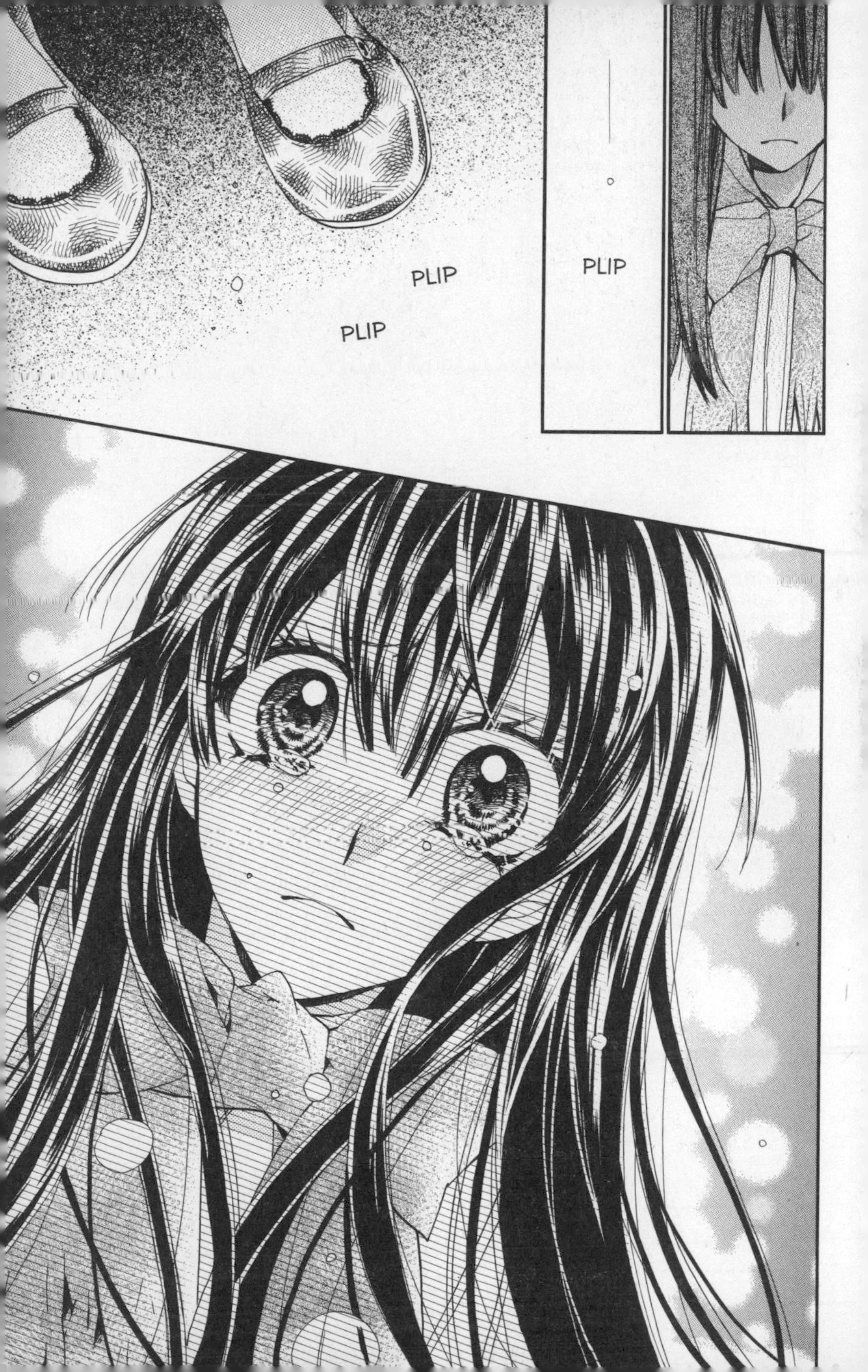
PLIP
PLIP
PLIP

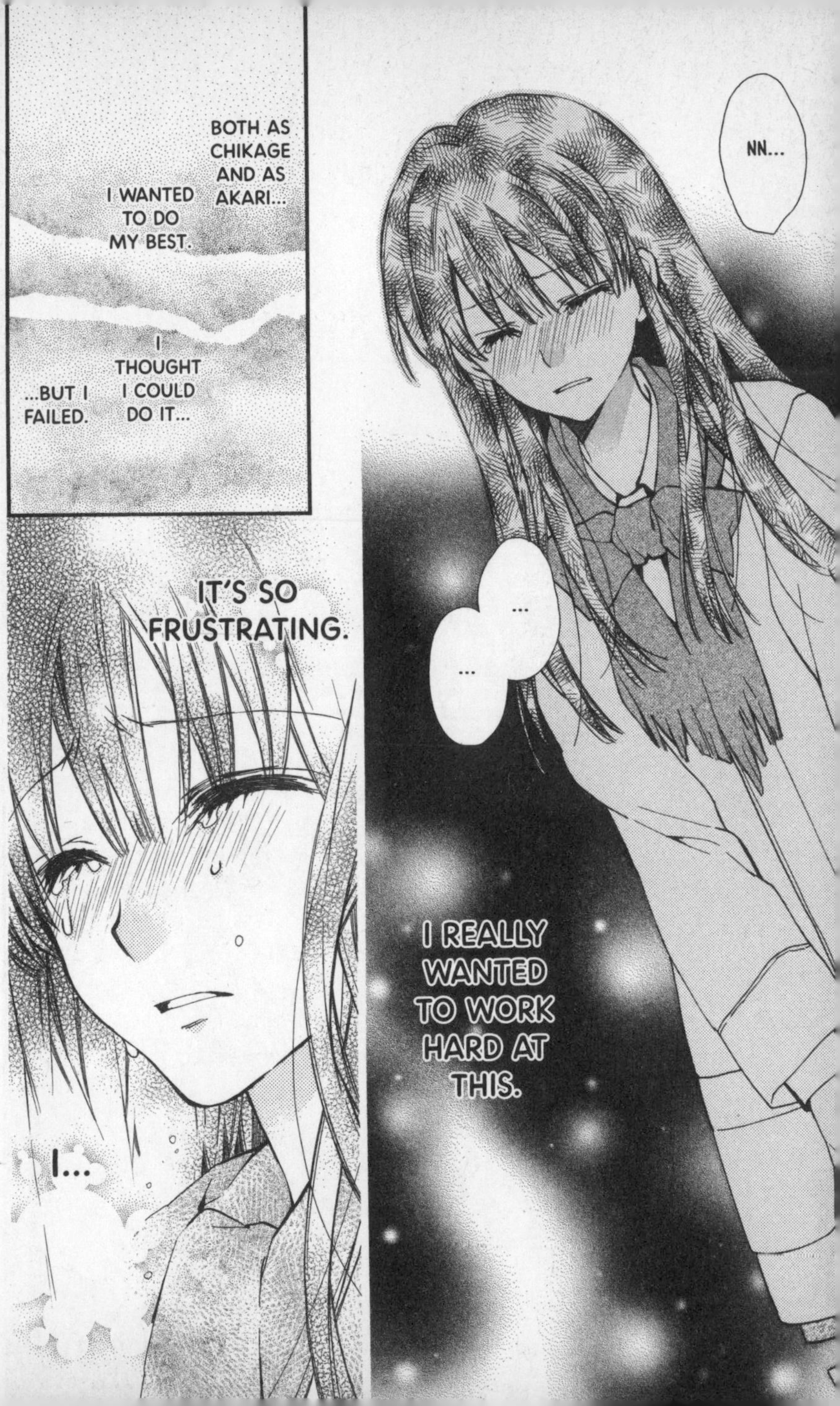
NN...
...
...
I REALLY WANTED TO WORK HARD AT THIS.
BOTH AS CHIKAGE AND AS AKARI...
I WANTED TO DO MY BEST.
I THOUGHT I COULD DO IT...
...BUT I FAILED.
IT'S SO FRUSTRATING.
I...

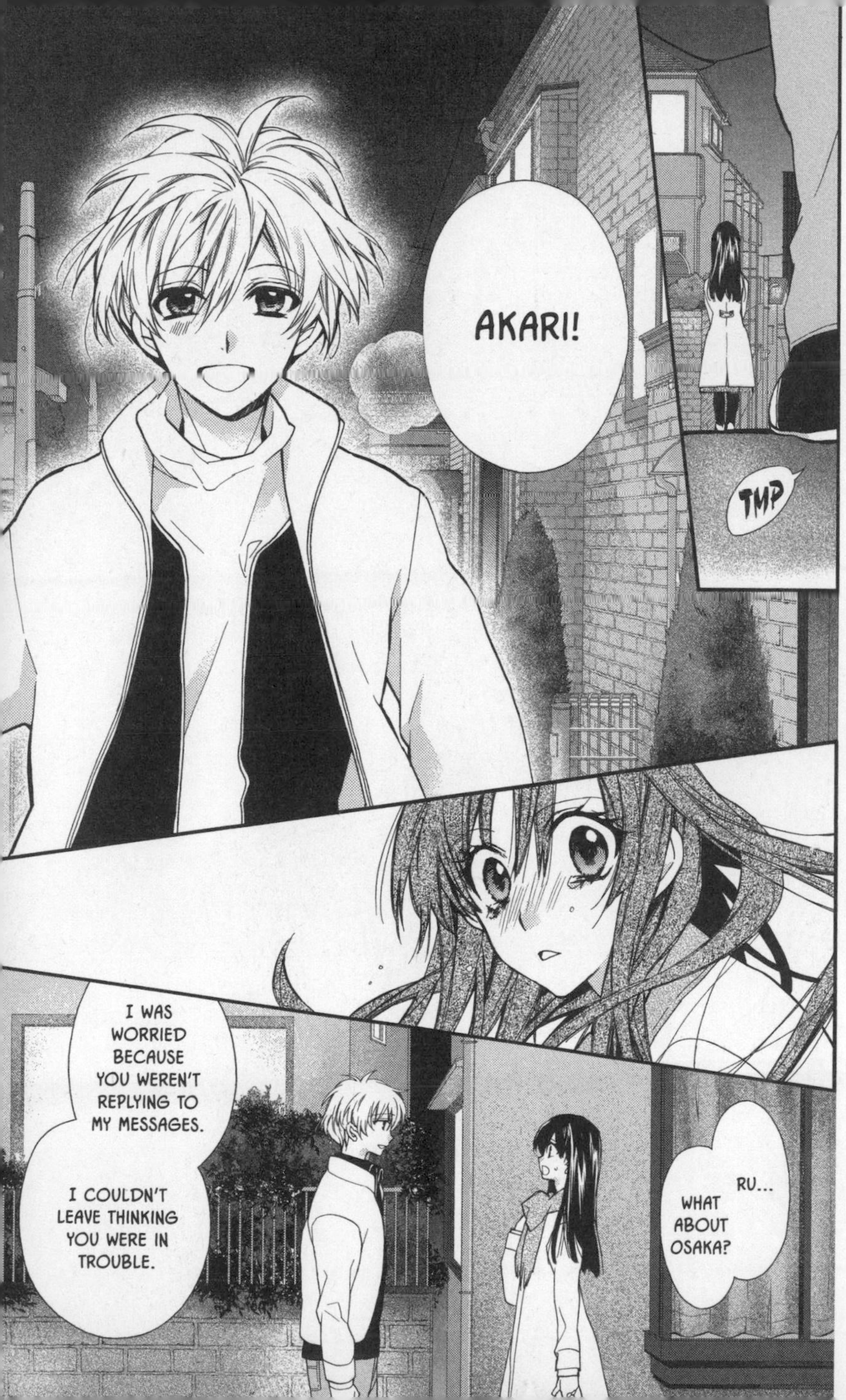
TMP
AKARI!
RU... WHAT ABOUT OSAKA?
I WAS WORRIED BECAUSE YOU WEREN'T REPLYING TO MY MESSAGES.
I COULDN'T LEAVE THINKING YOU WERE IN TROUBLE.

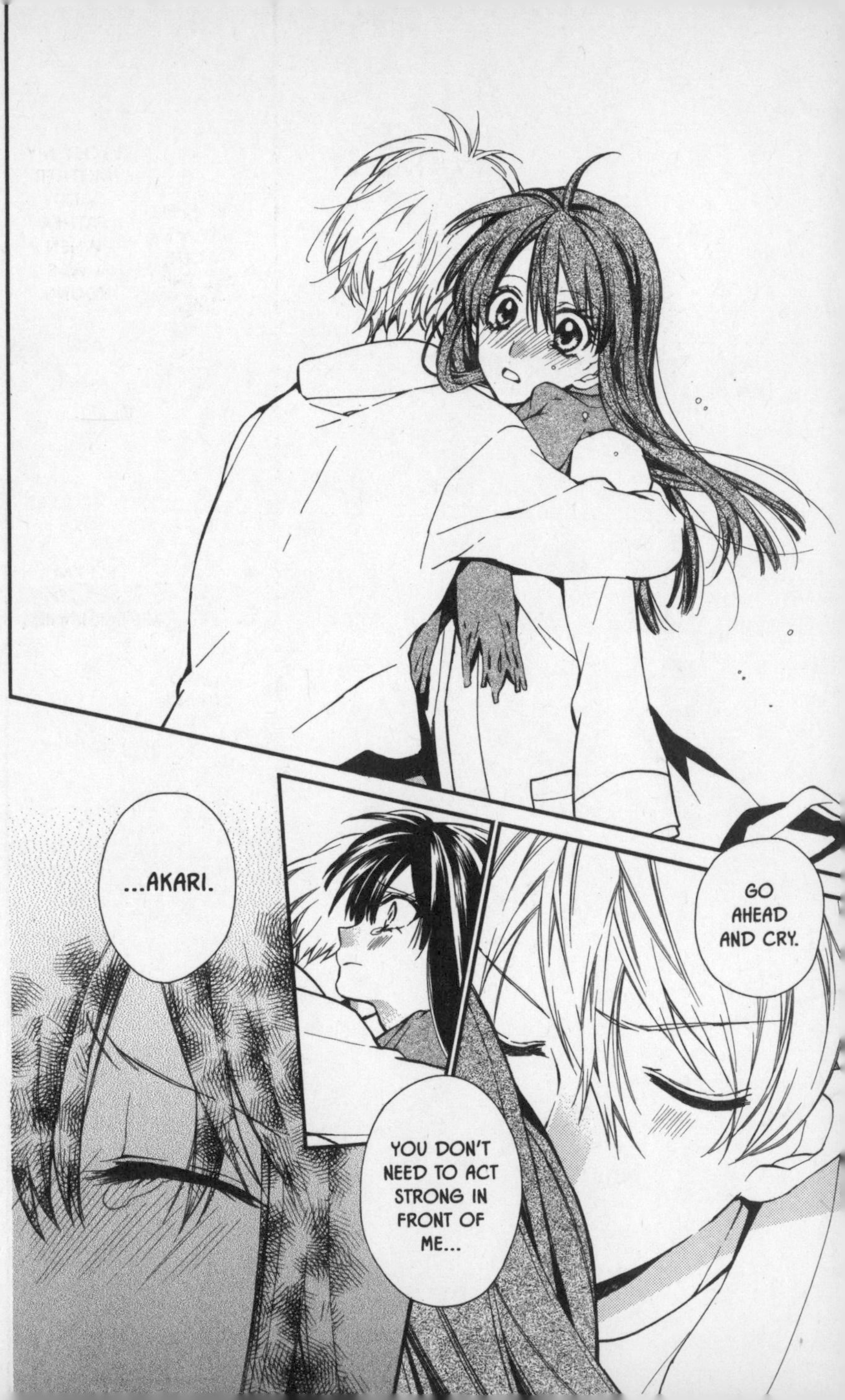
GO AHEAD AND CRY.
YOU DON'T NEED TO ACT STRONG IN FRONT OF ME...
...AKARI.

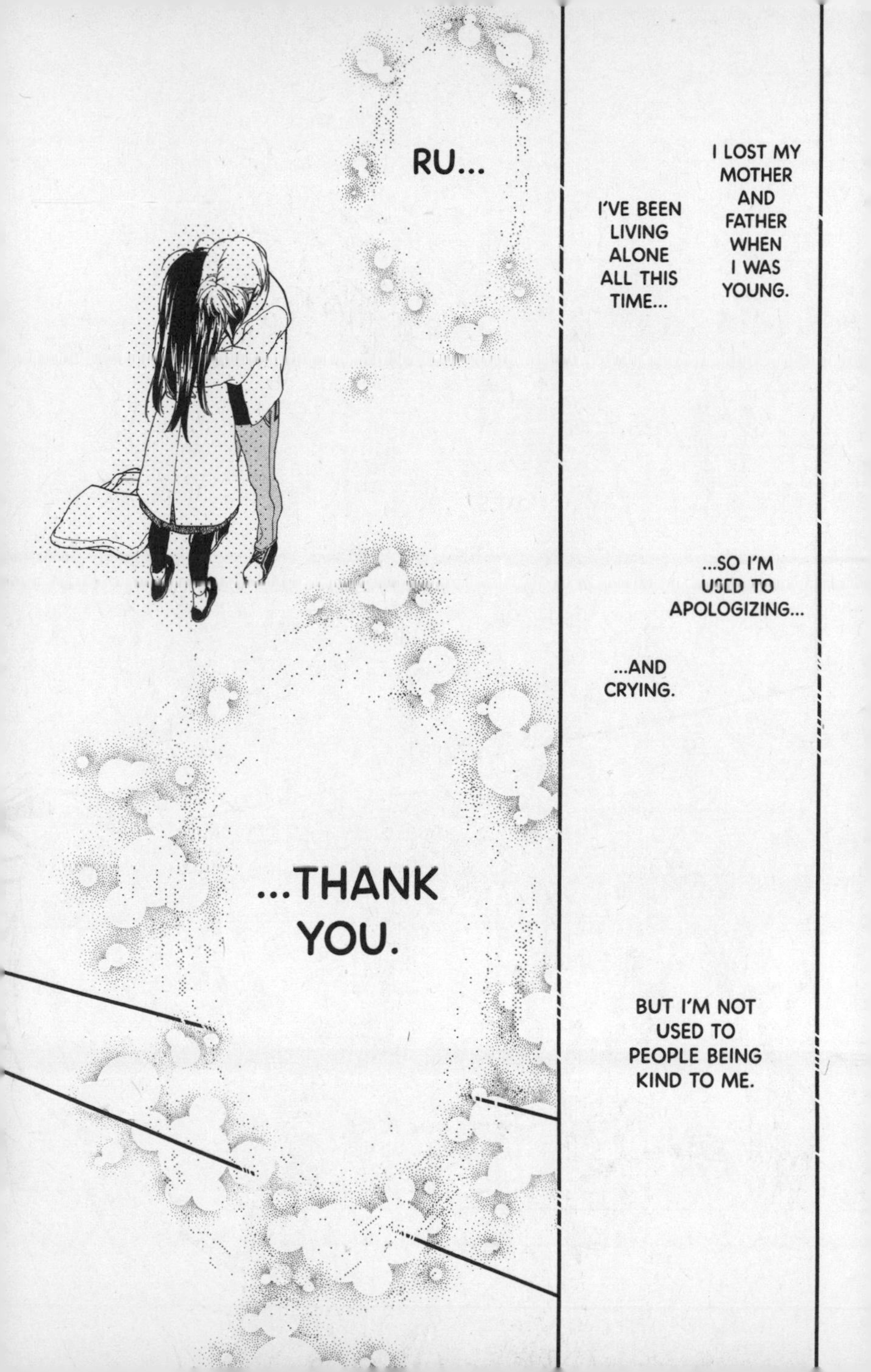
I LOST MY MOTHER AND FATHER WHEN I WAS YOUNG.
I'VE BEEN LIVING ALONE ALL THIS TIME...
...SO I'M USED TO APOLOGIZING...
...AND CRYING.
BUT I'M NOT USED TO PEOPLE BEING KIND TO ME.
RU...
...THANK YOU.

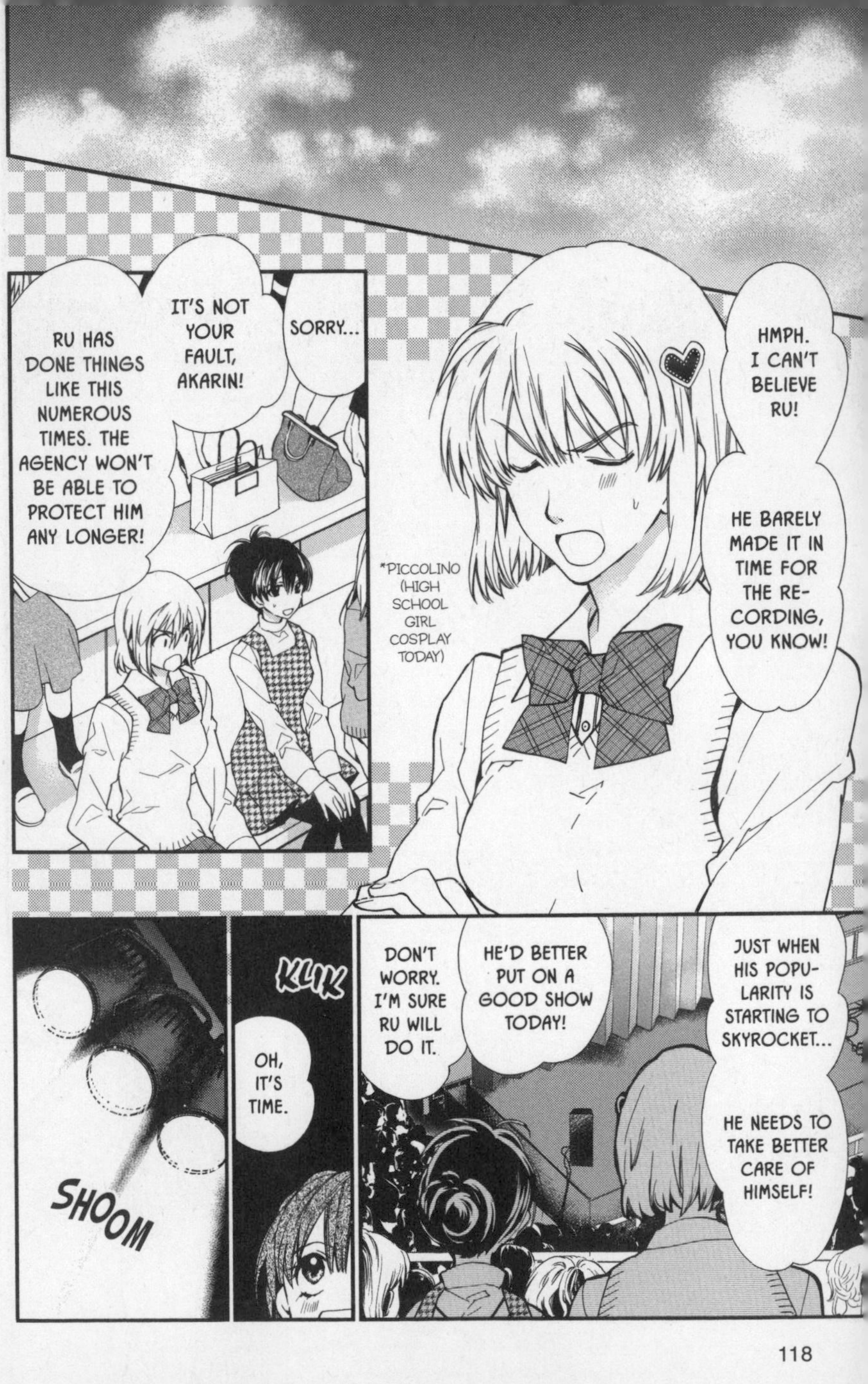
HMPH. I CAN'T BELIEVE RU!
HE BARELY MADE IT IN TIME FOR THE RE-CORDING, YOU KNOW!
*PICCOLINO (HIGH SCHOOL GIRL COSPLAY TODAY)
SORRY...
IT'S NOT YOUR FAULT, AKARIN!
RU HAS DONE THINGS LIKE THIS NUMEROUS TIMES. THE AGENCY WON'T BE ABLE TO PROTECT HIM ANY LONGER!
JUST WHEN HIS POPU-LARITY IS STARTING TO SKYROCKET...
HE NEEDS TO TAKE BETTER CARE OF HIMSELF!
HE'D BETTER PUT ON A GOOD SHOW TODAY!
DON'T WORRY. I'M SURE RU WILL DO IT.
KLIK
OH, IT'S TIME.
SHOOM

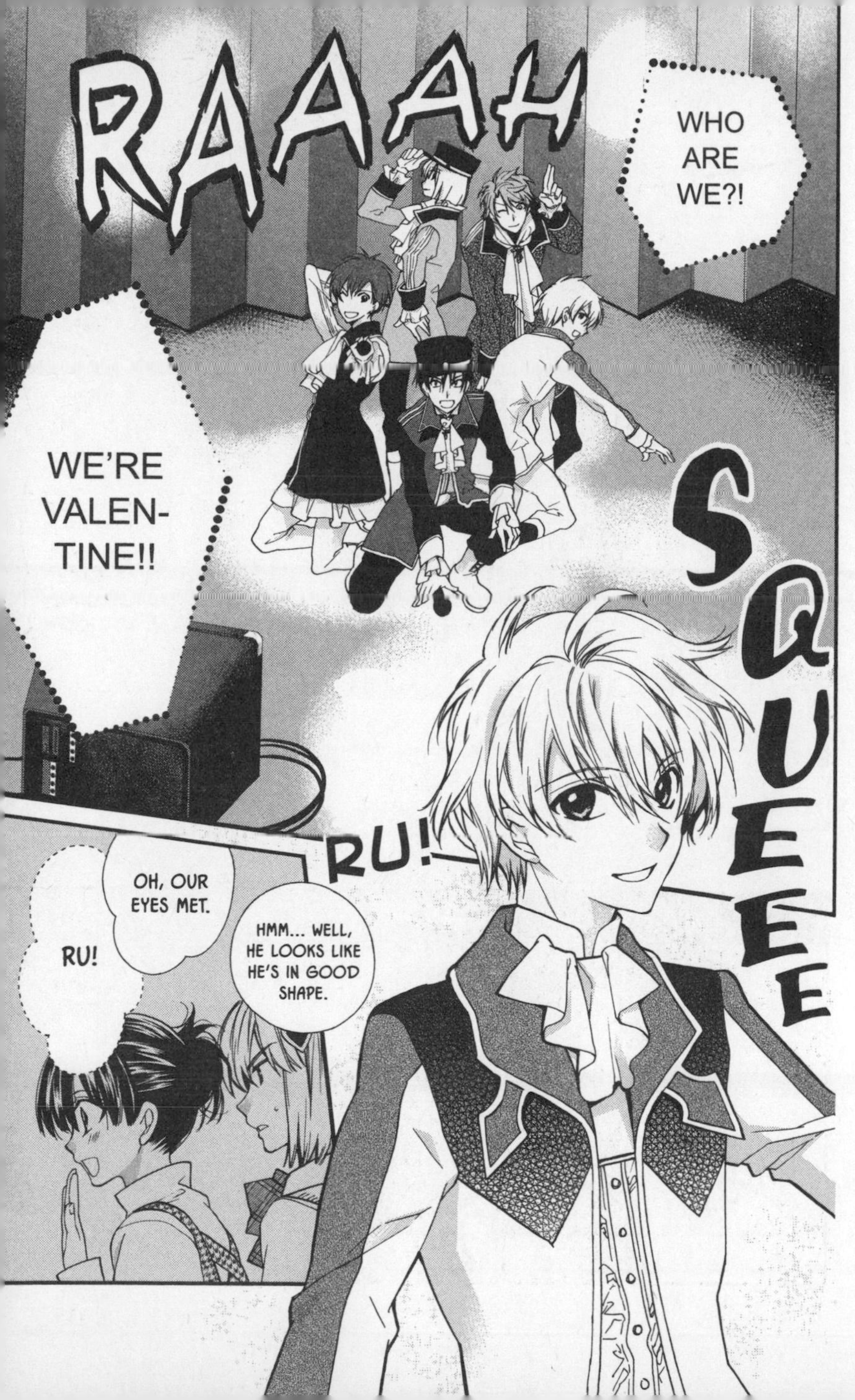
WHO ARE WE?!
RAAAH
WE'RE VALENTINE!!
SQUEEE
RU!
HMM... WELL, HE LOOKS LIKE HE'S IN GOOD SHAPE.
OH, OUR EYES MET.
RU!

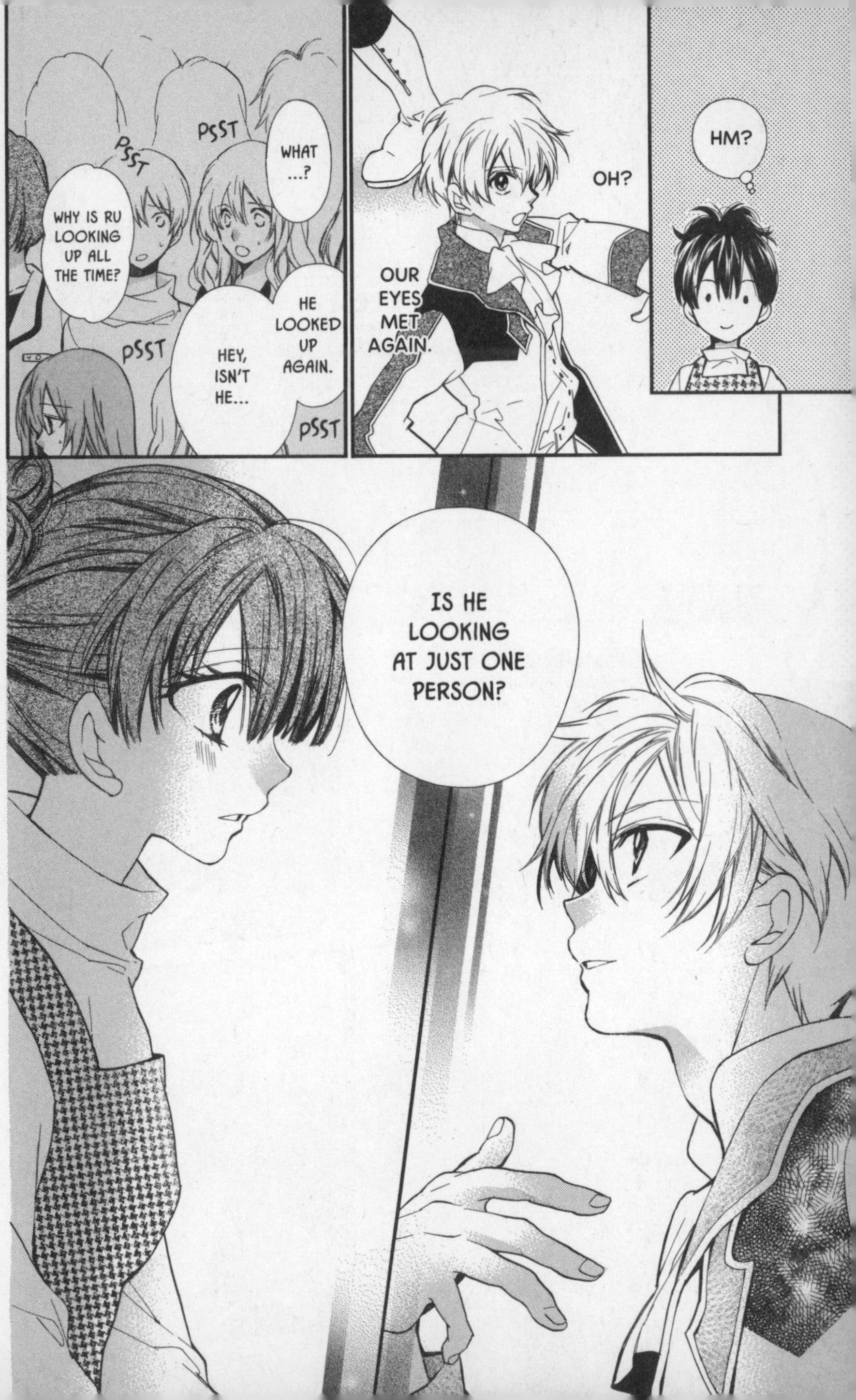
HM?
OH?
OUR EYES MET AGAIN.
WHAT ...?
PSST
PSST
WHY IS RU LOOKING UP ALL THE TIME?
HE LOOKED UP AGAIN.
HEY, ISN'T HE...
PSST
PSST
IS HE LOOKING AT JUST ONE PERSON?

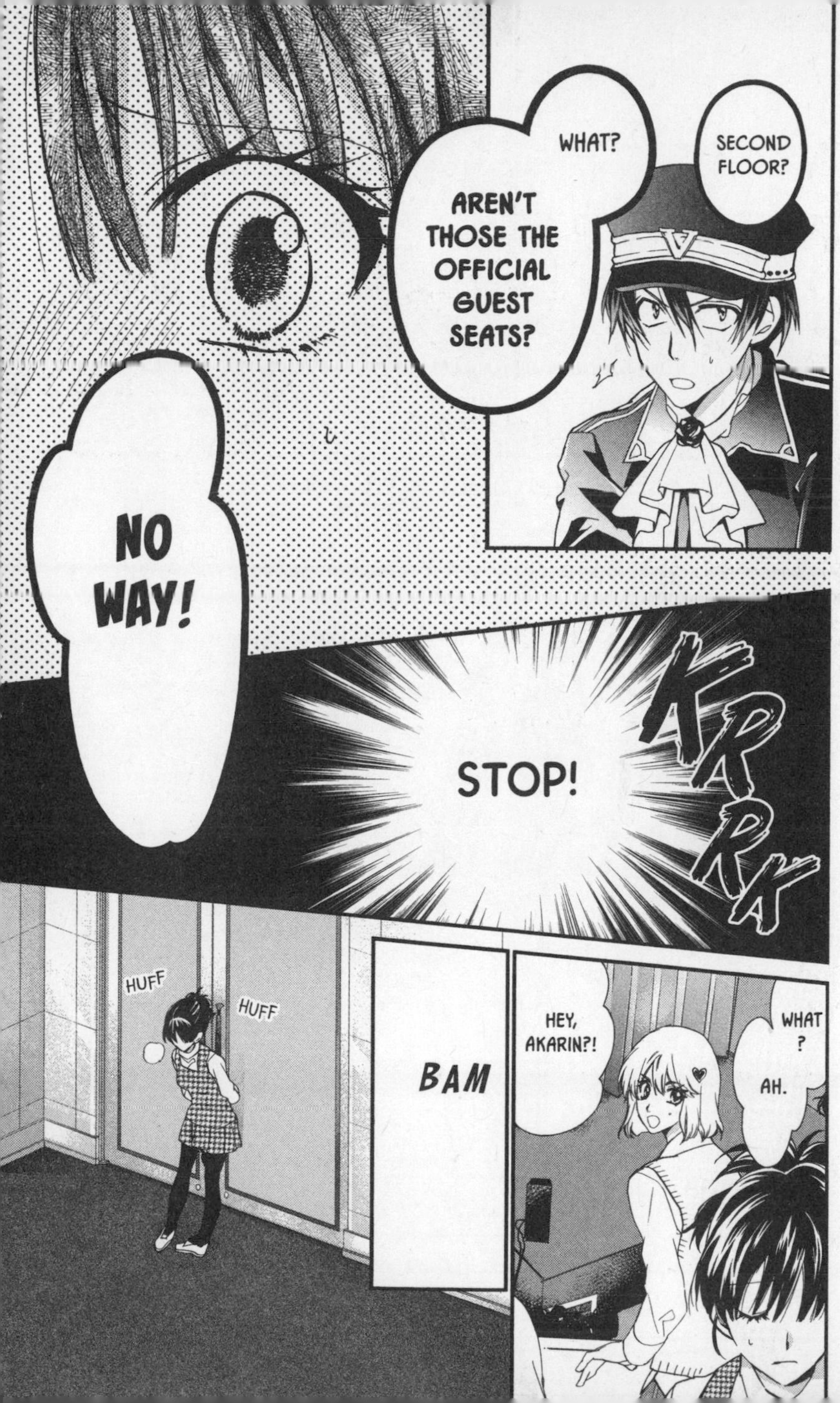
SECOND FLOOR?
WHAT?
AREN'T THOSE THE OFFICIAL GUEST SEATS?
NO WAY!
STOP!
KRRK
WHAT?
HEY, AKARIN?!
AH.
BAM
HUFF
HUFF

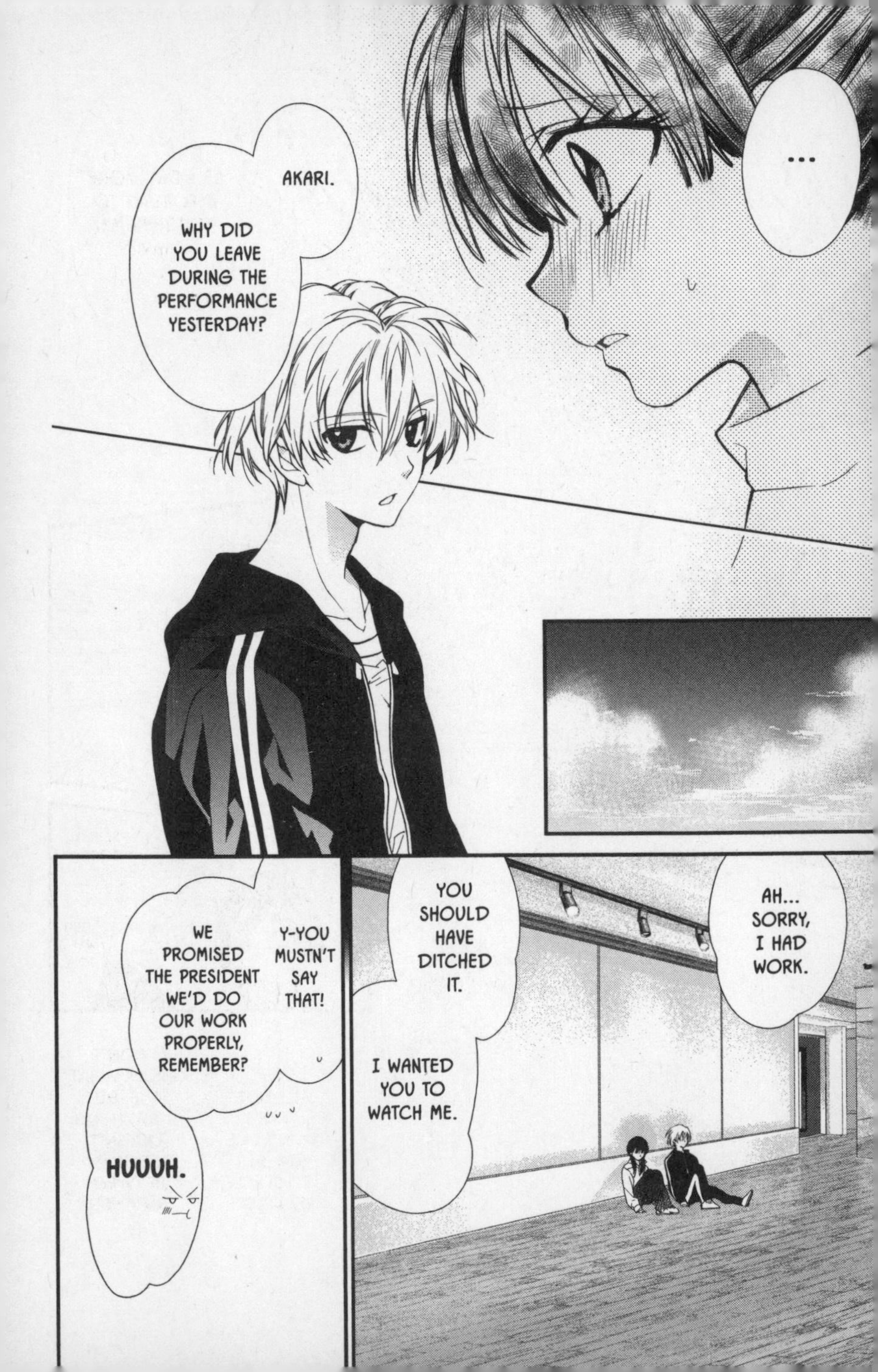
...
AKARI.
WHY DID YOU LEAVE DURING THE PERFORMANCE YESTERDAY?
AH... SORRY, I HAD WORK.
YOU SHOULD HAVE DITCHED IT.
I WANTED YOU TO WATCH ME.
Y-YOU MUSTN'T SAY THAT!
WE PROMISED THE PRESIDENT WE'D DO OUR WORK PROPERLY, REMEMBER?
HUUUH.

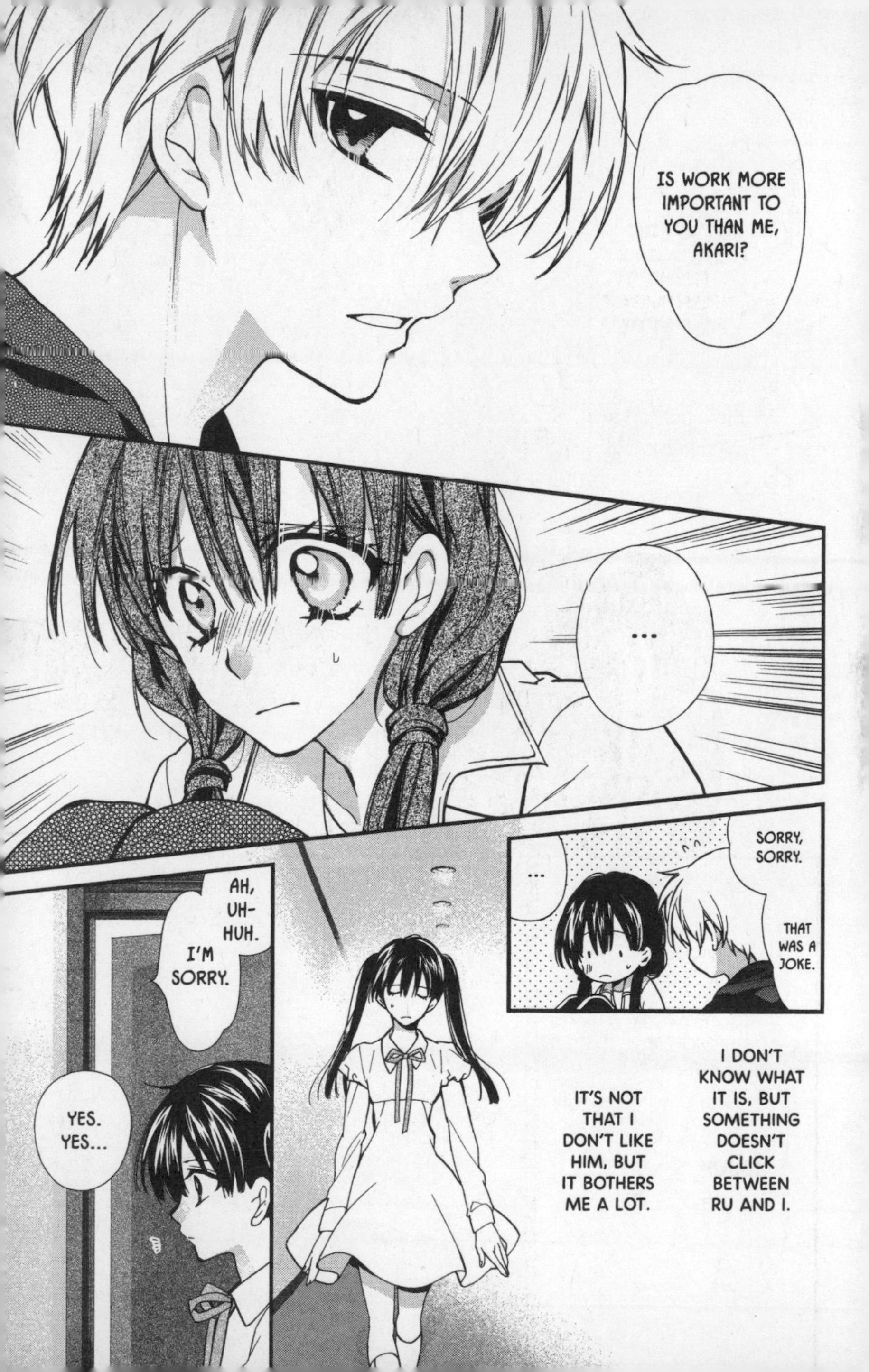
IS WORK MORE IMPORTANT TO YOU THAN ME, AKARI?
...
SORRY, SORRY.
...
THAT WAS A JOKE.
I DON'T KNOW WHAT IT IS, BUT SOMETHING DOESN'T CLICK BETWEEN RU AND I.
IT'S NOT THAT I DON'T LIKE HIM, BUT IT BOTHERS ME A LOT.
AH, UH-HUH. I'M SORRY.
YES. YES...

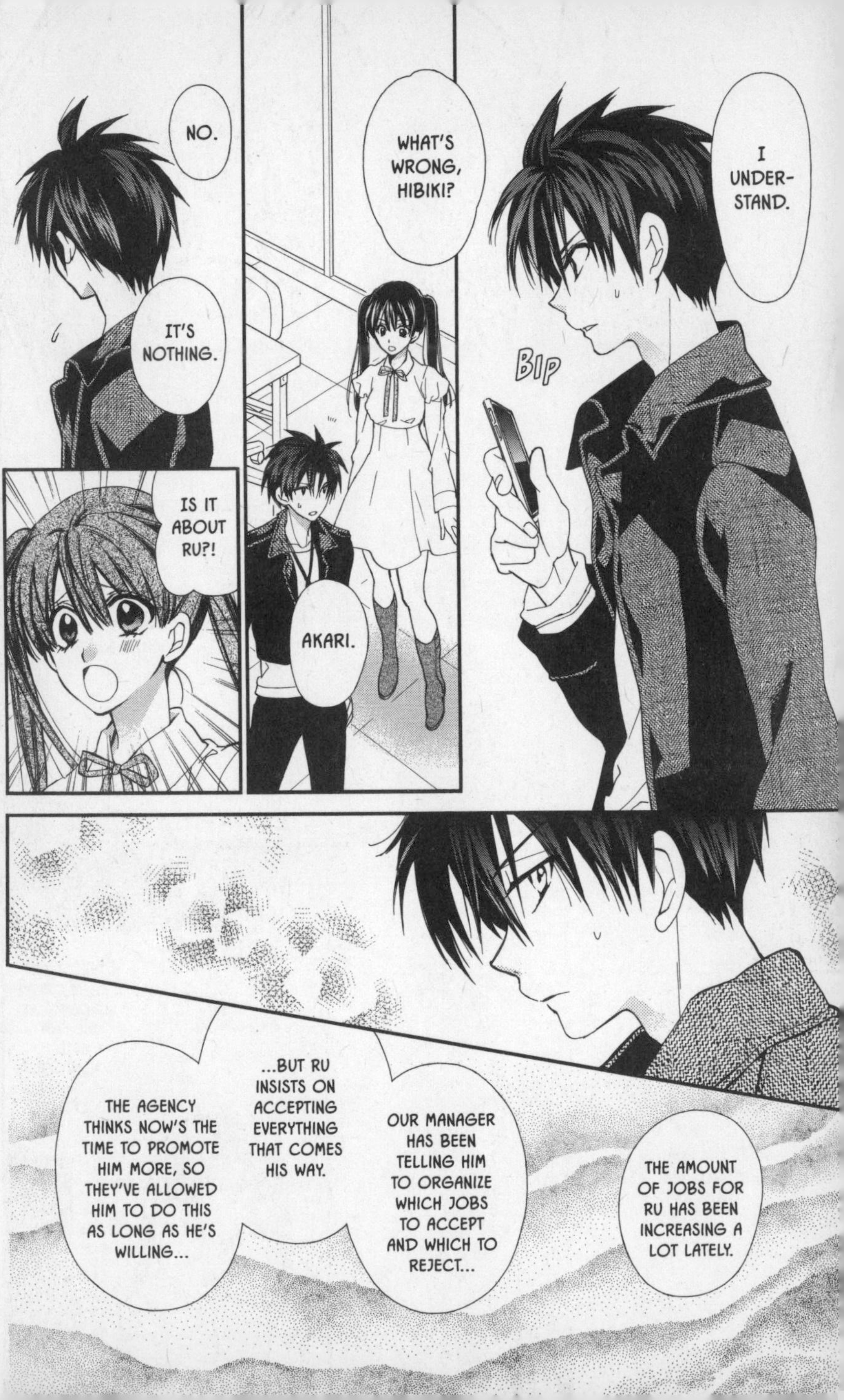
I UNDERSTAND.
BIP
WHAT'S WRONG, HIBIKI?
AKARI.
NO.
IT'S NOTHING.
IS IT ABOUT RU?!
THE AMOUNT OF JOBS FOR RU HAS BEEN INCREASING A LOT LATELY.
OUR MANAGER HAS BEEN TELLING HIM TO ORGANIZE WHICH JOBS TO ACCEPT AND WHICH TO REJECT...
...BUT RU INSISTS ON ACCEPTING EVERYTHING THAT COMES HIS WAY.
THE AGENCY THINKS NOW'S THE TIME TO PROMOTE HIM MORE, SO THEY'VE ALLOWED HIM TO DO THIS AS LONG AS HE'S WILLING...

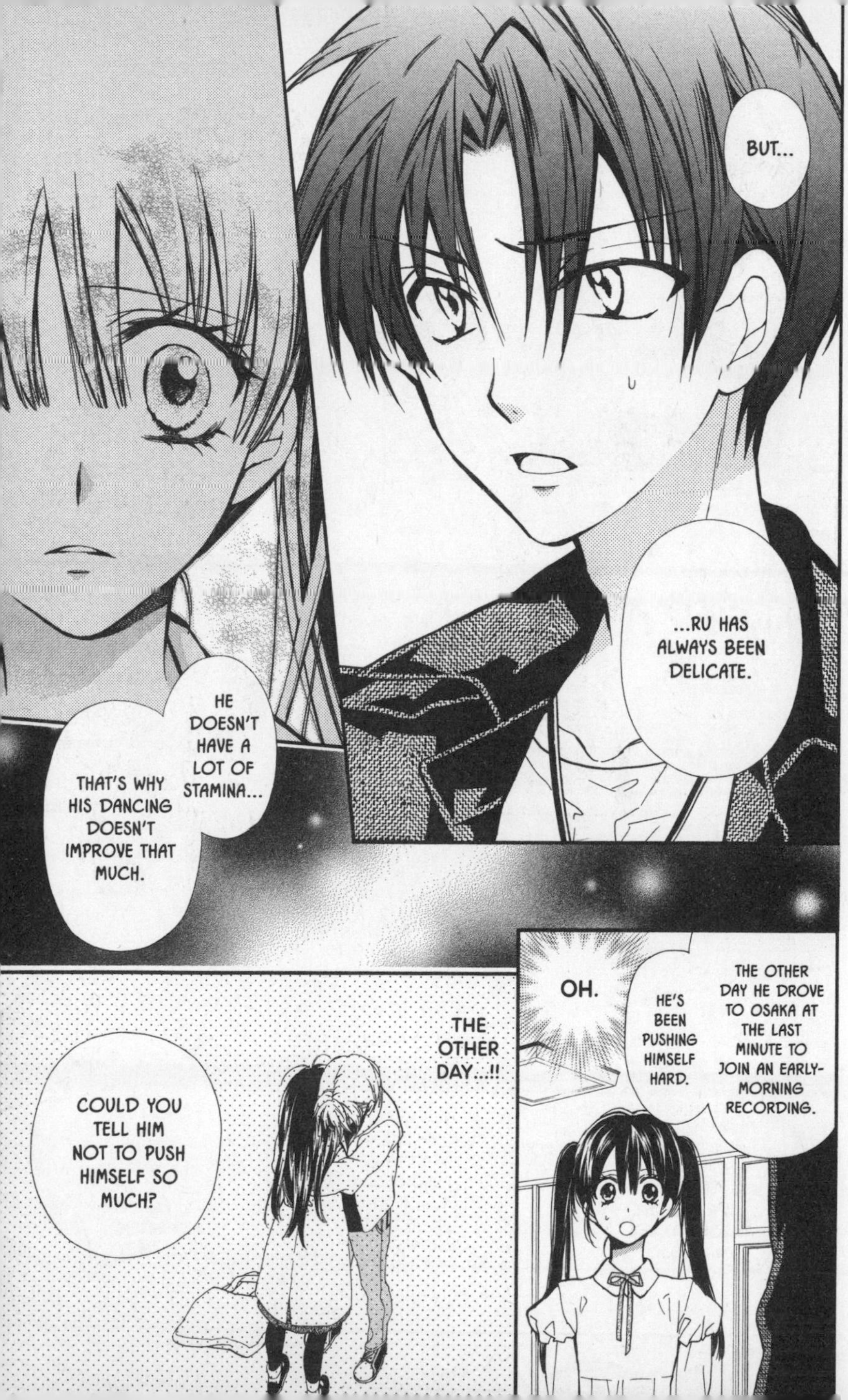
BUT...
...RU HAS ALWAYS BEEN DELICATE.
HE DOESN'T HAVE A LOT OF STAMINA...
THAT'S WHY HIS DANCING DOESN'T IMPROVE THAT MUCH.
THE OTHER DAY HE DROVE TO OSAKA AT THE LAST MINUTE TO JOIN AN EARLY-MORNING RECORDING.
HE'S BEEN PUSHING HIMSELF HARD.
OH.
THE OTHER DAY...!!
COULD YOU TELL HIM NOT TO PUSH HIMSELF SO MUCH?

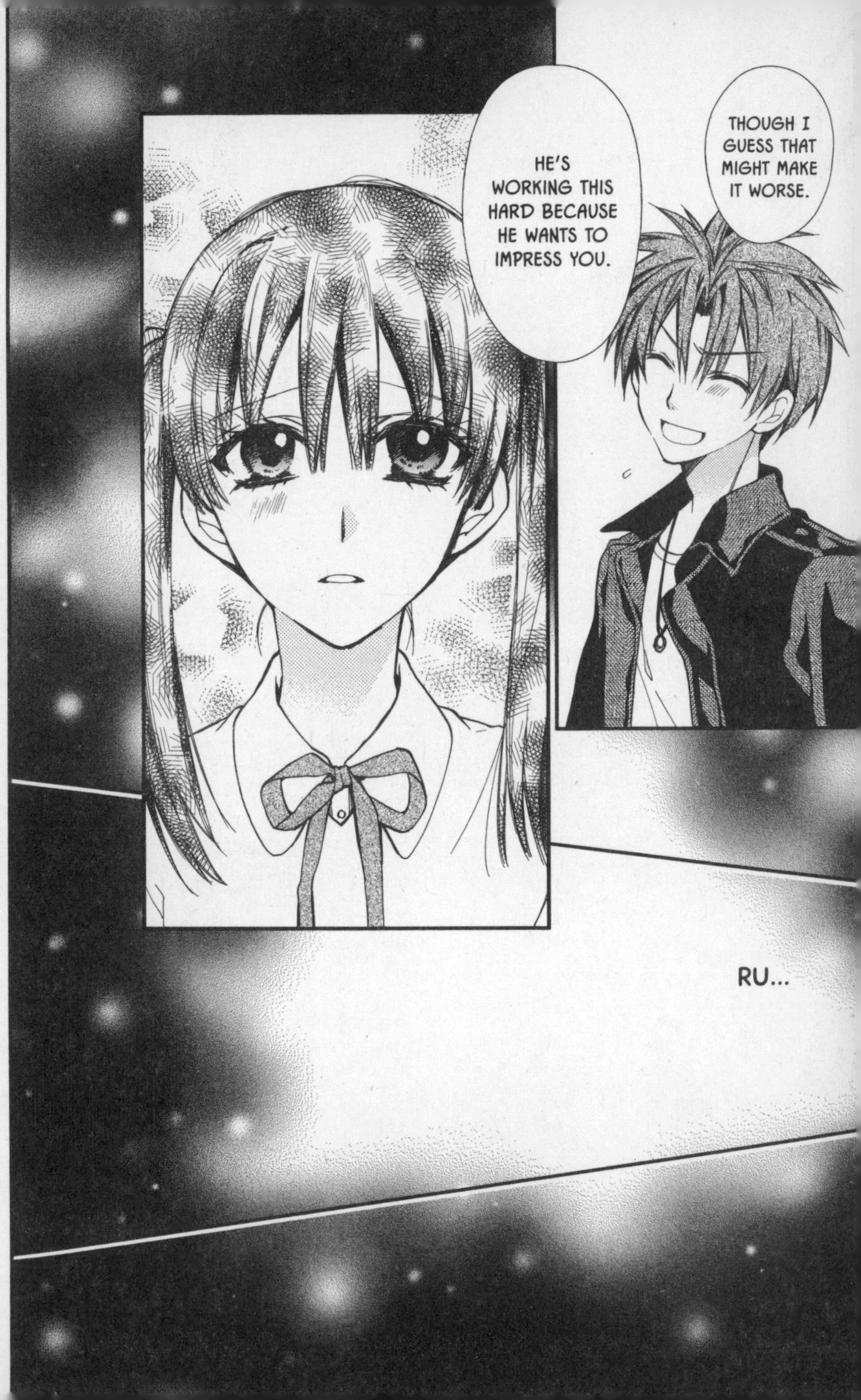
HE'S WORKING THIS HARD BECAUSE HE WANTS TO IMPRESS YOU.
THOUGH I GUESS THAT MIGHT MAKE IT WORSE.
RU...

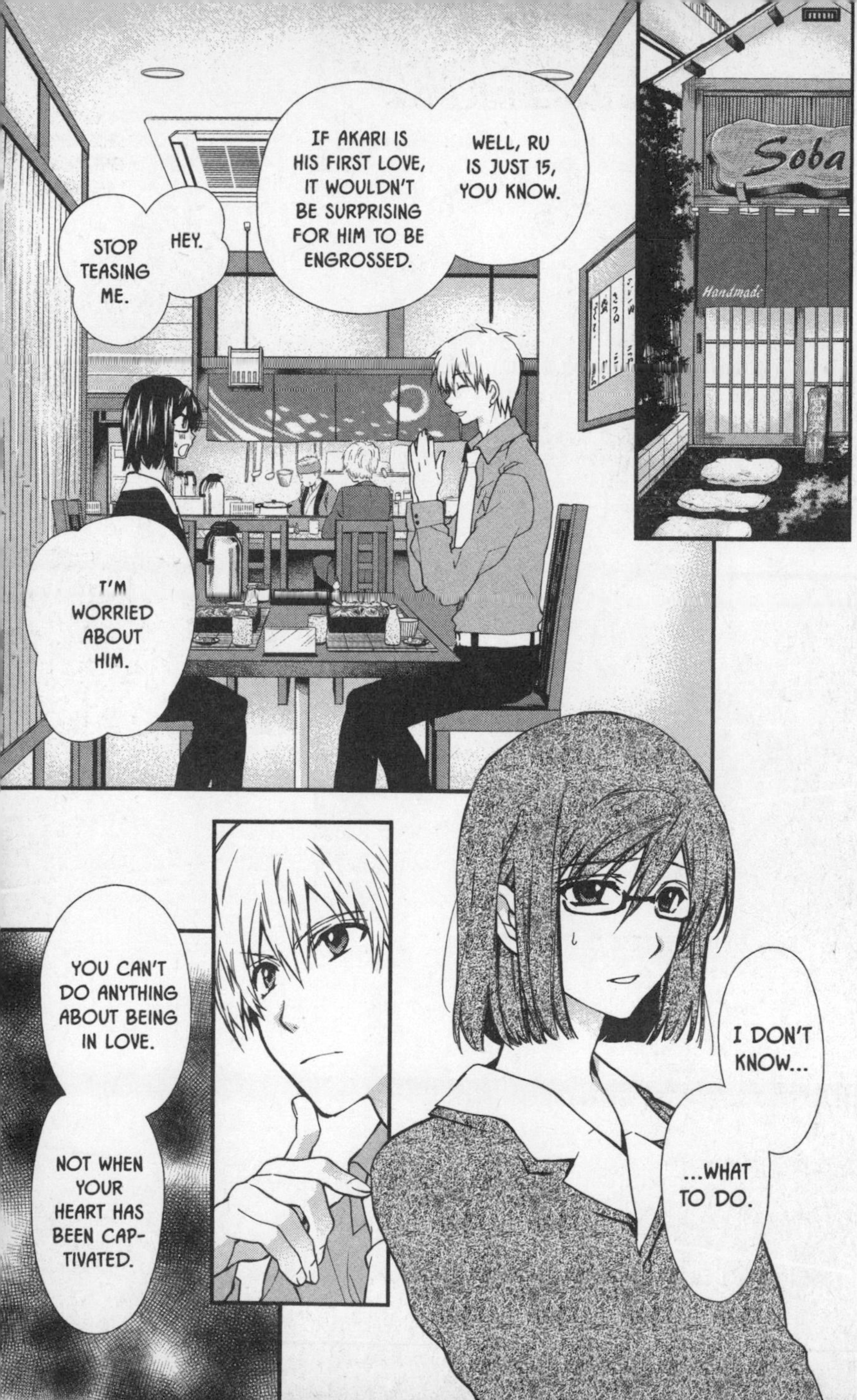
Soba
Handmade
WELL, RU IS JUST 15, YOU KNOW.
IF AKARI IS HIS FIRST LOVE, IT WOULDN'T BE SURPRISING FOR HIM TO BE ENGROSSED.
HEY.
STOP TEASING ME.
I'M WORRIED ABOUT HIM.
I DON'T KNOW...
...WHAT TO DO.
YOU CAN'T DO ANYTHING ABOUT BEING IN LOVE.
NOT WHEN YOUR HEART HAS BEEN CAP-TIVATED.

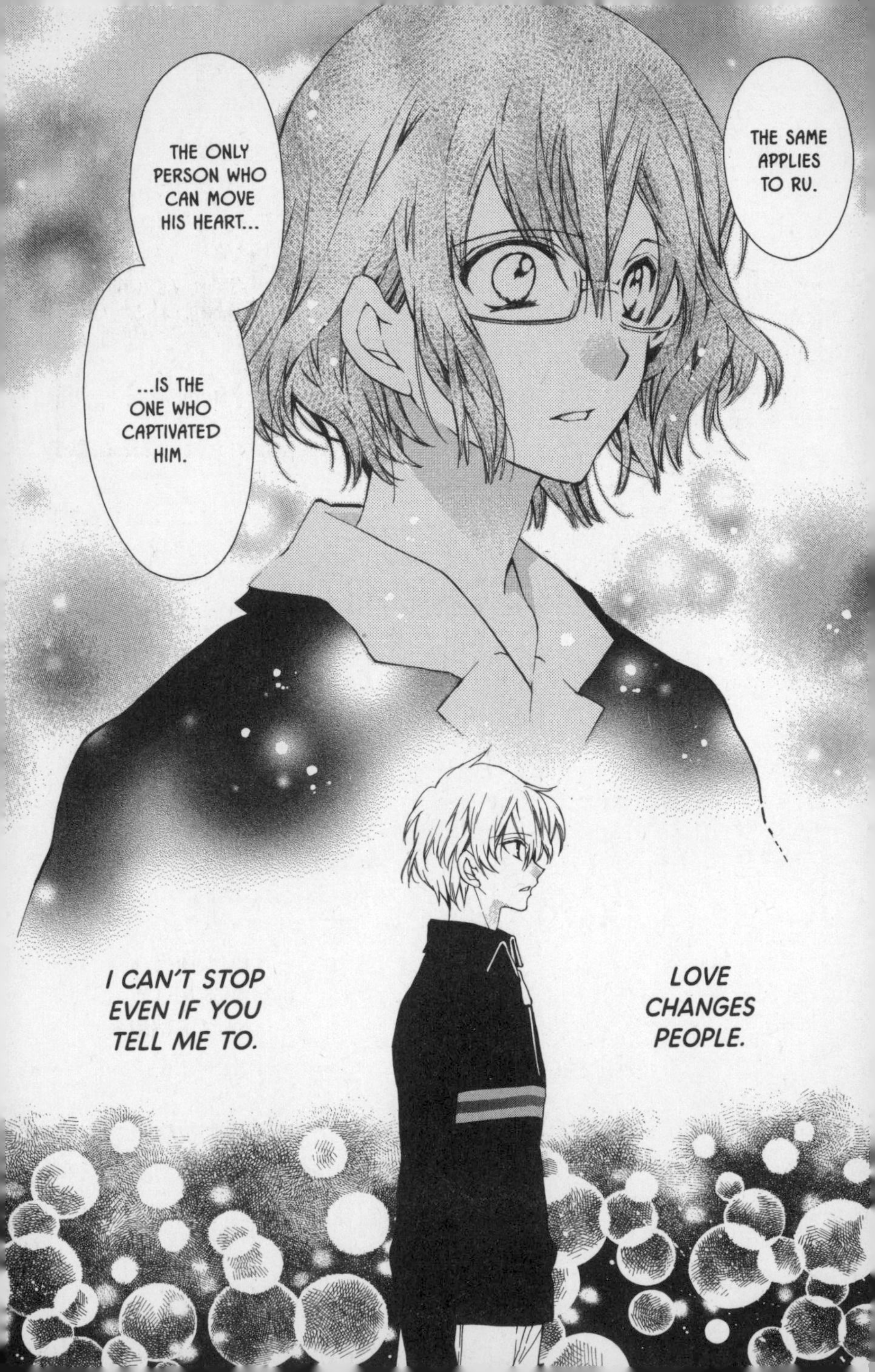
THE SAME APPLIES TO RU.
THE ONLY PERSON WHO CAN MOVE HIS HEART...
...IS THE ONE WHO CAPTIVATED HIM.
LOVE CHANGES PEOPLE.
I CAN'T STOP EVEN IF YOU TELL ME TO.

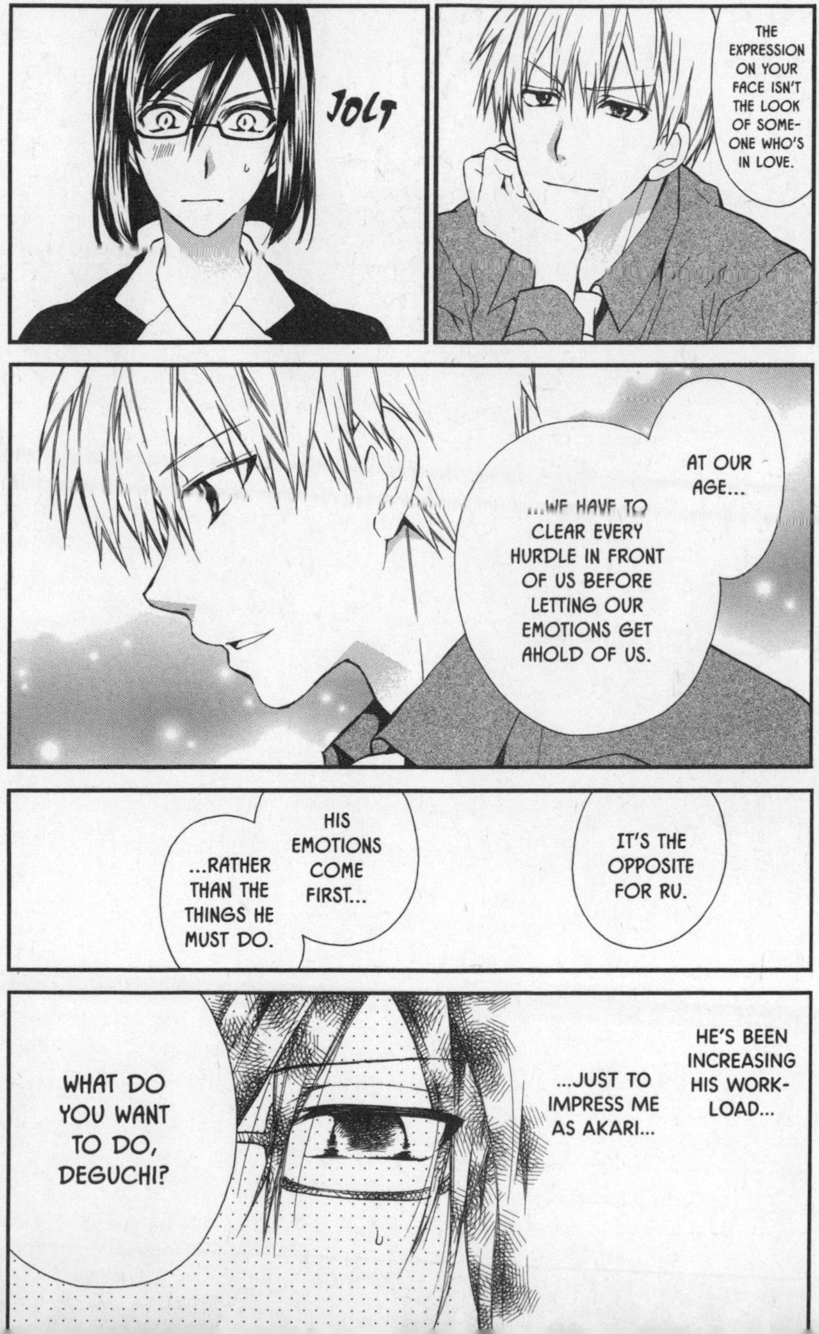
THE EXPRESSION ON YOUR FACE ISN'T THE LOOK OF SOME-ONE WHO'S IN LOVE.
JOLT
AT OUR AGE...
...WE HAVE TO CLEAR EVERY HURDLE IN FRONT OF US BEFORE LETTING OUR EMOTIONS GET AHOLD OF US.
IT'S THE OPPOSITE FOR RU.
HIS EMOTIONS COME FIRST...
...RATHER THAN THE THINGS HE MUST DO.
HE'S BEEN INCREASING HIS WORK-LOAD...
...JUST TO IMPRESS ME AS AKARI...
WHAT DO YOU WANT TO DO, DEGUCHI?

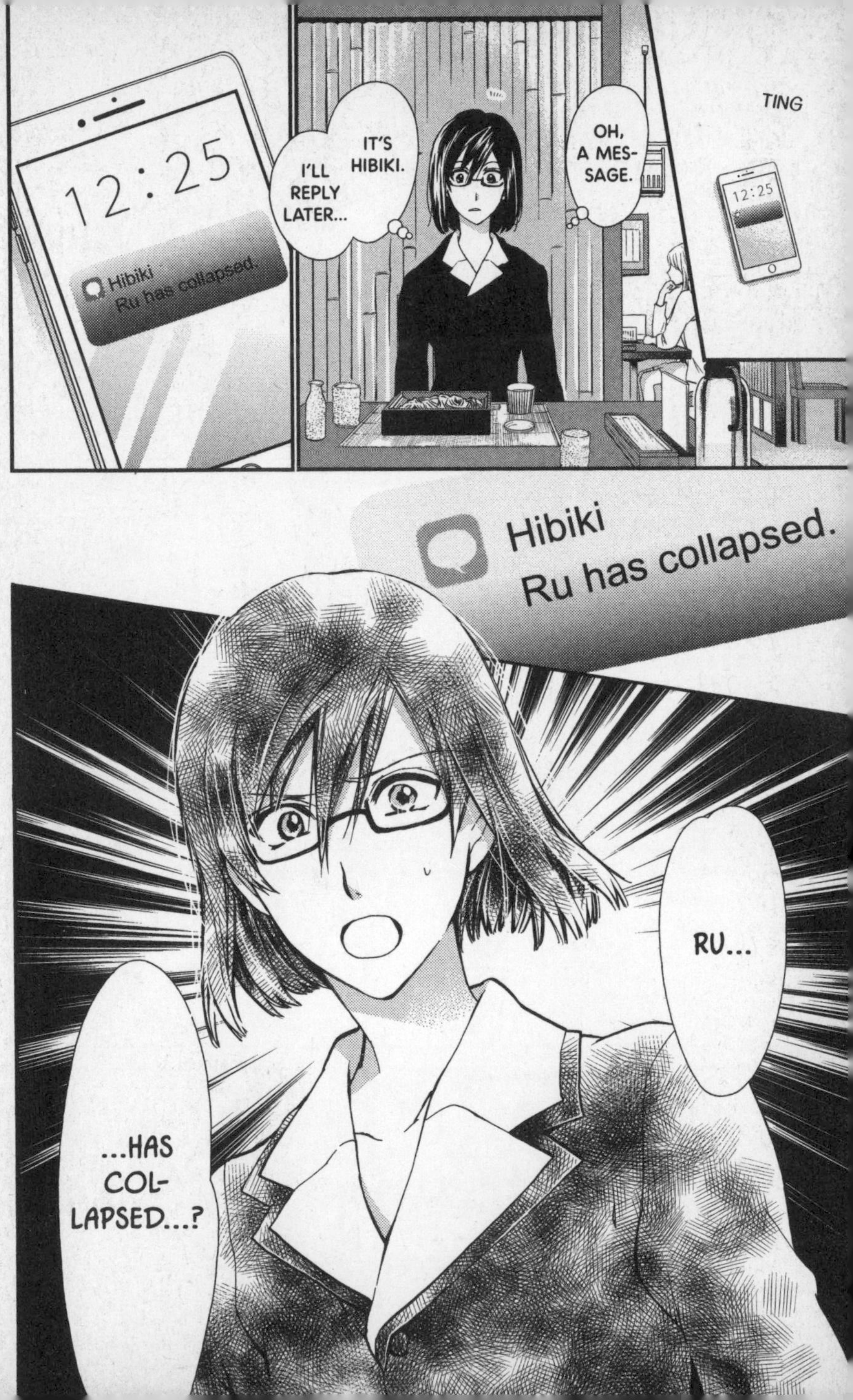
TING
12:25
OH, A MES-SAGE.
IT'S HIBIKI. I'LL REPLY LATER...
12:25
Hibiki
Ru has collapsed.
Hibiki
Ru has collapsed.
RU...
...HAS COL-LAPSED...?

Chapter 20

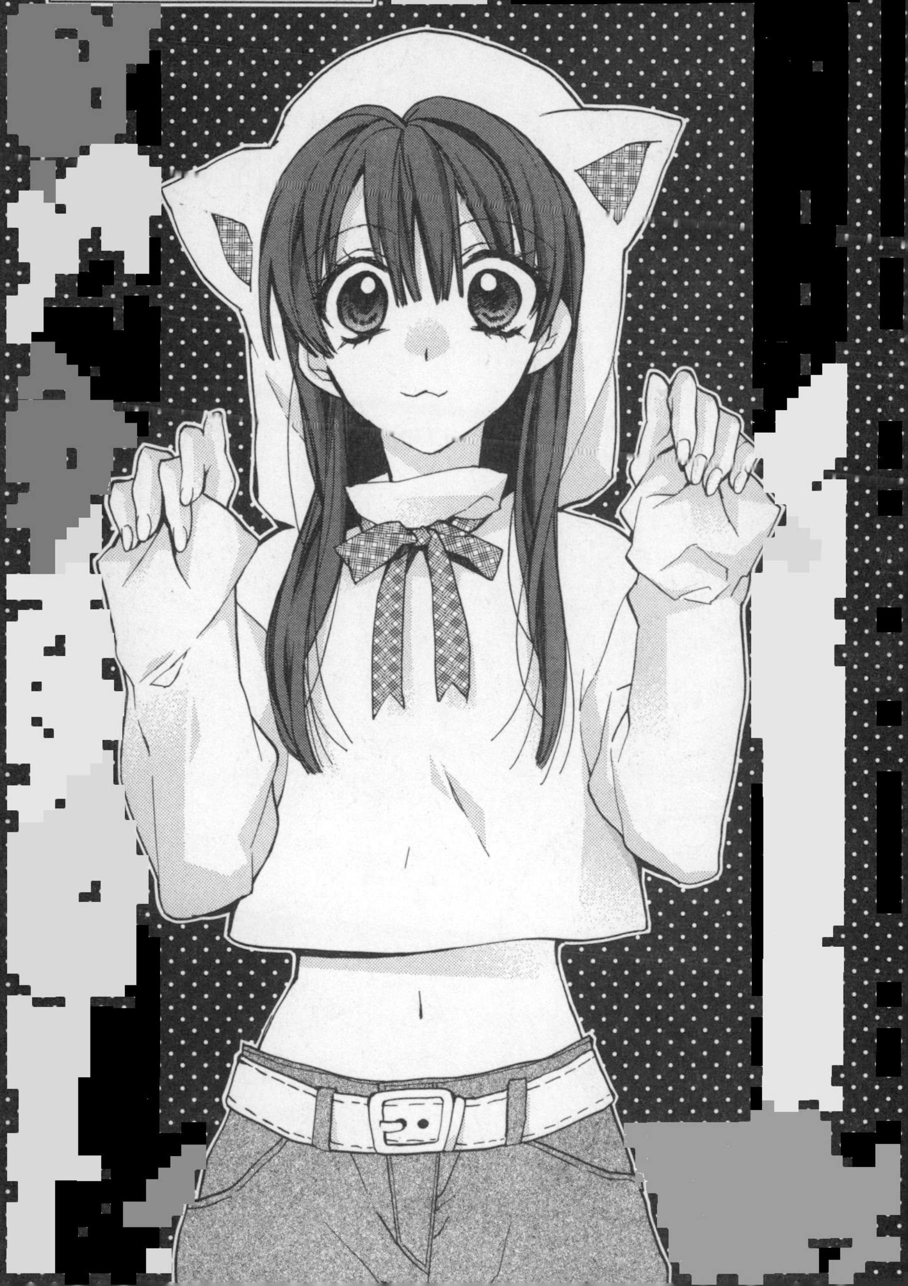

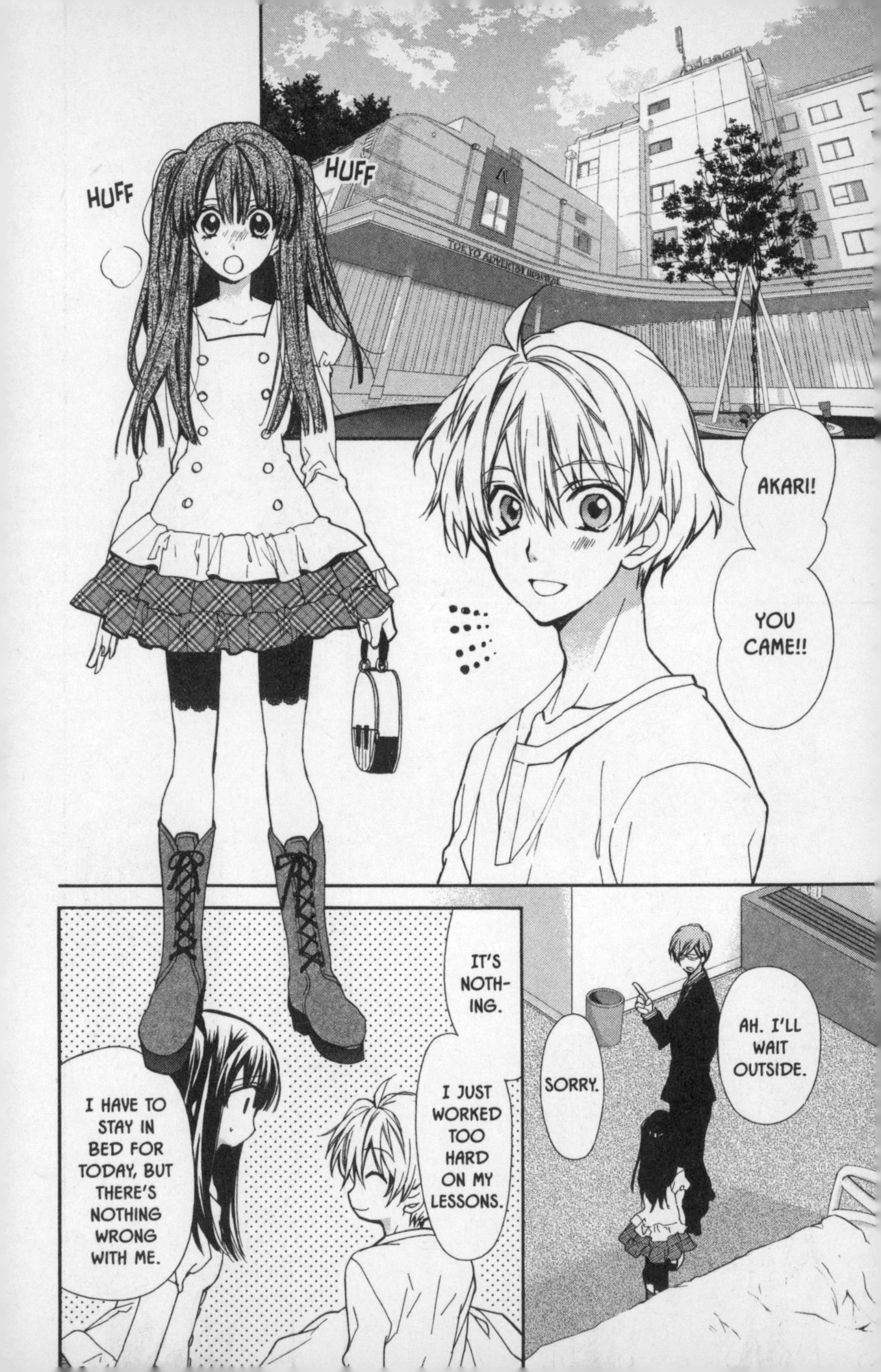
HUFF
HUFF
AKARI!
YOU CAME!!
AH. I'LL WAIT OUTSIDE.
SORRY.
IT'S NOTHING.
I JUST WORKED TOO HARD ON MY LESSONS.
I HAVE TO STAY IN BED FOR TODAY, BUT THERE'S NOTHING WRONG WITH ME.

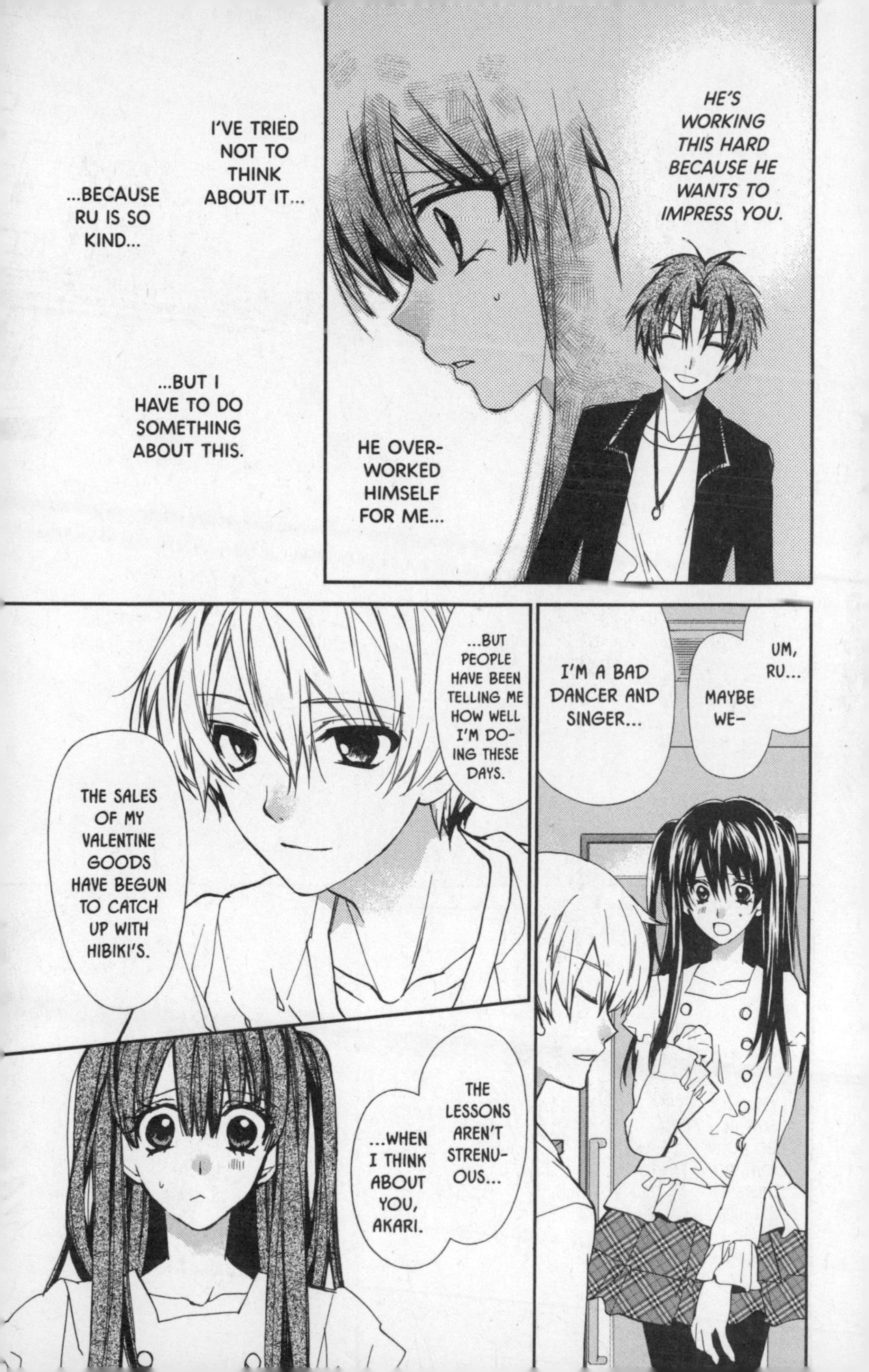
HE'S WORKING THIS HARD BECAUSE HE WANTS TO IMPRESS YOU.
HE OVER-WORKED HIMSELF FOR ME...
I'VE TRIED NOT TO THINK ABOUT IT...
...BECAUSE RU IS SO KIND...
...BUT I HAVE TO DO SOMETHING ABOUT THIS.
UM, RU... MAYBE WE-
I'M A BAD DANCER AND SINGER...
...BUT PEOPLE HAVE BEEN TELLING ME HOW WELL I'M DO-ING THESE DAYS.
THE SALES OF MY VALENTINE GOODS HAVE BEGUN TO CATCH UP WITH HIBIKI'S.
THE LESSONS AREN'T STRENU-OUS...
...WHEN I THINK ABOUT YOU, AKARI.

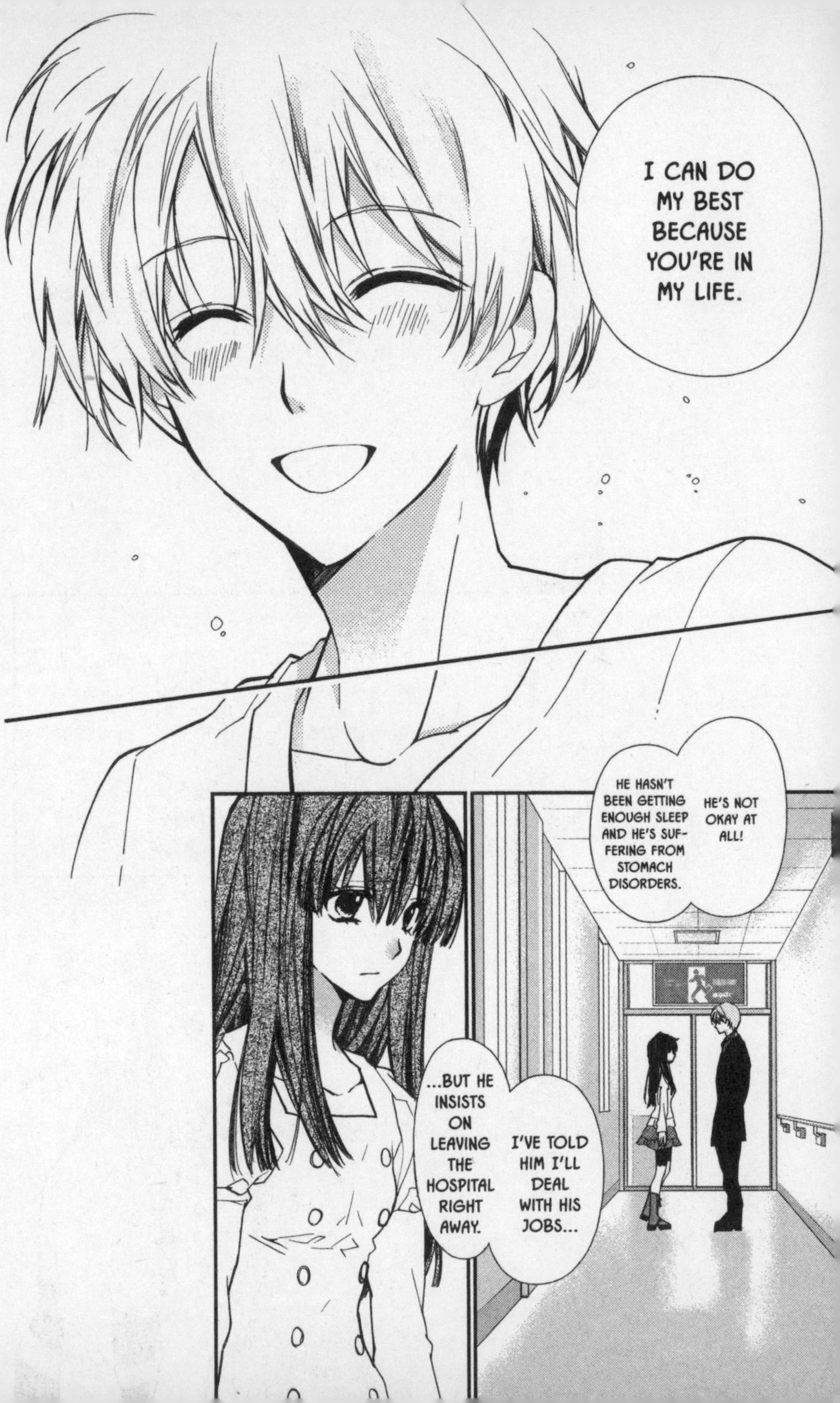
I CAN DO MY BEST BECAUSE YOU'RE IN MY LIFE.
HE'S NOT OKAY AT ALL!
HE HASN'T BEEN GETTING ENOUGH SLEEP AND HE'S SUF-FERING FROM STOMACH DISORDERS.
I'VE TOLD HIM I'LL DEAL WITH HIS JOBS...
...BUT HE INSISTS ON LEAVING THE HOSPITAL RIGHT AWAY.

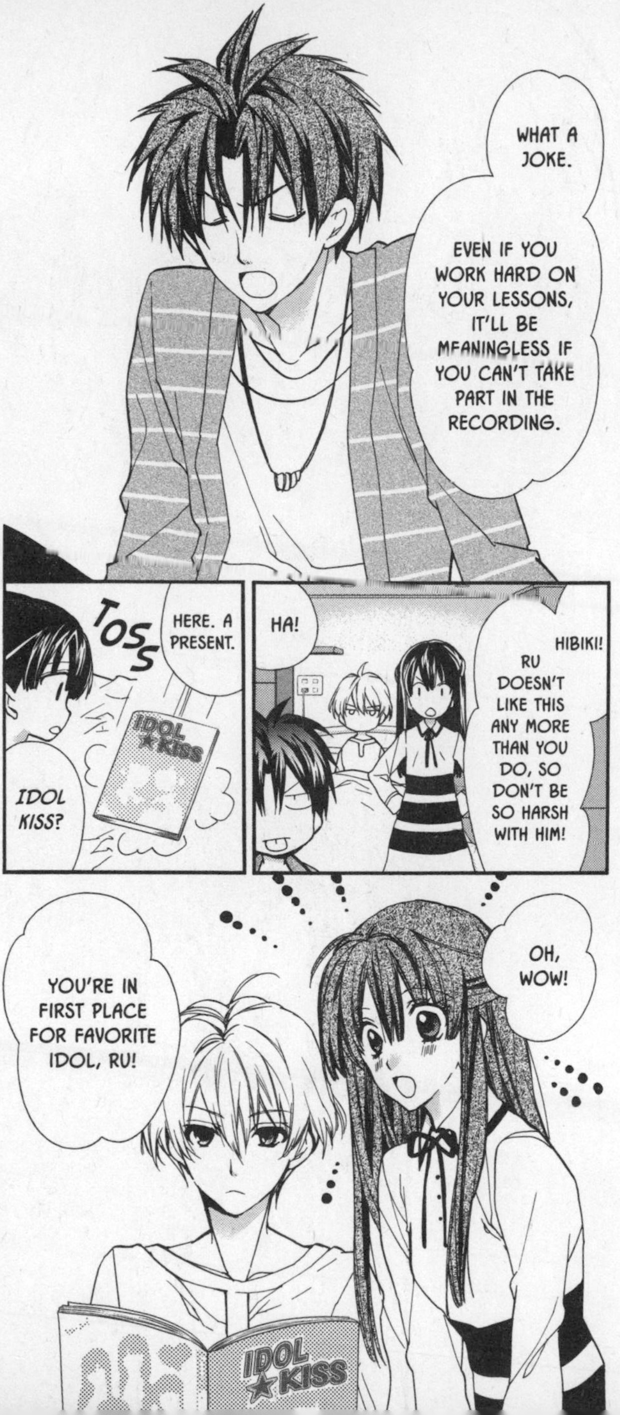
WHAT A JOKE.
EVEN IF YOU WORK HARD ON YOUR LESSONS, IT'LL BE MEANINGLESS IF YOU CAN'T TAKE PART IN THE RECORDING.
HIBIKI! RU DOESN'T LIKE THIS ANY MORE THAN YOU DO, SO DON'T BE SO HARSH WITH HIM!
HA!
HERE. A PRESENT.
TOSS
IDOL KISS
IDOL KISS?
OH, WOW!
YOU'RE IN FIRST PLACE FOR FAVORITE IDOL, RU!
IDOL KISS

IDOL dreams

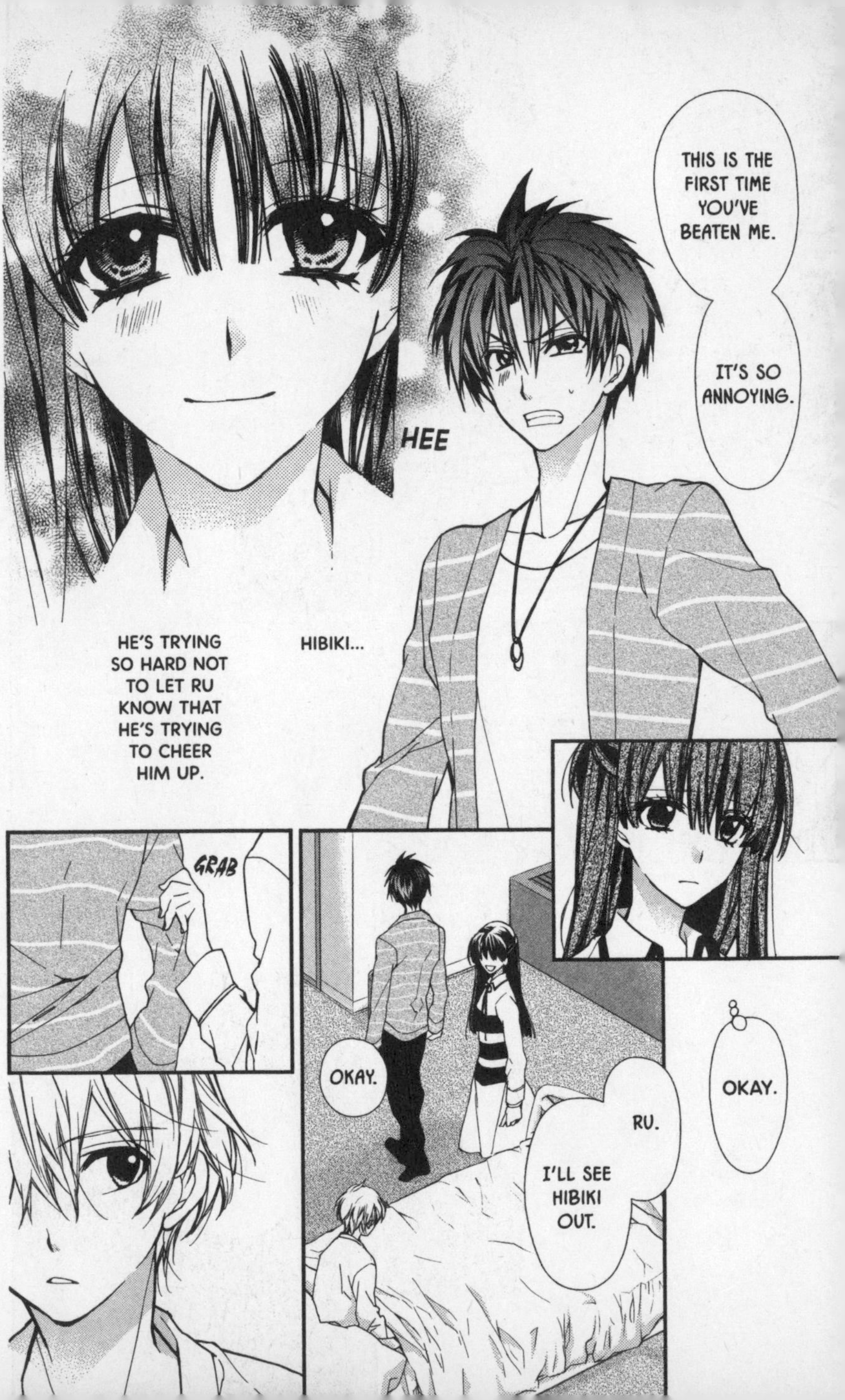
THIS IS THE FIRST TIME YOU'VE BEATEN ME.
IT'S SO ANNOYING.
HEE
HIBIKI...
HE'S TRYING SO HARD NOT TO LET RU KNOW THAT HE'S TRYING TO CHEER HIM UP.
OKAY.
RU.
I'LL SEE HIBIKI OUT.
OKAY.
GRAB

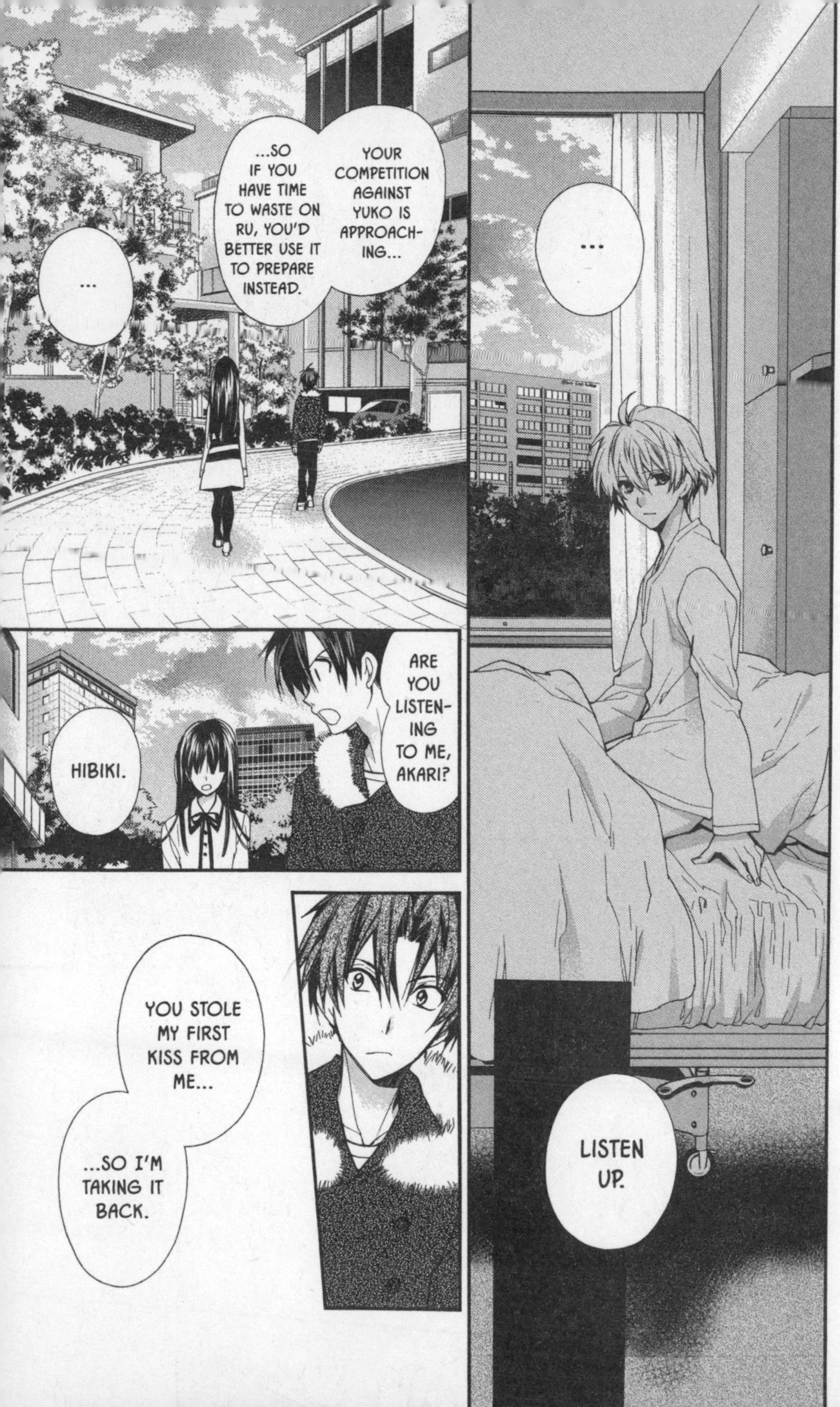
...
LISTEN UP.
YOUR COMPETITION AGAINST YUKO IS APPROACHING...
...SO IF YOU HAVE TIME TO WASTE ON RU, YOU'D BETTER USE IT TO PREPARE INSTEAD.
...
ARE YOU LISTENING TO ME, AKARI?
HIBIKI.
YOU STOLE MY FIRST KISS FROM ME...
...SO I'M TAKING IT BACK.

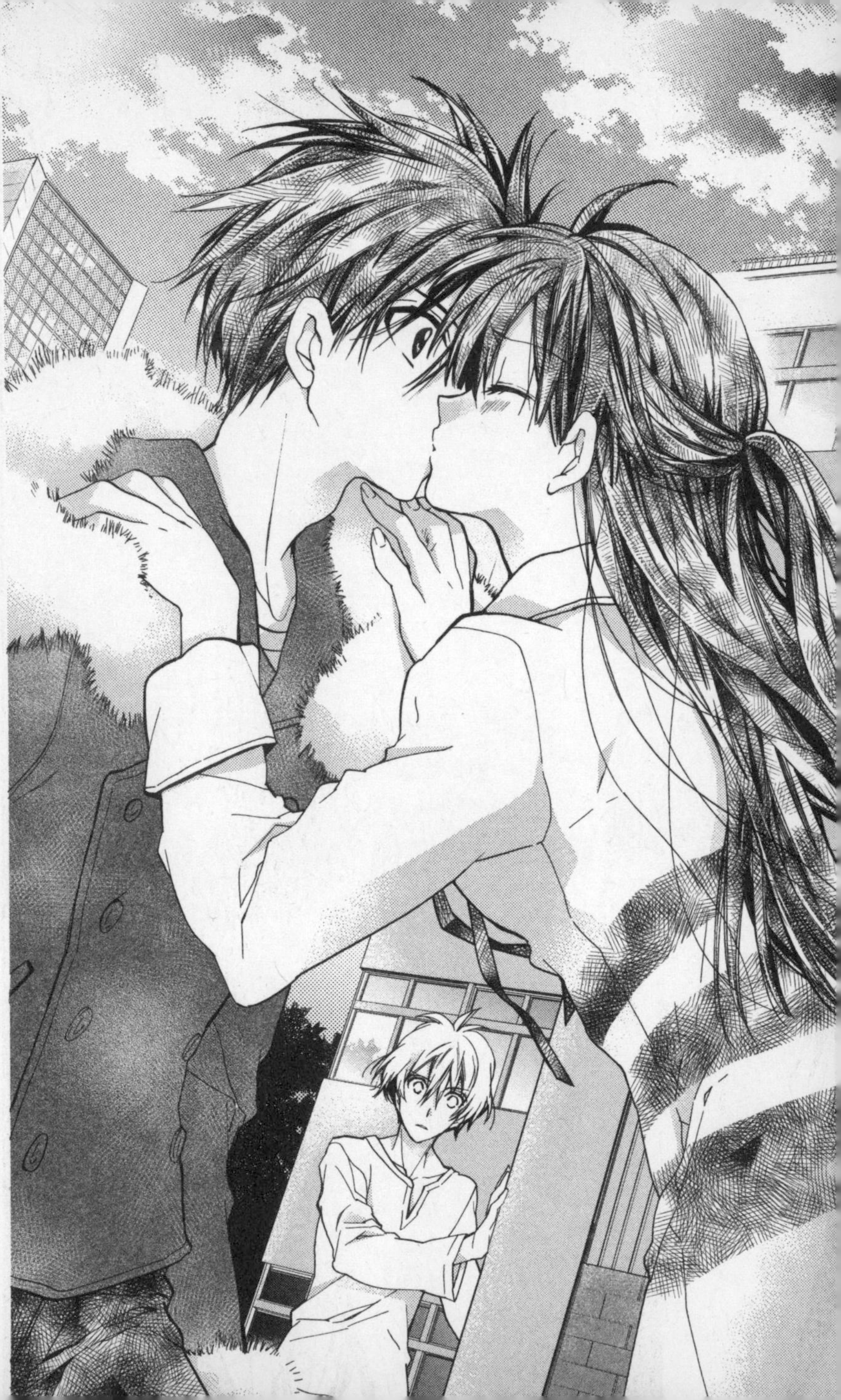

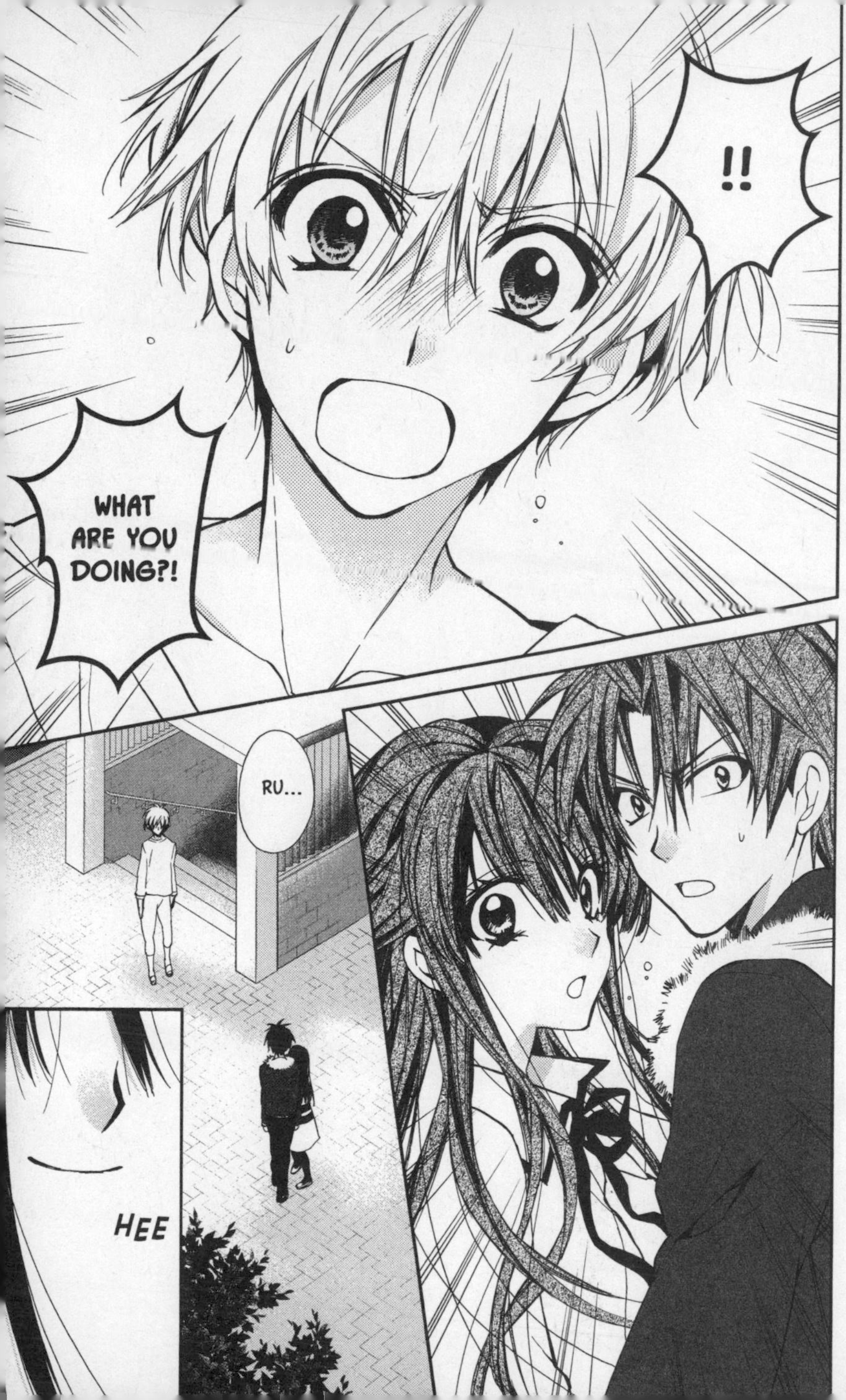
!!
WHAT ARE YOU DOING?!
RU...
HEE

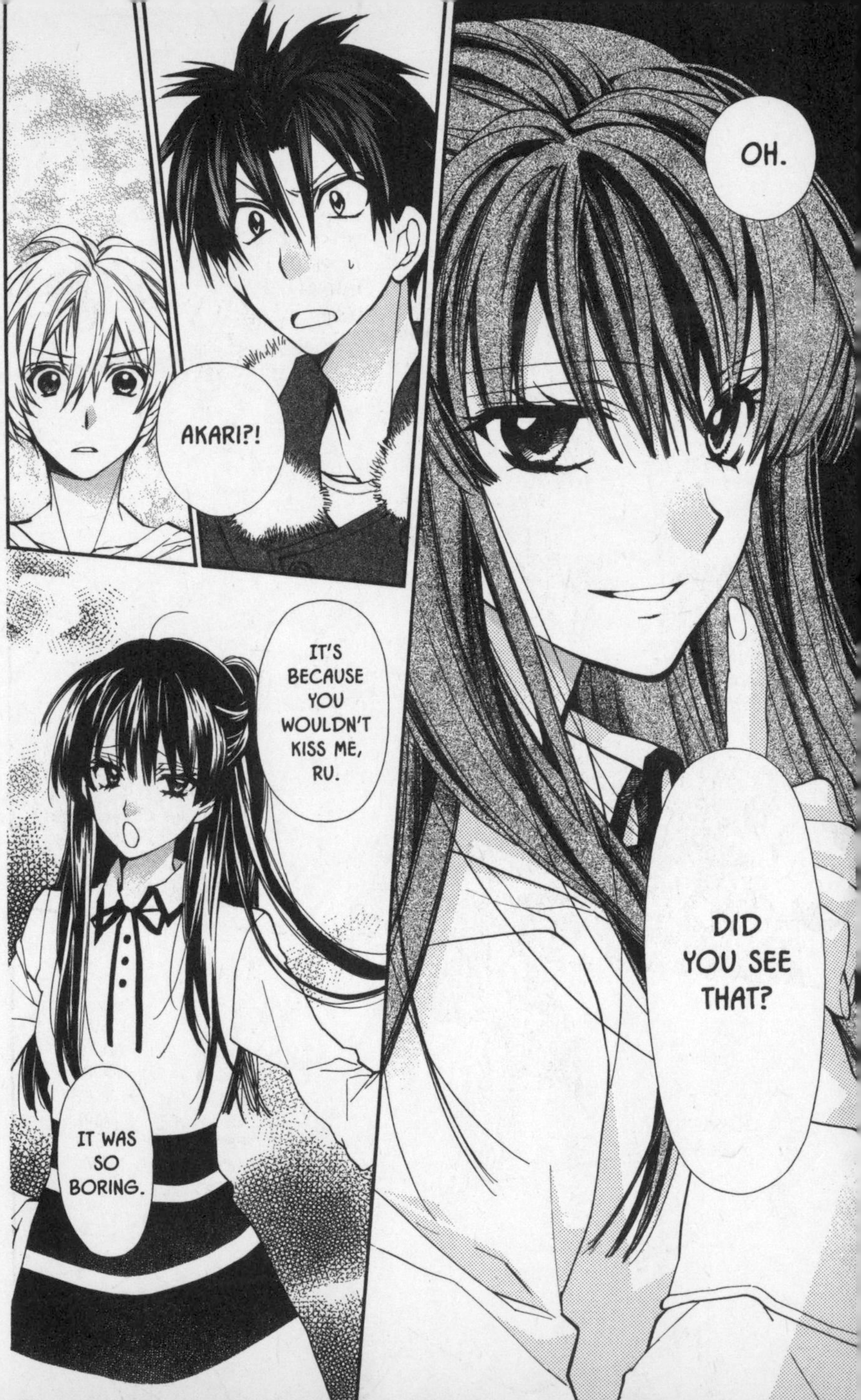
OH.
DID YOU SEE THAT?
AKARI?!
IT'S BECAUSE YOU WOULDN'T KISS ME, RU.
IT WAS SO BORING.

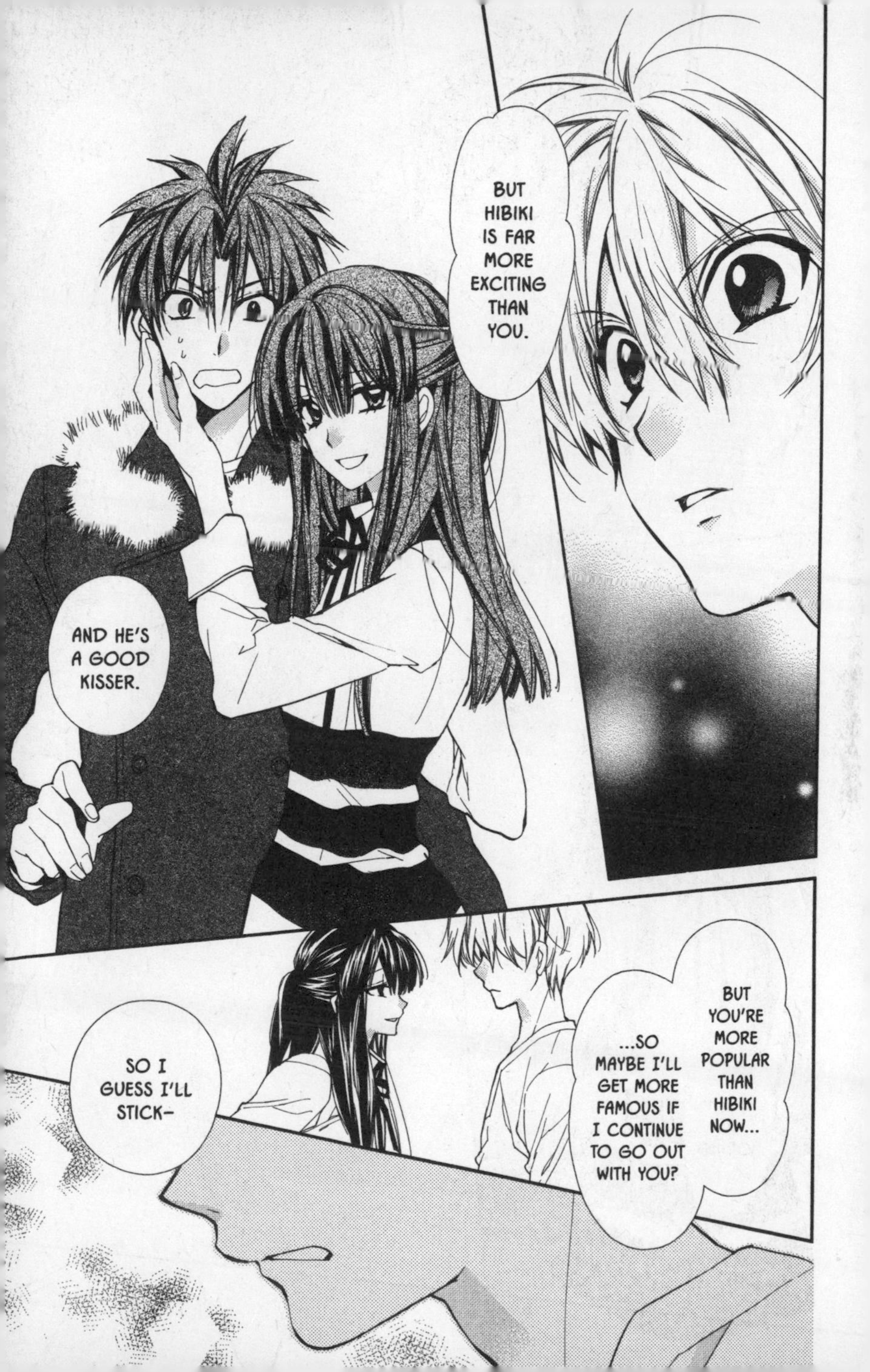
BUT HIBIKI IS FAR MORE EXCITING THAN YOU.
AND HE'S A GOOD KISSER.
BUT YOU'RE MORE POPULAR THAN HIBIKI NOW...
...SO MAYBE I'LL GET MORE FAMOUS IF I CONTINUE TO GO OUT WITH YOU?
SO I GUESS I'LL STICK–

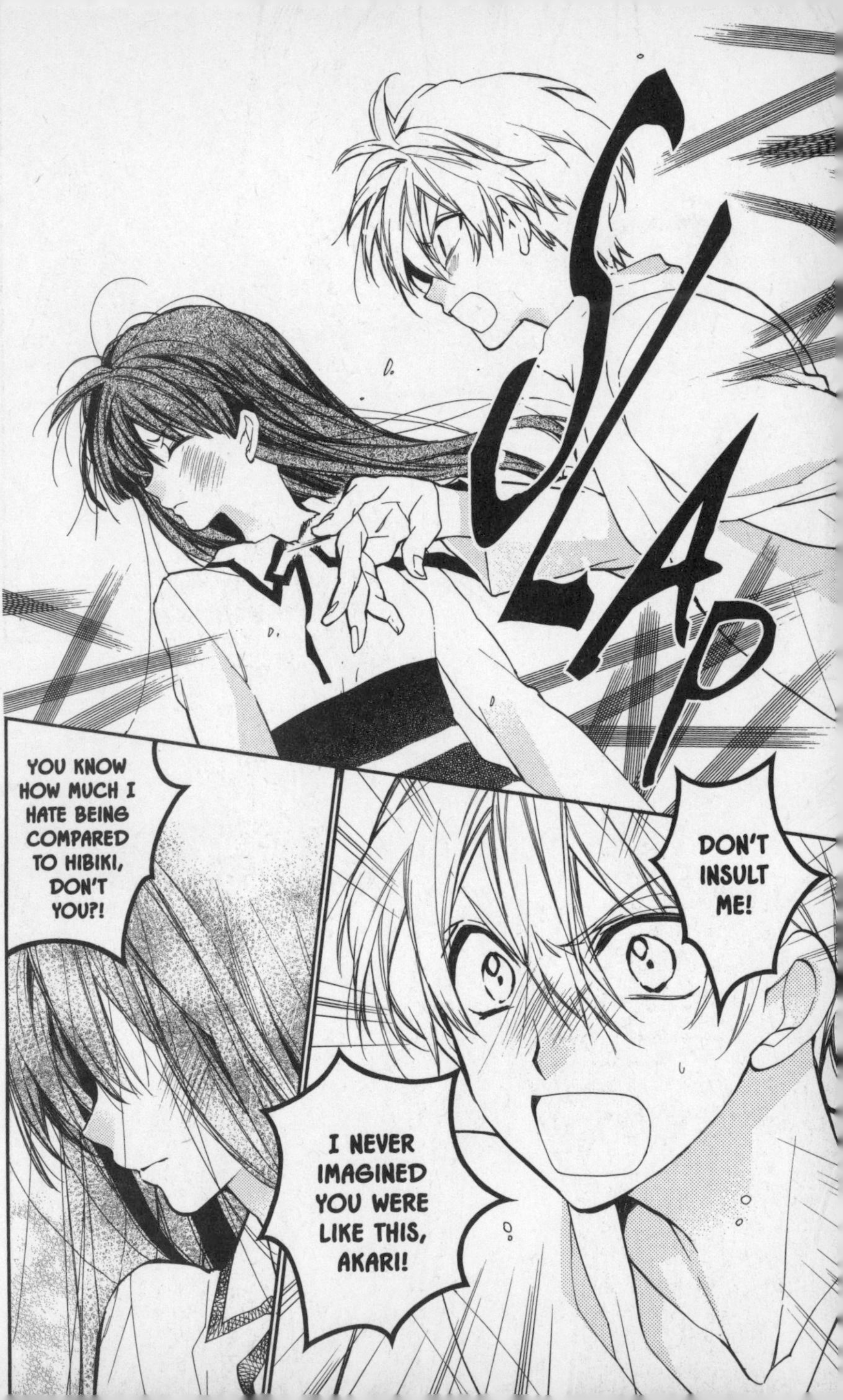
SLAP
DON'T INSULT ME!
I NEVER IMAGINED YOU WERE LIKE THIS, AKARI!
YOU KNOW HOW MUCH I HATE BEING COMPARED TO HIBIKI, DON'T YOU?!

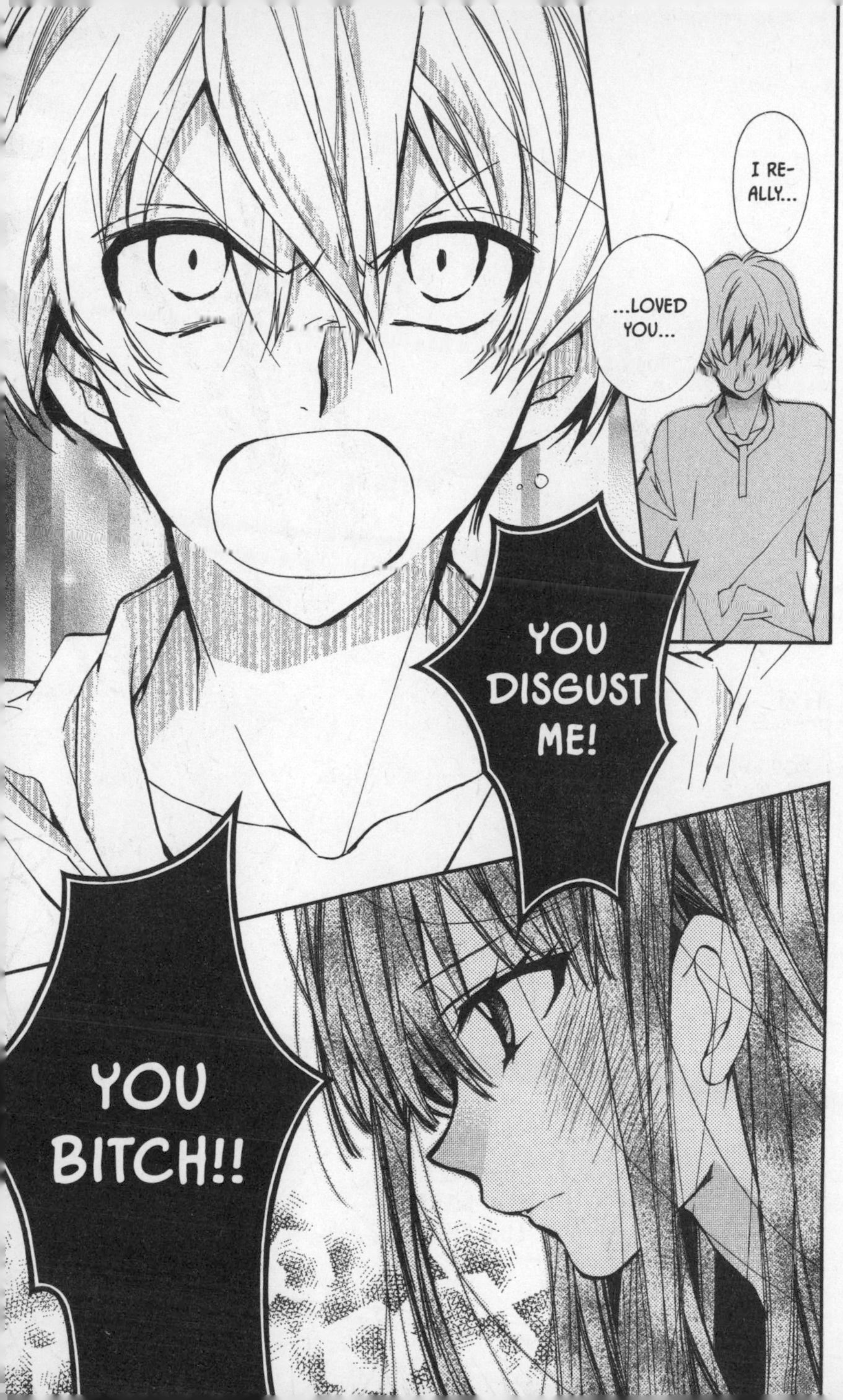
I RE-ALLY...
...LOVED YOU...
YOU DISGUST ME!
YOU BITCH!!

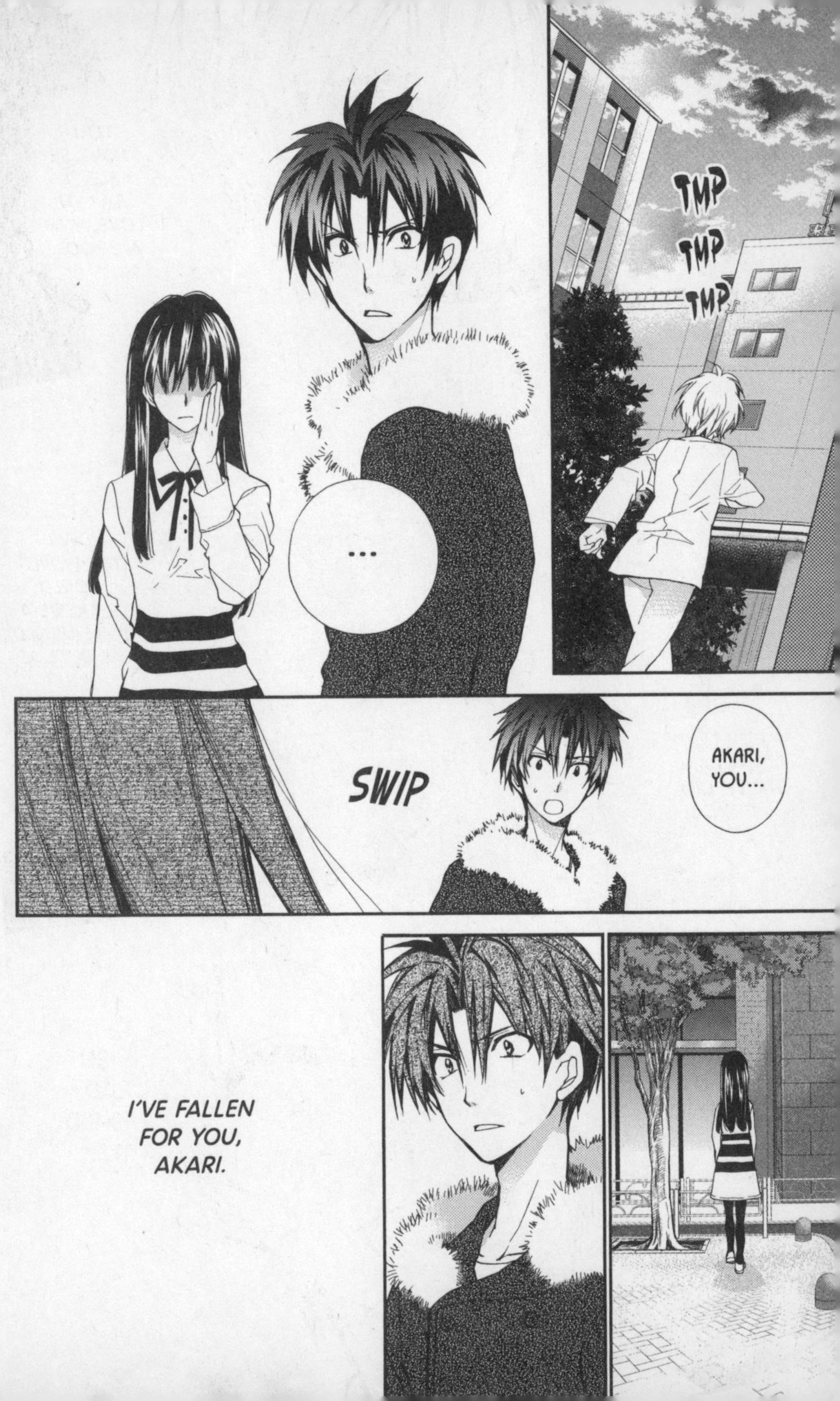
TMP
TMP
TMP
...
AKARI, YOU...
SWIP
I'VE FALLEN FOR YOU, AKARI.

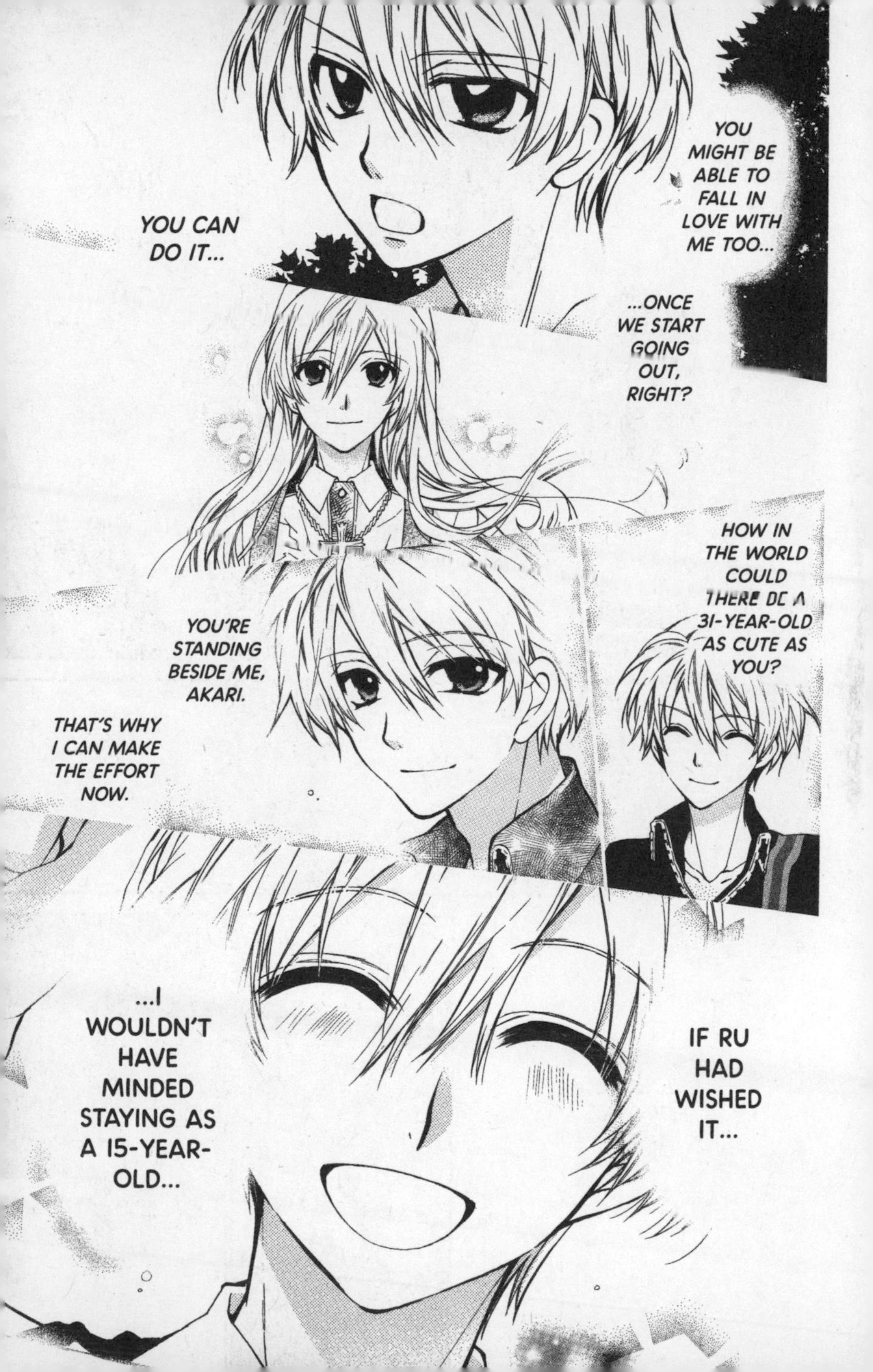
YOU MIGHT BE ABLE TO FALL IN LOVE WITH ME TOO...
YOU CAN DO IT...
...ONCE WE START GOING OUT, RIGHT?
HOW IN THE WORLD COULD THERE BE A 31-YEAR-OLD AS CUTE AS YOU?
YOU'RE STANDING BESIDE ME, AKARI.
THAT'S WHY I CAN MAKE THE EFFORT NOW.
IF RU HAD WISHED IT...
...I WOULDN'T HAVE MINDED STAYING AS A 15-YEAR-OLD...

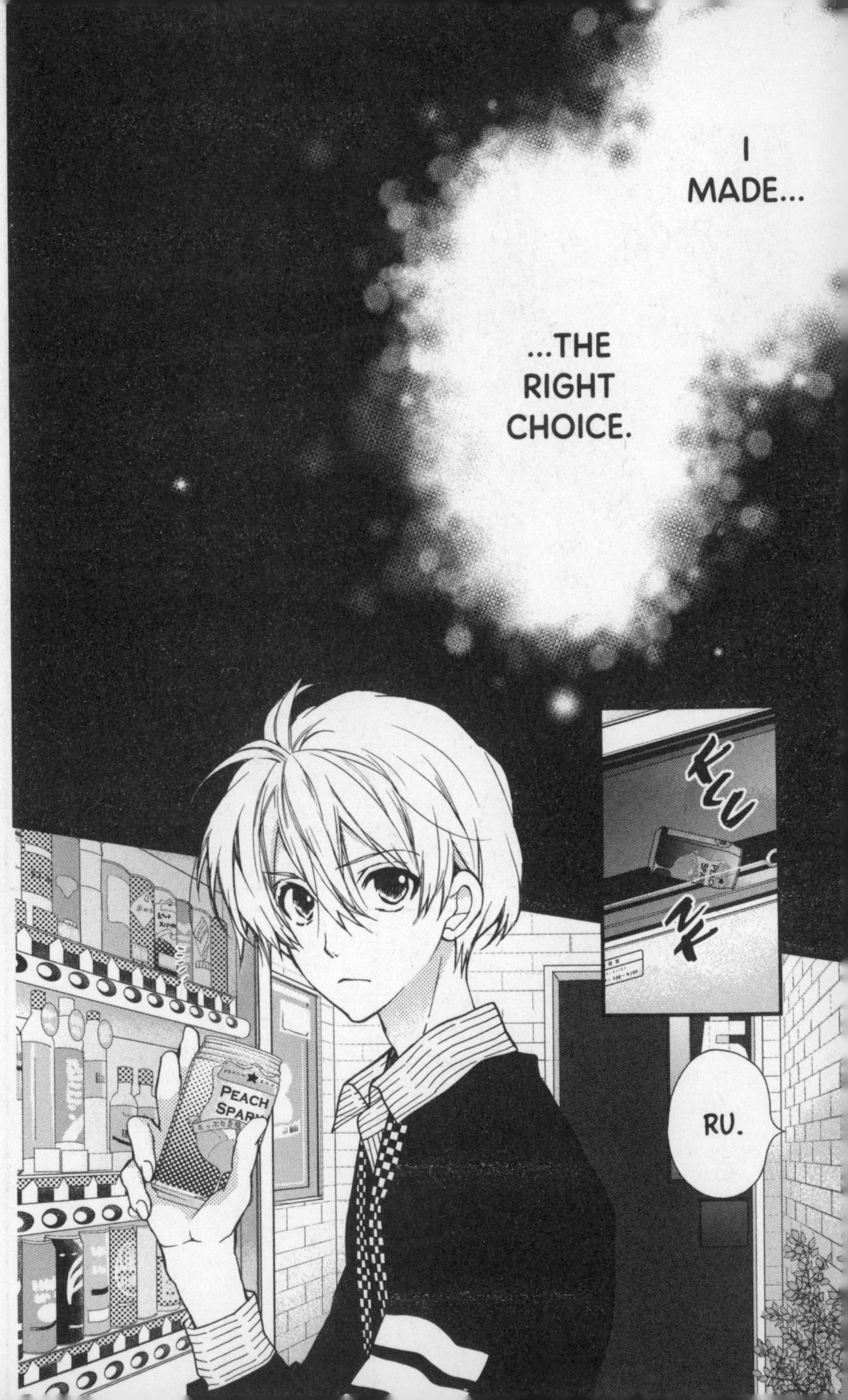
I MADE...
...THE RIGHT CHOICE.
KLUNK
RU.

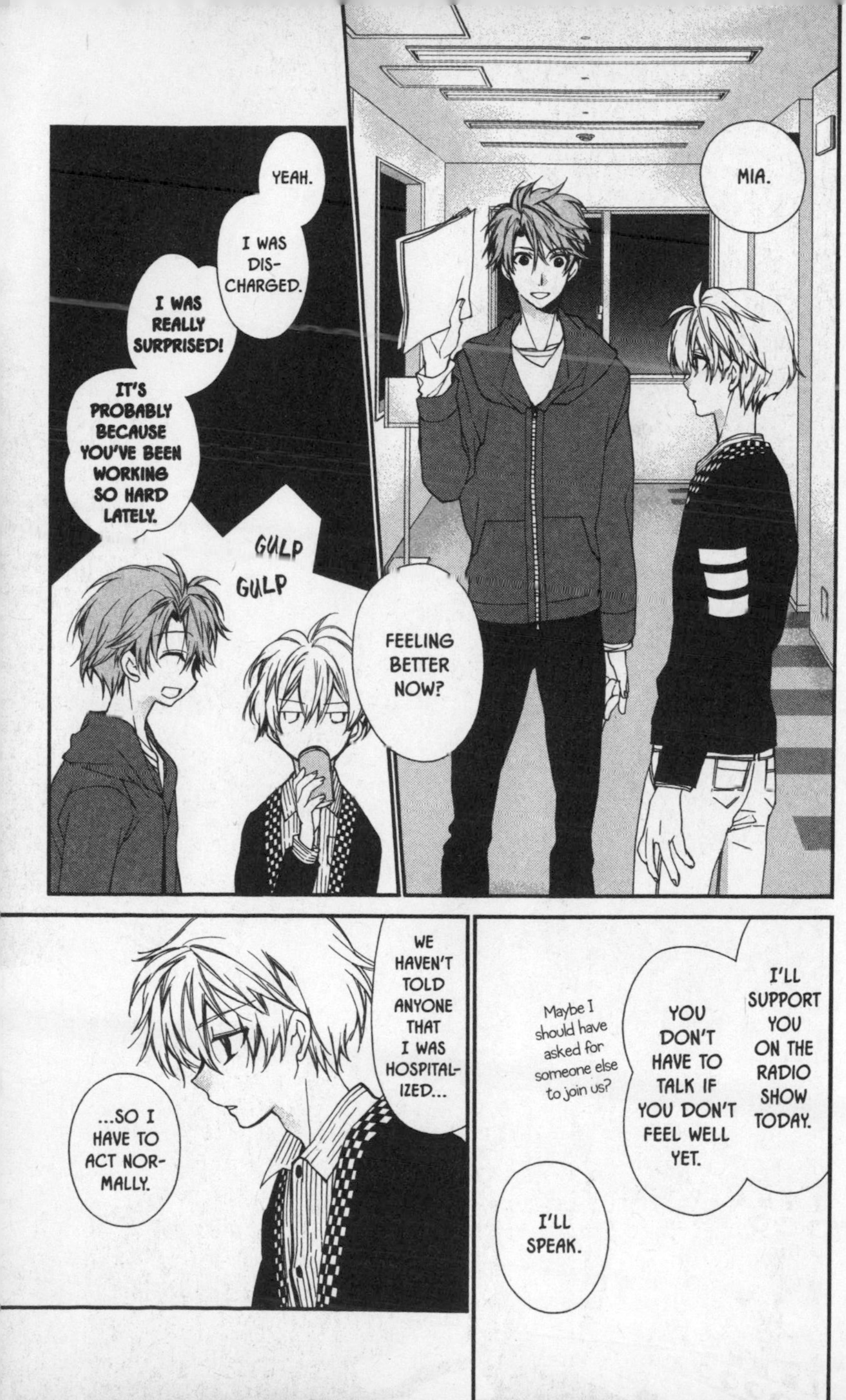
MIA.
FEELING BETTER NOW?
YEAH.
I WAS DIS-CHARGED.
I WAS REALLY SURPRISED!
IT'S PROBABLY BECAUSE YOU'VE BEEN WORKING SO HARD LATELY.
GULP
GULP
I'LL SUPPORT YOU ON THE RADIO SHOW TODAY.
YOU DON'T HAVE TO TALK IF YOU DON'T FEEL WELL YET.
Maybe I should have asked for someone else to join us?
I'LL SPEAK.
WE HAVEN'T TOLD ANYONE THAT I WAS HOSPITAL-IZED...
...SO I HAVE TO ACT NOR-MALLY.

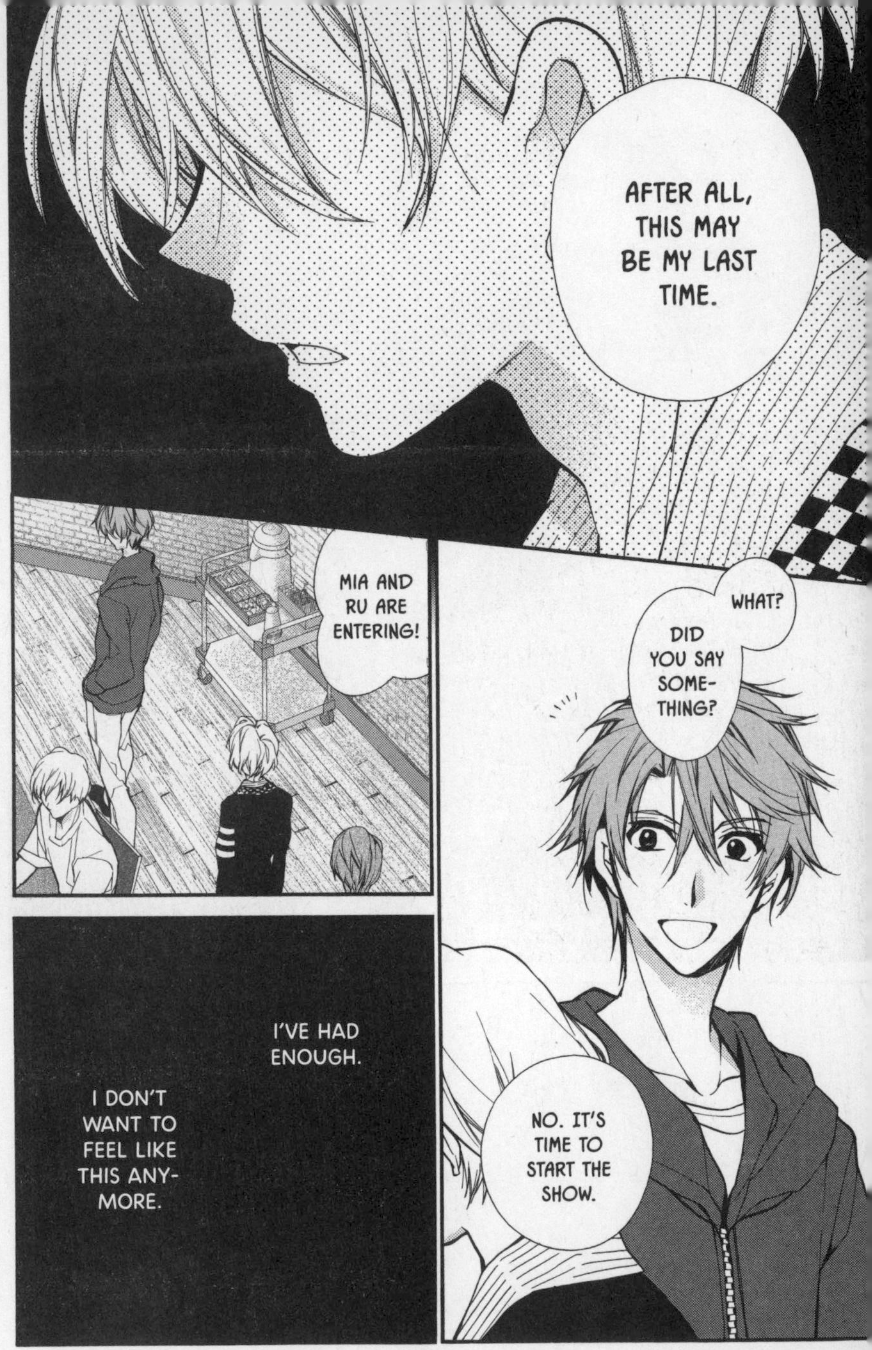
AFTER ALL, THIS MAY BE MY LAST TIME.
WHAT?
DID YOU SAY SOME-THING?
NO. IT'S TIME TO START THE SHOW.
MIA AND RU ARE ENTERING!
I'VE HAD ENOUGH.
I DON'T WANT TO FEEL LIKE THIS ANY-MORE.

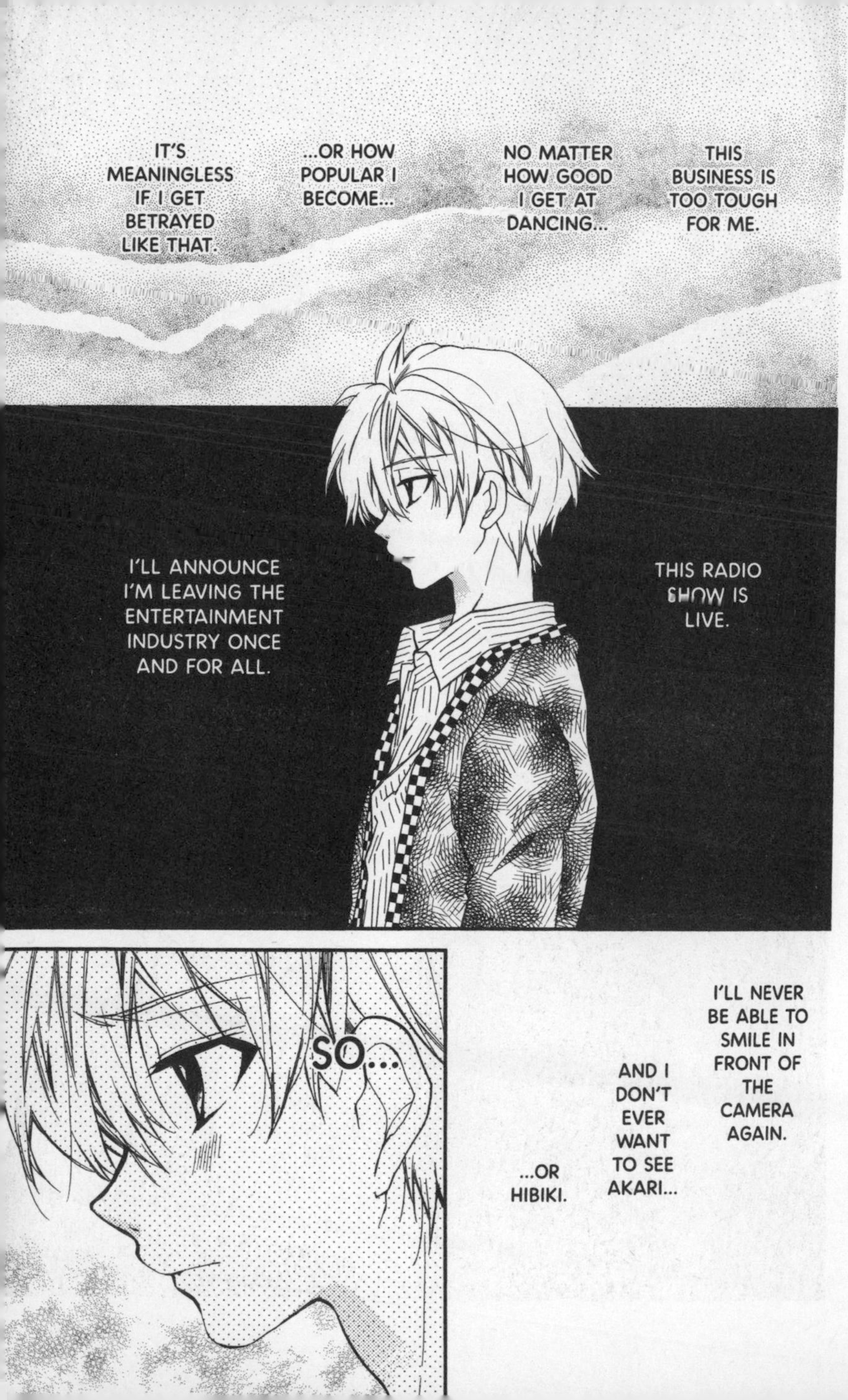
THIS BUSINESS IS TOO TOUGH FOR ME.
NO MATTER HOW GOOD I GET AT DANCING...
...OR HOW POPULAR I BECOME...
IT'S MEANINGLESS IF I GET BETRAYED LIKE THAT.
THIS RADIO SHOW IS LIVE.
I'LL ANNOUNCE I'M LEAVING THE ENTERTAINMENT INDUSTRY ONCE AND FOR ALL.
I'LL NEVER BE ABLE TO SMILE IN FRONT OF THE CAMERA AGAIN.
AND I DON'T EVER WANT TO SEE AKARI...
...OR HIBIKI.
SO...

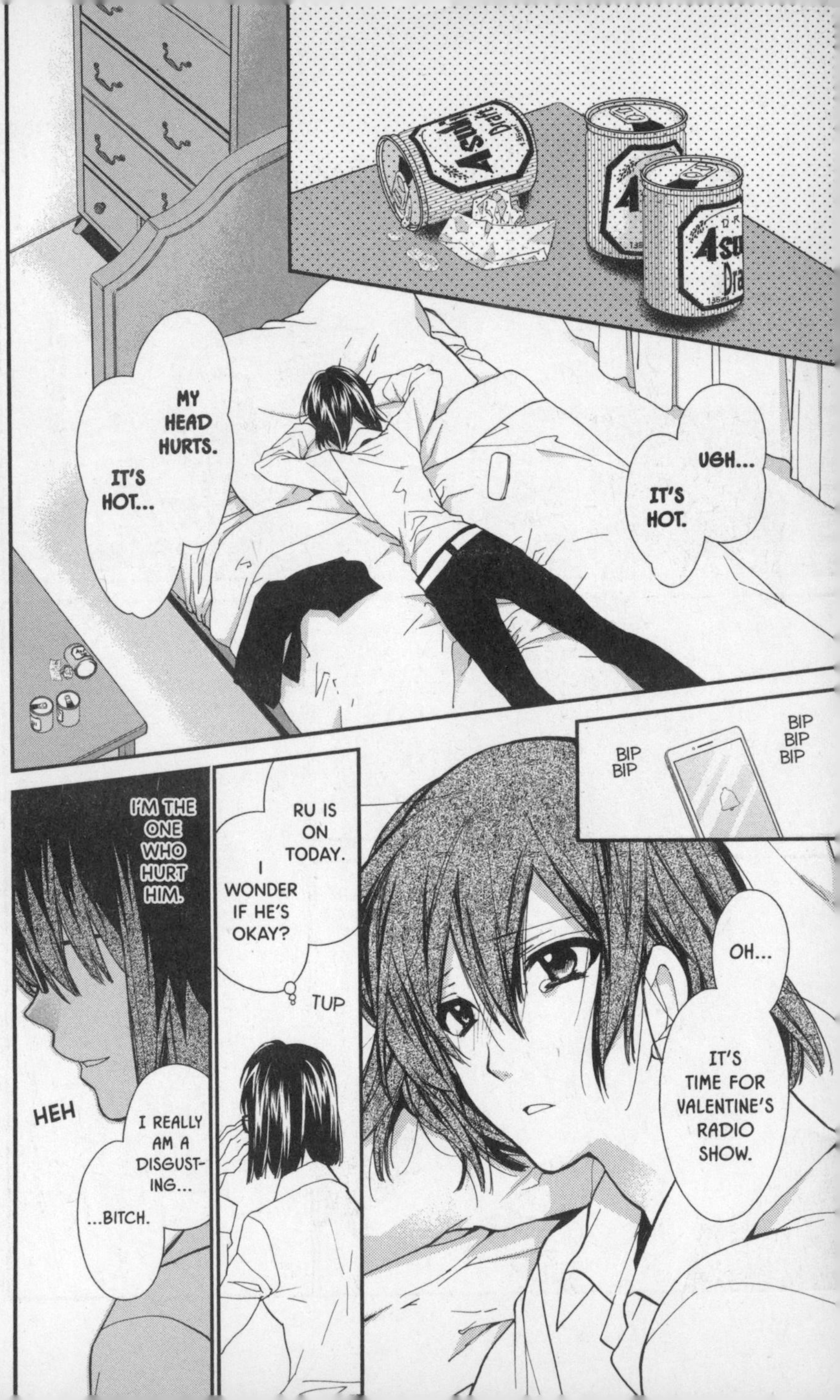
UGH... IT'S HOT.
MY HEAD HURTS. IT'S HOT...
BIP BIP BIP
BIP BIP
OH...
IT'S TIME FOR VALENTINE'S RADIO SHOW.
RU IS ON TODAY. I WONDER IF HE'S OKAY?
TUP
I'M THE ONE WHO HURT HIM.
HEH
I REALLY AM A DISGUST-ING...
...BITCH.

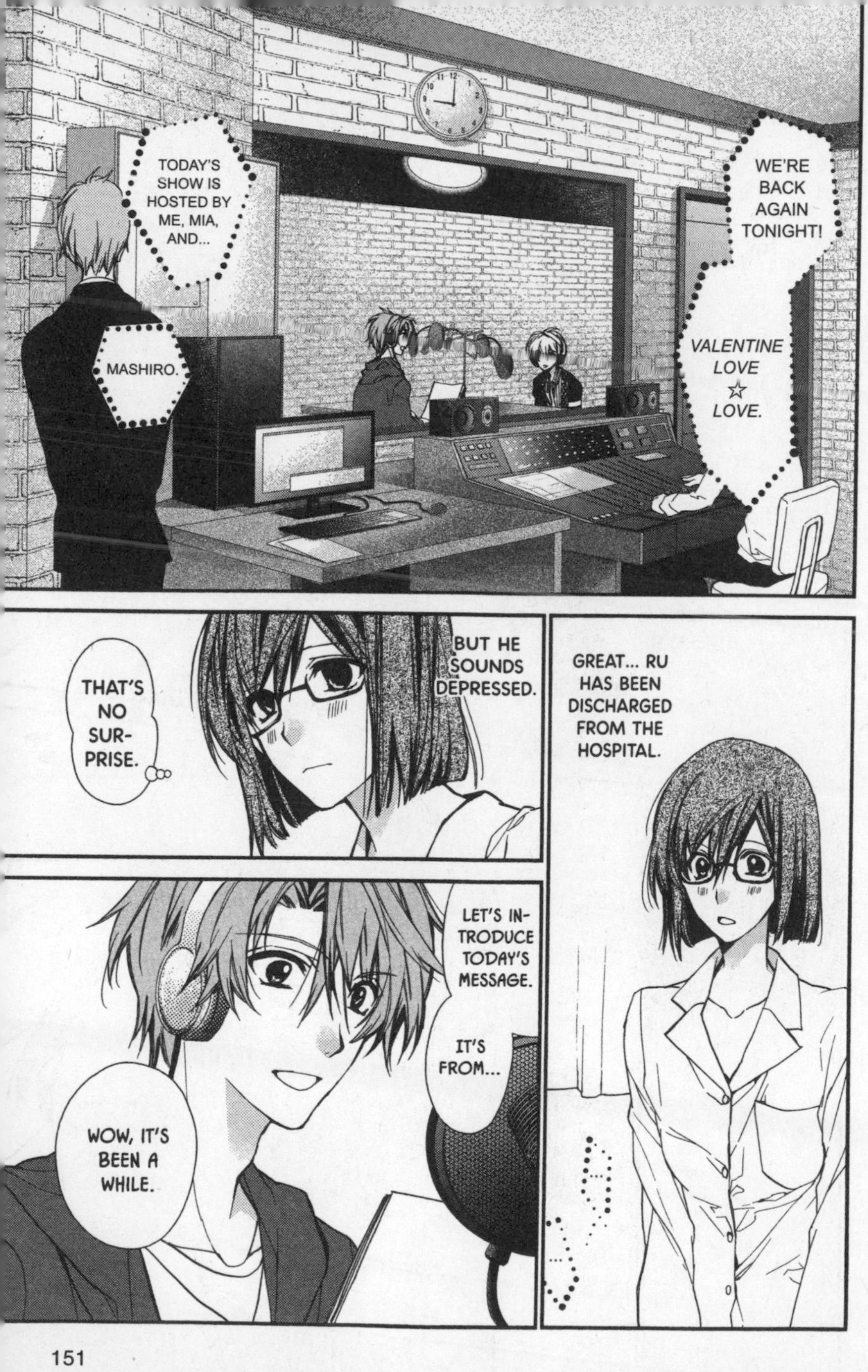
WE'RE BACK AGAIN TONIGHT!
VALENTINE LOVE ☆ LOVE.
TODAY'S SHOW IS HOSTED BY ME, MIA, AND...
MASHIRO.
GREAT... RU HAS BEEN DISCHARGED FROM THE HOSPITAL.
BUT HE SOUNDS DEPRESSED.
THAT'S NO SUR-PRISE.
LET'S IN-TRODUCE TODAY'S MESSAGE.
IT'S FROM...
WOW, IT'S BEEN A WHILE.

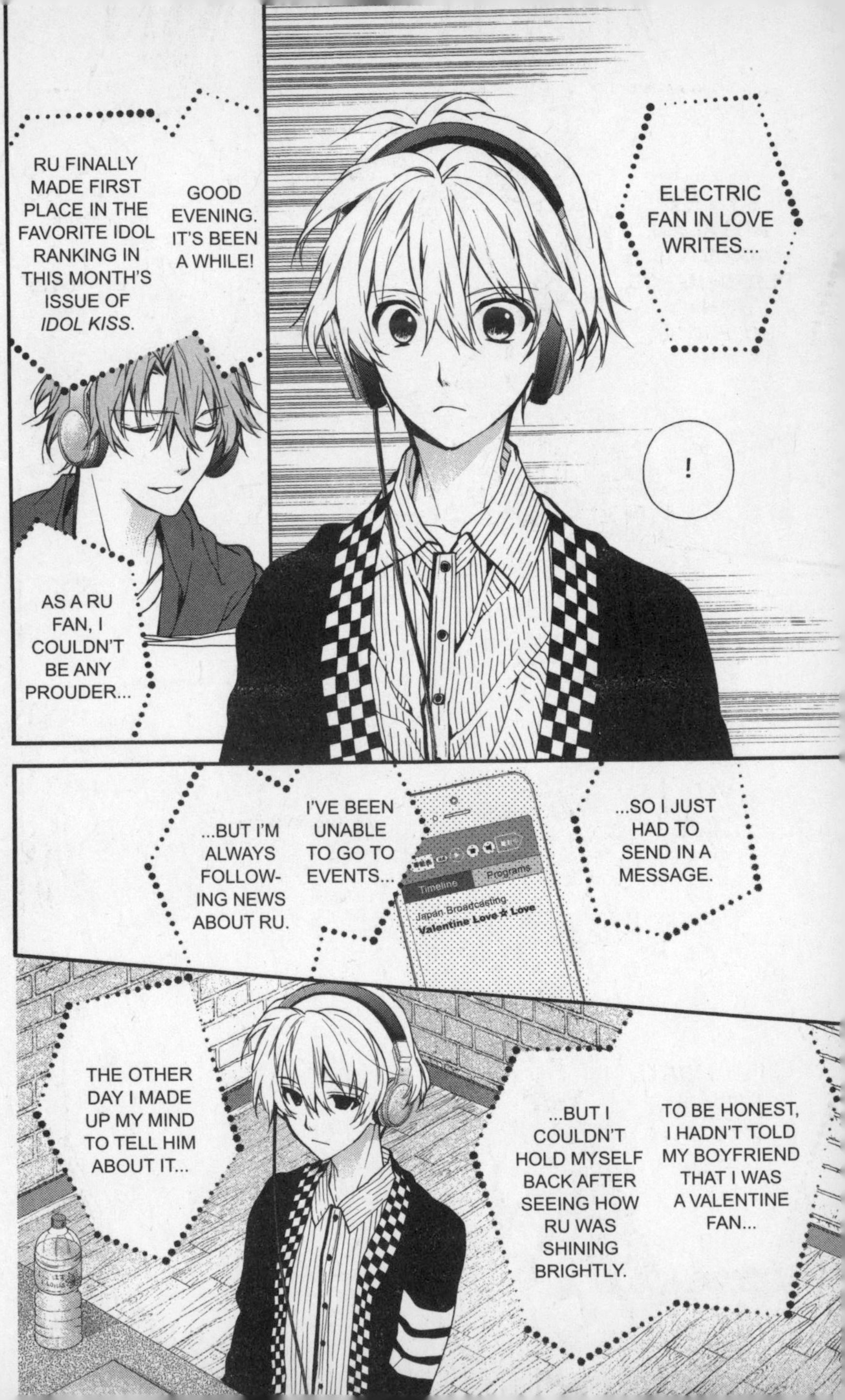
ELECTRIC FAN IN LOVE WRITES...
!
GOOD EVENING. IT'S BEEN A WHILE!
RU FINALLY MADE FIRST PLACE IN THE FAVORITE IDOL RANKING IN THIS MONTH'S ISSUE OF *IDOL KISS*.
AS A RU FAN, I COULDN'T BE ANY PROUDER...
...SO I JUST HAD TO SEND IN A MESSAGE.
I'VE BEEN UNABLE TO GO TO EVENTS...
...BUT I'M ALWAYS FOLLOW-ING NEWS ABOUT RU.
Timeline
Programs
Japan Broadcasting
Valentine Love☆Love
TO BE HONEST, I HADN'T TOLD MY BOYFRIEND THAT I WAS A VALENTINE FAN...
...BUT I COULDN'T HOLD MYSELF BACK AFTER SEEING HOW RU WAS SHINING BRIGHTLY.
THE OTHER DAY I MADE UP MY MIND TO TELL HIM ABOUT IT...

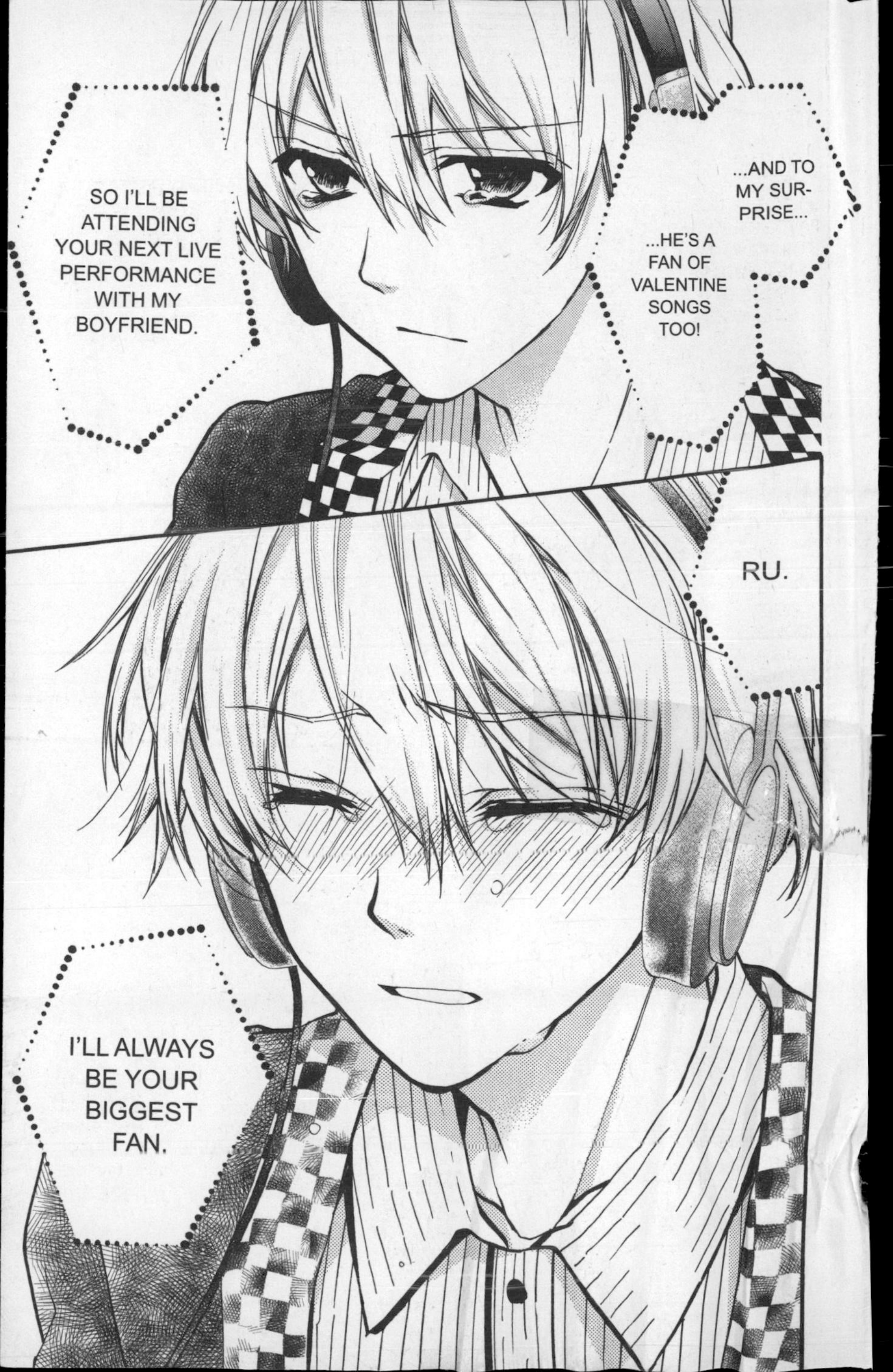
...AND TO MY SUR-PRISE...
...HE'S A FAN OF VALENTINE SONGS TOO!
SO I'LL BE ATTENDING YOUR NEXT LIVE PERFORMANCE WITH MY BOYFRIEND.
RU.
I'LL ALWAYS BE YOUR BIGGEST FAN.

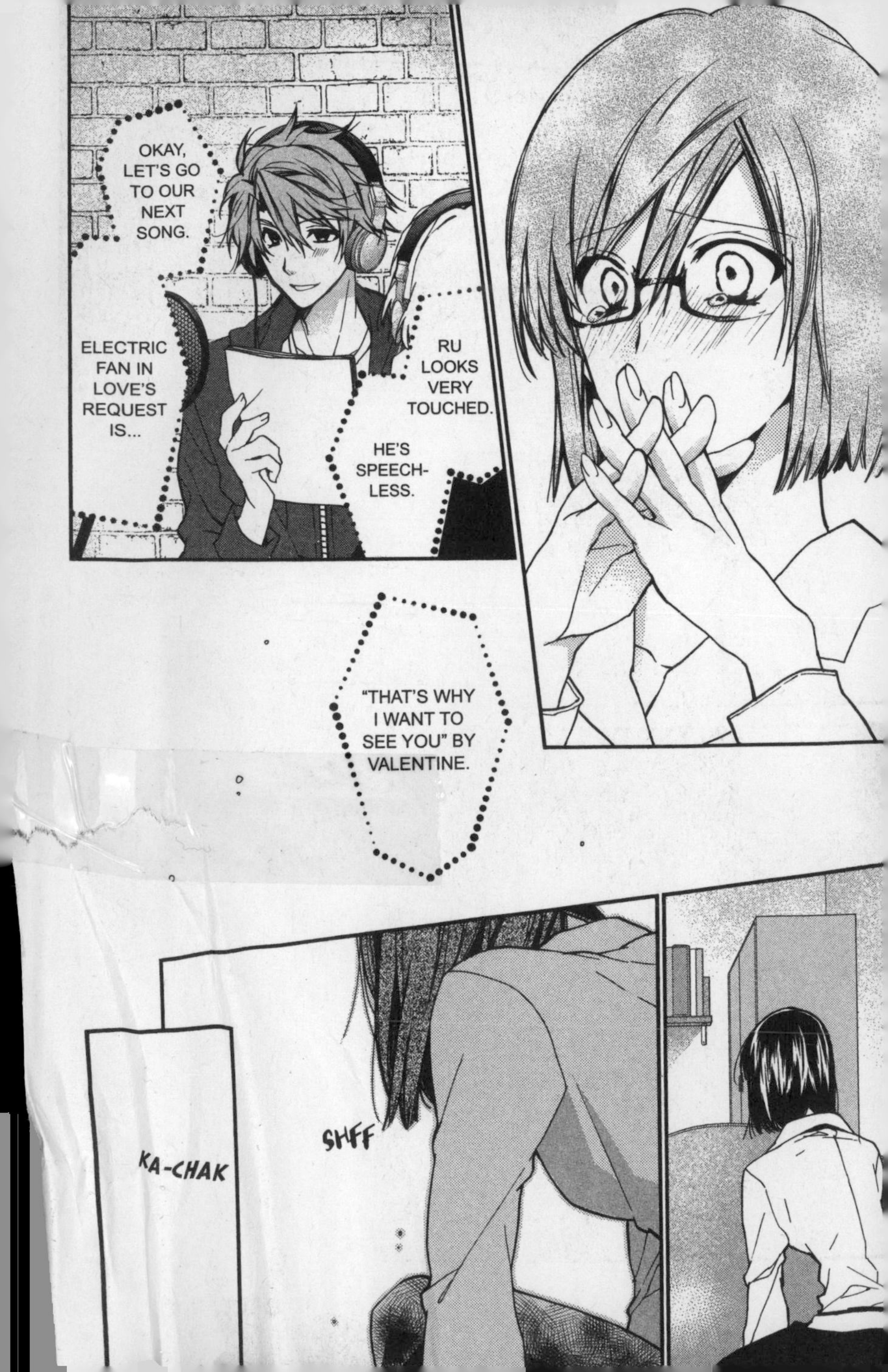
OKAY, LET'S GO TO OUR NEXT SONG.
RU LOOKS VERY TOUCHED.
HE'S SPEECH-LESS.
ELECTRIC FAN IN LOVE'S REQUEST IS...
"THAT'S WHY I WANT TO SEE YOU" BY VALENTINE.
SHFF
KA-CHAK

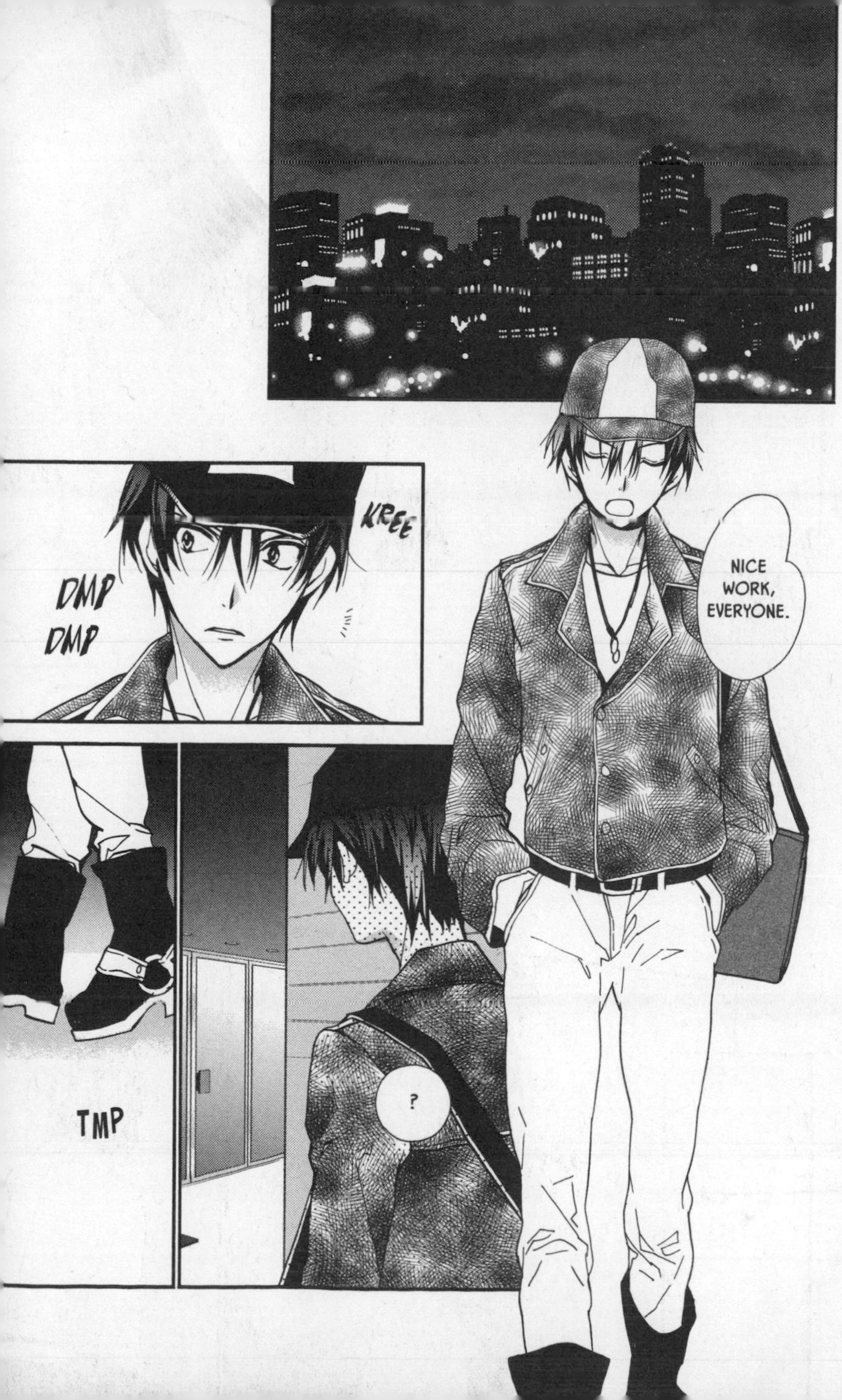
NICE WORK, EVERYONE.
KREE
DMP DMP
?
TMP

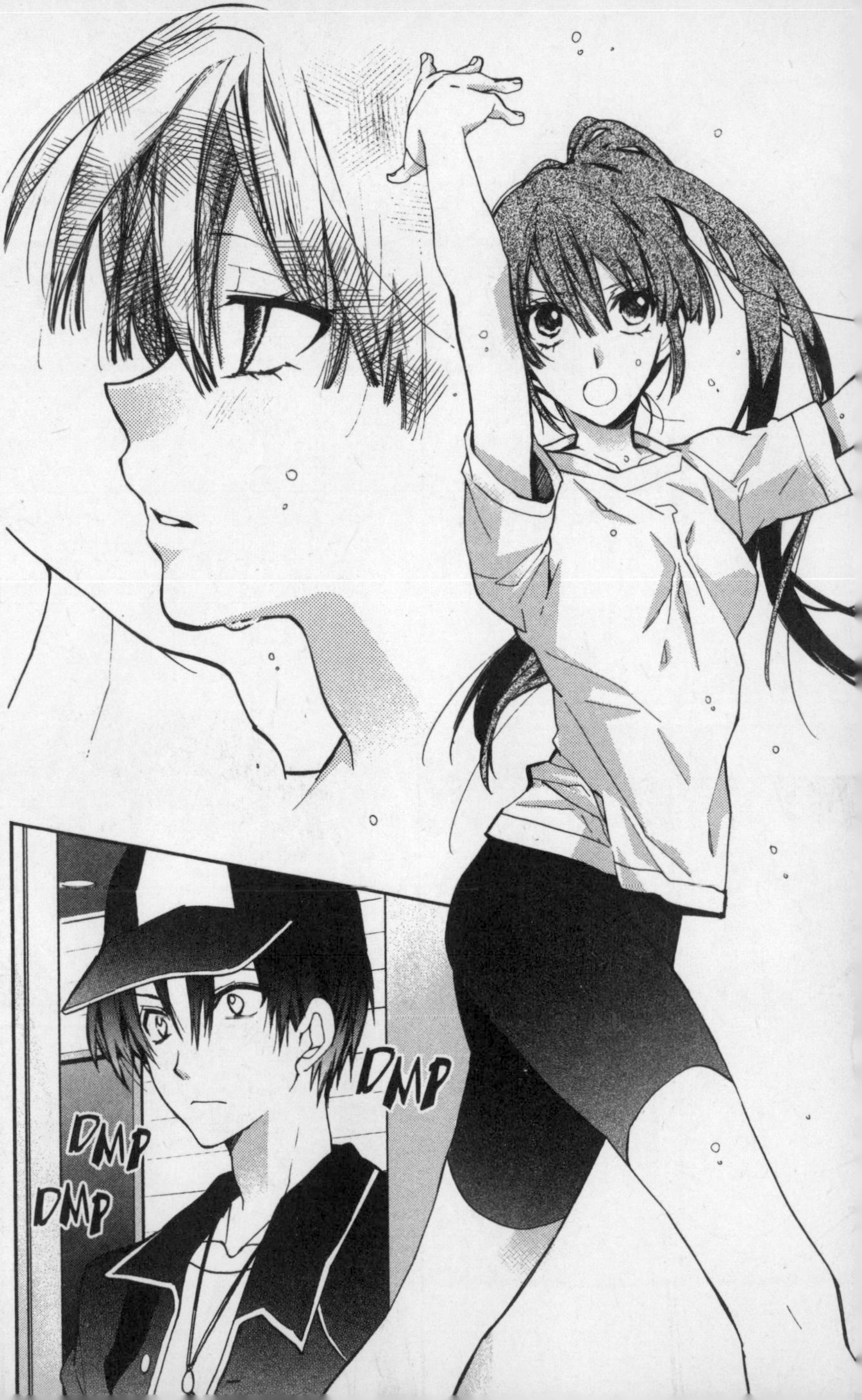
DMP
DMP
DMP

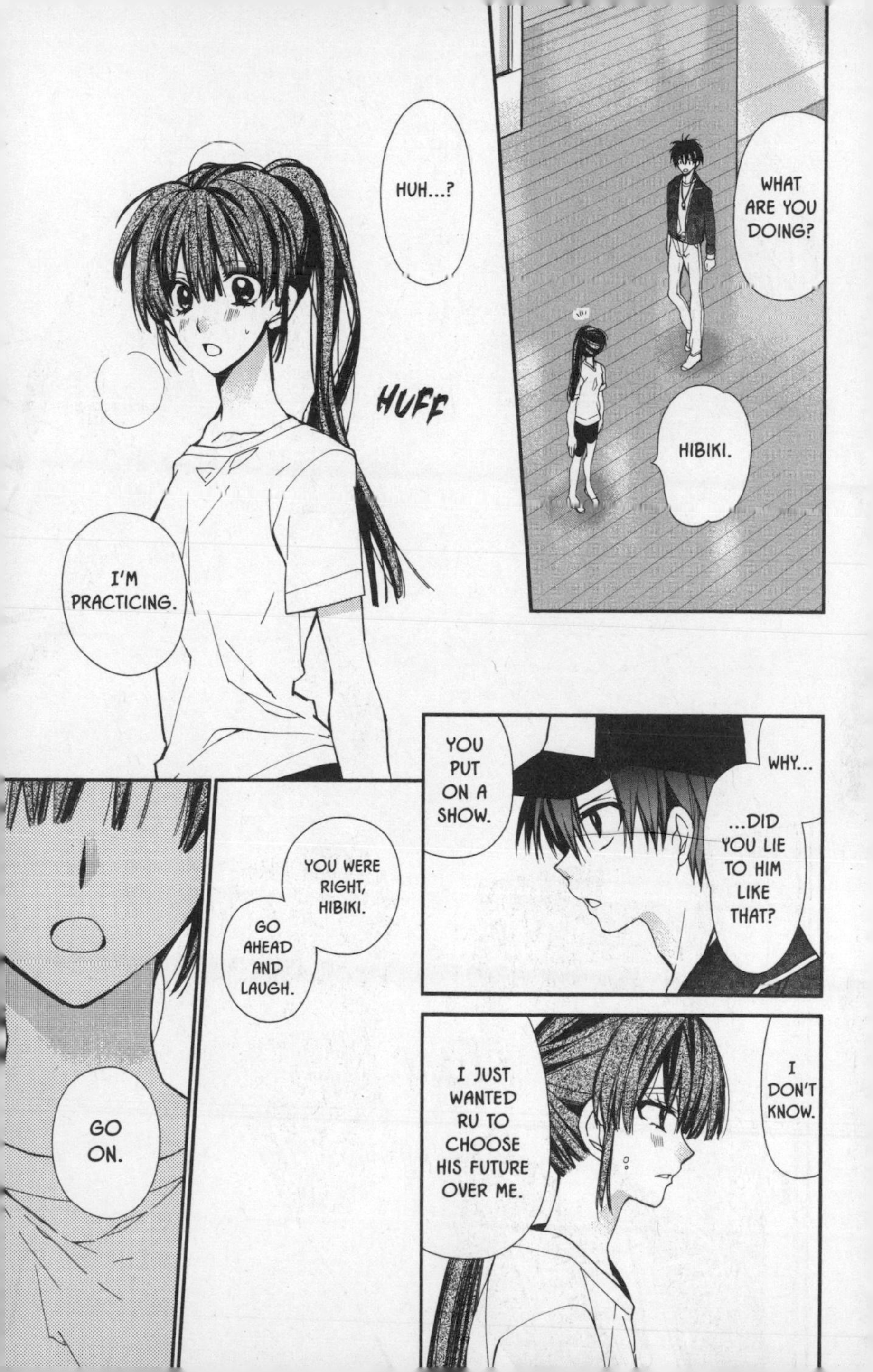
WHAT ARE YOU DOING?
HIBIKI.
HUH...?
HUFF
I'M PRACTICING.
WHY...
...DID YOU LIE TO HIM LIKE THAT?
YOU PUT ON A SHOW.
I DON'T KNOW.
I JUST WANTED RU TO CHOOSE HIS FUTURE OVER ME.
YOU WERE RIGHT, HIBIKI.
GO AHEAD AND LAUGH.
GO ON.

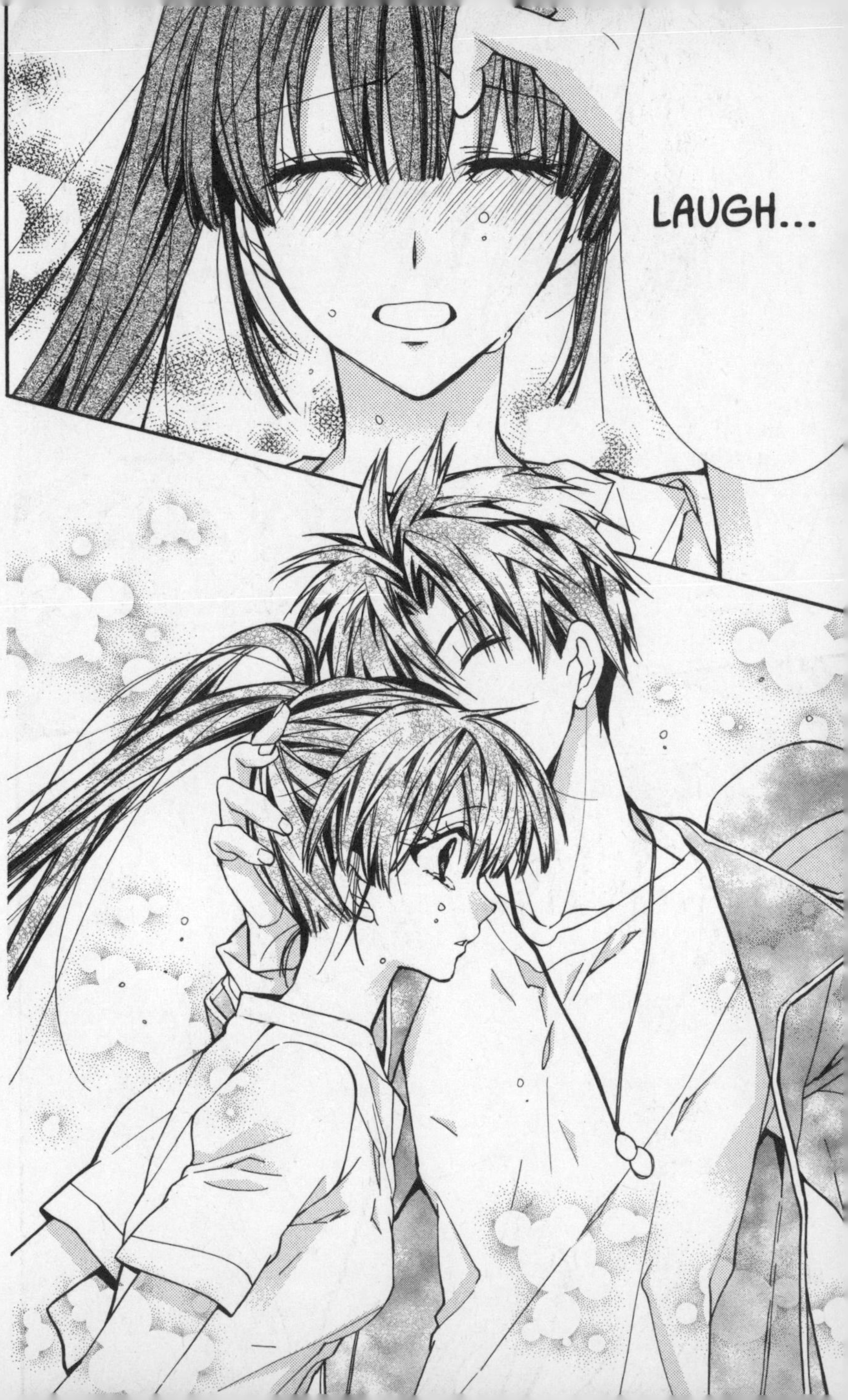
LAUGH...

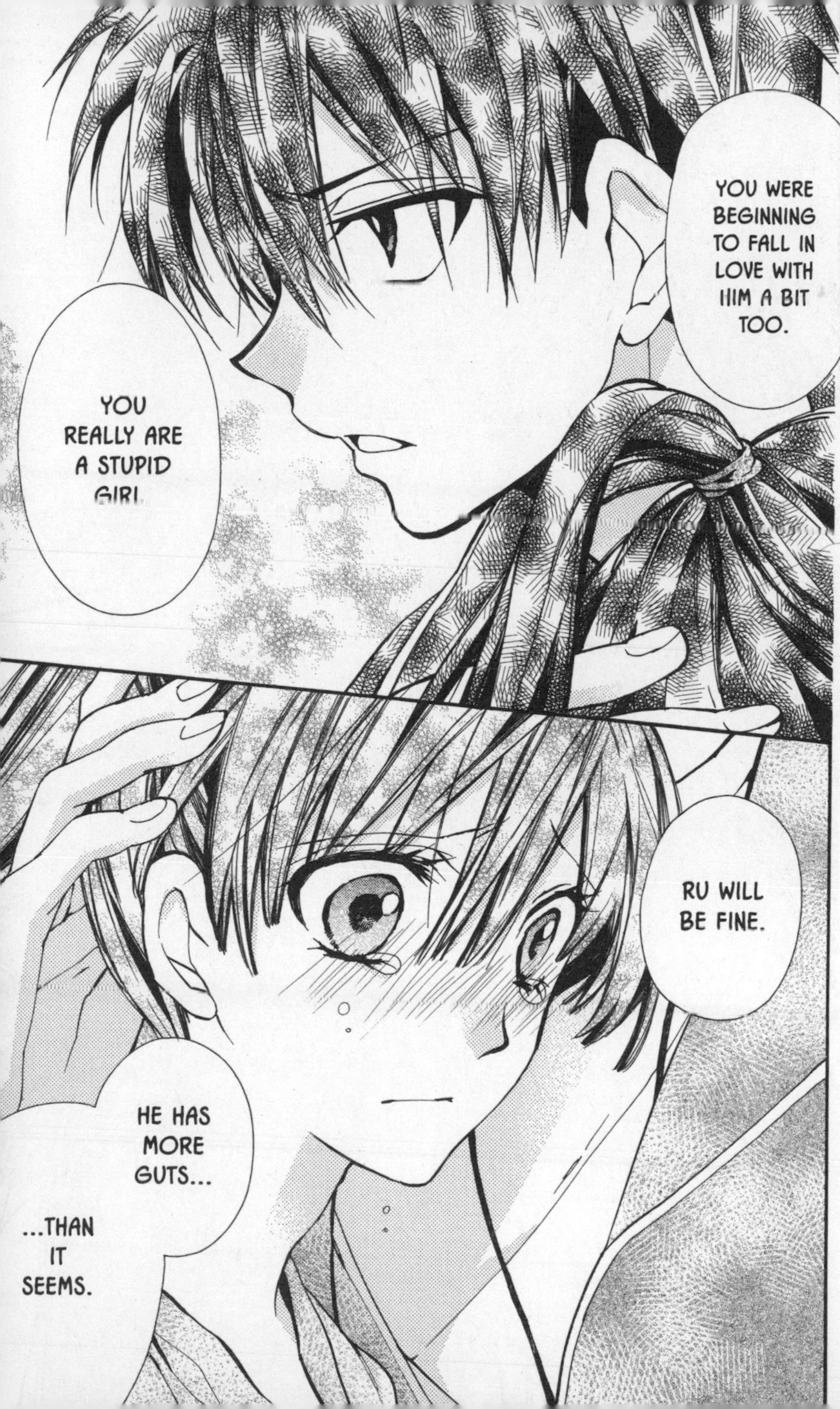
YOU WERE BEGINNING TO FALL IN LOVE WITH HIM A BIT TOO.
YOU REALLY ARE A STUPID GIRL.
RU WILL BE FINE.
HE HAS MORE GUTS...
...THAN IT SEEMS.

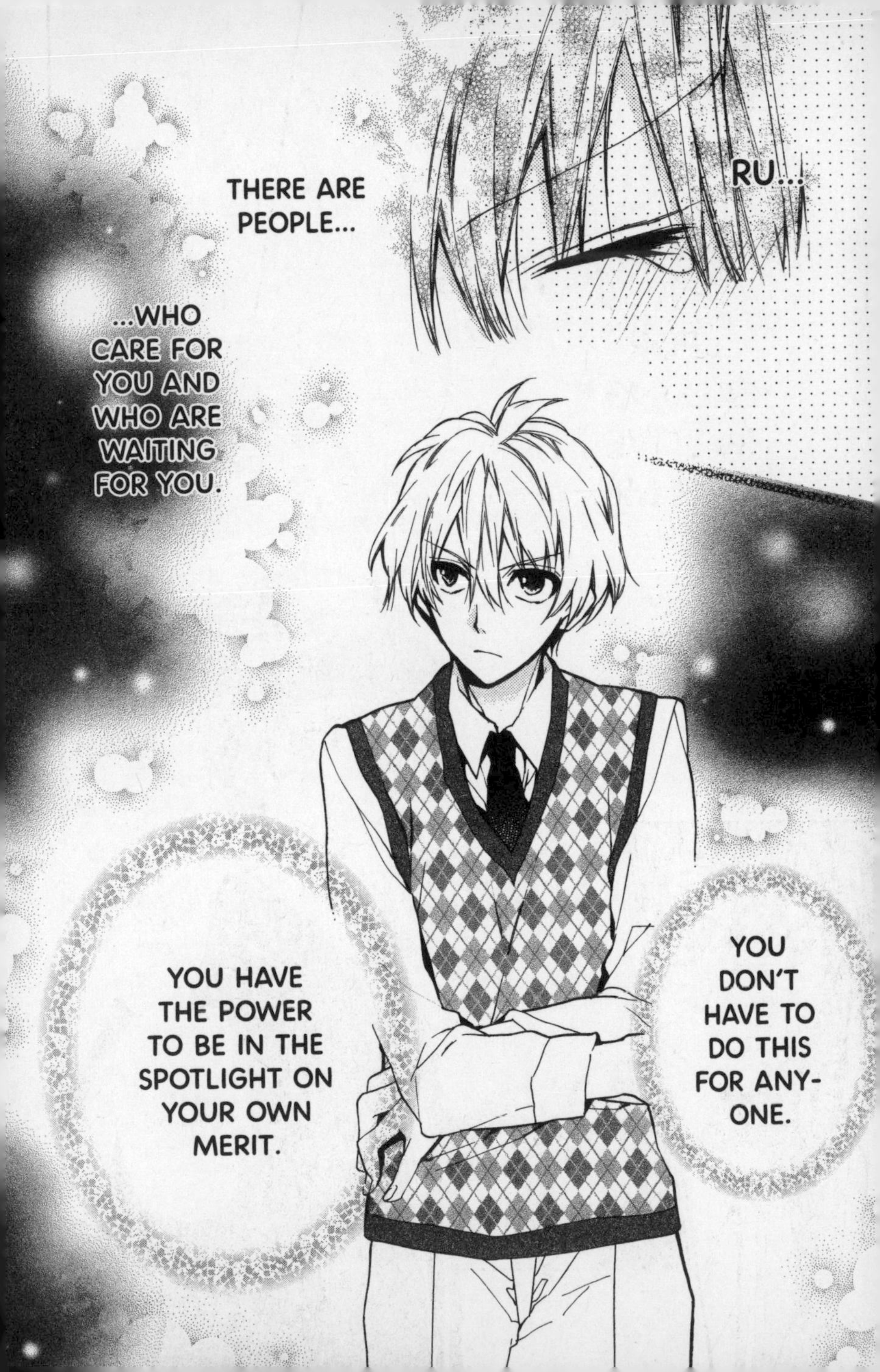
RU...
THERE ARE PEOPLE...
...WHO CARE FOR YOU AND WHO ARE WAITING FOR YOU.
YOU DON'T HAVE TO DO THIS FOR ANY-ONE.
YOU HAVE THE POWER TO BE IN THE SPOTLIGHT ON YOUR OWN MERIT.

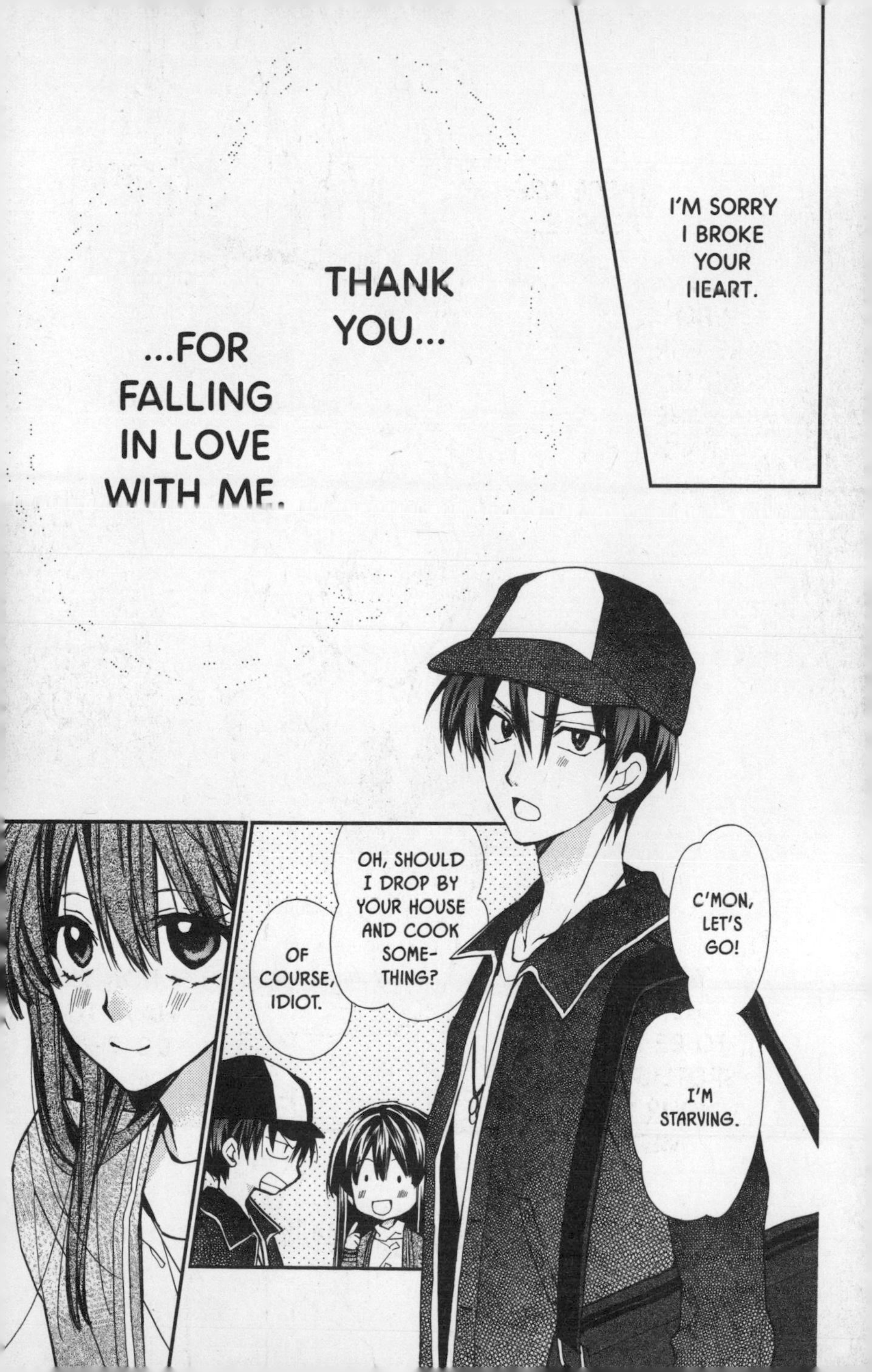
I'M SORRY I BROKE YOUR HEART.
THANK YOU...
...FOR FALLING IN LOVE WITH ME.
C'MON, LET'S GO!
I'M STARVING.
OH, SHOULD I DROP BY YOUR HOUSE AND COOK SOME-THING?
OF COURSE, IDIOT.

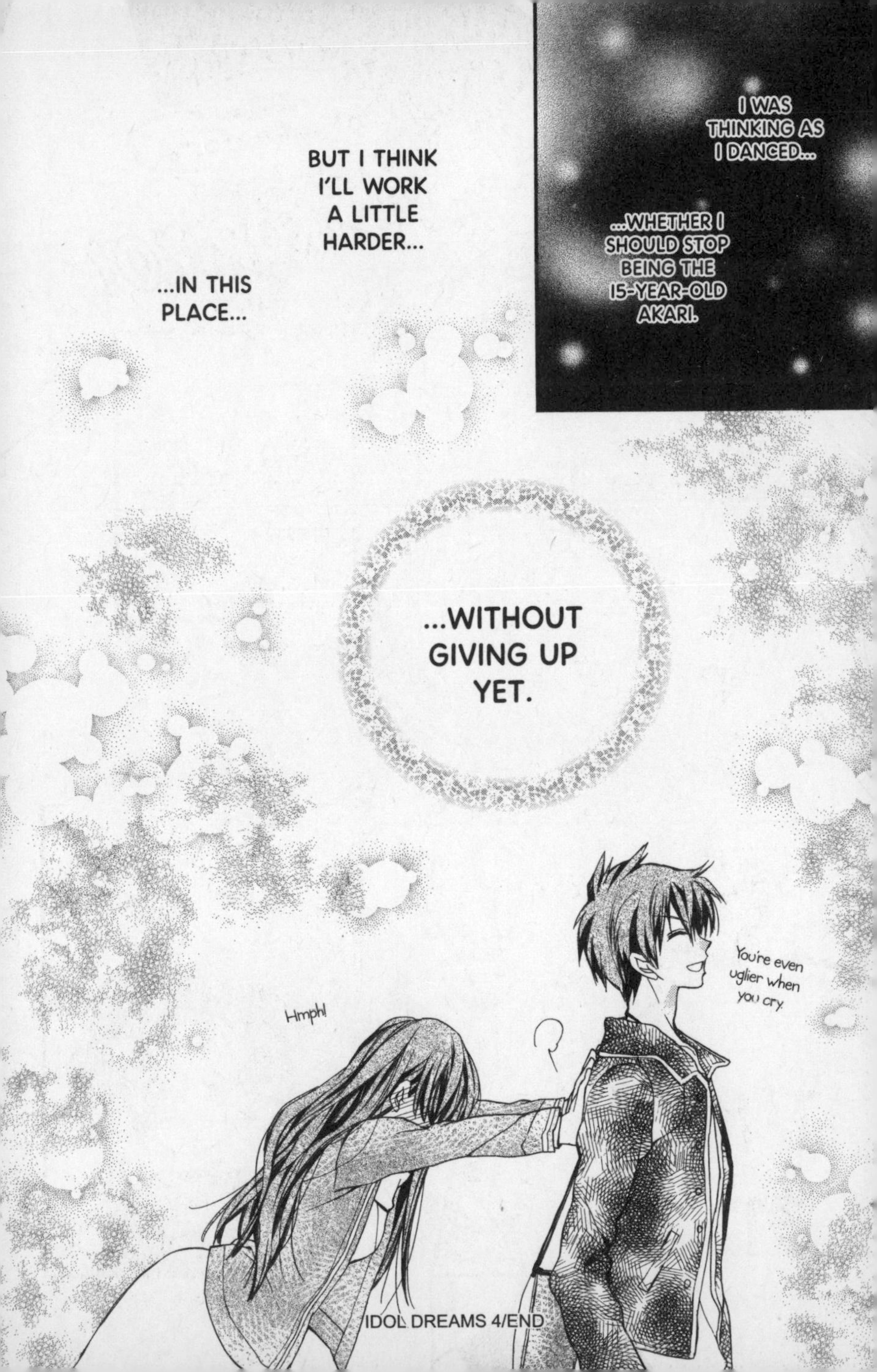
I WAS THINKING AS I DANCED...
...WHETHER I SHOULD STOP BEING THE 15-YEAR-OLD AKARI.
BUT I THINK I'LL WORK A LITTLE HARDER...
...IN THIS PLACE...
...WITHOUT GIVING UP YET.
You're even uglier when you cry.
Hmph!
IDOL DREAMS 4/END

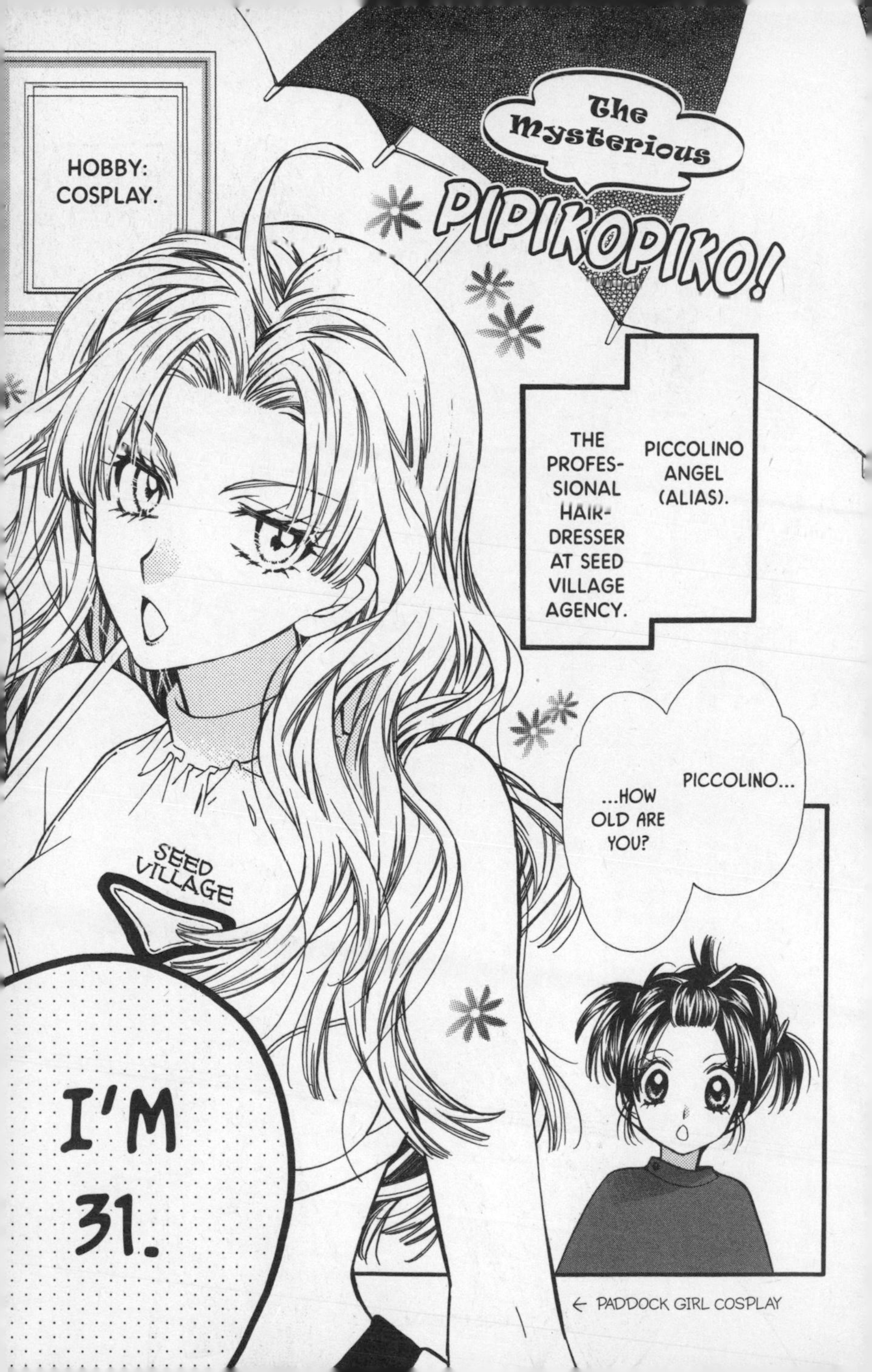
The Mysterious
PIPIKOPIKO!
PICCOLINO ANGEL (ALIAS).
THE PROFES-SIONAL HAIR-DRESSER AT SEED VILLAGE AGENCY.
HOBBY: COSPLAY.
PICCOLINO...
...HOW OLD ARE YOU?
SEED VILLAGE
I'M 31.
← PADDOCK GIRL COSPLAY

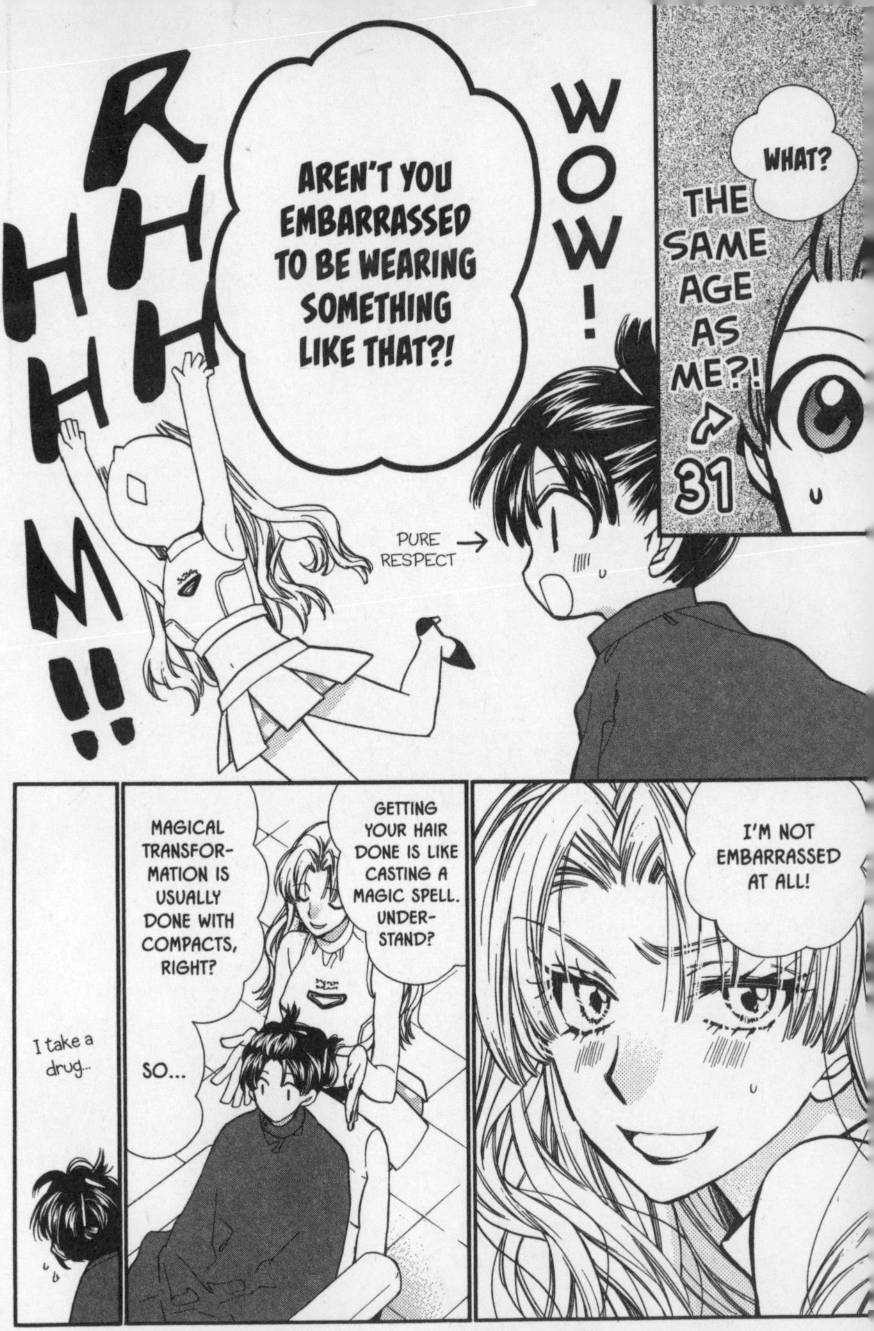
WHAT?
THE SAME AGE AS ME?!
31
WOW!
AREN'T YOU EMBARRASSED TO BE WEARING SOMETHING LIKE THAT?!
RHHHHM!!
PURE RESPECT
I'M NOT EMBARRASSED AT ALL!
GETTING YOUR HAIR DONE IS LIKE CASTING A MAGIC SPELL. UNDER-STAND?
MAGICAL TRANSFOR-MATION IS USUALLY DONE WITH COMPACTS, RIGHT?
SO...
I take a drug...

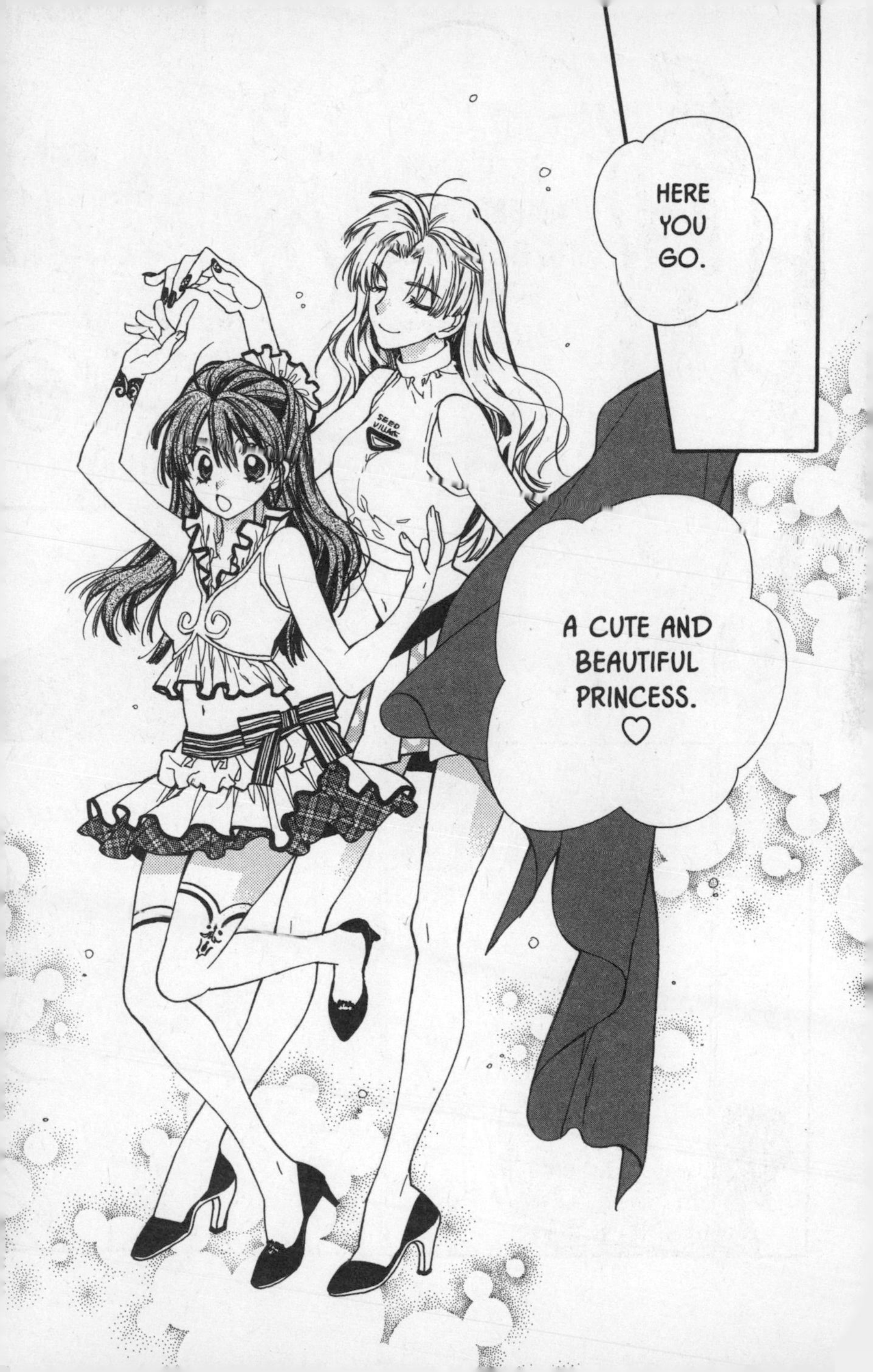
HERE YOU GO.
A CUTE AND BEAUTIFUL PRINCESS. ♡

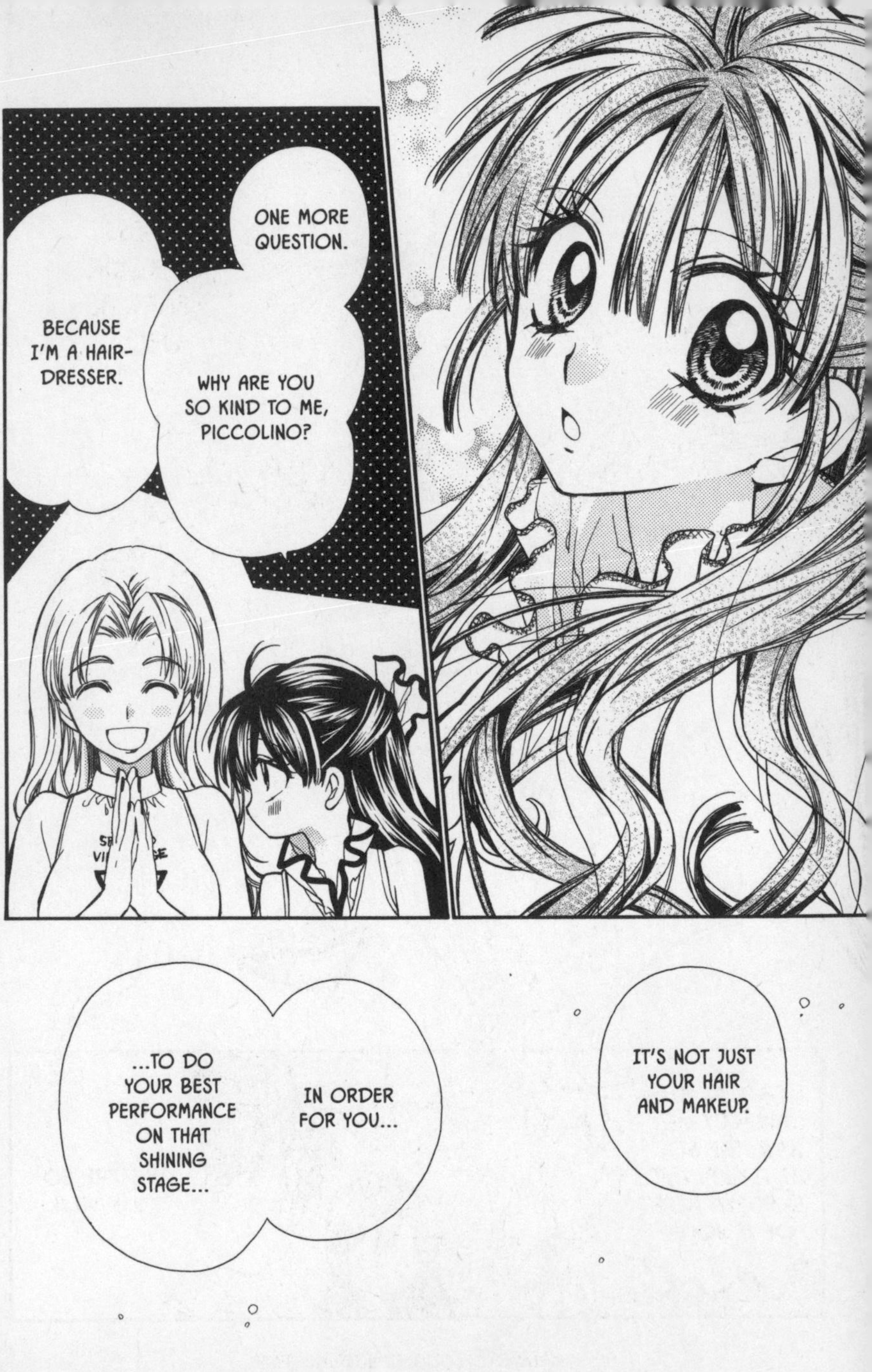
ONE MORE QUESTION.
WHY ARE YOU SO KIND TO ME, PICCOLINO?
BECAUSE I'M A HAIR-DRESSER.
IT'S NOT JUST YOUR HAIR AND MAKEUP.
IN ORDER FOR YOU...
...TO DO YOUR BEST PERFORMANCE ON THAT SHINING STAGE...

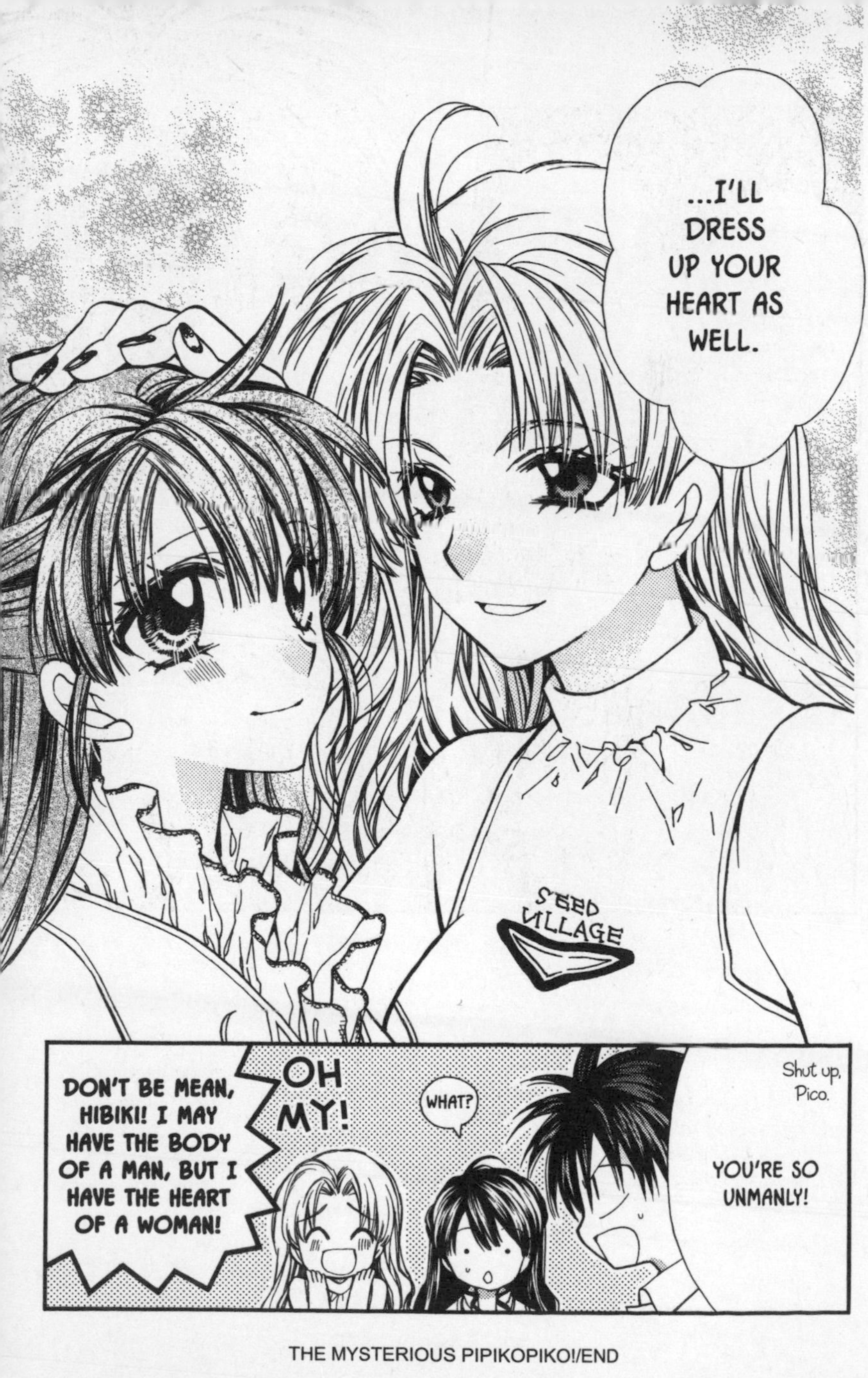
...I'LL DRESS UP YOUR HEART AS WELL.
SEED VILLAGE
Shut up, Pico.
YOU'RE SO UNMANLY!
OH MY!
WHAT?
DON'T BE MEAN, HIBIKI! I MAY HAVE THE BODY OF A MAN, BUT I HAVE THE HEART OF A WOMAN!

THE MYSTERIOUS PIPIKOPIKO!/END

This volume is centered around Ru.
Although it seems like an arc about Akari,
I feel that it's actually about Ru growing up.
Hibiki is watching over the whole thing for a
certain reason, so they don't really enter a love
triangle, but I hope their relationship continues
like this from now on. The next volume may
turn out to be the biggest climax of *Idol Dreams*.
Or maybe it will be sheer carnage? Don't miss it.

ARINA TANEMURA

Arina Tanemura began her manga career in 1996 when her short
stories debuted in *Ribon Original* magazine. She gained fame with the
1997 publication of *I·O·N*, and ever since her debut Tanemura has
been a major force in shojo manga with popular series *Phantom Thief
Jeanne, Time Stranger Kyoko, Full Moon, The Gentlemen's Alliance †* and
Sakura Hime: The Legend of Princess Sakura. Both *Phantom Thief Jeanne*
and *Full Moon* have been adapted into animated TV series.

SHOJO BEAT EDITION

STORY & ART BY ARINA TANEMURA

TRANSLATION **Tetsuichiro Miyaki**
TOUCH-UP ART & LETTERING **Inori Fukuda Trant**
DESIGN **Shawn Carrico**
EDITOR **Nancy Thistlethwaite**

Thirty One Idream by Arina Tanemura
© Arina Tanemura 2016
All rights reserved.
First published in Japan in 2016 by HAKUSENSHA, Inc., Tokyo.
English language translation rights arranged with HAKUSENSHA, Inc., Tokyo.

The stories, characters and incidents mentioned
in this publication are entirely fictional.

Printed in Canada

Published by VIZ Media, LLC
P.O. Box 77010
San Francisco, CA 94107

10 9 8 7 6 5 4 3 2 1
First printing, November 2017

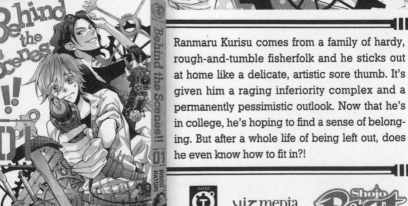

Now available in a 2-in-1 edition!

Maïd-sama!

As if being student council president of a predominantly male high school isn't hard enough, Misaki Ayuzawa has a major secret—she works at a maid café after school! How is she supposed to keep her image of being ultrasmart, strong and overachieving intact once school heartthrob Takumi Usui discovers her double life?!

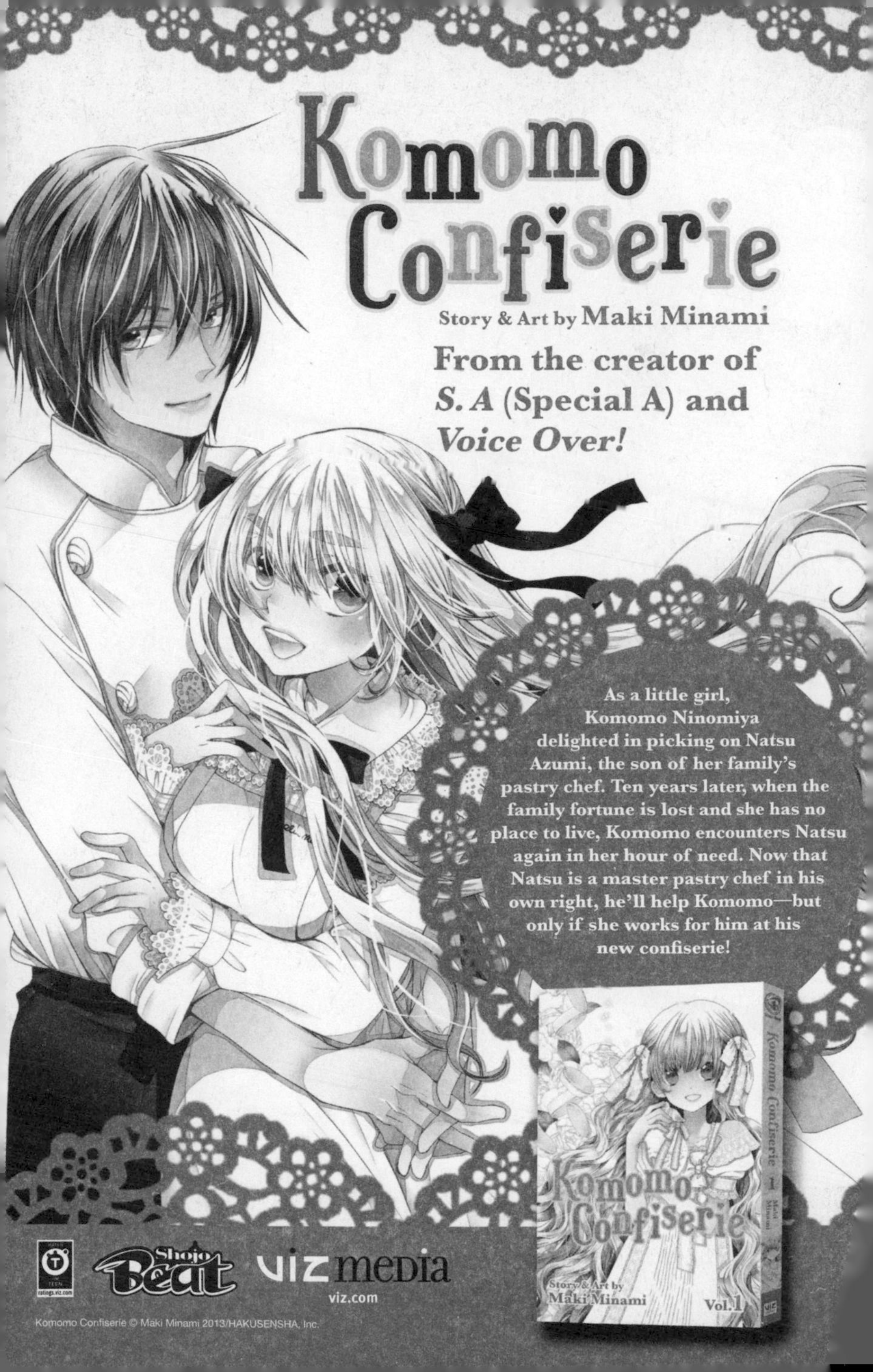
Komomo Confiserie
Story & Art by Maki Minami
From the creator of S. A (Special A) and Voice Over!
As a little girl, Komomo Ninomiya delighted in picking on Natsu Azumi, the son of her family's pastry chef. Ten years later, when the family fortune is lost and she has no place to live, Komomo encounters Natsu again in her hour of need. Now that Natsu is a master pastry chef in his own right, he'll help Komomo—but only if she works for him at his new confiserie!
Komomo Confiserie 1
Story & Art by Maki Minami
Vol. 1
Shojo Beat
VIZ MEDIA
viz.com
TEEN
ratings.viz.com
Komomo Confiserie © Maki Minami 2013/HAKUSENSHA, Inc.

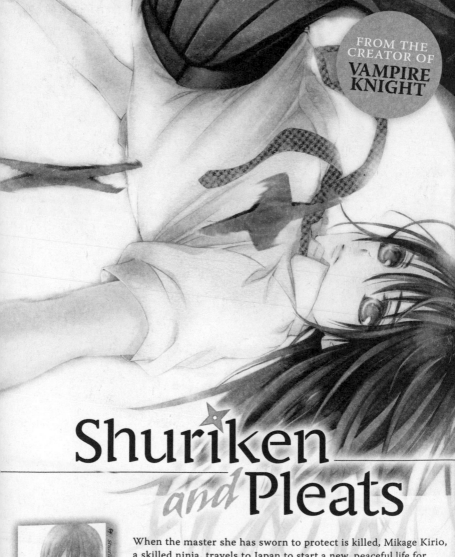

Shuriken *and* Pleats

When the master she has sworn to protect is killed, Mikage Kirio, a skilled ninja, travels to Japan to start a new, peaceful life for herself. But as soon as she arrives, she finds herself fighting to protect the life of Mahito Wakashimatsu, a man who is under attack by a band of ninja. From that time on, Mikage is drawn deeper into the machinations of his powerful family.

www.viz.com
ratings.viz.com

STOP!
YOU MAY BE READING THE WRONG WAY!

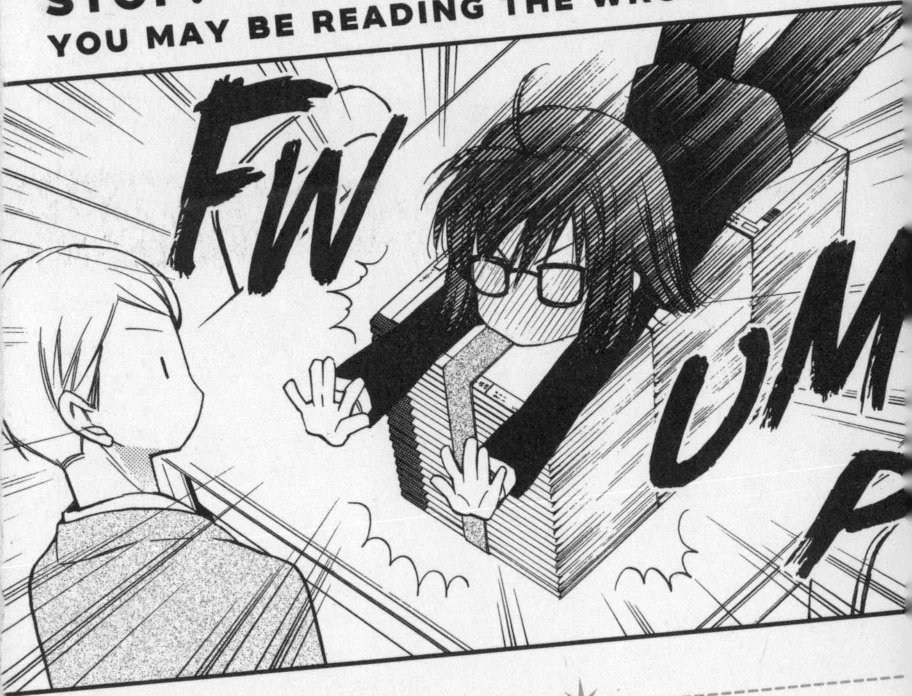
FWOMP

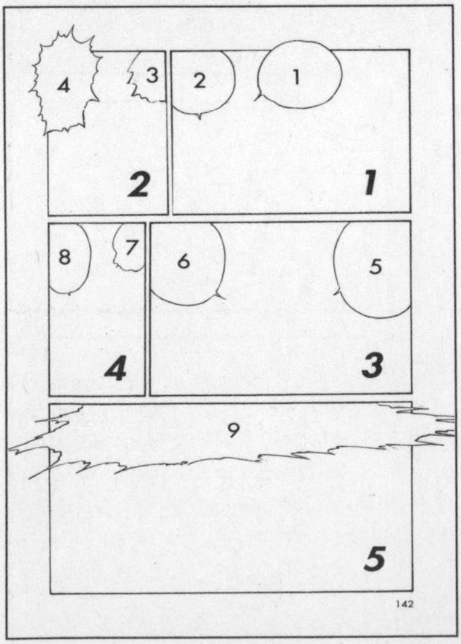
1
2
3
4
1
2
5
6
7
8
3
4
9
5
142

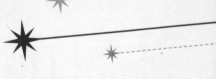

In keeping with the original Japanese comic format, this book reads from right to left—so action, sound effects and word balloons are completely reversed to preserve the orientation of the original artwork.

Check out the diagram shown here to get the hang of things, and then turn to the other side of the book to get started!